D0536502

Scotland in a Global Economy

Scotland in a Global Economy

The 2020 Vision

Edited by

Neil Hood, Jeremy Peat, Ewen Peters and Stephen Young

First published 2002 by
PALGRAVE MACMILLAN
Houndmills, Basingstoke, Hampshire RG21 6XS and
175 Fifth Avenue, New York, N.Y. 10010
Companies and representatives throughout the world

PALGRAVE MACMILLAN is the global academic imprint of the Palgrave Macmillan division of St. Martin's Press, LLC and of Palgrave Macmillan Ltd. Macmillan® is a registered trademark in the United States, United Kingdom and other countries. Palgrave is a registered trademark in the European Union and other countries.

ISBN 0–333–96454–3 hardback

This book is printed on paper suitable for recycling and made from fully managed and sustained forest sources.

A catalogue record for this book is available from the British Library.

Library of Congress Cataloging-in-Publication Data
Scotland in a global economy: the 2020 vision / Neil Hood ... [et al.].
    p. cm.
'This volume is a follow-up to an earlier project ... entitled Industry, policy, and the Scottish economy ... 1984'—Introd.
Includes bibliographical references and index.
ISBN 0–333–96454–3
1. Scotland—Foreign economic relations.   2. Industrial policy—Scotland.
3. Industries—Scotland.   4. Corporations—Scotland—Management.
5. Scotland—Economic Globalization—Economic
aspects—Scotland.   I. Hood, Neil.

HF1537 .S36 2002
337.411—dc21

                                                                    2002074835

10   9   8   7   6   5   4   3   2   1
11   10   09   08   07   06   05   04   03   02

Printed and bound in Great Britain by
Antony Rowe Ltd, Chippenham and Eastbourne

Sir Kenneth Alexander

This book is dedicated to the memory of Professor Sir Kenneth Alexander who died while we were writing it. We do so because of his outstanding contribution to Scotland in so many fields and over such a long period of time. He had many characteristics of the renaissance man, though in his modesty he would have shunned such a suggestion. His career embraced universities, public life, business, arts and culture, and so much more. Following teaching posts at the Universities of Aberdeen, Leeds and Sheffield, he was Professor of Economics at the University of Strathclyde for many years. He subsequently became Principal and Vice Chancellor of the University of Stirling; and then Chancellor of the University of Aberdeen. His public service was extensive, and included holding the chairmanship of the Highlands and Islands Development Board, membership of the board of the Scottish Development Agency and economic consultant to the Secretary of State for Scotland. In business, he was equally active with directorships that included Upper Clyde Shipbuilders, Govan Shipbuilders, Scottish Television, Stakis, and many others. His arts and culture interests ranged from the Edinburgh Book Festival to the National Museums for Scotland. Fittingly, he listed his recreation as Scottish antiquarianism.

Ken was honoured by many universities, learned institutions and other bodies for his many contributions. He wore all such recognitions lightly. Always an encourager, approachable, yet challenging in his analysis, he brought a superb mind to so many of the problems that we address in this book. His contributions were both intellectual and practical. Had he been with us we would have welcomed his views on its contents. These we do not know, but we write in the assurance that the future of Scotland, in all dimensions, was always close to his heart. He might not have welcomed all that we say, but he would have welcomed that we had done it.

The Editors

Contents

List of Tables	xiii
List of Figures	xv
List of Case Studies	xvii
List of Maps	xviii
Acknowledgements	xix
Foreword	xx
List of Contributors	xxii

1 Introduction		**1**
Neil Hood, Jeremy Peat, Ewen Peters and Stephen Young		
Industry, policy and the Scottish economy		2
Scotland in a global economy: the 2020 view		4
A brief chapter overview		5

Part I Contextual		**11**
2 The Scottish Economy		**13**
Brian Ashcroft		
Introduction		13
The way we were		14
Where we are now		17
So, what accounts for Scotland's mediocre economic performance?		17

3 The National and European Dimension		**32**
Gavin McCrone		
The trading environment		32
European and national policies		36
The Scottish Executive and Parliament		44
Conclusion		46

4 Scotland's Economy and Benchmarks **49**
Jonathan Star
Introduction 49
A note on benchmarking 49
Scotland's comparative performance 50
Country and regional comparators 57
Brief lessons from comparators 63
Conclusion: What sort of economy should Scotland become? 64

5 The Labour Market **68**
David Bell
Introduction 68
The OECD jobs strategy 69
Trends in employment and unemployment 70
Sectoral trends 73
Demographic trends 74
Participation 77
Private sector employment 79
Flexibility of working time 80
Training and education 83
Active labour market policies 85
Conclusion 87

Part II Industries, Technologies and Groupings **89**

6 Scotland's Biotechnology Cluster:
Strategic Issues and Responses **91**
Ewen Peters and Neil Hood
Introduction and context 91
What are biotechnology's main economic
features and boundaries? 91
Biotechnology's economic boundaries 92
Scotland's biotechnology cluster 93
Key trends and issues 97
Implications for future policy 106

7 Creative Industries **112**
Brian McLaren
Introduction 112
Global drivers 116

Future opportunities and threats 122
Creating future success 124
Conclusions 128

**8 The Future of ICT Industries in Scotland:
Towards a Post-branch Plant Economy? 130**
Ross Brown
Introduction 130
The evolution of 'Silicon Glen' in Scotland 130
An overview of the current ICT sector in Scotland 131
Cluster analysis of the electronics sector 134
SWOT analysis of Scotland's electronics industry 137
Key strategic trends and issues for the future 142
Policy implications 144
Conclusions 145

9 Financial and Business Services 149
Jeremy Peat
Introduction 149
Statistical description 150
Multiplier and head office impacts 155
Business services – key issues and challenges
    for the sector in Scotland 158
The financial sector and the Scottish economy 159

10 The Scottish Food and Drink Industry 165
Susan A. Shaw and Jonathan Tait
Introduction 165
The Scottish food and drink industry 165
External challenges and the Scottish food and drink industry 168
The pace of development by sector 1992–1998 169
Survival and growth strategies 1992–1998 171
Evolving business structures 174
Competitive position of Scottish
    food and drink 175
The food cluster strategy 177

11 A Vision of Tourism in 2020 182
Brian Hay
Introduction 182
Overview of world tourism 182

Tourism to the UK and Scotland   183
Review of past data trends   186
Review of key trends affecting the growth of tourism in
    Scotland   189
A 2020 scenario for tourism in Scotland   191
Strategic implications for the development of tourism in
    Scotland   193
Policy implications for the development of tourism   195

12 The Energy Industry   199
Stephen Boyle
Introduction   199
Defining the scope of the sector   200
Energy and the Scottish economy   201
Economic characteristics of the energy sector   204
Strategic trends and issues – looking to 2020   206
Competition policy and economic regulation   206
The future of oil and gas   210

**Part III Corporate Scotland:
          Established and New Firm Strategies   215**

13 Scotland's Established Corporate Base   217
Jonathan Slow and Diane Gordon
Introduction   217
Definition and impact   217
Impact   221
How does this compare?   222
SWOT analysis of established Scottish companies   225
Characteristics of success   231
Policy effects   231
Conclusion   235

14 The Growth and Development of New Firms   237
Neil Hood and Calum Paterson
Introduction and context   237
Business birth rate in Scotland   238
Business growth in Scotland   241
Technology, commercialisation and global companies   242
Case studies   245

Policy alternatives 252
Conclusions 253

Part IV   Policy Issues for the Scottish Economy **259**

15   Globalisation and the Knowledge Economy **261**
Stephen Young and Ross Brown
Introduction and context 261
Scotland's performance in the global
    knowledge economy 263
The 'international' policy of Scottish Enterprise and
    the Scottish Executive 273
Policy conclusions 275
Conclusions 277

16   Strategic Partnership and the Future
of Clusters in Scotland **280**
Ewen Peters
Introduction and context 280
Developing and implementing the cluster approach 280
The future of the cluster approach 285
Conclusion 290

17   Commercialising Scottish Knowledge **296**
Charlie Woods
Introduction 296
Knowledge and place 297
What drives the knowledge commercialisation? 302
Key challenges for Scotland 305
Recent Scottish policy and initiatives 306
The impact of commercialisation initiatives 310
Looking forward to 2020 311

18   Economic Governance and the Scottish Economy:
1980–2020 **313**
John R. Firn
Corporate Governance and Economic Development 314
Post-1975 economic governance in Scotland 316
Key business and industrial governance issues 323
Scottish economic governance to 2020 327

19   Networks and Relationships:
   The Scottish Diaspora   **331**
   Alf Young
   Population and growth   331
   Images of Scotland   336
   Tapping into the Scottish diaspora   337

Part V   The Future of the Scottish Economy:
   International Perspectives   **341**

20   Conclusions   **343**
   Neil Hood, Jeremy Peat, Ewen Peters and Stephen Young
   Introduction   343
   Recurring themes   344
   The shape of Scotland in 2020   349
   Concluding remarks   353

Index   354

List of Tables

3.1 Scotland's manufactured exports – percentage share (1999)   33
3.2 Scotland's manufactured exports by destination (1999)   33
3.3 Regional selective assistance grants (2000–2001)   37
3.4 Allocations to Scotland from the EU structural funds (2000–2006)   42
4.1 Population (between ages of 25 and 64) that has attained a degree, diploma, or equivalent   54
5.1 Wage premium for different types of school education/area of work   75
5.2 Share of temporary jobs   82
5.3 Distribution of highest qualification of labour market participants   83
6.1 Number of organisations (and jobs) in the Scottish biotechnology cluster   94
6.2 Number of drugs in clinical trials (Phase 1–4)   95
6.3 Annual change in biotechnology companies and employment (2000/2001)   96
7.1 Employment in the creative industries (1998)   114
8.1 Leading companies in Silicon Glen   132
8.2 Indices of output (1993–1997): by electronic groups and total manufacturing index values (1995 = 100)   133
8.3 The cluster's main characteristics   136
9.1 Scottish GDP: gross value added at basic prices by category of output   151
9.2 Number of enterprises with Scottish employment and their total Scottish employment for financial and business services (November 1997, 1998 and 1999)   153
9.3 Scotland business services sector exports (1997–1999)   154
9.4 Scotland financial services sector exports (1997–1999)   155
10.1 Manufacture of food products, drinks and tobacco (1998)   167
10.2 Sales by Scottish food and drink manufacturers 1998 – percentages to different destinations   168
10.3 Scottish food manufacturers and changing downstream food supply chains   170
10.4 Scottish food industry trends (1992–1998)   170
10.5 The action goals   178

11.1 International tourism in the 1990s   183
11.2 The UK share of world overseas tourist trips   183
11.3 English residents holiday tourism in Scotland   184
11.4 Scottish residents holiday tourism in Scotland and
      holiday spend overseas   184
11.5 Overseas tourism in Scotland   185
11.6 Employment in tourism-related industries in
      Scotland ('000)   186
11.7 Tourism businesses in Scotland   186
11.8 Long-term data on tourism spending in Scotland
      (£million)   187
11.9 Growth in tourism in selected destinations
      (trips million)   188
12.1 Gross value added, Scotland (1998)   202
12.2 Structure of demand, Scotland (1998)   202
12.3 Employment in energy, Scotland (1998)   203
12.4 Unit costs of fields at 2000 prices   210
13.1 Top Scottish companies (turnover >£0.5 billion)   218
13.2 Top 15 US companies (turnover >$0.5 billion)   223
13.3 Industry composition of the largest 100 TNCs for 1999   225
15.1 Scorecard for Scotland in the global knowledge economy   265
15.2 Policies and institutions for international development   274
15.3 Policy guidelines for Scotland in the global
      knowledge economy   276
16.1 Examples of main first year achievements against
      cluster action plans   284

Appendix 10.1 Companies mentioned in Chapter 10   181

List of Figures

4.1   Average annual GDP growth (1985–2001)   51
4.2   Average annual rate of unemployment – ILO-based
      measure (1991–1999)   52
4.3   Labour productivity 1998 (UK = 100)   53
4.4   R&D as a percentage of GDP (1999)   53
4.5   Exports as a percentage of GDP
      (annual average, 1994–1998)   55
4.6   DTI connectivity indicator   55
4.7   Global entrepreneurship monitor 2000: index of
      total entrepreneurial activity   56
5.1   Annual growth rate in employment (1994–2000)   71
5.2   Per cent reduction in unemployment rates (1994–2000)   72
5.3   Trends in employment (1989–2000)   74
5.4   Net migration to/from Scotland   75
5.5   Pension age dependents per 1000 working
      population (2000–2001)   76
5.6   Activity rates (1985–2000)   78
5.7   Male sickness/disability rates (1992–2000)   78
5.8   Proportion of males employed in the private
      sector (1994–2000)   80
5.9   Proportion of females employed in the private
      sector (1994–2000)   80
5.10 Distribution of weekly hours: males (1997–2000)   81
5.11 Distribution of weekly hours: females (1997–2000)   81
6.1   The new drug-development process   100
7.1   Creative industries supply chain   118
7.2   Scotland's creative industries: SWOT summary   123
8.1   Scotland's electronics cluster map   135
8.2   SWOT analysis of the Scottish electronics cluster   138
10.1 Scotland's food and drink cluster (1999)   166
11.1 Scottish tourism – SWOT analysis   188
14.1 Growth and development of new firms in
      Scotland: alternative policy scenarios leading
      to 2020   254
15.1 Scotland and the global knowledge economy   264
15.2 Scottish export performance (1995–2000)   267

15.3 Businesses that allow customers to order goods and
services online (%) 271

15.4 Migration rates in the UK 272

17.1 Net movement of graduates as a proportion of
graduate output (1997–2000) 298

17.2 Proportion of working age population by highest
and lowest qualification (2000) 299

17.3 R&D spend as percentage of GDP (1998) 299

17.4 Industry – academic links 300

17.5 Business registrations (1998) (per 10 000 population) 300

17.6 Balanced scorecard 311

List of Case Studies

14.1 Indigo Vision   247
14.2 Kymata   248
14.3 TeraHertz Photonics   249
14.4 Quadstone   250
14.5 Provis   251

List of Maps

3.1 The assisted areas (2000/2006)   39
3.2 Scotland – structural funds (2000–2006):
     Areas eligible under Objectives 1 and 2   43

Acknowledgements

The editors would like to express their sincere appreciation to the Royal Bank of Scotland plc, Scottish Enterprise and Strathclyde International Business Unit (SIBU) for their financial support for this project. Particular thanks go to the Royal Bank and the Scottish Development Agency (the predecessor to Scottish Enterprise) who were also among those providing financial assistance to the earlier project on *Industry, Policy and the Scottish Economy* (Edinburgh Press, 1984) in which two of the present editors were involved.

This volume was a large undertaking, involving 20 authors in total, from varying backgrounds and fields of activity. Finding the time to fit this project within their full-time employment was not easy, and we are grateful to the authors for their continuing interest despite the demands we placed upon them. The burden of supporting the authors fell largely upon Ewen Peters, who was employed as Senior Research Fellow within SIBU for the duration of the project and did a really excellent job; and to Irene Hood, who undertook all the secretarial and administrative work for the volume. The number of times in which Irene, secretary to Professor Neil Hood, has undertaken this same role now runs into double figures; she performed her work with the quiet efficiency and meticulousness we have long come to expect.

Neil Hood, Jeremy Peat, Ewen Peters and Stephen Young
March 2002

Foreword

In the Introduction, Neil Hood and his colleagues note that the Scottish Parliament provides a potential focus for economic and industrial development policy which was previously absent. As a member of that Parliament, and as Minister for Enterprise, Transport and Lifelong Learning, I am determined to make sure that this is not a matter of potential but of reality.

The Scottish Executive has committed itself to the achievement of social justice. This is our vision and the vision informs our aims and objectives. But how do we get there? A strong economy, a wealth-creating economy is key. It is not sufficient in itself but it is the basis. We need economic growth and, if it is to be sustained, under-lying improvements in productivity are necessary. While increased investment and innovation may lead to reductions in job numbers in specific instances, they promote the growth that creates wealth and employment.

Some will argue that it is the UK Government which holds the important levers in economic policy and that the Socittish Parliament has little room for manoeuvre. It would be foolish to dispute the importance of decisions at UK level and in the last five years they have provided us with a positive and stable economic climate. But it is equally foolish to suggest the the Scottish Parliament and the Scottish Executive do not have a vital role to play. Whether directly by the Executive or through our agencies, we take decisions on and fund investment in human capital, and physical infrastructure and we sup-port companies – through information, advice and finance – in making their own decisions on their future.

In exercising the powers available to Ministers and Parliament we do not only take decisions. We make choices. For too long in the past, Ministers' choices were not informed by an overarching economic policy or strategy for Scotland. As this book recognises, we now have a *Framework for Economic Development in Scotland* (Scottish Executive, 2000) and *A Smart, Successful Scotland* (Scottish Executive, 2001) which set out our ambitions for the Enterprise Networks. The Executive and our agencies will make choices within the context of the philosophy and priorities set out in these documents. I will work to achieve consensus around this approach. But I think more is needed. Our strategic thinking needs to have more depth and the debate to achieve that depth needs to be a broad one. It needs to be a debate that goes outside the Executive and the Enterprise Networks – to business and to a wider group of academics. It needs to take on board our commitment to sustainable development. This book will, I am sure, play a crucial part in encouraging and stimulating discussion.

Of course, the cold hard look which a book such as this should encourage can be double edged. It can lead, via debate, to well thought-out plans for action or it can lead to pessimism, to suggestions that problems are intractable. Such pessimism consigns us to failure. The creativity that we need is promoted by confidence. The confidence to acknowledge both what has gone right and what has gone wrong, the confidence to learn from others and to take our own path.

I am confident that, for example, the Enterprise Networks are in better shape than they have been before. There is strategic focus and a clear commitment to effective delivery. But we still need to learn – and perhaps look more to those nearer our doorstep than we have in the past. The DTI's recent publication, *The Government's Manufacturing Strategy* (2002), tells us much about drivers of growth in Europe and the USA. We are part of that bigger world as the title of this new book makes clear. I want Scotland to be part of that global economy in a positive and pro-active manner.

Iain Gray
Member of Scottish Parliament
Minister for Enterprise, Transport and Lifelong Learning

List of Contributors

Brian Ashcroft, University of Strathclyde, UK
David Bell, University of Stirling, UK
Stephen Boyle, Scottish Enterprise, UK
Ross Brown, Scottish Enterprise, UK
John R. Firn, Firn Crichton Roberts Limited, UK
Diane Gordon, Scottish Enterprise, UK
Brian Hay, VisitScotland, UK
Neil Hood, University of Strathclyde, UK
Gavin McCrone, University of Edinburgh, UK
Brian McLaren, Scottish Enterprise, UK
Calum Paterson, Scottish Equity Partners Limited, UK
Jeremy Peat, Royal Bank of Scotland plc, UK
Ewen Peters, Ewen Peters Associates/University of Strathclyde, UK
Susan A. Shaw, University of Strathclyde, UK
Jonathan Slow, Scottish Enterprise, UK
Jonathan Star, Scottish Enterprise, UK
Jonathan Tait, Scottish Enterprise, UK
Charlie Woods, Scottish Enterprise, UK
Alf Young, The Herald, UK
Stephen Young, University of Strathclyde, UK

1
Introduction

Neil Hood, Jeremy Peat, Ewen Peters and Stephen Young

This volume has been prepared at an exciting and fascinating time in the economic history of Scotland. The country's first Parliament for nearly 300 years came into being at Holyrood, Edinburgh, in 1999, potentially providing a focus for economic and industrial development and policy which had been absent hitherto. At the same time globalisation, the revolution in information and communications technologies (ICT), and the increasingly critical role of knowledge in wealth creation provide an enormously demanding global environment for business and for the economy and its management; yet this environment also provides huge opportunities. Domestically, the transformation from a traditional to a modern industrial structure has largely been completed, mainly through the inflow of capital into the electronics and related sectors and the continuing evolution from manufacturing to services. It now, however, faces the requirement for a new and wider transformation as the electronics industry has turned from saviour to sinner with the commoditisation of the hardware sector. The question is whether the Scottish Executive and Parliament and Scottish business can respond to these challenges and position Scotland on the global map, or whether the forces of insularity and, therefore, peripherality will prevail.

The aims of this volume are as follows:

- To enhance the understanding of the dynamics of industrial and commercial activity in Scotland in the early years of the new century, using clusters, sectors or companies as the unit of analysis as appropriate.
- To evaluate the policy and governance environment in which these value-adding activities take place, paying especial attention to the effect which different levels of policy will have on the Scottish economy.

1

- To set all the analysis within a global context wherever relevant, with the emphasis on issues of global competitiveness.
- To take a future-looking perspective, proposing policy measures to meet the challenges of the new century.

The book is of major interest to policy-makers, business people, academics and students, and commentators in Scotland itself. However, it is also highly relevant to similar audiences in other regional economies and small nations, particularly in Europe. All are facing the same challenges posed by the global, virtual, multicultural digital age, while building their local identities and encouraging technological agglomerations and global competitiveness.

Industry, policy and the Scottish economy

This volume is a follow-up to an earlier project in which two of the present editors were involved, entitled *Industry, Policy and the Scottish Economy* (Hood and Young, 1984), and follows suggestions from various quarters that the subject might be revisited to reflect the current shape of the Scottish economy and to facilitate an assessment of contemporary and future policy issues. In introducing the present volume, therefore, it is interesting to review the issues and findings for industry and policy in Scotland as observed over 20 years ago. The objectives of the earlier work were to evaluate industrial performance and industrial policy in Scotland; and to point the way ahead by the formulation of possible new initiatives which might enhance future performance. The opening lines of *Industry, Policy and the Scottish Economy* began with the view that:

> There seems little doubt that the 1970s will be seen as a turning-point in the history of the modern world economy. Events which took place during this period – successive oil price shocks, breakdown of the old international monetary order, the rise of the 'new protectionism', the enlargement of the European Community, the growing competitiveness of the newly industrialised countries, and the diffusion of the ubiquitous electronics technology – conspired to send shock waves around the globe.

Seen from a distance of 20 years, however, these changes seem insignificant. Political events have led to the fall of the Berlin Wall and the growing integration of the countries of Central and Eastern Europe within a further enlarged European Union (EU). Marketisation policies in China and the country's entry into the World Trade Organisation (WTO) are opening up a huge market, while also creating a major competitor for trade and investment. The UK itself and subsequently the rest of the world (albeit insufficiently in the Eurozone perhaps) witnessed an era of privatisation, deregulation and market opening which is continuing to the present time; while Japan has gone from world-beater to world-laggard. Globalisation, the information technology revolution and falling transport and communications costs are having ubiquitous effects. Impacts include increasing growth rates via enhanced productivity and flexibility and a shrinking globe for business people, tourists and refugees alike; global supply chains and global corporate restructuring; but also rising problems of drugs, crime and terrorism, an increasing emphasis on the environment and the problems of the poorest countries, and growing financial instability. Meantime, new institutions such as WTO may have a major role in what can be claimed as a possible new world order, provided the competing challenges of regionalisation and unilateralism do not take hold.

Contrasting with these regional and global influences on Scotland in the millennium, location has re-emerged as an issue of major importance in local economic development. The reinvention of agglomeration economies has focused attention on the role of geographic clusters of technologically related activities, and of created assets in economic rejuvenation.

Despite the vastly different environmental circumstances, many of the conclusions of the earlier volume still resonate today. For example, *Industry, Policy and the Scottish Economy* (Hood and Young, 1984) highlighted the lack-lustre performance by leading domestic companies within highly concentrated industries. Management weaknesses of Scottish industry were pervasive, with many companies appearing to be ignorant of the market and the technological environment surrounding their businesses. Traditional industries such as the food and fish processing sector were characterised by a lack of expansionist ambitions among companies; limited geographic vision; and the marketing of traditional, undifferentiated products. In general, company linkages into the international economy were constrained by operating from a home base with a persistently low rate of economic growth. The electronics industry was an exception to the generally gloomy picture; it contributed to the healthy performance of the foreign-owned vis-à-vis the indigenous manufacturing sector, although the warning bells were already being sounded in the observation concerning the limited embeddedness of the industry within the economy.

The previous volume also provides interesting contextualisation in respect of public policy. It is perhaps depressing to find how little has changed over 20 years. In the early 1980s, the largest constituent of expenditure on economic development was that associated with Regional Selective Assistance, as part of UK Regional Policy. Although regional aid made a significant contribution to industrial transformation in Scotland, some of the problems of the Scottish economy (and of the Assisted Areas in general) were relatively unaffected by Regional Policy. These included 'an unfavourable rate of product innovation; a relatively low rate of employment in the business services sector; occupational structures with a low proportion of managerial and professional jobs; and a high level of dependence for manufacturing employment on branch plants of international companies, whose UK headquarters and research and development (R&D) facilities are concentrated in the South-East' (Hood and Young, 1984, p. 400, citing a study from the UK Department of Trade and Industry).

At a specifically Scottish level, the impact of policy measures was constrained by the fact that the proportion of total identifiable public expenditure on industrial policy was so limited. Thus the effects 'in terms of the profitability, competitiveness and adaptability of the productive sector in Scotland [could] only be judged as small' (Hood and Young, 1984, p. 402). Concerning the role of economic development institutions in Scotland, the 1984 book commented on the 'the emergence of positive signs from some sectoral efforts [of the Scottish Development Agency (SDA)], but the danger of trying to undertake too many projects with limited managerial resources' (Hood and Young, 1984, p. 404). It also observed that 'institutional effectiveness requires efficient and harmonious relationships between the two major institutions [Industry Department for Scotland and the SDA] in Scotland. It is in this area that there is perhaps room for greatest improvement' (Hood and Young, 1984, p. 405). These observations on the limited level of public expenditure on industrial and technological development, the fragmentation of initiatives, and the necessity for constructive relationships among the principal institutions (now including the Scottish Parliament) still ring very true today.

Scotland in a global economy: the 2020 view

Deciding upon the appropriate structure and content for the present volume proved a challenging task when so much (and yet so little) has changed over the years since the last exercise. In particular, it is less meaningful to think solely in sectors when so many have been converging, and a series of common issues and themes pervade the entire volume. The latter include themes such as entrepreneurship, commercialisation, cluster development and globalisation.

In the end we settled upon a volume comprising five parts and 20 chapters. Part I is entitled *Contextual*: the focus in the four chapters is upon the historical development of the Scottish economy and its policy drivers and determinants; and an assessment of the country's position and performance within the world. Part II on *Industries and Technologies* comprises seven chapters, with contributions relating to a range of both new and emerging sectors and technologies and traditional industries. Part III on *Corporate Scotland: Established and New Firm Strategies* comprises two chapters relating to the characteristics and performance of Scotland's established corporate base, and to the birth, growth and development of indigenous enterprises. In Part IV, on *Policy Issues for the Scottish Economy*, a different approach was taken and encouraged, both in terms of subject and style. The five chapters provide a series of contributions on the domestic and international policy challenges to be tackled if Scotland is to thrive rather than languish in the twenty-first century. Finally, Chapter 20 attempts the task of drawing from the wide ranging contributions in the volume to provide coherent policy conclusions and recommendations.

Despite the overall number of chapters, we have had to be selective in coverage and, thus, some important areas have been omitted. These include textiles and clothing, and there is little on the natural-based sector, but both are significant especially in the context of the decline of rural economy jobs. Similarly, value-added engineering is not covered, although there are still significant niche activities in a number of areas.

Whereas adopting this structure was more relevant to the needs of the time, it was also more challenging to identify appropriate authors who could devote their time and skills to this project. We were very fortunate, therefore, to have obtained the support of experts from a variety of fields and backgrounds, including business, the public sector, consultancy, academia and journalism.

A brief chapter overview

In the first of the contextualisation chapters, Brian Ashcroft (Chapter 2, *The Scottish Economy*) provides a broad overview of the Scottish economy, past and present, with views forward to 2020. It stresses the need to create, nurture and develop dynamic entrepreneurial firms; and to develop and integrate policies towards the tradable service sector with those on manufacturing. Gavin McCrone (Chapter 3, *The National and European Dimension*) follows with a discussion of the policy context, including comment on major issues such as Scotland and the euro, UK regional development policy and the role of the Scottish Executive and Parliament. Despite resource limitations, he sees potential for the latter through prioritisation on small business and human capital development. In Chapter 4, *Scotland's Benchmarks*, Jonathan Star benchmarks the performance of Scotland with other countries and regions, including Ireland, Finland, Cambridge (UK) and Singapore. The common thread linking the latter are systems – education, communications, transport and business support – that result in highly productive and flexible economic assets. Aside from applying such lessons, he emphasises the need for Scotland to promote flexibility, distinctiveness and ambition. Concluding this scene-setting, David Bell (Chapter 5, *The Labour Market*) highlights a range of weaknesses in the Scottish labour market, including weak employment growth, declining self-employment, the problems of an ageing population and the low participation of older males. He calls for sound evidence on which to base policies to increase the stock of human capital.

The overall perspective from Part 1 is of Scotland as a modestly performing – even bit-part player – on a world stage.

Part II commences with Ewen Peters and Neil Hood on *Scotland's Biotechnology Cluster* (Chapter 6). They identify a relatively unique and growing opportunity and support the cluster approach as a mechanism to exploit these opportunities. A basic problem is, however, how to turn the spin-outs and start-ups into well-founded, multiproduct companies. In Chapter 7, Brian McLaren critically evaluates Scotland's *Creative Industries*, a sector in which the country 'can lay claim to some emerging strengths and a growing international reputation in some niche areas'. Focus, commitment and sustained investment are needed if Scotland is to compete long term. In *The Future of ICT Industries in Scotland* (Chapter 8), Ross Brown presents ideas for a successful transition to a post-branch plant economy, with a shift away from the low cost, high volume production model of the past. Jeremy Peat (Chapter 9, *Financial and Business Services*) argues that Scotland has significant potential to build upon its existing comparative advantage, benefiting from strong branding and 'the reputation of the prudent, competent and highly educated Scot'. He bemoans the lack of attention paid to financial services given its size and growth record. Skilled management, dynamism and creativity from the leading Scottish companies are viewed as the key for continued future expansion. Susan Shaw and Jonathan Tait evaluate the circumstances of *The Scottish Food and Drink Industry* (Chapter 10), a heterogeneous sector which still makes a significant contribution to the economy. Accepting the competitive weaknesses of the industry, they place qualified faith in the food-cluster strategy as a policy tool for revitalisation. Brian Hay's *A Vision of Tourism in 2020* (Chapter 11) recognises the significant challenges facing the industry, but sees complementary opportunities in targeting new segments, and new countries and in offering a range of new niche products. Quality across all aspects of the product is regarded as crucial. The final contribution in Part II is that of Stephen Boyle on *The Energy Industry* (Chapter 12). His perspective is that the industry will evolve in response to developments in public policy, and markets and technology; but, on the evidence of the last 20 years, perhaps in radical ways that cannot be anticipated. However, by 2020 a smaller but more efficient and still significant offshore industry is predicted to exist.

The chapters in Part II suggest significant potential in both established (financial services) and emerging sectors (biotechnology, creative industries). Achieving this requires management dynamism and ambition, with the public sector as an essential partner through its role in the provision of created assets. Meantime problem areas such as electronics require major restructuring. Tourism too is bedeviled by problems of quality and service.

The evidence of the two chapters in Part III on *Corporate Scotland* indicates the need for more of both large established firms, preferably head-officed in Scotland, and, particularly, new firms. As Jonathan Slow and Diane Gordon (Chapter 13, *Scotland's Established Corporate Base*) show, Scotland compares unfavourably with, for example, the USA in terms of the size and impact of its 'established firm' base. Critical requirements include increased spending on R&D, a focus on creating value, improvements in internal entrepreneurship and skills, and greater utilisation of e-business. Neil Hood and Calum Paterson (Chapter 14, *The Growth and Development of New Firms*) are quite unequivocal: 'the central economic development challenge . . . lies in the area of accelerating the birth, growth and development rates of indigenous business'. But, reflecting a theme which is implicit in a number of chapters in the volume, the companies need to have the ambition to grow and be increasingly innovative.

In the penultimate section of this book (Part IV, *Policy Issues for the Scottish Economy*), the objective was to encourage a variety of different approaches to the wide ranging policy challenges facing Scotland. Steve

Young and Ross Brown argue that Scotland's fundamental weaknesses in respect of *Globalisation and the Knowledge Economy* (Chapter 15) lie in the area of soft skills, connections and multiculturalism; Scottish Development International, as a newly created organisation of government, has the opportunity to tackle these. Ewen Peters' Chapter 16 provides a thoughtful contribution on *Strategic Partnership and the Future of Clusters in Scotland*. His view is that the cluster approach will require modification, with the concept of a 'local milieu' as a more appropriate focus. One important determinant of Scotland's future in the knowledge economy is the scale and pace of commercialisation. In Chapter 17 (*Commercialising Scottish Knowledge*), Charlie Woods suggests that the impact of initiatives to commercialise knowledge in Scotland has been encouraging; and he presents a balanced scorecard framework to consider ways of achieving maximum success in commercialisation into the future. For John Firn (Chapter 18, *Economic Governance and the Scottish Economy: 1980–2020*), however, the problem is that of too many initiatives and excessive tinkering with the economic policy framework, problems which are exacerbated by the absence of a coherent long-term economic vision for the country. He poses critical questions about the need to secure agreement on 'what type of Scotland we are seeking by 2020; what are the strategic priorities to achieve this; and what is then the post supportive governance framework?' Alf Young's Chapter 19 (*Networks and Relationships: The Scottish Diaspora*) provides a stimulating end to this section, discussing Scotland's image in the world – 'irredeemably but wholesomely old-fashioned' – and its failure to capitalise upon its global diaspora. He comments that by comparison with the Irish, 'we Scots can seem like blundering amateurs'. He criticises the history of under-resourced private initiatives, expensive research and competing ministerial initiatives. Such a viewpoint is widely shared in respect of many areas of economic development and not simply that of utilising the Scottish diaspora. The editors provide the finishing touches to the volume in Chapter 20 with focused recommendations on a way forward to 2020.

The findings of these chapters are invariably realistic – sometimes brutally so – and recognise that there is no magic wand to advance Scotland from its position as a small moderately performing player in a peripheral location at the edge of Europe. A start needs to be made, however, requiring an urgent debate on what we want Scotland to be and the priorities to get there. This vision and the strategies stemming from it must have buy-in from and partnership with all stakeholders in society. Government interventions have to be sharply focused, and rigorously evaluated and prioritised against the test of market failure. They also have to be based upon an acceptance that their impact is inevitably limited.

Reference

Hood, N. and S. Young (1984) (eds), *Industry, Policy and the Scottish Economy*, Edinburgh: Edinburgh University Press.

Part I
Contextual

2
The Scottish Economy

Brian Ashcroft

Introduction

Studying the Scottish economy is a little like watching and supporting a beloved yet mid-ranking football team. There is much to impress but quality is lacking in key areas. Performance can be variable, occasionally world class, but frequently mediocre and sometimes very poor. However, the importation of foreign talent has prevented a much worse outcome and the hope remains that some of the skills brought from across the water might rub off on the local players. Club policy continues to seek the best players from far and wide but given the rising costs and risks of relying on foreign players there is an increasing emphasis on directly improving domestic skills and developing home grown talent. But much remains to be done before the team can mount a sustained competitive challenge to teams higher up the league.

This chapter seeks to provide a context for the rest of the book by first describing the path taken by the Scottish economy to arrive at its present position. A brief survey of the modern economic history of Scotland is important because many of the problems that still confront the Scottish economy are a product of that historical legacy. Economists give this a fancy name and call it 'path dependency'. The second section briefly outlines where the Scottish economy currently stands in terms of its absolute and comparative performance. The next section then asks what the drivers of change are in modern economies and from that conceptualisation identifies some of the key strengths and weaknesses that are currently affecting the performance of the Scottish economy. The fourth and final section of the chapter seeks to assess, in the light of the earlier discussion, the appropriateness of industrial policy in Scotland. Recent thinking is outlined on policies to enhance Scottish industrial competitiveness given the imperatives of the global economy at the start of the twenty-first century.

The way we were

The story of the Scottish economy in the twentieth century is one of glory, followed by rapid demise, resurrection and consolidation.[1]

Scotland was at the forefront of the industrial revolution. In the late eighteenth century, development was initially centred on textiles with some subsequent production of textile machinery. Shipbuilding and the linked development of the iron and steel, marine engineering and coal industries followed, based on local supplies of coal, iron ore and water. As the twentieth century dawned, Scotland had a dominant position not only in the British market but also in several world markets. On the eve of the First World War, Clyde-built ships accounted for one-third of British shipping tonnage and nearly one-fifth of the world's total shipping output. The unemployment rate stood at only 1.8 per cent, whereas in London the rate was 8.7 per cent. But the glory soon faded.

Even before the First World War some of the traditional staples had begun to decline. The textile industry reached its employment peak in the mid-nineteenth century, losing 60 000 jobs by 1914, and the related clothing trades reached peak employment at the turn of the century. Yet, as the storm clouds of war rumbled out of Sarajevo, the textile and clothing sectors still accounted for about 12 per cent of Scottish jobs. After the war, the demise continued as the other staples began to decline. By 1923, Scottish unemployment stood at 14.3 per cent compared to 11.6 per cent in the UK as a whole. The process accelerated from the mid-1920s to the early 1930s after the return to the gold standard and the subsequent tough UK exchange rate regime.

Competitive advantage was lost as tastes and technology changed and as competition increased from new suppliers emerging first in Europe, then in Asia and the rest of the world. The vulnerability of the Scottish economy was further enhanced by disproportionate specialisation, compared with other UK nations and regions, in a narrow range of linked export industries producing simple capital goods that could easily be imitated by foreign competitors. Moreover, there was a general failure in the traditional industries to realise new productive opportunities by introducing new products, processes and organisational arrangements.

This situation was reinforced by the failure during the inter-war years to generate and attract the 'new' consumer-based industries and services such as motor vehicles, electrical engineering, chemicals, cycles, and furniture and upholstery. A key factor in this relative lack of success was the small size of the Scottish market for consumer goods and services and the relatively low income per head of the Scottish consumer. Added to this was the 'pull' effect of the growing market agglomeration of consumers and suppliers in the Greater London sub-region. The perceived advantages of a London or south-east location more than outweighed the attractions of lower labour costs in Scotland, which in any event did not fully reflect the imbalance in demand between labour markets due to the effect of national wage bargaining in narrowing wage differentials. Overall, there were no significant cost advantages in Scotland to offset the barriers to entry and the attractions of the south.

In sum, the combination in the inter-war years of declining traditional industries in Scotland, the regions of northern and western Britain and the growing market concentration in London and the south-east, laid the foundation of Britain's regional problem. Scotland had become an economic problem region of the UK.

After the brief resurgence experienced by Scotland's heavy industries during, and for a short time after the Second World War, the demise continued, slowly at first, but then rapidly as international competition increased and as direct state support for the declining sectors was withdrawn. Scottish industry was down and the referee was counting. However, it wasn't the bell that saved the Scottish economy. Salvation came from afar, beneath and within!

After the Second World War, industry generally became more mobile as production conditions and organisational structures changed. The relative significance of transport costs fell, standardised flow production procedures became more important and more professionally managed firms became organised along divisional and subsidiary lines. These changes allowed the separation, when profitable, of the production unit of a firm from its other key functions, which usually remained at the location of the company's headquarters. Faced with a deteriorating regional problem in the late 1950s, government offered differential regional policy incentives to induce mobile firms to locate in the assisted areas. Scotland benefited appreciably, particularly through its success in attracting foreign mobile firms. Between 1945 and 1971, Scotland attracted more than 40 per cent of all UK employment from this source. The number of overseas-owned manufacturing units in Scotland rose more or less consistently from 65 in 1950 to 357 in 1994 accounting for 12 per cent of the number of Scottish manufacturing plants and 28 per cent of manufacturing employment.

The scale and sectoral composition of this investment contributed both to the growth and to the restructuring of the Scottish economy. Incoming foreign firms were concentrated in the fastest growing sectors of the economy and particularly in 'high-tech' sectors such as electronics, which accounted for some 36 per cent of the employment in foreign manufacturing investment in 1992.

The discovery and development of North Sea oil and gas is estimated to have contributed more than 110 000 jobs to the Scottish economy, and around 7 per cent to income generated in Scotland's Gross Domestic Product (GDP). However, much of this development was made possible by foreign enterprise and capital. It has been calculated that between 1972 and 1989 no more than 23 per cent of the £13.5 billion orders to construct, equip and instal Scottish North Sea platforms were placed in Scotland. The benefits to Scotland of North Sea oil have been substantial but they did not result in the transformation of Scottish industry.

Financial and business services constitute the other pillar in the resurrection of the Scottish economy. In 1901 the sector accounted for less than 1 per cent of Scottish employment, by 1961 its share had risen slightly to just under 2 per cent; but by 1996, with employment of more than 200 000, its share had grown to 14 per cent, while its contribution to GDP stood at 20 per cent. By the 1990s, the sector was providing the principal impetus to economic growth in Scotland. So, for example, between 1991 and 1995 the sector contributed 27 per cent of Scottish GDP growth. The manufacturing sector, principally electronics, contributed 17 per cent to growth during the period, followed by education, social work, and so on, with a 14 per cent contribution and electricity, gas and water which contributed 11 per cent. In the more narrowly defined financial services, the sector constituted one of the main powerhouses of growth in the Scottish economy in the late 1990s. Between 1995 and 1999 net output in the sector grew at 5.4 per cent per annum, more than twice the Scottish average and second only to electronics in its contribution to overall Scottish growth. As a recent study by the Fraser of Allander Institute (FAI)[2] has shown, by the year 2000 financial services was contributing 7 per cent of Scotland's GDP, providing 91 000 full-time equivalent jobs directly and supporting through its local spending a further 89 000 elsewhere in Scottish industry. Ten of the top 20 companies located in Scotland were in the financial services sector. In terms of fund management centres, Edinburgh/Glasgow ranked sixth in Europe by institutional equity holdings, while in banking, Scotland again ranked sixth in Europe by market capitalisation when the nationality of the top 30 banks is considered.

Where we are now

The changes that have taken place in the Scottish economy during the last 40 years have been enormous. Between 1963 and 1996 the share of GDP contributed by manufacturing fell from just under 31 per cent to 22 per cent, the share of construction fell slightly from just under 8 per cent to 6 per cent, the share of agriculture also fell a little from just over 5 per cent to 3 per cent, while the share of the service sector rose from 50 per cent to 63 per cent. Moreover, the changes were not simply structural. Today, the average Scottish household enjoys a higher standard of living than ever before. However, by international standards and even by rest of UK standards, Scotland must be classified as a mid-ranking economy.

The trend rate of economic growth is comparatively low. Between 1964 and 1998 the average rate of growth of GDP was 2.1 per cent per annum in Scotland compared to 2.4 per cent for the UK as a whole.[3] In a recent publication from Scottish Enterprise (SE), which sought to chart the performance of the Scottish economy, Scotland was benchmarked against a number of selected regions and countries on a selection of indicators during the mid- to late-1990s.[4] Scotland appeared to have above average performance on labour market activity rates, export activity, and R&D expenditures by higher education; about average performance on unemployment rates and R&D expenditures by government; a little below average on GDP growth rates and corporate Information and Communications Technology (ICT) connectivity (broadly internet use); and much below average on investment, labour productivity[5] and R&D expenditures by business enterprises. Such comparisons should be viewed cautiously, since they depend on the choice of comparator areas, indicators and the time period covered. Nevertheless, they do accord with other benchmarking comparisons. For example, Huggins' (2000) composite index[6] of knowledge-based competitiveness of the UK regions ranks Scotland as 7 out of 12. On this measure, Scotland stands at 95.1 per cent of the UK, with similar-sized nations such as Ireland (102.9 per cent), Denmark (104.5 per cent), and Finland (111.8 per cent) exhibiting higher competitiveness ratings. By comparison, the USA stands at 134.8 per cent of the UK using the same measurement procedures.

So, what accounts for Scotland's mediocre economic performance?

Why we could do better

Many people have theories and views that seek to account for the under performance of the Scottish economy since its glory days. Most views are based on an implicit model that would be better articulated and subject to proper test, either through logical or statistical analysis, or preferably through both. However, it is fair to say that the specification and testing of a model adequate enough to embrace the principal structural and behavioural relationships affecting Scotland's economic development is a tall order, to say the least. A modest step along the way is to specify, or conceptualise, the principal drivers of change[7] and then seek to establish how they have affected the performance of the Scottish economy.

Economists conventionally divide the drivers of change within an economy into those influencing the demand side and those influencing the supply side. Demand-side drivers embrace those factors that help determine how much is spent on the output of firms producing in the domestic economy. Changes in the components of demand are normally considered to have only a transitory impact on output and employment due to a process of crowding out that occurs as prices rise through the direct and indirect effects of the initial demand stimulus. However, demand influences may have a long lasting effect if they lead to a change in the supply potential of the economy. Economies that experience a prolonged deficiency of demand, due for example to the decline of traditional industries, may experience an erosion of their skills base. Alternatively, the level of capital available may be permanently reduced if it is either tied up in specific assets that cannot be sold or recycled, or if the assets are transferred elsewhere.[8]

It follows from this that it is principally supply-side drivers that influence the long-run performance of an economy. Supply-side drivers can be grouped into two types: (i) those that raise the level and quality of productive capacity thus raising both inputs and outputs; and (ii) those that lead to existing capacity being used more efficiently thus raising the quantity of output alone. Net investment, additions to the transport and communications infrastructure, net in-migration, increased activity rates and labour retraining are typical examples of the former category. In addition, investment in R&D and innovation can be used to raise the quality of inputs. An improvement in the efficiency of use of existing productive capacity, on the other hand, can be obtained by enhancing competition in product markets, improving regulation and arguably by developing trust and improved information flows through networks and other social mechanisms. The removal of rigidities in the labour market, by a better matching of job vacancies to the unemployed, for example, will also enhance the efficient use of existing capacity.

Unfortunately, this categorisation of supply-side drivers lacks the richness of detail to take us far in an analysis of the reasons for Scotland's mediocre economic performance. It is, for example, quite clear that investment, R&D and innovation in Scotland are generally low, but it is less clear why. Some insights are, however, provided by reflection on five stylised facts concerning the Scottish economy.

First, in common with most modern economies, Scotland has been subject to unremitting economic change, with the ability to adapt and adjust being at a premium. Indigenous Scottish industry has not always shown the flexibility or entrepreneurship necessary to deal successfully with change. This was evident in the 1930s in the failure of the traditional industries to adapt, in the failure to develop new industries and in the relatively slow rate of adoption of new techniques. It appears evident today in the continuing low rates of new firm formation, R&D expenditure and product, and process innovation within much of the economy, particularly in manufacturing (Ashcroft, 2000). R&D and innovation in Scottish manufacturing has improved in recent years but Scottish performance is weaker, particularly in smaller establishments employing 10–19 employees, than in much of the rest of the UK, the Republic of Ireland and the key German regions of Bavaria and Baden Württemberg. Take-up of new technologies also tends to be slower here especially in locally owned firms compared to international best practice, although the take-up appears to be faster than in both parts of Ireland. Scottish manufacturing firms also appear less likely to form collaborative innovation links with other firms and organisations than international best practice (Fraser of Allander Institute, 2001). The result is that much of 'traditional' manufacturing competition, in Scotland, is still too much focused on the basis of price rather than on product differentiation and innovation. Consequently, the sector is less able to withstand exogenous price and cost shocks. The damaging effect of the rise in sterling in the late 1990s on Scottish textiles provides a comparatively recent example.

Secondly, the economy is small accounting for about one-twelfth of UK GDP and the workforce in employment. Economic shocks such as new investments and plant closures consequently affect the performance of affected sectors significantly. Industries tend to be more volatile in Scotland than their UK counterparts. Small economies also tend to be more specialised due to the need to attain production economies of scale and the lowest unit costs. This can be seen in Scotland where 75 per cent of all manufactured exports are accounted for by just four sectors: office machinery and computers (35 per cent), radio, television and communications equipment (19 per cent), whisky (13 per cent) and chemicals (9 per cent). Specialisation brings many advantages but there is also the risk that the economy will be significantly affected by the fortunes of one sector. This is clearly the case in Scotland where the scale and performance of the electronics industry dominates manufacturing. Scotland has benefited considerably from the influx and growth of electronics plants but remains vulnerable to a downturn in the sector, as recent performance has shown.[9]

Thirdly, the Scottish economy is peripheral to the principal markets in the rest of the UK and the global economy. Peripherality raises the transactions costs of serving distant markets, although technical change, such as the growth of the Internet, cheap air travel and containerisation, can help reduce these. Foreign market access costs are important for small economies that must inevitably trade with other economies, which leads on to the next stylised fact about the Scottish economy.

Fourthly, the Scottish economy is more open to trade flows and movements of labour and capital due to its small size and position as a nation within the UK. The ratio of external to total sales in Scotland is, for example, about 62 per cent compared to just below 30 per cent in the UK. So, the fortunes of the Scottish economy depend much more on what happens outside its borders than nations and countries of greater scale. As we have seen, Scotland's participation in an increasingly integrated global economy has led to a significant inflow of foreign, and rest of the UK, investment in the form of new plants but also through the takeover of major Scottish companies. The foreign sector accounts for about a quarter of manufacturing employment, 35 per cent of gross value added (GVA) and 39 per cent of gross output. In terms of productivity – GVA per employee – the sector has levels on average 80 per cent higher than the rest of Scottish manufacturing. Higher productivity levels are to be found in almost every manufacturing sub-sector. Against this background it is no surprise to find that within the foreign sector in Scotland innovation activity, the adoption of best-practice techniques, and the use of innovation links, are generally superior to Scottish, and rest of UK, owned manufacturing plants (Fraser of Allander Institute, 2001).

Finally, the Scots appear to have a greater propensity to migrate for given economic conditions than the residents of the other nations and regions of Britain. For much of the twentieth century the Scottish economy has under-performed the UK as a whole. Job opportunities have been less, with the result that the greater propensity to migrate has produced significant net out-migration and a declining share of UK population. In 1861, the Scottish share of UK population stood at 12.5 per cent, by 1994 it had fallen to 8.8 per cent. Loss of population may be the result of poor relative economic performance but it is damaging to growth too. Recent research suggests that regions that lose population, often the 'best and the brightest', suffer from low business birth rates and a further reduction in economic growth (Ashcroft and Love, 1997).

It can be suggested that all of these five 'facts' have influenced the supply-side drivers determining Scotland's long-run economic performance, particularly investment and productivity. We can perhaps go further than this and suggest that since small scale, openness and peripherality are given, while migration is largely a consequence of comparative economic performance, then it is the first 'fact', weak entrepreneurship and a lack of flexibility/adaptability, particularly amongst indigenous Scottish manufacturing firms, that offers a key challenge to policy.[10]

Policy and the road to 2020

For many years the performance of the Scottish economy has been the subject of concern, not least by policy-makers at both the UK and the Scottish levels. The decline of the Scottish economy from the glories of industrial pre-eminence to a less favoured economic region of the UK has produced many policy responses. These ranged from the application of general UK regional policies[11] to the more Scottish-specific policies associated with the development agencies. The enterprise agencies sought to implement a rational approach to economic development in Scotland and many of their policies came to be viewed as best practice in the development world far outside Scotland. But something was always missing. The missing ingredient was the lack of a strategy from central government for economic development in Scotland.

However, following the creation of the Scottish Parliament, the Scottish Executive launched its *Framework for Economic Development in Scotland* (*FEDS*) in June 2000. The new *Framework* provides a rational approach to development policy: the vision underpinning the Scottish Executive's desire to stimulate economic development; the perceived drivers of economic change; specific outcome and enabling objectives; the role of economic development policy; and the inter-relationship with other policies. The *Framework* also seeks to encourage a debate on the approach to economic development, with a view to revising and focusing future policy. The *Framework* must therefore be viewed as both a dynamic and operational document and, unusually for government pronouncements, it does not claim a monopoly of wisdom. The document is honest about where the gaps lie and seeks to put in place mechanisms to improve the knowledge base on which it recognises policy should depend.

Moreover, the *Framework* is modest about the role of the Scottish Executive in promoting economic development, recognising that it is the private sector that plays the key role in promoting economic change. But at the same time it stresses the importance of the public sector in dealing with market and institutional failures as well as in the promotion of fairness and equity. Successful economic development therefore requires collaboration and partnership within a flexible policy framework able to respond and adapt to rapidly changing events.

The *Framework* was published to a mixed reception. The business community generally responded favourably, reflecting the extensive consultation that lay behind the document. It was recognised that the purpose of the exercise is essentially about the need for transparency, coherence and an evidence base[12] in the development of future economic policies, which cannot be effectively implemented without the collaboration of, and partnership with, the wider community. The *Framework* provides the signposts to how this might be achieved but the devil is in the detail so it was wise enough to signal that it represents the beginning of a process not a final outcome.

The next step in that process after subsequent consultation was the publication in February 2001 of *Smart Successful Scotland: Ambitions for the Enterprise Networks*. In this document the challenges confronting the Network in particular and Scottish economic policy in general, were identified as: productivity, entrepreneurship, skills and digital connections. Subsequent strategy documents and policy actions have been produced on skills,[13] digital connections,[14] the marketing abroad of Scottish ideas, products, production opportunities and tourist locations,[15] and the Business Birth Rate strategy has been reviewed leading to the announcement of a revised strategy placing a greater emphasis on the promotion of innovative high-growth starts.[16] *Smart Successful Scotland* also created a Joint Performance Team,[17] with the objective of identifying appropriate indicators and setting specific targets in each of three challenge areas[18] and these were announced in February 2002.

The current thrust of economic policy in Scotland is broadly consistent with modern thinking on the importance of supply-side drivers to economic development and the key roles played by entrepreneurship, skills, new technologies and appropriate infrastructure in stimulating output growth. However, several observations can be made that should be taken into account in the development and application of policy.

First, Scottish labour productivity is low by international standards but as the latest data indicate (Daffin, 2001) it is broadly comparable with the UK. Scotland's standard of living, as measured by GDP per head, is lower than the UK and this is principally because a smaller proportion of our population of working age is in employed or self-employed work. It follows, that we can reach UK standard of living levels by creating more jobs through greater investment even at current productivity rates. An increase in the productive stock of capital can be achieved through greater investment from abroad and/or increased indigenous investment from existing firms or through the creation of more firms. So, a prime policy objective should be to raise the rate of investment and the share of investment in GDP.[19] Moreover, given that foreign investment in Scotland is unlikely to return to the levels seen in the 1980s and 1990s in the foreseeable future, due to short-term cyclical factors and more importantly the changing structure of the global economy, then greater effort must be placed on securing increased investment from within Scotland. While this is no simple task, the policy issues raised are probably less complicated than those thrown up by the desire to raise international competitiveness.

Secondly, in seeking to raise productivity nearer to those of the leading world economies it must be remembered that average sectoral productivity levels in Scotland are bolstered, particularly in manufacturing, by the presence of a large cohort of foreign firms. Within most sectors there tends to be a long tail of under performing firms and these are in the main companies that are domestically owned and managed (Ashcroft, 2000). If foreign investment in Scotland does fall and continues to remain below earlier levels then the challenge facing the Scottish economy and hence policy is greater than implied by current productivity levels. This highlights, among other things, the need to capitalise on the current stock of foreign firms remaining in Scotland by encouraging technology transfer to domestic firms and by assisting local companies to plug into the supply chains of the external sector. Thirdly, there needs to be a greater appreciation of the role of *capabilities* in productivity growth and economic development. The work of Michael Best at the University of Massachusetts, Lowell (Best, 1990, 1995, 2000, 2001)[20] highlights the futility of accounting for productivity and competitive advantage in terms of measures of inputs, while ignoring the mediating role of capabilities. Best's research leads him to conclude that industrial growth depends on a *Capability Triad* embracing: the business model adopted by an economy's companies; production capabilities; and skill formation.

The change agent in this system is the dynamic entrepreneurial firm.[21] Such firms deploy a *business model* that is product rather than price led. The emphasis is not simply on products *per se* but rather on the continuing need to add features, improve performance, reduce prices more quickly, seek out new markets and even reinvent the company, over and over again. The adoption of high performance work systems (HPWS)[22] is also found to be a key feature of entrepreneurial firms, helping them *inter alia* to compress new product development cycle times. Firms' focus on developing core organisational capabilities and network for complementary capabilities. Core capabilities embrace innovation, product development and technology management. Technology management capabilities are crucial, for while it is generally accepted that technology is critical to rapid growth, the importance of the capability to develop, diffuse, adopt, adapt and combine technologies is less well-understood. In addition, the greater willingness to network and create open-system networks further links the firm to the rest of the economy enhancing the possibility of positive spillover effects and the ongoing development of the technological capabilities of the region. Both the corporate sector and policy-makers in Scotland perhaps need to see more clearly that successful exploitation of the knowledge economy comes in the main from the rapid diffusion, adoption and adaptation of new technologies and products developed elsewhere. This is how the term 'innovation' should be best understood. The development of completely new technologies and products within Scotland's borders is desirable and needs to be encouraged but it can never be the mainspring of growth because such opportunities will always be comparatively rare in Scotland as elsewhere.

In Best's approach, the adoption of an effective business model needs to be reinforced by *production capabilities* that allow the company to achieve performance standards required by the most appropriate best practice production principle. For example, an appropriate performance standard for modern manufacturing firms would be endogenous technology innovation with the production system based on cellular production,[23] on driving down manufacturing and design/manufacturing cycle times,[24] and systems integration,[25] particularly the integration of design and manufacturing (Best, 2000, pp. 15–25). Hence, the adoption of industrial policy approaches that promote productive excellence, such as the DTI's promotion of Regional Centres of Manufacturing Excellence in England and Wales, would appear to be an essential requirement for a 'Smart Successful Scotland'.

The final strand in Best's approach is the recognition that the links between technological change, innovation and regional economic growth go beyond the introduction of new technologies. Technology development and diffusion depend upon a regional skill formation process that allows the growth and spread of firms with the necessary technology management capabilities and a labour force with the requisite skills. This requires training and skill development within the firm but also the presence of an educational establishment within the region that can guarantee the supply of people with the appropriate science, engineering, financial and management skills. The availability of people with science and engineering skills in particular is a necessary requirement to sustain the growth process in knowledge-intensive firms and sectors in the region. Moreover, competitive advantage can be enhanced if economies can successfully develop skill formation processes that anticipate technological change and emergent technologies.

To sum up the implications of Best's approach, policy in Scotland must focus more on creating, nurturing and developing dynamic entrepreneurial firms. The stimulation of productivity is key, but not simply productivity growth through economising on inputs per unit of output. Rather, sustained productivity growth must be built on an efficient and effective regional innovation system[26] centred on highly competitive entrepreneurial firms. In Best's words:

> Industrial policy, to be successful, must be informed by these competitive dynamics. Too narrow a focus on either one-on-one technical help, or an exclusive focus on helping firms acquire state-of-the-art technology, does little to help improve their manufacturing processes nor does it diffuse technology in ever-widening circles. Product-led competition requires a corresponding production-focused industrial policy, one that focuses on building the capacity of firms and sectors to respond to global manufacturing challenges.
>
> (Best, 2000)

The final observation on the current approach to industrial policy in Scotland as we look forward to 2020, is that more steps need to be taken to develop and integrate policies towards the tradable service sector with those focused on manufacturing.

Manufacturing plays a crucial role in the economy, much more than its present share of about 22 per cent of GDP might imply. For example, the sector accounts for 70 per cent of Scotland's exports, is an important customer for domestic producer service industries, and offers a balanced mix of jobs paying both high and low wages. It is also a significant repository of tacit knowledge, which can often only be acquired by several years of 'learning by doing', thus competitive advantages once won are arguably more durable.[27] However, if the present weakening in the growth of manufacturing in Scotland from the highpoint of the mid-1990s heralds a return to the average growth rates achieved during the final 20 years of the twentieth century[28] then the share of manufacturing in GDP is likely to fall further to around 19 per cent by 2020, with the service sector share rising to 70 per cent (Ashcroft, 2000). In these circumstances, it is sensible to ask whether more can be done to promote the growth of the service sector given its significance to the overall growth of GDP.

The emphasis here has to be on tradable services[29] and of these two sectors stand out: tourism and financial services. Tourism is not strictly speaking a sector at all but is rather a category of expenditure, since it is spread across many sectors of the economy. In Scotland, this category is nonetheless important, about 4 per cent when expressed as a proportion of GDP and more important than in the UK as a whole where the proportion is about 3.5 per cent (Scottish Enterprise, 2001). With the creation of VisitScotland greater efforts are now being made effectively to promote Scotland as a tourist destination. But serious questions can still be asked about the quality of the Scottish tourism 'product' and the competitiveness of the suppliers of services to visitors. This too is an area where there is an evident lack of dynamic entrepreneurial firms and more needs to be done to encourage a culture of innovation within the sector.

The first part of this chapter highlighted the importance of financial services to Scotland's growth performance. In the light of this, it is reasonable to ask whether there is a case for greater involvement by the Scottish Executive and its policy agencies in promoting the development of financial services in Scotland. There is little doubt that the sector has further development potential. Financial services are in increasing demand as incomes rise generally and as tastes change in favour of greater private sector provision in areas such as pensions. However, the answer to the question turns principally on whether there are market or institutional failures constraining the sector's development in Scotland.

At the institutional level, it can be argued that the sector lacks champions from government in Scotland. The sector very rarely receives the attention from ministers that is given to electronics, e-commerce and other aspects of the knowledge economy. Finance may be 'old' economy but in its production, marketing and distribution it increasingly embraces many aspects of the 'new' economy, including on-line and telephone banking. For example, a recent study by the FAI for SE and Scottish Financial Enterprise (SFE) revealed that more than 17 per cent of the Scottish banks' commodity and service expenditures is spent on computer services and another 10 per cent is spent on post and telecommunications.

The official championing of electronics and the advantages of a Scottish location has worked well, helping to facilitate a large flow of inward investment. There is no reason why the same approach would not work in attracting inward investments in finance. Moreover, such an approach would appear to be increasingly essential as the role of mobile investment in the industry becomes more important through the trend towards outsourcing and the growth of investment administration activities.[30] As mobility within the industry increases, the efforts of SFE and Scottish Development International may increasingly have to be devoted not only to the attraction of inward investment but also to the retention of the existing stock of financial activities in Scotland. Such efforts may also assume a greater urgency due to the diminishing prospect of attracting inward manufacturing investments at the same rate as in the 1980s and 1990s.

What of market failure? Two aspects to this question are worth identifying. First, to what extent is market failure limiting the development of the sector in Scotland either generally, or specifically as a 'cluster'? Secondly, if market failures are found, is it worth devoting policy resources at the margin to removing these constraints?

An industry has the potential to be the motor of a cluster if its growth can generate substantial spillover benefits elsewhere in the economy and if the sector, in turn, can benefit from collaboration and potential synergies with competitors, suppliers, and institutions such as colleges universities and government. On the face of it, financial services offers many of the advantages that could be said to constitute a potential cluster: it is well integrated with the local economy, with the potential for further integration; competition is strong; it is dynamic and innovative; and it is geographically focused. However, the sector's future development is affected by current labour supply shortages both at the level of senior management and of intermediate skills.[31] This could be an area where government and the sector could collaborate to develop appropriate local training schemes to minimise the shortage to the sector and to the potential benefit of the wider economy.

The sector is also subject to other present and future threats. These include the threats posed by the risk of takeover of key local firms, the trend towards demutualisation, the lack of sufficient size and flexibility in key sub-sectors such as fund management, which is hampering performance, and increased competition due to the growth of e-commerce and on-line banking. Further study is required to establish whether market failure is exacerbating these threats and limiting the development of financial services in Scotland as a cluster. Such a study is necessary to gauge the nature and scale of the problems and the scope for state intervention. Scotland receives considerable benefits from the presence of financial services. What is required now is for the Scottish Executive to take a more active role and collaborate with the sector to ensure that financial services continues as a principal motor of the Scottish economy on the road to 2020.

Notes

1 Much of this section is drawn from my 1996 Inaugural Lecture, which is published in Ashcroft (1997).
2 Undertaken for SFE and SE in 2000.
3 Scottish Executive (2000), *Scottish Economic Report*, January.
4 Scottish Enterprise (2001), *Tracking the Bigger Picture*, March.
5 It should be noted that recent labour productivity data from the ONS (Daffin, 2001) indicate that in 1999 Scottish GDP per hour was slightly above that for the UK (100.9), GDP per job was slightly less (99.7), while GDP per head was lower (96.5). Productivity in Scotland on all three measures has fallen relative to the UK since 1996. Given the similarity in GDP per job between Scotland and the UK, the disparity in GDP per head is accounted for by the relatively lower employment rate in Scotland.
6 Huggins hypothesises that area competitiveness is the result of a complex interaction between input, output and outcome factors. A weighted average of six indicators is used. Three indicators are classified as inputs: firms per capita; knowledge-based firms as a proportion of all firms; and economic activity rates. One indicator represents output: GDP per head. The other two indicators are viewed as outcomes: average full-time earnings, and the rate of unemployment. Note that Scotland's ranking is likely to have been higher if GDP per job or GDP per hour had been used as an output indicator rather than GDP per head (see note 5).
7 This is undertaken in Annex 1 of *Tracking the Bigger Picture*, Scottish Enterprise (2001). The next two paragraphs draw on that Annex.
8 A positive influence of the growth of demand on economic growth is posited by cumulative causation theories where, for example, sustained export growth leads to an improvement in factor productivity and competitiveness as internal and external economies of scale are achieved. Hence demand affects growth but through its impact on the supply potential of the economy. Such approaches can be considered as providing a macro-theoretic justification for cluster-based policies.
9 Electronics output accounts for more than 26 per cent of Scottish manufacturing output (GVA). Between 1995 Q1 and 1999 Q3, electronics GVA grew by

a quarterly average of 2.82 per cent contributing to average quarterly growth in manufacturing of 0.83 per cent. In the later period, 1999 Q4 to 2001 Q2, electronics GVA fell by a quarterly average of −2.71 per cent and manufacturing GVA contracted by −1.26 per cent per quarter over the same period.

10 This should not, of course, be taken as implying that other factors affecting supply potential, such as the level and quality of labour skills and infra-structure, are unimportant to Scotland's economic development. Indeed, there may be strong links between them and effective entrepreneurship. But it can be argued that the case for policy intervention is strong in those areas where there is evidence of a considerable gap in Scotland's comparative performance.

11 Currently through the provision of Regional Selective Assistance to encour-age investment in EU approved Assisted Areas and a number of small-scale schemes to encourage innovation such as SMART and SPUR.

12 The evidence base has improved over the past few years with the production by the Scottish Office and the Scottish Executive of input-output tables, GDP statistics, and manufacturing export data. Further developments are under way to provide new statistics including, for example, disaggregated informa-tion on key sectors such as financial services, and environmental accounts. However, Scotland still compares unfavourably with the UK in official data provision, although the situation is much better here than in the other regions and territories of the UK. Of course an evidence base also requires policy analysis and evaluation and this is an area where much remains to be done.

13 Indicating a renewed priority for skills and learning with the creation of Careers Scotland, and Future Skills Scotland.

14 Scottish Executive (2001b), *Connecting Scotland*, and Scottish Executive (2001c), *Digital Inclusion*.

15 Principally through the creation of Scottish Development International by amalgamating Locate in Scotland and Scottish Trade International, and the creation of Visit Scotland through the reorganisation of the Scottish Tourist Board.

16 The new strategy has two other key objectives: encouraging more people generally to start businesses, and increasing the contribution of education to the development entrepreneurship.

17 Staffed by civil servants from the Scottish Executive and from SE.

18 Specifically, Growing Business, Global Connections and Learning and Skills.

19 In 1996, gross investment in Scotland amounted to 17.2 per cent of GDP compared to 18.4 per cent in the UK.

20 Best's ideas are not determined *a priori* but 'from close observation of enter-prises that have established industrial leadership positions from the early days of industrialisation' (Best, 2001, p. 241).

21 The idea of the entrepreneurial firm as an extension of the entrepreneurial function from an individual attribute to a collective or organisation cap-ability is developed in Best (1990).

22 A HPWS, involves work environments in which staff experience greater autonomy over their job tasks and production methods, greater opportunity to upgrade their skills, participate in integrating design and manufacturing,

and enjoy incentive pay schemes linked to company performance (Best, 2000, p. 84).

23   A plant layout designed for multiproduct, low-inventory production, often involving the co-location of the full range of machining activities required to make a part in a U-shaped configuration. Cellular production complements self-directed work teams and requires multiskilled workers (Best, 2000, p. 83).

24   The design/manufacturing cycle time is the time it takes to convert a new product design into a scaled-up plant capable of producing at competitive cost and quality standards (Best, 2000, p. 84).

25   Systems integration is the organisational capability to redesign production to exploit design changes in sub-systems in ways that take advantage of reciprocal or interactive effects.

26   A regional innovation system can be defined as 'a rich and rapid flow of information and knowledge leading to innovation, animated by the agglomeration of specialised skills, knowledge, public and private institutions and resources that make up the nation or region' (Feldman, 1994; Audretsch and Feldman, 1996).

27   For an interesting, if contentious, view of the dangers of relying on post-industrial services and the importance of manufacturing to future prosperity (see Fingleton, 1999).

28   During this period, the growth of manufacturing GVA averaged 0.8 per cent per annum compared to 2.2 per cent per annum growth in services (Ashcroft, 2000)

29   Non-tradable services are defined as those that compete for local expenditure with the result that the promotion of one activity is likely to displace others in the local economy; a classic example would be the creation of a new shopping centre.

30   Investment administration in Scotland is largely composed of new, inward investments undertaking 'back-office' operations frequently in call centres.

31   This is a particular problem in Edinburgh as identified in recent work by Scottish Enterprise Edinburgh and Lothian.

References

Ashcroft, B. (1997), 'Scotland's economic problem: too few entrepreneurs, too little enterprise?', Strathclyde Papers in Economics, 97/6, Glasgow: Department of Economics, University of Strathclyde.

Ashcroft, B. (2000), 'A perspective on Scottish manufacturing', Manufacturing 2020, The Royal Society of Edinburgh Foresight Seminar Series, 23 February.

Ashcroft, B. and J.H. Love (1997), 'Firm births and employment change in the British counties: 1981–89', *Papers in Regional Science*, 75, 4, pp. 483–500.

Audretsch, D.B. and M. Feldman (1996), 'R&D spillovers and the geography of innovation and production', *American Economic Review*, 86, 3, pp. 630–9.

Best, M. (1990), *The New Competition*, Cambridge: Polity Press.

Best, M. (1995), 'Competitive dynamics and industrial modernisation programmes: lessons from Japan and America', Annual Sir Charles Carter Lecture, Belfast: Northern Ireland Economic Council.

Best, M. (2000), 'The capabilities and innovation perspective: the way ahead in Northern Ireland', Research Monograph 8, Belfast: Northern Ireland Economic Council, p. 21.

Best, M. (2001), *The New Competitive Advantage*, Oxford: Oxford University Press.

Daffin, C. (2001), 'Introducing new and improved labour productivity data', *Economic Trends*, No. 570, Newport: Office for National Statistics. May, pp. 47–62.

Feldman, M. (1994), *The Geography of Innovation*, Dordrecht: Kluwer Academic Publisher.

Fingleton, E. (1999), *In Praise of Hard Industries*, London: Orion Business.

Fraser of Allander Institute (2001), 'Innovation activity in manufacturing: A comparison of Scotland, Bavaria and Baden-Württemberg', Report of research sponsored by Scottish Enterprise and the Scottish Executive.

Huggins, R. (2000), *An Index of Competitiveness in the UK: Local, Regional and Global Analysis*, Cardiff: Centre for Advanced Studies, Cardiff University.

Scottish Enterprise (2001), *Tracking the Bigger Picture: Baselines, Milestones and Benchmarks for the Scottish Economy, 2001*, Glasgow: Scottish Enterprise.

Scottish Executive (2000a), *Scottish Economic Report*, Edinburgh: Scottish Executive.

Scottish Executive (2000b), *A Framework for Economic Development in Scotland*, Edinburgh: Scottish Executive.

Scottish Executive (2001a), *Smart Successful Scotland: Ambitions for the Enterprise Networks*, Edinburgh: Scottish Executive.

Scottish Executive (2001b), *Connecting Scotland: our broadband future*, Edinburgh: Scottish Executive.

Scottish Executive (2001c), *Digital Inclusion: Connecting Scotland's People*, Edinburgh: Scottish Executive.

3
The National and European Dimension

Gavin McCrone

This chapter sets Scotland's economy in its international context and considers the effect that both European and UK policies have had on its development. It concludes with a discussion of the scope available to Scotland's devolved government and Parliament to assist that development.

The trading environment

With a population of only five million, international trade is of the greatest importance to Scotland's prosperity, and industries that have been successful therefore tend to be export oriented. For manufacturers this is demonstrated by surveys in which Scotland's exports are shown to be 40 per cent per head above the UK average (SCDI, 1999). Three quarters of these exports are accounted for by just four industries: office machinery and computers; radio and communications equipment; whisky; and chemicals (Table 3.1). In the rest of the economy too, international business is of major importance, especially in tourism, the financial sector (which has experienced very rapid growth) and, of course, the development of North Sea oil.

This dependence on international trade is not new; past industries such as shipbuilding, steel and heavy engineering also relied upon it. But the development of the EU, since Britain joined in 1973, and successive rounds of international tariff reductions have altered fundamentally the direction and scope for Scotland's exports.

As Table 3.2 shows, 62 per cent of Scotland's exports of manufactures now go to the 15 countries of the EU, with France taking the largest share – 17 per cent. And if countries that share in the EU's Single Market through the European Free Trade Association (EFTA) or the European Economic Area (EEA), such as Switzerland and Norway, are included, the

Table 3.1 Scotland's manufactured exports – percentage share (1999)

	%
Office machinery and computers	37
Radio and communications equipment	18
Whisky	10
Chemicals	10
Machinery/equipment, including electrical	6
Transport equipment	4
Food and drink (excluding whisky)	2
Other	15

Source: Survey of Scottish Sales & Exports, April 2001.

Table 3.2 Scotland's manufactured exports by destination (1999)

	Overall (%)	Sub-total (%)
France	17	
Germany	12	
Netherlands	8	
Italy	7	
Sweden	4	
Belgium	3	
Spain	4	
Denmark	2	
Ireland	2	
Other EU	3	
Total EU 15		*62*
European countries associated with EU	6	
Total EU + Associated		*68*
North America	12	
Asia/Pacific	9	
Others	11	
Total Non-EU		*32*
Total	100	

Source: Survey of Scottish Sales & Exports, April 2001.

EU and associated countries account for almost 70 per cent of Scottish exports. By contrast, the North American market, though important, is a long way behind at 11 per cent and the countries of Asia and the Pacific take 9 per cent.

The EU and associated countries give Scotland access to a market of 380 million people (*Eurostat*, 2000). And this market is not just free of tariffs but, as the European Single Market takes effect, free of nontariff barriers such as regulatory restrictions and nationalistic public purchasing, as well. If, as expected, the EU is enlarged, to include applicant countries from Eastern Europe, starting with Poland, Hungary and the Czech Republic during the present decade, the market could eventually extend to a population of around 500 million. Increasingly it is this large market, and not Scotland or even the UK, that firms based in Scotland must see as their home market, since that is what the Single Market legislation is intended to achieve.

Beyond the EU the scene is also transformed. The successive rounds of tariff reduction under the General Agreement on Tariffs and Trade (GATT) and now under the WTO have reduced the average industrial tariff on imports from about 40 per cent after the Second World War to about 4 per cent at the time of writing (Heidensohn, 1995). The last round under GATT – the Uruguay Round – was for the first time aimed at reducing agricultural protection and other nontariff barriers as well as industrial tariffs. This pattern is likely to be repeated if, following the recent WTO meeting in Doha, there is a further round of reductions.

This bonfire of measures to restrict trade has transformed the world from one of domestic markets, which were often quite small, to a truly global economy. Whereas firms used to think differently of the home market, in which they enjoyed some protection, and the export market, where they might have to overcome some trade barrier, this difference is now greatly reduced. This change has not been brought about without opposition, as the violent demonstrations at recent summits have demonstrated. But even if this pressure were now to halt or to slow the movement to a global economy, it is hard to see the liberalisation measures that have been taken so far being reversed.

What this means for Scotland is not only that the opportunities are greater than ever before, but the competition has also become more intense. Scotland's place in the EU is clearly of the greatest importance for its prosperity. But if the EU is further enlarged to include countries that are at present more disadvantaged than herself, Scotland must expect to receive less EU aid than in the past and she will have to face competition from countries where labour is both skilled and low cost. The new members will also be strong competitors for the international investment which has come to Scotland in the past. Scotland's competitive position in Europe and also in the wider international market will therefore depend increasingly on quality, entrepreneurship and showing that it can continue to be an attractive location for direct foreign investment.

Scotland and the euro

As the Single Market develops, companies will tend to specialise and concentrate more. No longer will they feel it necessary to have plants in several EU countries to spread risk. This will be particularly apparent in countries that have adopted the euro, as exchange rate risk was one of the main reasons for diversification. Competition between locations will therefore be intensified and this raises the issue of how Scotland will be placed if the UK were to remain outside the single currency.

Membership of the single currency is a difficult issue in economic terms, leaving aside the political and nationalistic overtones that seem to dominate the debate in the UK (McCrone, 1997; Taylor, 1995). Those countries that have joined see it as the coping stone of the Single Market. It eliminates exchange rate risk in a world in which exchange rates can cause market distortions as serious as tariffs or other protective measures, because they often do not properly reflect the fundamentals of a country's competitive position. It is therefore to be expected that the single currency will result not only in a fairer and more certain competitive environment throughout the EU, but also in larger flows of investment crossing internal EU boundaries. This is expected to intensify competition, leading to more concentration, large scale production and specialisation, features that are characteristic of the US economy. All of this is likely to benefit the EU economy as a whole, even if the effect on individual members cannot easily be forecast.

On the other hand the single currency will only work if member countries can live in the long term with a single monetary policy. This will require them to control their inflation sufficiently to maintain their competitive position one with another. In the absence of a large European budget with automatically stabilising fiscal flows, such as exist within a nation state, there could be serious problems if external shocks to the economy had strong asymmetric effects on member-states. Though little has been said about it so far, it seems inevitable that member-states will have to make greater use of countercyclical fiscal policy to control their economies. The conditions of the Growth and Stability Pact may make this difficult because of the fiscal rigidity imposed, and it is unlikely to be popular, especially when taxes are raised to damp the economy. But in the absence of national monetary policy there will be no alternative. It will be several years before a judgement on the success of monetary union can be made, because if inflation rates diverge, their effect on the competitive position of countries will be gradual. Just as the benefits of the European Monetary Union (EMU) are potentially large, therefore, so also are the risks.

But remaining outside is not without risk either. Britain's competitive position is greatly affected by sterling's exchange rate against the euro. Since the launch of the single currency in 1999, the euro has fallen and the pound, which many experts thought already overvalued against other European currencies, has further strengthened. A reasonable estimate is that at the start of 2002 it was between 10 and 20 per cent overvalued. Clearly this has serious adverse consequences for Britain's exports to Europe and it is not surprising that the performance of manufacturing has suffered. Foreign investors will also be concerned that the high exchange rate erodes the UK's competitive position and makes it less attractive as a location for investment. The decision by Motorola in 2001 to close its Bathgate mobile phones plant, when demand turned down, rather its plant in Germany, may be an indication of difficulties ahead.

With its higher export volume per head and its dependence on foreign investment, Scotland is even more vulnerable than the UK as a whole to anything that adversely affects its competitive position. The balance of benefit versus risk for Scotland may therefore be more in favour of joining the euro than for the UK generally, but only so long as entry could be obtained at a competitive exchange rate. The critical issue, therefore, especially for the UK where the economic cycle has tended to be poorly synchronised with Continental Europe, will be whether it is able to live with the European Central Bank's monetary policy, while maintaining its competitive position and controlling inflation, if necessary, by other means.

European and national policies

The encouragement of both foreign and domestic investment in Scotland has been the rationale behind both UK and EU regional policies. UK policy includes the assistance to qualifying investment in UK assisted areas and the help available through SE, Highlands and Islands Enterprise (HIE) and the Local Enterprise Companies (LECs). EU aid from the Structural Funds is also available in designated areas.

UK regional development policy

Regional policy in the UK has a long history. It has varied considerably in intensity, in the instruments used and the amount of funds provided.

Today the principal instrument is Regional Selective Assistance (RSA), available under section 7 of the Industrial Development Act 1982. This is normally provided as a grant to capital investment, although other forms of assistance such as guarantees or loans are permitted under the legislation.

RSA is provided in designated assisted areas, classified in two categories according to the severity of their problems, and at rates that vary accordingly. It is subject to tests of viability, employment creation or preservation and additionality – a requirement to demonstrate that the project would not go ahead, or would go ahead on a more restricted basis in the absence of assistance. RSA is available for both inward investment and indigenous projects to encourage them to set up, to expand and to modernise. Similar grants are available from HIE for projects in that body's area, though these tend to be somewhat wider in scope and may be more generous. SE also has powers to give limited grants under special approved schemes, notably to small business.

Public expenditure on regional assistance has fallen substantially from the peak levels of the 1980s, and in real terms at the start of the new century was below a quarter of what it had been 20 years earlier. In part this reflects the reduction in coverage of assisted areas in Scotland, but it is mainly a consequence of the phasing out of other forms of assistance, which were automatic and nonselective. Expenditure on RSA is currently around £70 million a year (Table 3.3) (House of Commons, 2001).

Estimates of the effects of this grant-based regional policy have been made in the past (Moore *et al.*, 1986; DTI, 1993). But such assessments

Table 3.3 Regional selective assistance grants (2000–2001). Offers accepted and payments in £000

	No.	Value	New employment	Safeguarded employment	Payments
Scotland					
UK owned	62	28 708	2 262	2 312	25 158
Foreign	54	76 042	7 377	3 251	44 689
Total	116	104 750	9 639	5 563	69 839
Great Britain					
UK owned	450	146 536	19 126	8 056	95 477
Foreign	122	261 069	20 405	11 305	124 217
Total	572	407 607	39 531	19 361	219 694

Source: Annual Report on the Industrial Development Act 1982, House of Commons paper 83, June 2001.

are difficult, and up-to-date estimates do not exist. What is clear to those that administer these schemes is that projects which have been aided by RSA or by HIE and SE would not have gone ahead without assistance, or would only have done so on a much reduced scale. Other areas of the EU with which Scotland is in competition for investment also offer financial assistance, sometimes on a more generous scale. And while financial assistance is only one of a number of factors influencing those who make such decisions, without it many fewer projects would have come to Scotland. Indeed, without it, Scotland would not have become a major centre for the electronics industry. Nor would many of the other industries, such as pharmaceuticals, wood processing and pulp and paper have expanded in Scotland on the scale that they have.

Changes were made to arrangements for RSA in 2000 and it is too soon to estimate their effects. The most significant was a cut back in the coverage of assisted area. The new designated areas not only take account of changes in economic circumstances, such as Scotland's greater prosperity, but also bring the top tier into line with the highest category of assisted area (Objective 1 Areas) under the European policy (Map 3.1). Tier 1, in which assistance is permitted up to 35 per cent up of capital cost, is based on EU regions with GDP per head of less than 75 per cent of the EU average.[1] While other parts of the UK qualify on this basis, no part of Scotland does.[2] This is, of course, a consequence of the way in which regions have been defined by government for the EU system. But the areas of Central Scotland most in need of assistance, the South West, the Borders and the Highlands and Islands are all covered by Tier 2, in which grant assistance may be up to a ceiling of between 10 and 20 per cent of capital cost; but, exceptionally, grants up to 30 per cent may be permitted in the Highlands and Islands in the period up to 2006. This tier does not have to be coterminous with EU assisted areas, though there is considerable overlap. The Scottish Executive seems confident that this will allow sufficient discretion to provide assistance at a level not very different from what was available before.

Scottish Enterprise, Highlands and Islands Enterprise, Locate in Scotland

The purpose of SE and HIE is to help to create jobs and increase prosperity in Scotland (SE, 2000; HIE, 2000). Their aim is to strengthen competitiveness, to attract and encourage new businesses, promote linkages between them and work with other organisations, such as education and training institutions, to improve the skill base of the economy. They have powers to give specific grant assistance, provide loans and take

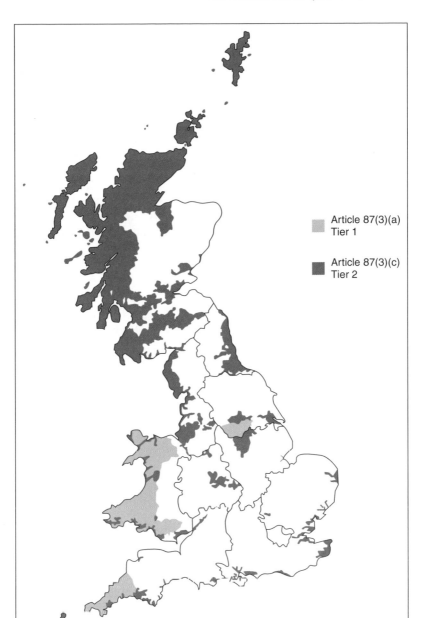

Map 3.1 The assisted areas (2000/2006).

Source: Annual Report of the Industrial Development Act 1982, 2001.

equity in companies; and they may undertake schemes of environmental improvement, particularly where this repairs the ravages of past economic activity and enhances an area's prospects of attracting new investment. They are responsible for assisting in training, the development of skills and for improving business infrastructure. Particular attention has been given to trying to improve Scotland's low business birth rate; and, jointly with the Industry Department of the Scottish Executive, to attracting inward investment and the promotion of exports. For this very wide remit SE has an annual budget of around £470 million and HIE around £80 million.

The attraction of inward investment has been a considerable success. Over the years 1991–2001 grant offers were made on 467 foreign-owned projects with projected employment (new and safeguarded) of 74 000 (House of Commons, 2001). This is a substantial number by any standards, even if past experience indicates that not all of the projects will go ahead on the scale anticipated. Some 23 per cent of those employed in manufacturing, about 80 000 jobs, and about one-third of the output is now accounted for by overseas owned companies (Scottish Office, 1999). Whereas originally these companies were predominantly from North America, there is now a wide spread of investors from Europe and Asia as well.

Of course, not all of the overseas projects that come to Scotland succeed; and, if there is a failure, this provokes much adverse comment, especially if the project is large. Sometimes it is asserted that too much attention and assistance is given to inward investors rather than indigenous companies. In 2000/2001 payments of RSA totalled £70 million of which £25 million was to UK firms and £45 million to overseas companies (Table 3.3). But overseas companies are not more generously treated – the rules for them are the same as for indigenous companies. It is simply that many projects by foreign-owned companies are large and involve substantial investment.

Nevertheless the birth rate of new indigenous business remains disappointing, among the lowest of UK regions. SE has developed a business birth rate strategy in an attempt to remedy this imbalance and work done by some of the LECs has been promising (SE, 1993).[3] But there is no reason to believe that any less effort in the attraction of inward investors would somehow result in more indigenous growth. Indeed, without inward investing companies, the economy would have been in a much worse plight over the last thirty years, as the traditional heavy industries declined. The effort to promote inward investment therefore needs to be maintained, and to achieve that

Scotland must remain a competitive location within the EU. At the same time, however, to strengthen policies that help to remedy the weakness in new firm formation and growth must be a high priority for SE and the Scottish Executive.

The European structural funds

In contrast to the expenditure on UK regional policy, European expenditure on the Structural Funds greatly increased in the 1990s and Scotland has been one of the principal parts of the UK to benefit. The European Regional Development Fund (ERDF) was set up in 1975 to assist both industrial investment and infrastructure in Europe's disadvantaged areas, and with the accession of Greece, Spain and Portugal in the 1980s, greatly increased impetus was given to the development of regional policy.

Since 1988 the Structural Funds – ERDF, the European Social Fund (ESF) and the guidance part of the European Agricultural Guarantee and Guidance Fund (EAGGF) have been brigaded together under the overall control of the Commissioner responsible for regional policy. A fourth fund, the Financial Instrument for Fisheries Guidance (FIFG), was added later, with power to help areas affected by the decline of the fishing industry. Finance for the Funds was doubled between 1988 and 1993, to help the weaker regions prepare for the Single Market; and in December 1992 it was decided to increase it again, by a further 50 per cent. By 1999 the Structural Funds were expected to take up some 35 per cent of the EU budget and the whole budget was to rise to 1.27 per cent of EU GDP.

Assistance is available to projects in designated areas across the EU. Since the reform in 2000, this is provided in accordance with three priority objectives, two of which are regionally specific: Objective 1 for lagging regions, where GDP is 75 per cent or less of the EU average per head; and Objective 2, for areas of industrial reconversion, rural areas and sparsely populated areas. Objective 1 areas are given the highest priority and receive about 70 per cent of total expenditure. Objective 3 provides assistance for human resource development, in particular training and retraining, throughout the EU.

Assistance can be provided for infrastructure, for industrial projects and for small and medium enterprises, for which purpose it is administered in global amounts to be disbursed through intermediary bodies such as the LECs, local authorities or enterprise trusts. But the assistance has to accord with priorities set out by member-states in their Single Planning Documents which are approved by the Commission and form the basis of a five-year allocation.

In addition to the bulk of the expenditure under these three Objectives, 5 per cent of the Structural Funds budget is allocated to four
Community Initiatives to fund projects that accord with priorities determined by the EU. These are: INTERREG to assist cross border activities;
EQUAL to tackle inequalities in the labour market; LEADER PLUS for
integrated rural strategies; and URBAN for the economic and social
regeneration of cities.

Over the period 1994–1999 Scotland received £1495 million or a
yearly average of nearly £300 million from the Structural Funds. In
this period, before the 2000 reform, the Highlands and Islands were
classified as an Objective 1 area and the greater part of Scotland was
covered by one Objective or another. The allocation for the period to
2006 is 1610 million euros (approximately £980 million at current
exchange rates) (Table 3.4). But this is mainly because of generous
transition arrangements for the Highlands and Islands and other areas
that have lost their status (Map 3.2).

The purpose of the changes introduced in 2000 was to simplify policy,
give it a sharper focus and to concentrate it. The net contributor countries had virtually reached the limit of what they were prepared to pay
and the entry to the EU of countries from Central and Eastern Europe,
all of which have low GDP per head compared with existing EU members and well below that of Scotland, would greatly add to the claims on
the Structural Funds. While Scotland will still receive substantial funds
under transitional arrangements up to 2006, the outlook thereafter must
be for substantially reduced assistance as the priority for EU policy shifts
to new member-states.

Table 3.4   Allocations to Scotland from the EU structural funds (2000–2006)
(million euro)

Area	Funds	Amount
Highlands and Islands: Transitional Programme	ERDF, ESF, EAGGF, FIFG	308
West of Scotland: Objective 2	ERDF, ESF	480
East of Scotland: Objective 2	ERDF	250
South of Scotland (Dumfries, Galloway & Borders): Objective 2	ERDF	73
All Scotland: Objective 3	ESF	499
Total	All Funds	1 610

Source: *European Funding and Scotland: A Guide to the Funding Process*, European Commission,
2001.

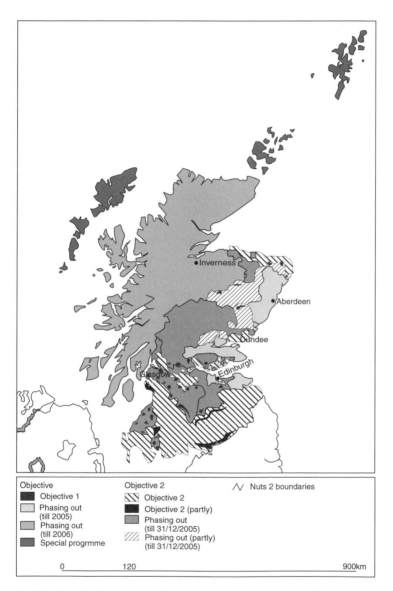

Legend:

Objective
- Objective 1
- Phasing out (till 2005)
- Phasing out (till 2006)
- Special progrmme

Objective 2
- Objective 2
- Objective 2 (partly)
- Phasing out (till 31/12/2005)
- Phasing out (partly) (till 31/12/2005)

∧∨ Nuts 2 boundaries

0   120   900km

Map 3.2   Scotland – structural funds (2000–2006): Areas eligible under Objectives 1 and 2.

Source: European Commission Representation in Scotland, 2001.
Reproduced with kind permission of the European Commission.

The large volume of EU funding can be seen, in part, as compensating for the decline in UK regional assistance. But two qualifications have to be made. First, much of the EU funding goes to infrastructure projects and, while welcome, is not comparable with UK regional assistance; and secondly there remains the vexed issue of 'additionality'. The EU has always maintained that it wanted to see its funds used for something that would not otherwise be affordable. This is relatively straightforward in countries that are net beneficiaries from the EU budget, but those that are net contributors have tended to try to use EU funding to refinance projects that would otherwise be paid for wholly from national funds. Eventually this issue came to a head in the UK and the present practice in Scotland is for a separate line for EU funding to be shown in the Scottish block allocation from the Treasury.

In practice this means that EU funding still scores as UK public expenditure and is subject to Treasury control. The Scottish allocation from the Treasury (known as the Departmental Expenditure Limit or DEL) is therefore no larger than it would otherwise be; but EU funds received, though part of the DEL, finance regional development projects in Scotland which would not otherwise be assisted. Since the Scottish block cannot be increased this means that the more EU money is received for qualifying projects, the less is available for other purposes. There is therefore additionality at the level of the project, but not at the level of the DEL. This bizarre arrangement has so far satisfied the EU, but it reduces the value of the aid to Scotland and remains in many respects unsatisfactory.

The Scottish Executive and Parliament

Devolution raised expectations that the Scottish Executive would adopt policies to improve the performance of the Scottish economy. Yet the powers of the Scottish Executive and Parliament in this area are constrained. The principal levers for influencing the economy, monetary policy, exchange rates, fiscal policy and regulatory policy, including monopoly and competition, necessarily remain on a UK basis. The Scottish Executive has taken over responsibility for those policies previously administered by the Secretary of State: Regional Selective Assistance (RSA); SE, HIE and the LECs; education and training; and the provision of infrastructure. But it cannot unilaterally alter the qualifying levels of RSA, the range of activities to which it applies or the coverage of assisted areas, since these have to be agreed on a UK basis to ensure fair competition across the UK. For similar reasons, the European Commission, which is concerned with competition across the EU, also has to approve the regime of assistance.

Nevertheless there is scope for effective action, if the powers available to the Scottish Executive and Parliament are wisely used. The key to this, and the thread that has been running through this chapter, is the need to maintain and improve Scotland's competitive position in Europe's Single Market, especially as it takes in more countries, and in the world's increasing global market.

The legislative powers of the Scottish Parliament and the independence of the Scottish Executive mean that some changes can be made for which it might previously have been hard to secure agreement at Westminster or legislative time. There is now greater freedom to alter the institutional arrangements. The public bodies charged with promoting economic development and tourism are the responsibility of the Scottish Executive and their form and constitution, or even their existence, can be altered by Scottish legislation. But there are dangers in this as well as potential benefits. Experience shows that Ministers are all too often prone to deflect criticisms directed at themselves by reorganising the public body in the area responsible. Seldom do they seem to appreciate the damage to morale or the loss of momentum that radical changes (often made for purely political reasons) cause. There are many examples of this in Scotland.[4] Staff morale nearly always suffers; key members of staff leave and are hard to replace; and it may take years for the new structures to bed in and become effective. There are of course cases where change is fully justified. But often it is not, and Ministers should satisfy themselves not only that real benefits will result, but that such benefits will outweigh the damage that change inevitably brings, before embarking on reorganisation.

Probably the most fruitful areas for action by the Scottish Executive are the fostering and promotion of small and medium enterprises, investment in human capital through improved education and training and investment in infrastructure that assists growth. All of these are within the Scottish Executive and Parliament's responsibility.

Scotland's relatively low birth rate for new businesses has already been referred to. It has been subjected to a lot of study. But despite the many schemes that exist to help small business both at the UK and Scottish levels, progress is slow and the results are disappointing. However, work by some of the LECs, notably that done by the Lanarkshire Development Agency, has been encouraging and may point the way forward for wider application (Talbot and Reeves, 1997).

Scotland's record in education and training is patchy. A total of 48 per cent of school leavers go on to university or further education, a substantially higher proportion than in the rest of the UK (Committee of Inquiry into Professional Conditions of Service for Teachers, 2000). A general shortage of graduates is therefore not the problem, although there may be a mismatch between subjects taken and career opportunities available. But the whole UK, including Scotland, still suffers from a low level of educational attainment among a large section of the population. This is particularly apparent in areas of deprivation, such as the peripheral urban housing estates, where many children leave school with few qualifications and some with none at all. Levels of numeracy and literacy are often not adequate to equip young people for jobs in a modern economy that is becoming increasingly knowledge based. Language ability, despite more than 25 years membership of the EU and freedom of movement in the Single Market, remains throughout the UK depressingly poor and certainly much inferior to levels achieved in other European countries.

Nor is the position better in vocational training. An out-of-date apprenticeship system that was based on time served and imposed unacceptable rigidity on the labour force, with the attendant ills of demarcation, has now largely gone. But too many of the schemes that replaced it were as much designed to get people off the unemployment register for political reasons as to provide effective and worthwhile training. And because many of the colleges that provided certificates and diplomas have sought and acquired university status, these qualifications have been seen wrongly as of lesser importance than a university degree. Yet it is lack of technicians, craftsmen and good vocational skills that too often hold up the growth of the economy.

Improvement in these areas, as well as investment in key well-chosen infrastructure, is of the greatest importance for the competitive strength of the Scottish economy. Such improvement will cost money but, if sensibly directed, it will pay dividends in improved economic performance. While the resources available to the Scottish Executive are limited, the essence of good government is to choose priorities well. Indigenous growth from small business and investment in human capital should therefore be amongst the highest priorities for those responsible for the government of Scotland.

Conclusion

This chapter has attempted to show that Scotland's future prosperity depends on its competitive strength, particularly within the European market, the destination for some 70 per cent of Scotland's exports of manufactures. Continued membership of the EU is therefore essential for Scotland; and for the overseas investment on which the economy heavily depends. Membership of the single currency at the right exchange rate would benefit Scotland and may become increasingly necessary. But it is not a simple matter and the risks are substantial.

Government and EU policies to promote regional development have been of major assistance in restructuring the economy and without them the electronics and associated industries, which are now so important to Scottish GDP, employment and exports, would never have developed to the extent they have. But both UK and EU regional policies have been curtailed and the focus of EU policies in the enlarged Union can be expected to shift to the new member-states. The maintenance of Scotland's competitive position will therefore in future depend more on action taken within Scotland.

The Scottish Executive and Parliament, though not responsible for monetary or fiscal policy, can take valuable action. A better performance from small business and a more skilled and vocationally qualified workforce would do much to enhance Scotland's competitive position in an increasingly competitive Europe.

Notes

1   Based on the EU's Nomenclature for Territorial Statistics (NUTS).
2   Coverage of Tier 1 includes Cornwall, Merseyside, part of South Yorkshire and West Wales, and the Welsh valleys, as shown in Map 3.1.
3   This strategy is considered in greater detail in Chapter 14.
4   The change from the Scottish Development Agency to Scottish Enterprise and numerous changes to the structure of Health Boards and Trusts are just some examples.

References

Department of Trade and Industry (1993), *Regional Selective Assistance: 1985–88: An Evaluation by PA Cambridge Economic Consultants Ltd.*, London: Her Majesty's Stationery Office. See also House of Commons (1995), *Regional Policy*, Fourth Report of the Trade and Industry Committee 1994–95, HC paper 356–1, London: HMSO.

European Commission (2001), *European Funding and Scotland: A guide to the funding process*, 5th edition, Edinburgh: European Commission Representation in Scotland.

Eurostat (2000), Yearbook, Luxembourg: Commission of the European Communities.

Heidensohn, K. (1995), *Europe and World Trade*, London: Pinter.

Highlands and Islands Enterprise (2000), Annual Report, Inverness: Highlands and Islands Enterprise.

House of Commons (2001), *Annual Report on the Industrial Development Act 1982*, by the Secretary of State for Trade and Industry, the First Minister of the

Scottish Parliament and the First Minister of the National Assembly for Wales for the year ended March 2001, HC paper No. 83, London: HM Stationery Office.

McCrone, G. (1997), *European Monetary Union and Regional Development*, Hume paper Vol. 5, No. 1, Edinburgh: Edinburgh University Press.

Moore, B., J. Rhodes and P. Tyler (1986), *The Effects of Government Regional Economic Policy*, London: Department of Trade and Industry.

Report of the Committee of Inquiry into Professional Conditions of Service for Teachers (McCrone Committee) (2000), *A Teaching Profession for the 21st Century*, Edinburgh: Scottish Executive.

Scottish Council Development and Industry (1999), *Survey of Scottish Manufacturing and Exports 1998/9*, Edinburgh: Scottish Council Development and Industry.

Scottish Council Development and Industry (2001), *Survey of Scottish Sales and Exports*, Edinburgh: Scottish Council Development and Industry, April.

Scottish Enterprise (1993), *Improving the Business Birth Rate: A Strategy for Scotland*, and the accompanying research paper *Scotland's Business Birth Rate*, Glasgow: Scottish Enterprise.

Scottish Enterprise (2000), Annual Report, Glasgow: Scottish Enterprise.

Scottish Office (1999), *Statistical Bulletin: Industry Series*, Edinburgh: Scottish Office.

Talbot, S. and R. Reeves, (1997), 'Boosting the business birth rate in Scotland: Evidence from the Lanarkshire Development Agency's Entrepreneurship Programme', *Quarterly Economic Commentary*, Vol. 22, No. 2, Glasgow: Fraser of Allander Institute.

Taylor, C. (1995), *EMU 2000*, Chatham House papers, London: Pinter, for Royal Institute for International Affairs.

4
Scotland's Economy and Benchmarks
Jonathan Star

Introduction

This chapter will bring an external perspective to the debate about Scotland's future economic prospects. In assessing these, it is important to look at economic policies and performance in other parts of the world. To achieve this, the chapter uses comparative information to help understand a little more about Scotland – where it has come from, where it sits today, and its prospects for the future.

This allows us to do three things:

1 To set in context the performance of Scotland's economy, comparing with other countries or regions.
2 To describe ways in which some other places have created success for themselves, including Ireland, Finland, Cambridge (UK) and Singapore.
3 To offer some thoughts about economic aspirations and direction for Scotland over the next 20 years.

A note on benchmarking

In a world increasingly characterised by global competition and knowledge, 'benchmarking' has become the conventional approach for comparing the performance of different entities (including teams, companies and countries). In Scotland, the current strategy for the Enterprise Networks (Scottish Executive, 2001a) has been given added focus by the publication of a set of target measures for achievement within the Scottish economy (Scottish Enterprise, 2001a). The overall aspiration is for Scotland to exhibit economic performance on a par with the upper quartile of Organisation for Economic Co-operation and Development (OECD) nations. Policy-making in Scotland is becoming more influenced by international benchmarking.

As its popularity suggests, the concept of benchmarking is very seductive, but it does raise some issues. There are problems of comparability, especially across countries because of differences in institutional arrangements. It can also lead to an overemphasis on the quantitative, leading to numeric targets and relative rankings being perceived as far more important than less tangible comparisons. Because of these difficulties, benchmarking is probably best used as a tool with which to learn about one's own position and challenges. It provides a useful, objective, external perspective about where you stand in relation to others.

But even then, there are real dangers in what to do about the findings. It is very tempting to look at well-performing comparators and feel that, by replicating what they do, Scotland could achieve higher levels of performance. But this is dangerous. It can lead to policy-makers pursuing very similar strategies in different regions. Scott observes that: 'policies should really encourage regional specialisation rather than the attempted duplication of economic achievements elsewhere' (Scott, 1998). Similarly, Kay suggests that: 'competitive advantage is based, not on doing what others already do well, but on doing what others cannot do as well' (Kay, 2000).

The focus of Scottish industrial policy must be on what Scotland does better. It follows that the real benefits of benchmarking must be to assess what is different, distinctive and valuable about Scotland.

Scotland's comparative performance

The following section places Scotland's economic performance in context, by providing some basic comparisons with other countries and regions. The choice of benchmark economies has been made on the basis of data availability, and an assessment of characteristics that seem particularly relevant to informing Scotland's policy choices of the future. Many of the comparisons have been taken from the *Tracking the Bigger Picture* work undertaken by the Fraser of Allander Institute (FAI) for SE (Scottish Enterprise, 2001a). They scored comparator economies against a list of criteria that included:

- Similar economic history;
- Similar contemporary economy;
- Socioeconomic indicators to which Scotland aspires;
- Similar drivers of change;

- Key current or future competitors;
- Relevant and innovative policies.

Scotland in context

The following figures show the most accepted indicator for the wealth and dynamism of an economy – the rate of economic growth. Because different countries will be at different stages of a business cycle, it is best to take some measure over a longer time period – in this case over 15 years – where data allows.

GDP growth

Scotland has historically grown at just over 2 per cent over the period 1985–2001, a similar rate to that within other European countries like Denmark and Switzerland. The UK and Finland have grown slightly more quickly, but the star performers over the period have undoubtedly been Ireland and Singapore (Figure 4.1).

Unemployment rates

Figure 4.2 shows comparative unemployment rates, measured by the accepted International Labour Organisation (ILO), over the 1990s. Scotland has a slightly higher average rate than the UK, but outperforms, on average, Ireland and Finland. Scotland also outperforms many other

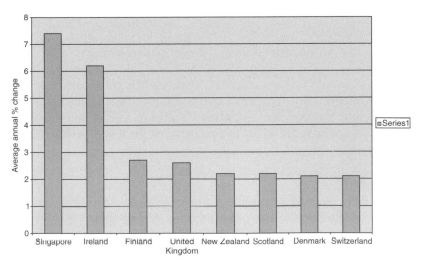

Figure 4.1   Average annual GDP growth (1985–2001).

Source: OECD Economic Outlook, 2001.

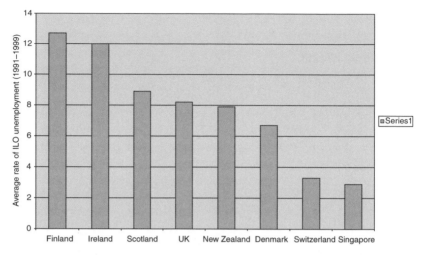

Figure 4.2 Average annual rate of unemployment – ILO-based measure (1991–1999).

Source: OECD, 2001.

regions of Europe, reflecting the rigidities in many European labour markets. But Scotland's job creation has not been good by international standards, particularly compared to the spectacular levels of job creation achieved in the US during the 1990s.

Labour productivity

One of the critical determinants of economic prosperity and living standards is labour productivity – the value added produced in an economy divided by the number of workers. It is commonly accepted that UK productivity in general lags behind our competitors in continental Europe and the USA. Two other UK regions (Wales and the North East) that are included in these comparisons lie below Scotland, plus New Zealand (Figure 4.3).

Spending on R&D

A major influence on productivity is spending on R&D. Here, data is available that provides a breakdown of R&D spending by its three major categories – businesses, government and higher education. Scotland performs well in the proportion of R&D funds that are spent in higher education institutions, and in government, but levels of business investment in R&D fall well short of comparator nations. Recent figures from the Office for National Statistics (ONS), find that Scotland spends

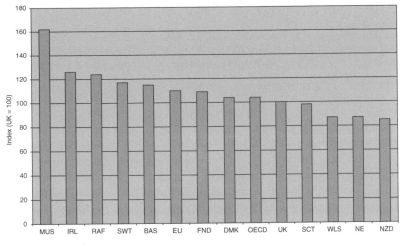

Figure 4.3 Labour productivity 1998 (UK = 100).

Source: Scottish Enterprise, 2001.

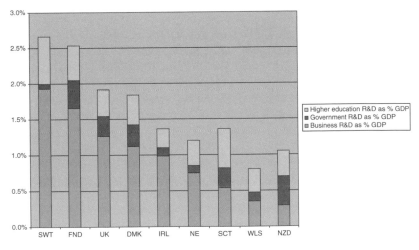

Figure 4.4 R&D as a percentage of GDP (1999).

Source: OECD, Scottish Enterprise, 2001.

0.6 per cent of GDP on business R&D, the US spends 2 per cent and Japan spends 2.1 per cent. The average UK spend is 1.2 per cent (Figure 4.4).

Table 4.1   Population (between ages of 25 and 64) that has attained a degree, diploma, or equivalent

	Diploma or equivalent (typically 2 years study) (%)	Degree or equivalent (typically 3 years study) (%)
United Kingdom	8	17
Finland	17	14
Switzerland	9	15
Denmark	20	7
New Zealand	14	13
Singapore	10	17
Ireland	10	11

Note: The UK emerges as a country with a very high proportion of graduates within its labour force, but it has a significantly lower proportion of population with a Tertiary Type B qualification – typically a diploma or other qualification which lasts for two years and has a focus on gaining practical, technical and occupational skills. Comparable figures are not available for Scotland, but other data suggest that the proportion of the Scottish population achieving these levels of education is two or three percentage points above the UK average.

Source: OECD, Singapore Statistics Office, 2001.

Skills and knowledge

In an economy where success is increasingly based on skills and knowledge, it is vital that Scotland continues to produce, and provide work for, highly skilled people. Table 4.1 provides international comparisons, in terms of the population that has attained high-level qualifications. This indicates that Scotland, alongside the UK, has a very high proportion of graduates within its core workforce. However, both the UK and Scotland tend to have a significantly lower proportion of population with a Tertiary Type B qualification – typically a diploma or other qualification which lasts for two years and has a focus on gaining practical, technical and occupational skills.

Exporting

Scotland exports a high proportion of its GDP, and shows up well in terms of the value of exports per worker. Much of this has been due to the dominance of electronics manufacturing in the structure of Scottish exports (Figure 4.5).

Digital connectivity

In 2001, the percentage of businesses 'connected' in Scotland stands at 83 per cent, a little below the UK average of 87 per cent (Scottish Enterprise, 2001b) (Figure 4.6).

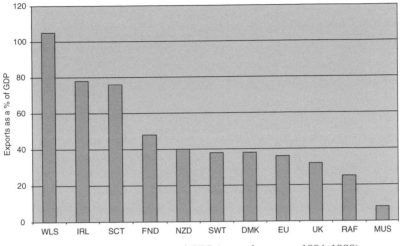

Figure 4.5 Exports as a percentage of GDP (annual average, 1994–1998).

Source: Scottish Enterprise, 2001.

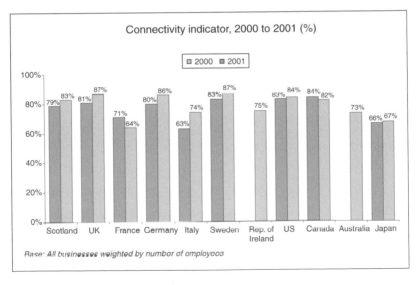

Figure 4.6 DTI connectivity indicator.

Source: Scottish Enterprise, DTI, 2001.

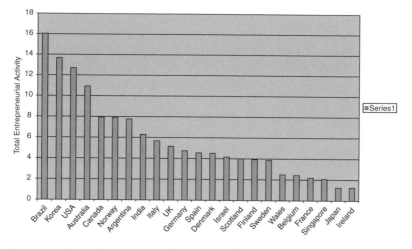

Figure 4.7   Global Entrepreneurship Monitor 2000: index of total entrepreneurial activity.

Source: Global Entrepreneurship Monitor, 2000.

Entrepreneurship

It is widely acknowledged that Scotland lags behind the UK average for new business starts *per capita*, but there is no internationally comparable definition that is appropriate. The Global Entrepreneurship Monitor (Levie and Stelle, 2000) is an ambitious attempt to provide this comparison. It shows Scotland as middle ranking in terms of entrepreneurial competitors. Their measure, Total Entrepreneurial Activity, is a sum of two measures:

1 The nascent entrepreneurial prevalence rate – that is, the proportion of working age adults actively involved in the creation of a firm which they would own in whole or in part
2 The new firm owner-manager prevalence rate, that is the proportion of working age adults owning and managing new firms (less than three years old).

Scotland lies well behind nations such as the US, Canada and the UK, but above Wales, France, Singapore, Japan and Ireland.

    This brief look through comparative data provides the following conclusions. Scotland can be described as open to global markets, slow growing, of average prosperity. Its labour market performs well, with strong performance in higher education, but less so at more intermediate levels. It is moderately entrepreneurial, and in common with other parts of the UK, productivity is low. Its R&D performance is mixed, with higher education doing well but businesses poorly.

Country and regional comparators

This section provides brief details of countries or regions that have succeeded economically over recent years. Many of them started off in positions less advantageous than Scotland, but they have fought to create strong successful elements within their economies. It focuses on six places where Scotland may have something to learn. Some of these comparators – Finland, Ireland and Denmark – are selected from the data comparisons. The others – Singapore, Cambridge (UK) and North Rhine Westphalia – have been chosen because they highlight other aspects of policy and economic history that may be particularly relevant for Scotland.

Ireland

Ireland's recent economic success has been striking. In 1975, its national wealth was two-thirds of the EU average. Today, it is 20 per cent richer than the average and still continuing to grow. In 2001, its growth in industrial production approached 14 per cent, compared to near zero in many European nations. However, more recent economic difficulties, particularly in the electronics sector, is sure to limit this growth in the near future.

There are many explanations for the Irish economic improvement. According to the OECD, recent surge in activity has been due to 'capital accumulation, productivity growth, technological change and a young, educated and growing population' (OECD, 2001a).

Its industrial policy has focused on developing a high-value added manufacturing base through foreign direct investment. To encourage this, some distinctive fiscal arrangements have been most helpful – notably the 10 per cent corporate tax rate. There has been a transformation in the make up of the Irish manufacturing base. Foreign-owned firms now account for more than 80 per cent of Ireland's manufacturing output, up from 60 per cent in 1983. The structure of Ireland's exports has changed. This boost to manufacturing through foreign direct investment (FDI) has ensured that manufacturing employment in Ireland has remained broadly the same in the last two decades, whereas in the UK and in Scotland, it has fallen by over 30 per cent.

The Irish approach to FDI has been highly targeted towards three key sectors – electronics, pharmaceutical and internationally traded services – which were likely to have the maximum impact on the Irish economy in terms of growth prospects, employment potential and links into domestic providers.

FDI is far from being the whole story of Ireland's economic success. Ireland's concentration on improving its overall education system has led to higher skill levels in the young workforce. Skill levels are now on a par with the EU average, but Ireland's advantage has largely accrued through unit labour costs. It has a quality workforce at a low cost. This ensures that goods are competitive in international markets.

But Ireland's industrial policy model is facing severe challenges. The concentration on inward investment is looking increasingly unlikely to sustain the number of jobs that it once did. The EU will be concentrating its support in enlargement to the east. As the market for FDI shifts to increasingly cost-competitive locations elsewhere, Ireland must look to higher value activities – and the domestic spirit of enterprise if it is to maintain its economic progress.

Finland

The story of Finland is instructive because it suggests how a sophisticated base of demand, coupled with a policy environment that encourages the right type of growth can lead to strong growth in certain industrial sectors.

The electronic equipment industry has been a major growth engine of the Finnish economy, and looks likely to remain so. Nokia, a mobile communications company, has provided much of this impetus and provides massive boosts to Finnish export growth. Government policy has played a role in this, by concentrating academic research in a limited number of centres, by providing an engineering-oriented education system, by early and far-reaching liberalisation of the telecommunications system and by allowing foreign competition in critical segments of the market.

However, growth and development in electronic equipment has had very little impact on productivity and economic performance in other sectors. The OECD notes that there is little evidence that ICT has become a main developer of the rest of the Finnish economy, with the possible exception of financial services. Annual average productivity growth was about 2.5 per cent between 1995 and 1999, but productivity growth in electrical and optical equipment was about 18 per cent (OECD, 2000).

Finland currently has very high levels of investment in R&D, but it has been two decades of intensive R&D spending, and a history of innovation that have been the main determinants of its recent success. This focus on innovation is particularly true in the high technology sector, but also in other areas such as engineering, forestry and product design.

Tekes – the national technology agency – has a driving role in developing the technology capability of firms in Finland. One example is that of Technology Clinics.

The Technology Clinic initiative was launched in 1992 by Tekes (the National Technology Agency). The main purpose of the initiative is to promote the adaptation of specified technologies for problem solving in small- to medium-sized enterprises (SMEs). The initiative aims to introduce SMEs to new technological sources and to raise awareness of external R&D resources. In essence, technology clinics are used to develop the demand (SMEs) and supply (technology providers).

A recent evaluation of the Technology Clinic programme operated by Tekes has also shown positive results. The main findings of the evaluation were the following:

- The clinics were easy to carry out with minimum bureaucracy/cost and the resulting technical success rate has been high;
- The clinic projects have helped some SMEs overcome their fears of using external technology support;
- There has been a permanent increase in the R&D budgets of the clinic customer companies after the clinics; and
- A variety of suppliers of technological expertise have greatly increased their understanding of, and ability to work with, SMEs and there is tangible evidence of further joint work being undertaken on a full cost basis after the clinics finished.

Finland has made the development of a well-educated, multilingual, motivated work force a national priority. The International Institute for Management Development (IMD) ranks Finland's employees first in the world in terms of effectiveness. Finland ranks third in terms of quality of management and sixth in terms of science and technology. The workforce is already generally proficient in several languages. The business culture in Finland is perceived to be collaborative – with knowledge sharing as a standard model of business. Collective pooling of resources, collaborative R&D, excellent links between academia and industry are the norm in Finnish industry. Collaboration also exists beyond national boundaries, as evidenced by co-ordination with other Nordic nations in developing telecommunications infrastructure.

Denmark

Denmark also offers some real lessons for Scotland. It is the same size – 5 million population – but it is one of the most productive, wealthiest nations in Europe. Denmark's continued success is based on investment in knowledge and innovation (Local Futures Group, 2000). Its future as a knowledge-driven economy is underwritten by its performance in education, where its high-performing schools, colleges and universities provide a continuous source of highly productive workers.

In common with Finland and Sweden, Denmark has the highest proportion of people employed in R&D in the EU. It has the highest rate of internet access both at home and at work. For figures in 1999, 37 per cent of the population had internet access at home, compared with around 15 per cent in the UK (Local Futures Group, 2000). It has a very advanced telecommunications infrastructure, with a fibre-optic network covering the whole country.

But the prosperity in Denmark has not been confined to a limited number of high-technology sectors. While ICT and biotechnology are driving growth, innovation in other sectors is a prevalent characteristic. This includes the food production sector, which remains Denmark's largest single sector.

Cambridge UK

The experience of Cambridge UK highlights the ways in which universities and research institutes have combined with other factors to create a dynamic cluster of high-technology start-up companies in the Cambridge area.

The 'Cambridge Phenomenon' has been well documented in two reports by Segal Quince Wicksteed (SQW, 1985, 2001). The earlier report concluded that the Cambridge area was already characterised by 'a significant and growing number of high-tech firms that were essentially based on the development and/or exploitation of research and technology.'

Over the last 20 years, Cambridge's economy has built on these foundations. The number of high-technology businesses in the area has risen from 30 to 1 450 in 2000. Now 30 000 are employed in high-technology industry, around 12 per cent of the local workforce (SQW, 2001). The more traditional sectors that gave Cambridge its initial technology edge – electronics, audio, instrument engineering and computer hardware – have evolved and in their place biotechnology, telecommunications and consultancy have emerged – all very high growth global markets throughout the 1990s.

There are strong reasons for believing that the Cambridge area now operates as a working 'cluster' for high-technology sectors. Not only does it contain large concentrations of such firms, but there are also signs of additional activity that bind the firms together and create the sparks for upgrading of the cluster. Technology consultancies, seed and venture capital providers and advanced business services, like management consultancies, are all well represented and offer a means of knowledge transfer within the cluster.

Universities have also played a significant role. Staff have been important as founders of new companies. Structural changes in departments have made them more accessible to industry. There has been a fairly liberal policy applied towards the ownership and exploitation of Intellectual Property. And there has been active encouragement of joint research with major scientific and technological firms.

This experience shows that universities and research establishments can help to create a dynamic that benefits the economy. Scotland has some world-class strengths in university research, in computing, biotechnology and optoelectronics. But the Cambridge story has a number of additional characteristics that Scotland must aim to put in place. SQW stress the importance of R&D consulting firms, the fact that industry spin-offs are more important than university spin-offs, and the fact that the fastest growing firms are 'technology-intensive', not necessarily 'R&D-intensive'.

Singapore

Singapore has been characterised by continual attempts to upgrade its industrial structure and economic performance in recent decades. Although it has suffered very recently in the global economic downturn of 2001, its rise to prominence over the last few decades has been staggering. The economic development regime in Singapore has always been more directive than in many areas. However, there is no doubt that, over the last 40 years, Singapore has moved from being a third world country to one of the richest, most competitive economies in the world.

Singapore has a very open economy with strong service and manufacturing sectors and excellent trading links derived from its sophisticated port facilities. The overwhelming feature of the Singaporean economy is its constant desire to improve and upgrade. The government is currently undertaking another wave of restructuring to ensure that its industries remain competitive (Financial Times, 2001).

The government is focusing its development efforts on four industrial clusters: electronics, chemicals, engineering and biomedical sciences. Support for services also remains vitally important. Singapore has always been a trading hub; today the Economic Development Board (EDB) sees its role as one of a logistics hub and education centre, characterised by very high levels of business activity in software and ICT industries.

The EDB has several investment arms that address gaps in funds in clusters by developing new capabilities, new technology projects and innovative start-ups. As an example: the EDB's coinvestment programme aims to strengthen Singapore's partnership with multinational companies and promising local enterprises in key industry clusters through equity coinvestments both in, and beyond, Singapore. The main investment vehicle for this programme is the Economic Development Board Investments (EDBI), a wholly owned subsidiary of the EDB.

EDBI manages more than S$2 billion through several funds – the Cluster Development Fund (CDF), two venture capital funds (EDB Ventures Pte Ltd. and EDB Ventures 2 Pte Ltd.), a dedicated biotechnology fund (Singapore Bio-Innovations Pte Ltd.), and a Regional Investment Company (RIC). These funds address gaps in Singapore's industrial clusters by developing new capabilities, new technology projects and innovative start-ups. The EDBI also coinvests in regional and overseas projects that foster strong economic ties with Singapore. At end of 1998, some $1.5 billion of the funds had been committed within 32 projects under the CDF.

In recent years the government has continued to focus on life sciences by putting resources into a range of initiatives: funding start-up companies who commercialise technologies developed locally, funding technology transfer joint ventures, and encouraging foreign life sciences companies.

There is no doubt that FDI – encouraged by the Singaporean government – has played a major role. But cleverly, the FDI that has been sought has always moved the economy onto a higher growth path, always looking to upgrade from basic manufacturing to higher value products and services. Where once incentives would have been in place for, say, pharmaceutical manufacturing, today the emphasis is very much on higher value activity – like clinical research and life sciences. This is particularly important for the long term, as many of Singapore's key industries are suffering badly with cyclical and structural slowdowns.

More importantly, industrial restructuring has always been put in place alongside very significant investment in the education infrastructure. In past decades, Singapore focused attention on improving literacy, numeracy and technical skills which enabled highly productive standard work. As work is becoming more knowledge-based, we see Singapore reacting by 'teaching' creativity and entrepreneurialism. There appears to be a real desire to lead the economy into new, more profitable directions. The government is even investing in upgrading the entrepreneurial talent within Singapore, and looking to recruit senior established managerial talent from across the globe.

North Rhine Westphalia (NRW)

It is also instructive to look briefly at comparator economies that operate as a region within a wider nation state. Such regions do not have the full range of flexible policy options open to them, and so must ensure that their competitiveness is driven by microeconomic factors, rather than relying heavily on adjusting tax rates or other macroeconomic variables. This brief section looks at the experiences of NRW, a resource-rich region of Germany. It also has a similar industrial history, and therefore structure, to that of Scotland.

NRW is the most populous of Germany's länder with 18 million inhabitants. It accounts for 25 per cent of German GDP. It was the main area for Germany's industrial development in the nineteenth century. Like other regions in Germany, it suffered profound economic transformations in the 1970s, as the heavy industries – coal and steel – lost competitiveness and shed jobs in their thousands. In the Düsseldorf region, 78 000 people worked in steel plants at the end of the 1970s. Today, the figure is 3000. New jobs have been created in the telecommunications sector, where employment has gone from 2500 to 42 000 over the same time period. Today about 60 per cent of NRW's workforce are employed in the service industry.

One particular feature of the region is the dense network of higher education institutions. There are 54 higher education institutions, trade and technical schools training half a million students each year for professional careers. This is complemented by a network of innovation and technology centres. The state is now projecting itself as a magnet for FDI, particularly from Japan.

Scotland and NRW have recently collaborated at a policy level, focusing their learning on four main areas: land reclamation and environmental renewal; clusters or 'competence fields'; sustainable development and environmental technologies; and entrepreneurialism and new business start-ups. Although there remain wider issues concerning the competitiveness of German labour markets, the experience of NRW highlights how a region can emerge stronger from a period of severe industrial restructuring.

Brief lessons from comparators

Benchmarking competitor locations provides two key pieces of information. It sets Scotland's performance in context, and it provides information to learn a little about the drivers of success in comparator locations. Scotland's economy performs moderately, but it has some world-class companies, research facilities and other advantages that can be developed for a more prosperous future. A brief look at some of the most successful comparable economies of recent years leads to the following observations.

Firstly, the economies have all benefited from having some *concentrations of industries that have grown strongly in global terms*. So Ireland, Singapore and the Scandinavian countries have experienced strong growth in ICT industries, fuelled mostly by the decade-long investment boom in the US. This, of course, has seen the rise to pre-eminence of Silicon Valley, Austin, and Ottawa as key North American regions that have grown accustomed to success recently. It will be instructive to see how such high-performing regions cope with the downturn in these growth markets. In previous decades, Germany and Japan have been held up as exemplars of countries with outstanding economic success.

Secondly, growth has been seen both in economies which have *targeted inward investment*, like Ireland and Singapore, and also in those which have focused more on the *development of local capability, connections and infrastructure* – such as Denmark, Finland and Cambridge. Scotland, in many ways like Singapore, has tried to pursue a policy that encompasses both of these elements, targeting inward investment while also boosting the indigenous capability. However, Scotland has simply not been able to see its industries 'upgrade' in the same way as those in Singapore.

Thirdly, most of the exemplar regions have benefited from a long-term policy of *high levels of investment in productive capacity*. This is most obvious in terms of investment in education, but we also see, in Singapore and the Scandinavia countries, a propensity to think and act long term to develop infrastructure for the twenty-first century.

Conclusion: What sort of economy should Scotland become?

There is no shortage of observers suggesting that Scotland needs a clearer 'vision' in terms of its future economic direction. With the advent of a devolved parliament in Scotland, policy-makers started to address this question more fully. *The Framework for Economic Development in Scotland* (Scottish Executive, 2000) was the first step towards providing a more integrated view of how economic development policy fitted with all other aspects of public policy. The publication of *A Smart Successful Scotland* (SSS, Scottish Executive, 2001a) indicates that the Government is looking to address many of the causes of Scotland's moderate economic performance – lagging productivity, low levels of business R&D, insufficient new business starts. But it also puts emphasis on some of the real opportunity areas, such as developing Scotland's global connections, digital connectivity and the commercialisation of university research in industries like biotechnology and communications technologies.

A vision of the possibilities for Scotland has been set out by Professor Gerry Rice (Rice, 1999). He describes the forces that are transforming economies across the world, and uses evidence and examples from comparator locations to set out his 'key characteristics for success'. He stresses six features that should provide Scotland with the opportunity to reap economic rewards in the decades to come. Scotland should be successful because (or if) it is:

1 Small – as the global economy is likely to reward speed and agility;
2 Wired – the future is about connections with other places;
3 Educated – an ability to learn – and relearn new concepts and skills;
4 Competitive – requiring improvements in productivity;
5 Sustainable – where economic progress coincides with social and environmental responsibility;
6 Run with high quality systems of governance.

The following points are worthy of addition to Rice's list. In a fast-changing world, an economy's ability to be *flexible*, adapt and reconfigure itself is of utmost importance. This involves learning systems that encourage creativity and flexibility from an early age. It requires physical and electronic infrastructure that can be upgraded when required. It needs mindsets that encourage rather than stifle change. The countries of Scandinavia have developed education systems that produce people with valuable, flexible skill sets. Cambridge UK has seen its high-technology cluster grow because of far-sighted and flexible approaches by universities and other institutions. Singapore has constantly sought to upgrade and reconfigure its economy to match market conditions and its aspirations. And it now realises that its education system needs an overhaul to meet the needs – creativity and flexibility – of the next couple of decades.

Scotland also needs to build on its success, and develop products, services and approaches that reflect its culture, values and reputation. These are what make Scotland truly *distinctive*. Charles Hampden Turner (1998) contrasts Scotland's values with those of other places. He finds that Scots are more community-oriented and are more likely to seek consensus than others in the UK (and the US). Another research-based study identified Scotland's values as: tenacity, integrity, inventiveness and spirit (Scottish Enterprise, 2000). A more recent report by the Scottish Council Foundation offers a more radical vision of how Scotland's economy might develop in line with its values. It may be characterised by innovation, an emphasis on reconciling wealth creation with social, environmental and cultural values, resource-use efficiency, remarkable global connections and new governance mechanisms (Leicester *et al.*, 2001).

Thirdly, Scotland's economy – its people, businesses and systems of governance – need to be more *ambitious*. Scotland's policy initiatives and approaches are often very similar to those happening in other places. In many cases they have brought reasonable levels of success. But there remains a feeling that Scotland has found difficulty in translating new approaches and policy ideas into sustained improvements in overall economic performance. In particular sectors and areas, it has proved difficult to create 'step-changes' in outlook and industrial performance. Scotland has great strengths in many exciting areas, like biotechnology, communications technologies and more general research strength in our universities. But these industries, and others, need to find ways to achieve a greater 'critical mass' so that this promise is translated into a fast-growing, dynamic economy.

References

Hampden-Turner C. (1998), *The Intelligent Economy: Culture, Value and Competitiveness*, Edinburgh: Scottish Council Foundation.

Kay, J. (2000), *The Economics of Business*, Oxford: Oxford University Press.

Leicester, G. *et al.* (2001), *Out of the Ordinary: the Power of Ambition in an Uncertain World*, Edinburgh: Scottish Council Foundation.

Levie, J. and L. Steele (2000), *Global Entrepreneurship Monitor – Scotland 2000*, Glasgow: University of Strathclyde/Hunter Centre for Entrepreneurship.

Local Futures Group (2000), *Report on a Study Visit to Denmark and Sweden* (unpublished work).

OECD (2000), *Economic Survey: Finland*, Paris: OECD.

OECD (2001a), *Economic Survey: Ireland*, Paris: OECD.

OECD (2001b), *Education at a Glance: Education and Skills*, Paris: OECD.

Rice, G. (1999), *Scotland's Global Opportunity: Seizing it or losing it?*, Glasgow: University of Glasgow Business School.

Scott, A.J. (1998), *Regions and the World Economy: The Coming Shape of Global Production, Competition and Political Order*, Oxford: Oxford University Press.

Scottish Enterprise (2000), *Project Galore*, Glasgow: Scottish Enterprise.

Scottish Enterprise (2001a), *Tracking the Bigger Picture: Baselines, Measures and Milestones for the Scottish Economy, 2001*, Glasgow: Scottish Enterprise Network.

Scottish Enterprise (2001b), *E-Business Benchmarking Study*, Glasgow: Scottish Enterprise.

Scottish Executive (2000), *The Framework for Economic Development in Scotland*, Edinburgh: Scottish Executive.

Scottish Executive (2001a), *A Smart Successful Scotland: Ambitions for the Enterprise Networks*, Edinburgh: Scottish Executive.

Scottish Executive (2001b), *Measuring Progress Towards a Smart Successful Scotland – Consultation Paper*, Edinburgh: Scottish Executive.

Scottish Executive (2001c), *Partners for Development: Opportunities for Collaboration between Scotland and North Rhine Westphalia*. Edinburgh: Scottish Executive.

Segal Quince Wicksteed (1985), *The Cambridge Phenomenon*, Cambridge: Segal Quince Wicksteed.

Segal Quince Wicksteed (2001), *The Cambridge Phenomenon Revisited*, Cambridge: University of Cambridge.

Financial Times (2001), Financial Times Survey, Singapore, 11 April.

5

The Labour Market

David Bell

Introduction

The national and international economic environment has changed radically since the publication of Neil Hood and Stephen Young's previous study of the Scottish economy in 1984. One of the most fundamental changes has been the recognition of the key role that the supply side of the economy plays in promoting economic growth. As a result, the labour market has moved to centre stage. When attention was focused on demand management, the labour market was simply an irritating source of inflationary pressure. Looking forward to 2020, its efficient operation will be seen as key to continuing economic growth and hence to further improvements in living conditions. Without an adaptable, innovative and well-trained labour force, the Scottish economy will be unable to support the changes needed to maintain competitiveness in an increasingly dynamic international marketplace.

The labour market also has a key role in other aspects of economic and social development. For example, Scottish Executive estimates for 1996/1997 suggest that around 25 per cent of all individuals and 34 per cent of children in Scotland live in poverty – they belong to households where net income (including benefits) is less than half of average income. Increasing the incomes of the adult poor by bringing them into the labour market is the most effective way to reduce poverty and social exclusion. In the UK as a whole, decreases in earned income account for 62 per cent of entries to poverty while increases account for 44 per cent of exits.

Another example of the role of the labour market is self-employment, which is important in stimulating business development. The formation of new firms intensifies local competition, which is a driver for innovation and efficiency. But growth in self-employment has been almost non-existent during the 1990s. This contrasts with employment, which grew by 85 000 between 1993 and 1999. Stimulating self-employment is one way to combat the sluggishness of the Scottish economy – but to do so requires an understanding of the labour market and the social and economic pressures that lead some individuals to become self-employed rather than employees.

A review of the labour market can only briefly touch on some of the main ways that it will relate to the development and performance of the Scottish economy over the next 20 years. Perhaps the best approach is to try the unfamiliar – to take an international rather than a UK perspective. During the last decade there has been a massive increase in the amount of labour market research. Not only national governments, but also international bodies such as the International Monetary Fund (IMF), the EU and particularly the OECD have been involved. The purpose of this research has been to discover which policies have been effective in the battle to reduce unemployment in the 1990s.

The OECD work has involved many comparative studies across industrial countries, which have brought out the importance of the institutional framework in which labour markets operate. Much of this work was crystallised in the OECD Jobs Strategy – a blueprint for the development of policy and particularly the reform of institutions that was intended to improve the effectiveness and efficiency of labour markets. The next section explains the background to this approach.

The OECD jobs strategy

At the beginning of the 1990s, unemployment was a serious problem throughout the developed world. In 1992 the unemployment rate in the USA was 7.5 per cent, in Germany 6.6 per cent, in France 10.4 per cent and in the UK 10 per cent.[1] The rate in Eire, with which Scotland is frequently compared, was 15.4 per cent. Problems of youth unemployment and long-term unemployment were more severe than in previous recessions.

Research into unemployment by the OECD resulted in a number of policy recommendations, which were brought together into what is now described as the 'OECD Jobs Strategy'. What lies behind this approach is an 'Anglo-Saxon' model of the labour market in which unemployment is reduced and employment increased by improving the *flexibility* of the labour market. It can be described as Anglo-Saxon because it broadly follows the policies followed by the USA and the UK during the 1980s and early 1990s. These policies were aimed at freeing up the labour market by reducing the role of institutions and removing legal barriers.

It would be wrong to suggest that there is complete agreement that this approach is the best way to deliver low unemployment. There are also reservations, particularly within Europe, that this model undermines some of the institutions of the labour market such as trade unions and leads to substantial gaps in wealth between rich and poor. Nevertheless the success of the USA and the UK in reducing unemployment relative to the major economies of mainland Europe during the last decade has proved a strong argument in its favour.

Some of the key policy recommendations of the Jobs Strategy are:

1 Increase flexibility of working time (both short-time and lifetime).
2 Nurture an entrepreneurial environment by eliminating impediments to, and restrictions on, the creation and expansion of enterprises.
3 Make wage and labour costs more flexible by removing restrictions that prevent wages from reflecting local conditions and individual skill levels, in particular of younger workers.
4 Reform employment security provision that inhibit the expansion of employment in the private sector.
5 Strengthen the emphasis on active labour market policies.
6 Improve labour force skills and competencies through wide-ranging changes in education and training systems.
7 Reform unemployment and related benefit systems – and their interaction with the tax system – such that society's equity goals are achieved in ways that impinge far less on the efficient functioning of labour markets.

How will the Scottish labour market in 2020 measure up in terms of these recommendations? What role is there for policy at the UK/Scottish level? These are the themes that this chapter considers. We begin by putting the Scottish Labour market in some context.

Trends in employment and unemployment

Although Scotland experienced some growth in employment during the 1990s, its performance compared poorly with other industrial economies. An average annual growth rate of 0.45 per cent in Scotland was less than one-tenth of the growth rate in Eire between 1994 and 2000

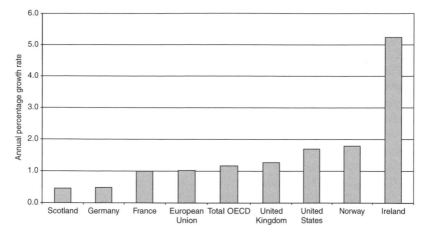

Figure 5.1 Annual growth rate in employment (1994–2000).

Source: Bureau of Labor Statistics, 2001.

(see Figure 5.1). Scotland also compared poorly with the EU as a whole. Its employment growth was on a par with Germany, which spent much of the 1990s trying to avoid recession.

In its defence, part of the reason for the slow growth of employment was demographic – Scotland's population remained virtually static during the 1990s, while population grew rapidly in growth economies like the USA and Eire. Even in the EU, population grew by nearly 10 million between 1990 and 1997. However, the causal relationship between employment and population runs in both directions. Employment cannot grow substantially without an expansion of the population, but one of the main reasons why population is not growing in Scotland is due to a lack of employment opportunities that would make it a desirable destination for migrants. These mechanisms are poorly understood in a Scottish context and are ripe for serious research.

Figure 5.2 shows the per cent reduction in unemployment rates between 1994 and 2000. It perhaps does a disservice to the USA, whose unemployment rate started at a much lower *level* than in most EU countries in 1994. Even in 2000, the standardised US unemployment rate (4.1 per cent) was half that in the EU (8.2 per cent). In contrast to the *employment* data, the *unemployment* rates show Scotland's performance in reducing unemployment during the 1990s is broadly similar to the EU as a whole and to the US. However, Scotland does not compare well with the UK as a whole and, once again, with Eire. Nevertheless, the

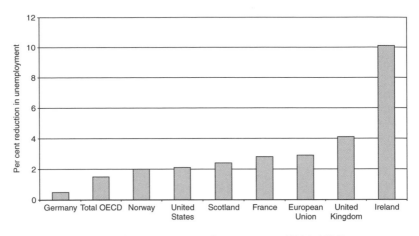

Figure 5.2   Per cent reduction in unemployment rates (1994–2000).

Source: Bureau of Labor Statistics, 2000.

unemployment *level* in Scotland in 2000 was below that in the major economies of mainland Europe – France, Germany, Spain and Italy. This could be seen as vindication of the labour market policies followed by successive UK governments.

Two words of caution however:

1   The figures shown in Figures 5.1 and 5.2 are not corrected for cyclical differences between countries. The UK and to a lesser extent Scotland experienced prolonged growth over this period, unlike most of the rest of Europe. This perhaps places a more negative gloss on the performance of the Scottish labour market.
2   Unemployment data do not give the full picture of the underutilisation of labour in the Scottish labour market. Particular groups with low rates of participation, such as lone parents or older males, may be part of the 'hidden unemployed'. We focus on one of these groups subsequently.

Scotland's performance during the 1990s in respect of employment growth and unemployment reductions leave it a long way short of the best performing economies during the decade, including the rest of the UK. However, this performance coincided with a period where labour market policy in Scotland contained many of the elements of the OECD Jobs Strategy.

As mentioned above, growth in self-employment has been particularly disappointing. Between 1994 and 2000, the number of self-employed in the Scottish economy fell from 224 000 to 208 000. Although the number of female self-employed is approximately one-third of the number of males, both genders experienced a significant decline over the period. And this comes at a time when international attention is increasingly focusing on the role of an entrepreneurial culture in promoting development. Audretsch and Thurik (2001) claim to have found international evidence linking higher rates of entrepreneurial activity with higher growth and lower unemployment. And Blanchflower and Oswald (1998) argue that in the USA, capital constraints may affect the level of entrepreneurship. Other things being equal, those who have received an inheritance or gift are more likely to enter self-employment. They also find that the self-employed generally exhibit higher levels of life and job satisfaction and that the likelihood of being self-employed cannot easily be explained by psychological characteristics. It is not evident that these findings would necessarily apply to Scotland, but they are certainly worthy of a careful analysis in a Scottish context. We now consider some of the factors that will influence how employment and unemployment will evolve in the next two decades and try, where possible, to relate these to the Jobs Strategy. We begin by considering sectoral trends.

Sectoral trends

The shift from manufacturing into services continued during the 1980s and 1990s. Partly this is the result of manufacturing companies 'contracting-out' services that were previously supplied in-house. But there has also been a significant shift of employment into areas such as financial services, education and health. Figure 5.3 shows how much the Scottish labour market is now dominated by employment in the service sector. In 1989, 70 per cent of workers were employed in the service sector and by 2000 this share had risen above 76 per cent: more than three out of four Scots are now employed in services, while only two in every 100 work in agriculture, forestry and fishing.

Should the shift to services be a concern to policy-makers? Not if the principle underlying policy is that intervention should occur only where there is market failure. Apart from the relatively large public sector, which is predominantly located in the service sector, the sectoral distribution of employment in Scotland is the outcome of market pressures. The ability of the Scottish economy to respond to the shift

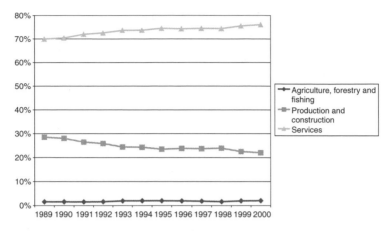

Figure 5.3 Trends in employment (1989–2000).

Source: Labour Force Survey, 2000.

away from primary and manufacturing industries partly depends on the flexibility of the labour market. Again, this resonates with the underlying philosophy of the Jobs Strategy.

Demographic trends

The labour market not only responds to market pressures, it also inter-acts with the size, structure and skills of the workforce. The size and structure of the workforce slowly changes as a result of demographic changes. Looking forward to 2020, two of the most important issues facing the Scottish labour market are migration and the ageing of the population.

Migration

For many decades emigration has held back the growth of the Scottish population. Whereas migration has had a positive effect on the supply of labour in the rest of the UK, it has resulted in an outflow of around 100 000 people from Scotland during the last two decades. From 1994 to 1999, there was no net outflow or inflow (see Figure 5.4).

However, the dynamic economies of the 1990s, ranging in size from the US to Eire, did attract a net inflow of migrants. Immigration not only adds to the potential stock of workers: it reinforces economic dynamism through the interchange of ideas and cultures that accompany it.

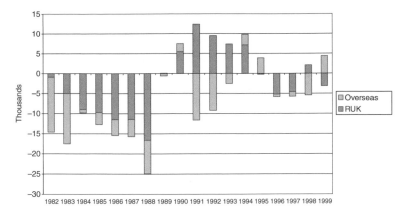

Figure 5.4 Net migration to/from Scotland.

Source: Registrar General for Scotland, 2000.

Migration is very selective. Those who leave Scotland tend to be the most able with the highest earnings potential. One way of calibrating this is to look at the premium that Scots-educated individuals earn in England, compared with what they earn in Scotland. Table 5.1 shows wage premiums earned by different categories of workers, based on the type of education they receive and where they work after correcting for individual characteristics such as age, education and industry. The wage premium measures – the increase in the wage relative to that earned by those who took Highers as their main qualification from school and who work in Scotland.

Males who took Highers while at school (and therefore probably went to school in Scotland) and then moved to work in England enjoy a weekly wage that is almost 28 per cent higher than otherwise similar individuals who took Highers but stayed to work in Scotland. The comparable figure for females is 22.8 per cent. These are very large

Table 5.1 Wage premium for different types of school education/area of work

Education	Living in	Wage premium (%)	
		Males	**Females**
Highers	England	27.7	22.8
'A' Levels	England	13.7	18.5
'A' Levels	Scotland	4.3	14.6

Source: Labour Force Survey and author's calculations, 2001.

margins, suggesting that well-qualified Scots can successfully adapt to the labour market in England. The linkage between labour markets in Scotland and the rest of the UK is under-researched even though it has important implications for the growth potential of the Scottish economy and for optimal levels of investment in training and education in Scotland (see below).

Ageing population

Another key concern about the future of the Scottish economy in the next two decades is the effect on the labour market of the ageing population. As birth rates fall, the average age of the population is inexorably rising. An ageing population inevitably impacts on retirement, savings, pension provision, public spending and healthcare. One of the key indicators of economic sustainability in these circumstances is the ratio of the working population to the elderly population. Projections for Scotland and the UK as a whole are shown in Figure 5.5. These indicate that the number of pensioners relative to the working population will rise by about 7 per cent during the next decade – the aftermath of the baby boom in the 1940s and 1950s – and then level out. The reason why the dependency ratio is projected to be greater in Scotland than in the UK has again to do with migration: migrants tend to be young and of working age. Therefore a net inflow of migrants reduces

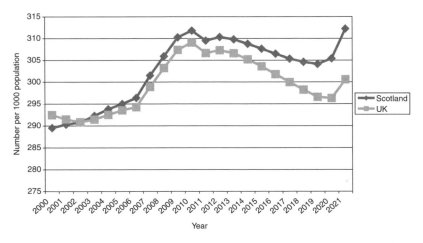

Figure 5.5   Pension age dependents per 1000 working population (2000–2001).

Source: Government Actuary's Department, 2001.

the dependency ratio. These projections assume zero net migration into Scotland over the period. But if past history is repeated and there is net emigration, the problem of dealing with an elderly population will be more difficult than Figure 5.5 suggests.

A higher dependency ratio means that Scottish society will have to devote more resources to looking after the elderly, unless it is willing to contemplate a reduction in their average standard of care. Unless there is a substantial increase in savings, private consumption will have to be reduced to meet the additional costs of looking after the elderly, probably through increases in taxes.

Nevertheless the increase in Scotland will be modest compared with some of the world's major economies. In Italy, the population over 65 is expected to climb from 15 per cent of the total in 1990 to twice that in 2030. In Germany, the projected rise is from 15 per cent to 28 per cent and in Japan, from 12 per cent to 26 per cent. Though the problem of age dependency is likely to be greater in Scotland than in the rest of the UK, putting greater pressure on the caring professions, and public spending, nevertheless it is much less acute than that likely to be suffered in countries such as Germany, Japan and Italy.

Participation

As mentioned previously, unemployment is not the only way to measure slackness in the labour market. Another approach is to consider those of working age who are not participating in the labour market – neither working nor looking for work. Overall participation rates in Scotland increased during the last two decades (see Figure 5.6). Like those in the Rest of the UK, Scottish participation rates are high compared with the rest of Europe. This is principally because of the very high proportion of women working either full-time or part-time compared with the rest of Europe. In line with the Jobs Strategy, the provision of flexible working arrangements in Scotland helps a relatively high proportion of women find work.

Unlike the upward trend of higher female participation, male activity rates have drifted downwards in the last two decades. Two factors have contributed to this trend:

1 Higher rates of participation in post-school education have reduced the numbers of younger workers going into full-time employment.
2 Older males' participation in the labour market has dropped through a combination of early retirement and inactivity due to disability and

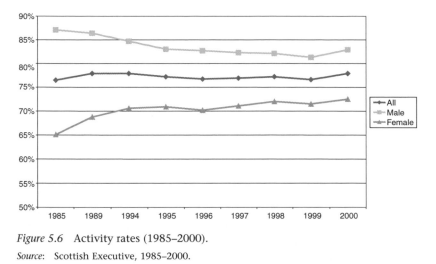

Figure 5.6 Activity rates (1985–2000).

Source: Scottish Executive, 1985–2000.

long-term ill health. Early retirement is more common among men than women because men are more likely to have built up substantial pension entitlement. However, there is also a significant problem of nonparticipation due to ill-health. This is particularly acute in Strathclyde. Figure 5.7 shows the proportion of males by age group absent from the labour market due to ill-health or disability.

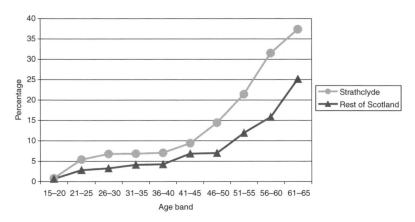

Figure 5.7 Male sickness/disability rates (1992–2000).

Source: Labour Force Survey, 1992–2000 (author's own calculations).

The gap between Strathclyde and the rest of Scotland grows dramatically for males aged more than 45. For the 56–60 age band, 32 per cent of males in Strathclyde claim to be unable to participate in the labour market due to ill-health, almost double the equivalent proportion for the rest of Scotland. The problem is even worse for those with few educational qualifications. For the entire group of males aged over 50 in Strathclyde, who left school aged 16 or less, rates of absence from the labour market due to disability averaged 30 per cent during the 1990s. This group is much more likely to be reliant for support on benefits rather than occupational pensions. They are often overlooked in labour market policy, which has tended to concentrate on the problems of young labour market entrants. Part of the challenge for 2020 is to identify such groups and find strategies that will bring them back into some form of labour market participation. For older poorly educated males, such policies will require 'joined-up' thinking that involves both healthcare workers and those concerned with training and job placement in trying to find solutions. Such policies fall within the ambit of Active Labour Market Policies (ALMPs) that are discussed in the Jobs Strategy. Their status in Scotland is described subsequently.

Private sector employment

The Jobs Strategy emphasises the importance of an entrepreneurial private sector labour market, unimpeded by excessive government regulation. The share of workers in the private sector (see Figures 5.8 and 5.9) is significantly lower in Scotland than in England, both for males and for females. The proportion of males working in the private sector is much higher than females because occupations such as teaching and the caring professions are both female dominated and mainly in the public sector. The lower share of private sector employment in Scotland is the outcome of higher levels of *per capita* public spending – which in turn reflect both Scotland's relatively poor economic performance and perhaps a relatively greater demand for public rather than private consumption in Scotland. Nevertheless, the share of private sector workers, both male and female, grew more rapidly in Scotland than in England during the 1990s.

One key question is whether the size of the public sector impedes expansion in the private sector, perhaps by competing for scarce skilled labour. Again, this is an issue about which little is known and which ought to be on the list of research questions that the Scottish Executive should address.

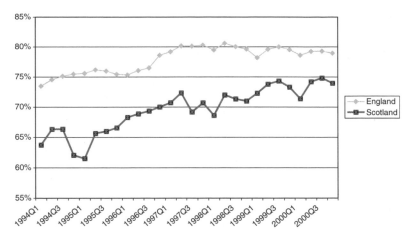

Figure 5.8   Proportion of males employed in the private sector (1994–2000).
Source: Labour Force Survey, 1994–2000.

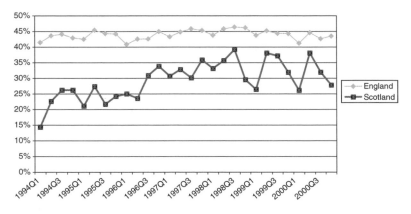

Figure 5.9   Proportion of females employed in the private sector (1994–2000).
Source: Labour Force Survey, 1994–2000.

Flexibility of working time

Another aspect of the Jobs Strategy is working time flexibility. This has several dimensions. Flexibility of working time during the working week is described in Figures 5.10 and 5.11, which show the distribution of employees across various lengths of working week. It is evident that Scottish workers are supplying a wide variety of weekly hours in their

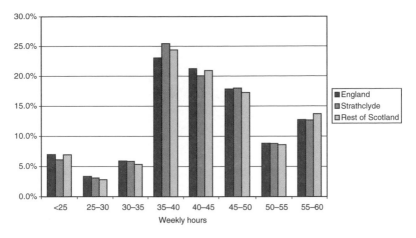

Figure 5.10   Distribution of weekly hours: males (1997–2000).

Source: Labour Force Survey, 1997–2000.

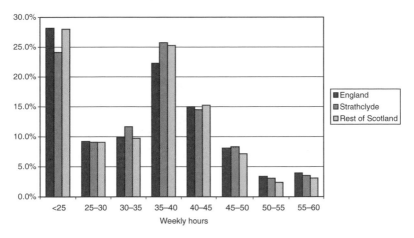

Figure 5.11   Distribution of weekly hours: females (1997–2000).

Source: Labour Force Survey, 1997–2000.

jobs. Males' typical workweek extends beyond 40 hours, while a large proportion of women work less than 25 hours. There is very little variation in the distributions between England, Strathclyde and the rest of Scotland, implying that this outcome is largely due to market and institutional pressures at a UK level. Compared with most major European economies, which are subject to greater legal and institutional constraints, the variation in hours worked is considerably larger both in Scotland and in the UK as a whole.

But the Jobs Strategy also refers to 'lifetime' working time flexibility. This implies flexibility to take career breaks for purposes such as enhancing skills or to make a career change. Although such breaks result in short-term costs, they may be in the long-term interest of the economy. This aspect of working time flexibility is much less developed in Scotland and the UK, perhaps because employers and employees are unwilling to incur the associated short-term costs for future benefits that cannot be guaranteed.

It may also be true that some aspects of working-time flexibility in the short-run act against long-run participation in the labour market. Workers who work long hours early in their careers may develop health problems or find it difficult to continue working at high intensity as they get older. Until there is greater flexibility to make career changes in later life, the outcome may be, as we have seen, falling rates of participation among those aged over 50.

Another perspective on lifetime flexibility comes from looking at the proportion of the workforce employed in temporary jobs. Nonpermanent jobs cover a range of working arrangements, such as fixed-term contracts. The proportion of workers who claim that their job is not permanent is shown in Table 5.2.

These proportions changed little during the 1990s, implying no upward trend in the use of temporary contracts by employers to avoid long-term commitments to workers. The proportion of nonpermanent contracts is slightly higher in Scotland than England, particularly for men. Interestingly although often characterised as the sector where jobs

Table 5.2   Share of temporary jobs

Category	England	Scotland
Male		
All	6.9	9.1
Private Sector	5.7	7.0
Public Sector	8.2	10.0
Female		
All	9.0	9.5
Private Sector	6.5	7.5
Public Sector	10.2	9.5

Source: Labour Force Survey, 1994–2000 and author's calculations.

are most stable, temporary contracts are more prevalent in the public sector than the private sector. Looking forward to 2020, temporary contracts are likely to remain a feature of the labour market. Employers might be less willing to offer short-term contracts if there is any significant extension to employment protection legislation (EPL), but this seems unlikely in the present political climate.

Training and education

Increasing the supply of human capital and therefore productivity levels is a mainstay of 'supply-side' policies. It is central to the Jobs Strategy. As well as providing competencies to carry out particular tasks, increased training and education improve the flexibility of the labour force by enhancing workers' skill and occupational mobility. But to argue in support of more education and training is like arguing in favour of motherhood and apple pie. Such arguments are all too often accepted uncritically. The efficacy of training and educational programmes is often accepted unquestioningly. The possibility of over-education is rarely discussed in policy circles, even though there is a respectable academic literature on the topic. Where the value of training and education is evaluated, the methods used are often inappropriate even though large amounts of resources are invested in such programmes. Looking forward to 2020, the competitiveness of the Scottish economy will continue to depend on its ability to produce skilled and adaptable workforce. But investment in education and training must be made more critically than the past.

We do know the starting point. The distribution of educational qualifications in the Scottish labour force is broadly similar to that in England (see Table 5.3). Although Scotland produces significantly more graduates than England given its population, a slightly higher

Table 5.3 Distribution of highest qualification of labour market participants

Qualification	Males (%)		Females (%)	
	England	Scotland	England	Scotland
Degree level and above	18.7	16.0	15.3	15.2
Up to HNC, HND	8.8	16.3	9.6	22.7
Up to 'A' Level/Higher	11.4	14.0	13.8	17.4
Up to 'O' Level	61.1	53.6	61.2	44.7

Source: Labour Force Survey, 1999–2000 and author's calculations.

proportion of the workforce in England have degrees, which is consistent with a net outflow of graduates from Scotland to England. Among current cohorts of school leavers, 47 per cent are entering higher education, a higher proportion than any other European nation and well above the 32 per cent in England. It is reasonable to ask why there are, as yet, no readily apparent economic benefits from this investment in skills.

Where Scotland does considerably better is in the proportion of the workforce qualified at Higher National Certificate (HNC) and Higher National Diploma (HND) level. And with Highers more common amongst the Scottish workforce than are 'A' levels in England, the proportion of the workforce with qualifications above 'O' Level is considerably higher in Scotland than in England. The qualifications of the Scottish workforce are substantially more concentrated in intermediate levels of education than is the case in England.

These distributions are not simply the outcome of market forces. Because the private market does not provide socially desirable levels of education, state intervention can be justified. In Scotland, expenditure on education is approximately 20 per cent per head higher than in England. Table 5.3 gives some idea of what this extra investment is buying – a better-qualified workforce at all levels up to degree level.

The skills of the 2020 workforce are already partly known. Many of those working in 2001 will still be working in 2020. By then, the proportion of graduates in the workforce will increase substantially.

However, the intervening period does give an opportunity to influence the distribution of skills for those already working, joining or returning to the labour market. This policy framework should include policies to attract skilled workers to Scotland. Many countries have already developed policies for this purpose, including the USA, Ireland, Canada and Italy. These are aimed at: (i) increasing the stock of human capital; (ii) responding to labour market shortages; and (iii) encouraging the circulation of knowledge and innovation. Specific measures include subsidising foreign students to study at local universities and developing centres of research excellence as ways of attracting the brightest and best qualified into the local labour market. While it is encouraging that enterprise and higher education are now contained within a single department in the Scottish Executive, it is not yet evident that such a policy framework for the attraction and retention of skilled workers has been developed. Whereas some attempts are being made to attract successful Scots to return, little progress has been made on policies to encourage skilled foreign workers to come to Scotland. Evidence from the USA suggests that international centres of excellence in science and technology have strong drawing power for the brightest foreign students, who then often remain within the local labour market. This has important lessons for the university sector in Scotland. For the last two decades, Scottish universities have competed in a costly competition for research funds known as the Research Assessment Exercise (RAE). Its underlying assumption was that all institutions could achieve international excellence in research. Each university acted in what it perceived to be in its own best interest to attract these funds. But the outcome of these independent actions has not necessarily been to the benefit of the Scottish economy. The 2001 RAE did not include one Scottish University in the top 15 research institutions in the UK. If the US evidence is correct, then higher education policies in Scotland do not appear to be delivering the strong research base necessary to attract the best international researchers. This issue should be investigated by the Scottish Executive as a prelude to developing a coherent strategy for attracting and retaining high-level skills in Scotland.

Another key factor, and one that has received almost no research interest, is the role played by wage levels in attracting and retaining skilled labour. Such workers operate in an increasingly well-informed global labour market. Competitor countries are willing to provide both wage and nonwage incentives to attract such workers. Corresponding remuneration packages must be available in Scotland. Unfortunately some of the workers will be employed in the public sector, which is notoriously poor at setting wage levels close to those that would pertain in the market. A coherent skills strategy must seriously consider mechanisms to make public sector pay more closely reflect conditions in the market.

Active labour market policies (ALMPs)

A final component of the Jobs Strategy is the promotion of ALMPs. These typically comprise a mixture of 'carrot and stick' approaches to labour market participation such as reducing benefits if the unemployed do not actively search for work and providing tax credits for those on low incomes. Several ALMPs are in place in Scotland. Since they are closely linked to the benefit system, which is a reserved matter, these policies are largely applicable throughout the UK. For example, the Working Families Tax Credit (WFTC) was introduced in 1999 and is designed to ensure that low-income families that have at least one adult working for more than 16 hours a week have a minimum weekly income of £200. WFTC is withdrawn at a much slower rate than the benefit it replaces – Family Credit – and so should maintain the incentive to work as earnings increase.

Another ALMP is the New Deal for Young People (NDYP), which is mainly aimed at the young unemployed. Since April 1998 all individuals aged between 18 and 24 claiming unemployment benefit ('Job Seekers Allowance') must enter the New Deal programme. It comprises two stages. In the 'Gateway' stage, a personal adviser gives the claimant intensive help with job search. If no unsubsidised employment results from this process, the claimant then enters the second stage where a number of options are available. These comprise:

1   Subsidised full-time training/education;
2   Wage subsidy paid to employers willing to hire the claimant;
3   Voluntary work; or
4   Environmental Task Force (government provided employment).

Failure to progress through the scheme can result in sanctions – mainly in the form of benefit withdrawal. Job search is also monitored. There is no option to remain on benefit. US evidence (Ashenfelter *et al.*, 1999) suggests that assistance with job search is an effective method for increasing labour market participation. But Scarpetta (1998) argues that subsidies to employment are not generally effective in increasing permanent private sector employment. Van Reenan (2001) argues that the sanctions embodied in the New Deal programme have not deterred participation.

So far NDYP has helped around 38 000 young people back into work in Scotland. The New Deal also comes in other flavours, including New Deal for those aged 25+, 50+ and Lone Parents. These follow the same pattern as NDYP but are on a much smaller scale. Van Reenan's cost-benefit analysis of the scheme suggests that its social benefits modestly outweigh its costs. This contrasts with the analysis of similar US schemes, although these perhaps deal with a more disadvantaged segment of the population than the New Deal in the UK.

One new ALMP comprises the creation of 15 'Employment Zones', which target participants aged 25 years and over, who have been receiving income-based Job Seeker's Allowance for a long period of time – the long-term unemployed. Participation is mandatory. In Scotland, one zone has been created in Glasgow City and is run on a commercial basis by a partnership that includes the private sector. The target in Glasgow is to make 5000 placements in jobs.

These policies are the latest in a sequence of ALMPs that have been introduced in the UK. Although Scarpetta (1998) argues that the evidence of the effects of ALMPs on aggregate unemployment is mixed, we can expect continuing efforts by government to fine tune these policies to achieve the objective of reducing unemployment at minimum cost to the public purse. The reason that the evidence is mixed is partly due to the diversity of the schemes that have been introduced. And the methodologies used to evaluate the schemes range from the very crude to the highly sophisticated. Nevertheless, taking the 2020 vision, it is likely that ALMPs will form a continuing and significant part of the labour market policy framework, whether applied from Westminster or Edinburgh.

Conclusion

The Scottish labour market has not performed well during the last decade. Employment growth has been poor, the reduction in unemployment has been average by international standards and the decline in self-employment disappointing. This has been the outcome even though the existing policy framework has been in many ways consonant with the OECD Jobs Strategy. This does not necessarily reduce its credibility, since the same policy framework applies in the rest of the UK, which has performed well by international standards. Instead it should lead one to question what have been the particular failings of the Scottish economy that have led to this relatively poor outcome. There are obvious candidates: the failure to produce sufficient entrepreneurs is a well-worked criticism, and a greater reliance on public sector employment than in the rest of the UK has been highlighted here. But looking forward to 2020, it is imperative that such explanations are more thoroughly researched if the next two decades are to be significantly more prosperous than the 1990s. Labour market policy is likely to continue along the lines set out in the Jobs Strategy. Most of the industrial countries have adopted some, if not all, of its tenets. Its success at UK level means that it will not be readily abandoned by Westminster, which is likely to continue to set the major parameters for labour market policy within Scotland. A more distant possibility is that the EU will play a stronger role. It already influences working time regulations, but EU interference in benefits and aspects of ALMPs is likely to be strongly resisted, not only in the UK.

The Scottish Executive and SE are still likely to be able to play important supporting roles. There are particular problems that will arise which perhaps require particularly Scottish solutions, or at least a distinctively Scottish input into the policy process. For example, the problems of dealing with an aging population or of the problems associated with failure of older males to participate in the labour market due to ill-health are sufficiently distinct in Scotland to make it worth considering specifically Scottish responses. And with Scotland able to determine its own education and training policies, there is an important opportunity that should not be missed to focus on the objective of increasing Scotland's stock of human capital in ways that contribute to its economic health.

Such policies must be based on sound evidence. Evaluation methodologies must be built into the design of policy. And it is essential to take a strategic view of policy formulation. Although 2020 may seem a distant prospect, many of the pressures on the Scottish labour market at that time can reasonably be anticipated now. Its ultimate health may depend on taking a view that goes beyond the short-term horizon that politicians find so distracting.

Note

1   Source: OECD Standardised Unemployment Rates.

References

Audretsch, D. and R. Thurik (2001), 'Linking entrepreneurship to growth', STI Working Paper No. 2001/02, Paris: OECD.

Ashenfelter, O., D. Ashmore, O. Dechenes (1999), 'Do unemployment insurance recipients actively seek work? Randomized trials in four U.S. States', Working Paper No. 6982, Boston, Mass.: National Bureau of Economic Research.

Blanchflower, D. and A. Oswald (1998), 'What makes an entrepreneur?', *Journal of Labor Economics*, January 16, 1, pp. 26–60.

Scarpetta, S. (1998), 'Labour market reforms and unemployment: Lessons from the experience of OECD countries', Working Paper No. 382, Washington, DC: Inter-American Development Bank.

Van Reenan, J. (2001), 'No more skivvy schemes? Active labour market policies and the British New Deal for the young unemployed in context', Working Paper 01/09, London: Institute for Fiscal Studies.

Part II
Industries, Technologies and Groupings

6
Scotland's Biotechnology Cluster: Strategic Issues and Responses

Ewen Peters and Neil Hood

Introduction and context

The focus of this chapter is the future growth and development of the Scottish biotechnology cluster, the strategic issues which will help to shape that future and the role of public policy in this process.

In the foreseeable future, related public policy in Scotland will be developed in a wider UK and European context that already recognises the long-term importance of biotechnology to international competitiveness; where the traditional role of inward investment in local economic development of peripheral regions is changing; and where there is a need within more devolved political structures for regional policy to encourage stronger and more dynamic indigenous innovation.

The latter, in particular, would place a high premium on the more rapid formation and growth of specialised indigenous firms that are science-based, innovative and internationally oriented. For policy-makers in Scotland, biotechnology represents a relatively unique and growing opportunity across these dimensions. The chapter begins, however, by considering some basic points of definition that are material to policy-makers and by characterising the existing Scottish biotechnology cluster.

What are biotechnology's main economic features and boundaries?

Main economic features

Modern biotechnology[1] dates back only a few decades and as such is at the early stage of its economic lifecycle. Currently, the economics of biotechnology remains closely linked to the economics of drug development and are distinctive. For example, the industry literature (The Boston Consulting Group (BCG), 2001; Ernst and Young, 2000; Robbins-Roth, 2000; Carroll, BioIndustry Association (BIA), 1997) reveals that drug development:

- *Is highly regulated* (because of the public health considerations);
- *Operates on an extended timescale*: the average time-to-market was 15 years during the 1990s and, despite greater regulatory efficiency, has increased in each decade since the 1960s;
- *Is expensive*: typically it costs over £600 million to successfully commercialise a drug, requiring pharmaceutical companies, especially Big Pharma,[2] to plough as much as 15 per cent of sales revenue back into drug discovery; and
- *Is risky*: in the US for example, for every 250 lead candidate drugs in preclinical testing only one drug will achieve approval from the US Food and Drug Administration and once any patent has run out, cheap generic drugs may flood the market.

As will become apparent, these economic fundamentals, though changing at the margin, will continue to have a profound effect on the development of biotechnology, at least for the foreseeable future.

Biotechnology's economic boundaries

The Department of Trade and Industry (DTI, 1999a) estimates that the industries for which biotechnology holds most promise currently account for nearly a quarter of industrial output, employment and export earnings in the UK. Accordingly, the DTI suggests that biotechnology is perhaps best defined as an 'enabling technology' rather than a distinct industrial sector. This definition is now gaining wider acceptance in Europe (European Commission, 2002a) and is a useful starting point for any high-level description as it captures the increasingly ubiquitous nature of biotechnology applications.

Organisationally, biotechnology related activity is also becoming increasingly complex, inter-related and systemic. A number of factors are contributing to this including: the rate of life-science advance and the increasingly multidisciplinary nature of the science underpinning biotechnology; the blurring of traditional distinctions between the pharmaceutical industry and biotechnology;[3] the widening and deepening of the process whereby life science advance is transformed into successful biotechnology products and services;[4] the strengthening of organisational trends such as downsizing, outsourcing and increased specialisation; finally, the interaction of biotechnology with a wider range of key product markets (for example, clinical health care, agriculture, food and drink, oil and gas, other environmental industries and aerospace) and key factor markets (for example, semiconductors, opto-electronics, information technology and global financial markets). Accordingly, the cluster approach (Porter, 1990) with its systems orientation, its emphasis on innovation, and its recognition of multiple linkages between multiple actors across related industries, is especially well suited to the needs of biotechnology.

Scotland's biotechnology cluster

Pioneering the cluster approach

In a UK context, Scotland has led the development and application of cluster thinking to better exploit the development potential of biotechnology, largely through the work of SE. The starting point has been the recognition that while Scotland has important assets on which to build, notably the excellence of its life sciences, the Scottish biotechnology cluster has still to achieve critical mass, a higher level integration both locally and internationally, and factor conditions that are increasingly specialised and advanced and capable of rapid and continuous upgrade. SE has adopted a broad-based and inclusive approach to development to achieve these ends. This also allows the new competitive synergies associated with current strategic trends to be exploited in a creative and defensible way. The present cluster strategy, launched by SE in 1999, aims within four years to double the number of core biotechnology companies from 50 to 100; to double the number of support and supply organisations from 180 to 360 and double related employment from 12 000 to 24 000. By early 2002, good progress had been reported towards meeting these targets.

Cluster definition, measurement and characterisation

The cluster definition developed by SE includes: core companies (where Scotland has a growing strengths in drug discovery), support and supply companies (where Scotland has world class capability in contract research, clinical trials, biomanufacturing and medical device manufacture) and basic science and research institutions (where Scotland has internationally recognised centres of excellence in a number of important areas including cancer, heart disease, neurology and some infectious disease). Official statistics have yet to be published on Scotland's biotechnology cluster

Table 6.1 Number of organisations (and jobs) in the Scottish biotechnology cluster

	Core companies	**Support and supply**	**Medical devices**	**Academic/ research**	**Total**
Mar 1999	49 (3 211)	93 (2 976)	90 (4 000)	25 (2 542)	257 (12 729)
Mar 2000	68 (3 344)	135 (4 780)	90 (4 000)	37 (2 735)	330 (14 859)
Sep 2000	74 (3 677)	163 (4 969)	92 (4 771)	53 (5 013)	382 (18 430)
Mar 2001	81 (3 743)	178 (5 129)	94 (5 774)	48 (7 654)	401 (22 270)
Sep 2001	86 (3 897)	192 (5 571)	99 (6 714)	51 (8 224)	428 (24 406)

Source: Scottish Enterprise, 2001.

but SE has started to publish statistics on a bi-annual basis for two key variables, namely company numbers and employment.

Results from SE's latest survey (see Table 6.1) show that as at September 2001, the Scottish biotechnology cluster comprised 428 companies and institutions employing 24 406 people. New unpublished estimates (Peters, 2002) suggest that sales for the trading component of the Scottish biotechnology cluster were worth over £1.2 billion to the Scottish economy in 2000. Recent growth has apparently been dynamic: since early 1999 the number of companies and institutions has increased by around 66 per cent and employment has almost doubled. This growth can be attributed to new company formation, to existing business growth, to an increase in the number of organisations choosing to participate in the biotechnology cluster, and improved data collection.

Biotechnology's organisational complexity limits the usefulness of general classification systems. Thus, additional cluster features to note would include the following:

● With respect to its vertical configuration, the Scottish biotechnology community has important linkages with both traditional (for example, agriculture, marine life, and food and drink) and nontraditional (for example, North Sea oil and gas and other environmentally sensitive industries) markets. However, human health care remains the dominant market driver.

● As such, the activities of most biotechnology companies and organisations functionally align with the main process of drug discovery, development and delivery; most companies specialise and aim to occupy a specific space in the system, such as discovery (for example,

Pantherix), development (for example, Strakan), delivery (for example, CeNes), contract services including biomanufacturing (for example, Q-One Biotech), and clinical trials management (for example, Quintiles). Other companies operate in related sub-sectors such as diagnostics (for example, Axis-Shield), and medical devices (for example, Aortech).

- Downstream from the science base, inter-firm linkages within and between these functional specialisms are strengthening, though the overall pattern, like most developing biotechnology clusters, remains fragmented and partially integrated.

- Related to the above, and with few exceptions (for example, PPL Therapeutics), Scottish biotechnology companies are not pursuing integrated business models and a natural focus of international product strength has yet to emerge. Accordingly, the average size of core companies tends to be relatively small: only 15 core companies currently employ more than 50 people and only a small cadre of core companies is publicly listed (that is, Aortech, Axis-Shield, CeNeS, Meconic, NMT and PPL Therapeutics). Again, the above features are by no means atypical of developing clusters in Europe.

- The corollary to this is that Scotland has yet to nurture a large 'flagship firm' (D'Cruz and Rugman, 1993) such as Irish-based Elan (which now has annual sales of over £1 billion). However, the strength of Scotland's drug development pipeline (see Table 6.2) suggests that some of the more established core companies have the potential of becoming more substantial businesses with an international orientation.

- Important local linkages have also been established with the Scottish life science and research base, Scottish education, the public sector and specialist sources of risk capital – and these are being developed further. Some important horizontal linkages also exist with leading biotechnology clusters (for example, Maryland in the US); other related and supporting industries (for example, Big Pharma and the

Table 6.2 Number of drugs in clinical trials (Phase 1–4)

United Kingdom (excl. Scotland)	76
Scotland	20
Ireland	20
Sweden	15
Switzerland	14
Denmark	11
France	10

Source: Ernst and Young, 2001; Scottish Enterprise, 2001.

information industries including opto-electronics); and some related emerging technologies (for example, nano-technologies).

● Foreign ownership, though significant, is not a dominant feature of the Scottish biotechnology cluster: SE estimates that around one-third of employment is in companies that are overseas owned. This percentage is somewhat less than the 50 per cent typically associated with branch-plant clusters (Birkinshaw and Hood, 1998) but more than the average for Scottish manufacturing which currently stands at around 22 per cent (Scottish Executive, 2001).

● Recent growth has been relatively dynamic. As Table 6.3 shows, the annual growth in the number of core companies and related employment has been above the European average for entrepreneurial life science companies in recent years. New firm formation made a significant contribution to this. But existing companies have also contributed. For example, Strakan (£45.5 million), Cyclacel (£34 million), Ardana Bioscience (£13.3 million) and Pantherix (£10.25 million) have all recently raised substantial funding from international venture capitalists. These commitments represent some of the largest biotechnology investments in Europe in 2001.

In summary, when assessed against the cluster dimensions identified by Enright (1999), the Scottish biotechnology cluster presents a mix of features. In a Scottish context, the core (that is, drug discovery and development) of the cluster is relatively dynamic and innovative. But the core is small relative to the ring (that is, services and support including medical devices) and both are geographically dispersed and local linkages are still developing. The core and ring are both activity rich but have yet to develop the scale, density and depth associated with fully developed industrial clusters (Porter, 1990). Moreover, the Scottish life science and research base is an important driver of new firm formation. As noted elsewhere, this base is well aligned with a number of major health concerns and emerging technologies. These will continue

Table 6.3 Annual change in biotechnology companies and employment (2000/2001)

	Companies (%)	**Employment (%)**
Scotland	19	12
Europe	16	6

Source: Ernst and Young, Scottish Enterprise, 2001.

to drive fundamental research and drug discovery and offer scope for further commercialisation in the future. However, in common with other developing biotechnology clusters, the main engines of business growth and development lie beyond the cluster's local boundaries.

Key trends and issues

The focus of attention in this section is on the range of trends and issues that will shape the Scottish cluster in the medium and long term. Put another way, the extent to which this industry grouping is material to Scotland in 2020 will to a large degree be determined by how these are addressed by the various actors involved, hence the emphasis on both implications and responses in each case.

Market factors

Estimates published by the European Commission (2002b) indicate that by 2010, global markets where life science and biotechnology constitute the major proportion of new technology applied could be worth over £1200 billion. Pharmaceuticals are expected to be the single largest component, accounting for 75 per cent of this market by value. Within pharmaceuticals, the rapid growth of biopharmaceuticals has been a key feature as more therapies emerge from biotechnology laboratories, including blockbusters such as Epogen and Neupogen.[5] Biopharmaceuticals now make up 13 per cent of new therapies in development compared with the 5 per cent share that typified the 1990s, and this percentage is expected to rise further to around 25 per cent by 2010 (BioIndustry Association, 1998). Furthermore, most commentators expect this percentage to rise further to around 25 per cent by 2010. Current technology trends and the strong growth in the number of new drug discovery firms, especially in Europe, would encourage this view (Ernst and Young, 2000).

More specific trends and issues can also be identified from analysis of the current drug development pipeline, which is a useful lead-indicator. These include the following:

- Therapeutic proteins are the drug category of primary interest: it is estimated that between 250 and 370 of these could be under development (Bridgehead Technologies, 1999; *Datamonitor*, 2000). This position is regarded as robust by historic standards. The strong sales growth experienced by therapeutic proteins throughout the late-nineties has, however, begun to plateau as manufacturers try to consolidate existing market positions (*Datamonitor*, 2000).

- In the medium term, monoclonal antibodies is the product class within therapeutic proteins offering the greatest growth potential because of their versatility and their precision as a targeting mechanism. This opens up the possibility of treating a large number of diseases by a wider range of therapies.
- Looking to the far horizon (for example, ten years ahead), the growing research effort that the public and private sector is devoting to gene and stem-cell therapy is expected to limit the long-term market growth in therapeutic proteins.
- In a UK context, the bulk of premarket demand (66 per cent) has been for preclinical material that to date has not necessarily had to meet the highest regulatory standard known as current Good Manufacturing Practice (cGMP). This percentage is not forecast to change in the short to medium term (DTI, 1999a).
- Much of the UK's contract manufacturing capability, however, is geared to producing material for clinical trials to cGMP standard. This is a highly competitive international market: typically over 50 per cent of the sales of the UK's leading contract manufacturers are generated overseas. This has resulted in more UK biotechnology companies attempting to meet their need for pre-market material from US sources. Much of the available biomanufacturing capacity in the US has, however, been taken up by approved and late-stage products, largely as a result of the FDA Modernisation Act. This has created a serious bottleneck.

Implications and responses

It follows from the above that benefits will accrue in the short- to mid-term if Scotland's more internationally oriented service and support companies can align themselves with the growth anticipated in therapeutic proteins in general and monoclonal antibodies in particular. The existing shortfall in premarket material provides Scotland with a potentially important opportunity to build on existing strengths in bio-manufacturing and thereby add further mass and functional capability to the cluster. SE has sought to address this need through a strategic initiative to create a new bio-manufacturing campus at Gowkey Moss, near Edinburgh.

The long-term implications are perhaps less easy to specify. There is a need, however, to continue to monitor and assess developments in gene and stem-cell research to ensure that Scottish biotechnology companies are well placed to exploit emerging opportunities and avoid the pitfall of becoming locked-in to products and technologies that may become obsolete.

Scientific and technological advance

The completion of the sequencing of the human genome was a landmark event that is driving fundamental changes in the way that drug discovery will be undertaken over the next 5–10 years. New functional specialisms are emerging, underpinned by an increasingly powerful range of new platform technologies. These specialisms are also increasingly IT-dependent. This has helped to create the new domain of bioinformatics that has mathematics, computer science and biology as its knowledge wellspring. Current estimates suggest that between 2001 and 2010, bioinformatics sales will grow globally from £332 million to £4.1 billion (Frontline Strategic Management Consulting, 2001). Other important convergences are also occurring with nanotechnology (nanobiotechnology) and opto-electronics (bio-photonics). These changes are captured in Figure 6.1 which presents a characterisation of the new drug discovery process envisaged by leading industry analysts.

Technological convergence is opening up the possibility of cheaper and more effective and narrowly targeted therapies (aimed primarily at the genetic component of disease and handicap) that will eventually displace the current markets for therapeutics and diagnostics (Roger Tym and Partners, 2000). Convergence is also providing vital new test beds and production methods for such therapies. Moreover, if existing hurdles and bottlenecks can be overcome, Boston Consulting Group (2001) has calculated that genomics technologies could reduce drug-discovery costs by around £200 million and bring down the average timescale by around two years. Such an efficiency gain would add significantly to shareholder value.

Whether these gains can be fully realised will in large part be down to a new breed of technology-based companies that have begun to emerge. Many of these companies are relatively small but highly specialised and known within the industry as 'toolkit companies'. Others are larger and more fully integrated. For example, Massachusetts-based, Vertex Pharmaceuticals has been singled out by many established drugs companies as a technology company at the leading edge of industry best practice (The Economist Technology Quarterly, 2001). Vertex has pioneered many of the IT-enabled techniques that are now entering the mainstream of drug discovery and development.[6] Despite such rapid technological progress, commentators have also noted that there is no early evidence of a rapid and significant increase in the number of new drugs being discovered (The Economist Technology Quarterly, 2001).

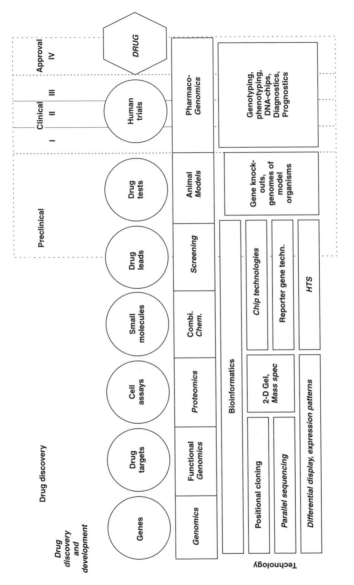

Figure 6.1 The new drug-development process.

Source: Burrill & Company, 1999.

Implications and responses

The functional specialisms of the post-genomic era represent a potentially important opportunity for Scotland to extend the range and scale of its specialist high-value services with international potential. This will require better exploitation of the relevant specialist knowledge and research that already resides within Scottish Universities and Research Institutes.[7] Steps have already been taken to develop an appropriate infrastructure and institutional landscape around some of these areas. Moreover, Scottish expertise is already beginning to emerge in the commercial domain. For example, Edinburgh BioComputing Systems – a recent university spin out – has developed a new system for sequence analysis on a general-purpose computer, rather than an expensive parallel supercomputer.

However, to achieve a 'step change' in the level of commercial activity associated with these areas of technology, Scotland must, *inter alia*, stimulate the formation of many more science-based new ventures, accelerate business building and ensure that Scotland's intellectual property is well protected. Moreover, the mix of competences, scale of activity and level of integration of Vertex remain a benchmark for Scottish biotechnology companies.

Big Pharma and biotechnology

Strategic alliance with the pharmaceutical industry is one of the major determinants of success for specialist biotechnology companies serving the healthcare sector: more than half of the biopharmaceutical drugs approved in 2000 in the USA were either codeveloped or marketed by pharmaceutical companies (Ernst and Young, 2001). The nature of this relationship and its implications for the development of the Scottish biotechnology cluster will now be considered.

Big Pharma shareholders expect robust growth in investment values. Delivering this will be a major challenge. For example, the next ten years will see a series of patent expiries on drugs whose current annual sales are worth over £23 billion (Ernst and Young, 2001). This will require a growth rate in excess of 10 per cent per year to compensate. To sustain double-digit growth, however, the average pharmaceutical company will need to develop three or four new drugs per year capable of generating sales of up to £650 million or more while the average pharmaceutical company currently only produces one new drug per year from in-house development. Thus, significantly raising the productivity of drug discovery and development is one of the biggest challenges facing pharmaceutical and biotechnology companies alike. Two basic responses have been apparent.

First, Big Pharma has spun-out noncore activity, pursued a series of mergers and acquisitions, and become more active in corporate venturing. These trends continue today driven by the need: to achieve greater scale (for example, Roche/Corange, Elan/Sano); to achieve greater customer focus (for example, Merck/Medco, Lily/PCS); to protect patents (for example, Bayer/Schein, Hoescht/Copley); or to enhance innovative capacity (for example, Glaxo/Powder Jet, Searle/ Epimmune). Secondly, Big Pharma has outsourced much of its research and development activity to more productive biotechnology compan- ies, either as deals and alliances or as contract research and manufacture. This has created a multi-billion pound global market that is forecast to expand further.

Restructuring has already progressed to such an extent that these two industries are now highly interwoven and much of biotechnology's growth continues to be driven by demand from the pharmaceutical sector. This restructuring, combined with current technology trends, has created an increasingly complex and fast changing economic space for biotechnology companies to operate in. Biotechnology companies have responded in a variety of ways. Some have become drug discovery boutiques, others have become toolbox companies or information specialists while others have become more service oriented. And a few have tried to try to capture maximum value by becoming as vertically integrated as resources will allow.

Implications and responses

Distance from Big Pharma's centre of decision-making could impair Scotland's ability, firstly, to influence the relocation of in-house bio- related functions and/or the relocation of any bio-related spin-outs and, secondly, to fully exploit outsourcing trends. Distance from the centre may also compound the problem of becoming an accepted insider in high-level business networks. Adoption of e-business models relevant to the European life sciences sector (Ernst and Young, 2000), may help to offset some of the disadvantages of distance. This will require new investment in appropriate skills, equipment and infrastructure to enable rapid uptake. However, while early adoption may be an advantage, speed of uptake cannot by itself guarantee the creation of sustainable competitive advantages (Porter, 1997). It is also unclear that by 'going virtual' more Scottish-based firms will achieve the legitimacy needed to become a respected insider at the industry's highest level.

Access to capital

Biotechnology companies require large sums of specialised long-term, high-risk capital to realise their full business potential. Europe has taken strides recently to develop its venture capital industry, but the US still invests three times as much in technology venture capital: the European relative is even less favourable in biotechnology. Against this backdrop, the recent creation of new and relatively large biotech funds in Europe is encouraging: during 1999–2000, for example, 57 specialist funds raised £4.8 billion, 14 of these had funds in excess of £125 million (Deloitte and Touche, 2001). This scaling up has had a knock-on effect on the size of investments made by venture capitalists that has benefited a number of Scotland's leading biotechnology companies.

In common with other competing locations, Scotland has also been developing its capital infrastructure. For example, 'Proof of Concept Funding' has provided new biotechnology ventures with vital prestart and early stage funding. Business angels have also actively supported start-up activity. This combination has contributed to the higher rate of new firm formation that Scotland has achieved in biotechnology recently. The resultant 'nursery' of new ventures now require seed capital to develop further. Unpublished analysis (Scottish Enterprise, 2001a) indicates that only five seed-stage deals worth £9.35 million were completed in the three-year period to 2001. Moreover, at the beginning of 2002, 18 biotechnology companies were looking for early stage funding worth £44.4 million.

Lack of investor readiness has been cited as the primary reason for such ventures failing to secure the finance needed and support to address this issue (for example, the Biotech Business Advisers Initiative) has been made available. Other important factors implicated in this problem include the following:

- Seed funds have not performed well recently. Combined with the 'scaling up' that has taken place this has led biotechnology funds to pursue opportunities that are nearer-to-market and offer a more attractive balance of risk and return.
- In 2001, capital markets experienced unprecedented shocks and risks that were especially high and unsystematic and specialist venture capitalists adjusted biotechnology portfolios by pursuing nearer-to-market investment opportunities.
- Biotechnology investment clearly requires specialist skills and deep industry knowledge to evaluate intellectual property, technology offerings and related market potential. The major cost of investing

is the remuneration of specialist executives and the additional diligence needed. Thus, irrespective of deal size, transaction costs are relatively high and fixed and this could foster risk adverse attitudes.

Throughout the 1990s enthusiasm for biotechnology stocks on the public equity markets has been cyclical with particular peaks in 1991–1992, 1996 and 2000. As with most technology stocks, 2001 was an especially difficult year for biotechnology: the average value of a biotechnology initial public offering (IPO) was less than many private venture capital deals over the same time frame. Accordingly, trade sales to Big Pharma and Big Bio have been the preferred exit route for venture capitalists.

Implications and responses

Like most developing biotechnology clusters, Scotland's overall risk exposure is high: Scotland's growing cadre of drug discovery companies remains relatively small; most companies typically have only one or two drugs under development at any one time; and while Scotland's position relative to the near competition in Europe is strong, the absolute number of drugs that have progressed to the second and third phase of clinical trials remains small. Accordingly, the opportunity cost of providing public sector support for drug discovery (compared with other growth opportunities within biotechnology and elsewhere) can be expected to remain a material point of discussion for Scottish policymakers. This is likely to place a premium on the more rapid development of innovative approaches that will help spread and reduce risk for the key actors involved.

Were the apparent lack of early stage funding to continue indefinitely then the progress of recent years could be jeopardised. Investor readiness among young ventures must be commensurate with international best practice and SE should be encouraged to take forward its efforts in this regard. A key related challenge is to help these companies put in place the management teams and skills needed to support the next phase of their development. Local venture capitalists must also ensure that biotechnology investment appraisal and funding techniques also reflect international best practice.[8] Furthermore, if trade sales remain the preferred exit route for venture capitalists, this could threaten Scottish ownership and control.

The risk aversion and lack of depth in European public capital markets is likely to remain a constraint on post-IPO company development in biotechnology. Moreover, Scotland's public companies can expect to face significantly more competition from the growing number of

European public companies that will be seeking follow-on investment. Thus, the investor readiness of these companies must be world class to ensure that the range of funding options available to them are maximised. This is an important prerequisite if Scotland is to maintain the long-run prospect of producing a large independent biotechnology company that is locally headquartered.

International competition

The US is the most advanced and developed centre for biotechnology. Seventy-five per cent of all commercialised biopharmaceutical products have been discovered and developed there. Around 1400 specialist biotechnology companies employ 174 000 people and generate annual turnover of around £17 billion in the US: while the European industry has more companies, the level of employment and turnover is 33 per cent and 20 per cent of the respective US totals (Ernst and Young, 2001). Moreover, around 55 per cent of the employees in US biotechnology companies work in drug discovery and development and 17 per cent work in biomanufacturing: in 1990 the equivalent employment figures were 72 per cent and 5 per cent, respectively.

The life science base in the US is focused on centres of research excellence in locations such as San Francisco, Seattle, Boston, Maryland and North Carolina. Though relatively localised, this base is exceptionally well resourced, especially through the support of government bodies and departments such as the National Institutes of Health, the US Department of Agriculture and the National Science Foundation. Effective technology transfer mechanisms, allied to a strong entrepreneurial culture and laws that bring clarity to intellectual property (IP) ownership, income and equity among the main actors involved in commercialisation are all key factors that have contributed to America's success. Accordingly, the US industry remains the benchmark to which the international competition aspires.

Thus, biotechnology has been identified as a strategic priority by a growing number of countries across the globe. The list currently includes Japan, Korea, Taiwan and Singapore in the Far East and the UK, Ireland, Sweden, Denmark, France and Germany in Europe. However, the competition starts from a long way behind: for example, the US may have as much as a ten-year lead over the UK, its nearest European competitor (DTI, 1999a). Moreover, none of Europe's second generation biotechnology products have achieved blockbuster status and the capitalisation of Amgen, the corporate bell-weather of biotechnology in the US, is only slightly smaller than the combined value of all of Europe's publicly quoted biotechnology companies (Ernst and Young, 2001). A common feature has been the adoption of powerful financial incentives (for example, tax holidays and easy access to soft money, both loans and venture funding) as the favoured form of intervention by many countries playing catch up.

The biotechnology community in the UK is the most established in Europe, and accounts for almost 50 per cent of biopharmaceutical products in clinical trials and around 25 per cent of revenues. However, Germany has recently overtaken the UK as the European country with the largest number of specialist biotechnology companies following government intervention in the mid-1990s. This helps to explain why Europe currently has around 10 per cent more specialist biotechnology companies than the US and why European companies are generally much smaller.

Implications and responses

Scotland faces a major challenge in trying both to close the gap with the US and respond to the growing international competition identified above. For example, the level and type of financial support that Germany has provided, with EU approval, is something that Scotland would find difficult to justify given its stronger drug development pipeline. Nonetheless, the superior weight of German drug-development activity may well become telling. Moreover, under devolution major schemes of financial support for industry in the UK are determined centrally. Similarly corporate taxation rates are not within the locus of Holyrood. This makes it difficult for Scotland, for example, to respond directly to the Irish challenge.[9]

The present Government has, however, formally recognised the strategic importance of Scotland's capacity to undertake world-class science and research in biotechnologyrelated fields: the Scottish Executive (2001), for example, has identified bioscience, genomics and medical research as key priorities as part of its recently launched strategy to promote Scottish science. However, there are a number of other important policy steps that Scotland will need to take in order to press its claim for a significant stake in the future of biotechnology. These issues will now be taken up and developed in the final section.

Implications for future policy

Much of the analysis in this chapter has a future orientation. Given all the risks and uncertainties associated with this complex group of industries, it is impossible to predict the nature and shape of Scotland's contribution towards it by the year 2020. On the other hand, it is perfectly clear that without the type of concerted initiative that has been directed towards it in recent years, the opportunities that lie therein will not be exploited. There is therefore a sense in which for Scotland, as for many other countries, there is an option value in much of the investment in biotechnology. In the strategic search for a new basis for Scottish competitiveness in the early twenty-first century, it would be perverse not to make a major effort to build on the existing strengths that exist in biotechnology. Yet the risks are high and the uncertainties great.

Directionally, the cluster approach seems entirely appropriate for Scotland, not least because of the powerful corporate actors and major technological investments that take place elsewhere. In effect, this is necessary both for the development of the linkages within the industry and for the enhancement of its national and international visibility. Thus, while it is not possible to influence many of the forces shaping this industry, it is essential to have the potential Scottish contribution as well defined, prepared and presented as it can be to ensure a flexibility of response to major trends. Part of this lies in taking a focused approach to building on internationally recognised research strengths in areas such as cancer, heart disease, neurology and some infectious diseases. Within this it is ever more important to provide incentives to ensure higher levels of better prepared University spin-outs; and ensure that intellectual property rights are well protected.

Within this broader direction, there are many practical challenges. The way in which these are addressed will be very material in determining Scotland's role in biotechnology. For example, more spin-outs and start-ups are one thing, the effective consolidation of these into meaningful and well-founded companies is quite another. As of 2002, the structure is too fragmented and there are too many one-product companies. Part of this also lies in the need to achieve significant scale in drug-development activity. There is little doubt that drug discovery and development is the area exposed to the highest risk of technological and financial failure. The absence of flagship companies at this stage has already been observed, and while there are some potential candidates around in 2002, it is relatively early days for most of them. It is difficult to see Scotland being a credible world force in this industry without a number of them by 2020 – although, given the nature of restructuring in industry over that time frame, their ownership would be hard to call.

Another of the practical challenges lies in the provision of risk capital. While it is important, as part of the cluster development, to ensure adequate seed-corn and early stage finance which has local roots, the real test for this industry remains being able to access funds from the international specialist investors. This is not only a matter of the quantum of such funds and the capacity for risk within portfolios, it is also one of the endorsement of such funds.

Among the largest of these challenges between now and 2020 is the fact that many other countries are pursuing the development of biotechnology clusters, for exactly the same reasons as Scotland. Public policy in Scotland has in turn to match their innovation, although it is unlikely to be able to match the finance of some of them. Continued attention has to be given to the creation of a well-adapted infrastructure that (in the terms of this industry) is advanced, specialised and capable of rapid and continuous upgrading. Among the ingredients of this are top graduate level skills, quality technician training, high power computing, advanced communication platforms and a high level of expertise in both protecting intellectual property and in finding the best ways to commercially exploit it. More top entrepreneurs and business leaders will, however, also be needed to ensure that these ingredients are fully harnessed and exploited. There is also a list of things that Scotland should avoid doing in this area, including volume manufacture. On the other hand, being internationally recognised as a centre for contract research and manufacture would be desirable; as would the expansion of tool kit companies as part of a move into high-value specialist services that are both internationally attractive and competitive.

Notes

1　In the DTI's 'Sainsbury Report' biotechnology is defined as 'the application of knowledge about living organisms, and their components, to industrial products and processes'. This is similar to the definition offered by the OECD (1998). However, the OECD also distinguishes between 'traditional biotechnology', 'modern biotechnology' and 'gene technology'. While traditional biotechnology mainly uses naturally occurring organisms or their parts to make beer, bread, cheese and some drugs, modern biotechnology expands this definition to include genetics-based and other molecular biological methods (for example, hybridoma technology for the production of monoclonal antibodies). Gene technology is defined as the sum of all the methods for the isolation, characterisation and selective modification and transfer of a genetic make-up. Accordingly, gene technology is used to undertake fundamental research on the molecular mechanisms of vital functions and is also applied commercially in biotechnology and medicine.

2　Big Pharma (and Big Bio) are colloquial terms used to describe the cadre of very large multi-billion pound pharmaceutical companies (for example, Glaxo-SmithKline, Merck, Pfizer, and so on) and biotechnology companies (for example, Amgen and Genentech).

3 Convention has it that the molecules engineered by biotechnologists cannot be synthesised easily by the traditional chemical methods employed by
Big Pharma. Biotechnologists use recombinant DNA to engineer therapies
that utilise modified forms of the bodies own proteins to target natural
processes and are active at one thousandth of the dosage of conventional
drugs like Asprin. By contrast Big Pharma has historically used chemical
synthesis to produce small organic molecules that can only mimic the
active part of proteins. Today, however, some biotechnology companies
are working on small molecules and some pharmaceutical companies develop
proteins.

4 The main aspects of human healthcare with which the biotechnology community has recently been concerned includes: therapeutics, vaccines, diagnostics, drug delivery and cell and gene therapy (see Burrill & Co., 2000;
NASDAQ, 2000). However, in the US the technology convergence around
healthcare means that biology is a significant, but not the only, driver of
next generation products and services: medical devices, pharmacology, bioinformatics and nano-technologies are now regarded by industry practitioners
as complementary components that sit comfortably together in an emerging
'life science' portfolio.

5 Such drugs are helping to address some of the most serious health concerns
for which more conventional treatments have been found to be limited.
For example, despite years of effort, pharmaceutical companies have made
relatively little headway in cutting death rates from the three main killers in
the advanced economies namely: cardiovascular disease, cancer and stroke
(NASDAQ, 2000).

6 These techniques include, for example, molecular modelling, structure-based
design, virtual screening, efficient data mining and ADME and toxicity
prediction.

7 For example, genomics at the University of Edinburgh and the University of
Glasgow; and proteomics at the University of Aberdeen. Scotland will also
have to rapidly develop and exploit emerging research strengths in conver-
gent technologies. For example, bioinformatics at the University of Dundee,
University of Abertay, the University of Edinburgh, and Roslin Institute;
biophotonics at the University of Strathclyde; and nanotechnology at the
University of Glasgow and the University of Stirling.

8 According to Ernst and Young (2000), venture capitalists who can achieve
significant internal rates of return in months need to be encouraged to
adopt different ways of monitoring and measuring the value created by
their investments in biotechnology. Investments should be appraised not
on the basis of net international rates of return (IRR), but on investment
return multiples of over ten times the original investment over periods of
up to eight years.

9 The activity attracted by locations such as Ireland and Singapore may well
be larger-scale manufacture designed to meet the needs of the market place
and final stage clinical trials. As such, this could/should perhaps be interpreted as a continuation of the trend that saw the employment base in the
UK's pharmaceutical manufacturing sector contract by 15 per cent in the
five-year period to 1996 – and may not be an appropriate opportunity for
Scotland.

References

BioIndustry Association (1998), *Making the Manufacturing Breakthrough – an investigation into the UK Biopharmaceutical manufacturing requirements in the new millennium*, BioIndustry Association report, December.

Birkinshaw, J. and N. Hood (2000), 'Characteristics of foreign subsidiaries in industry clusters', *Journal of International Business Studies*, Vol. 31, No. 1 Quarter 1, pp. 141–154.

Boston Consulting Group (2001), 'A revolution in R&D: How genomics and genetics are transforming the biopharmaceutical industry', London: British Consulting Group.

Burrill & Co. (2000), 'Key trends in biotechnology', Edinburgh BioAlliance Launch, Edinburgh. (unpublished presentation).

Bridgehead Technologies (1999), *Pipeline Analysis*, Internal Report for Scottish Enterprise.

Carroll, M. (1997), 'Research cell to manufacturing reality', *Moving the Industry into the Manufacturing Phase*, BioIndustry Association, pp. 29–36.

Commission of the European Communities (2002a), 'Innovation and competitiveness in European biotechnology', Enterprise Papers, No. 7, Brussels.

Commission of the European Communities (2002b), *Life Sciences and Biotechnology – A Strategy for Europe*, COM (2002) 27 Final, Brussels, 23 January.

Datamonitor (2000), *Therapeutic Proteins, Key Markets and Future Strategies*, New York: Datamonitor.

D'Cruz, J.R. and A. Rugman (1993), 'Developing international competitiveness: The five partners model', *Business Quarterly*, Winter (Reprint Order BQ93206).

Deloitte & Touche (2001), 'Investment incentives to increase venture capital and private equity in biotechnology in Scotland', Report for Scottish Enterprise Deloitte and Touche (unpublished).

Department of Trade & Industry (1999a), 'Biotechnology clusters', *The Sainsbury Report*, London: Department of Trade & Industry.

Department of Trade & Industry (1999b), *Early Stage Biopharmaceuticals Manufacture, Manufacture for Biotechnology*, London: Department of Trade & Industry.

Enright, M.J. (1999), 'The globalization of competition and the localization of competitive advantage: Policies towards regional clustering', in N. Hood and S. Young, (eds), *The Globalization of Multinational Enterprise Activity and Economic Development*, London: Macmillan, pp. 303–331.

Ernst & Young (2000), 'Evolution, the seventh annual european life sciences', and, 'Convergence: Ernst and Young's biotechnology industry report', Millennium Edition. New York: Ernst & Young LLP.

Ernst & Young (2001), 'Focus on fundamentals, the biotechnology report'; and 'Integration, Ernst and Young's eight annual european life sciences report', Gt. Britain: Ernst & Young International.

Frontline Strategic Management Consulting (2001), 'The promise of bioinformatics: convergence of technology and health science', New Brief, London: Ernst and Young LLP.

NASDAQ (2000), *Biotech Industry Guide*, London: Forward Publishing.

OECD (1998), *21st Century Technologies – Promises and Perils of a Dynamic Future*, Paris: OECD Publications.

Peters, E.H. (2002), 'The economic impact of the Scottish biotechnology cluster: measures and approaches', Report for Scottish Enterprise, Scottish Enterprise (unpublished).

Porter, M. (1990), *The Competitive Advantage of Nations*, London: Macmillan.

Porter, M. (1997), 'Interview', in *Rethinking the Future*, Gibson, R. (ed.), London: Nicholas Brealey Publishing, p. 58.

Robbins-Roth, C. (2000), *From Alchemy to IPO*, Cambridge, Mass: Perseus Publishing.

Roger Tym & Partners (2000), Report on Bioinformatics for Scottish Enterprise, (unpublished).

Scottish Enterprise (2001a), *Biotechnology Investment Incentives Scheme* (Internal Paper).

Scottish Enterprise (2001b), *Biotechnology Scotland, Framework for Action 2001–2002*, Glasgow: Scottish Enterprise.

Scottish Executive (2001), *A Science Strategy for Scotland*, Edinburgh: Scottish Executive.

The Economist (2000), 'The World in 2001', London: The Economist Newspaper Ltd, p. 110.

The Economist Technology Quarterly (2001), 'Drugs ex Machina', London: The Economist Newspaper Ltd, 22 September, pp. 36–38.

7
Creative Industries
Brian McLaren

Introduction

The creative industries have been attracting growing interest at policy levels and are seen as being important to the development of a global knowledge-based economy.

Recent forecasts estimated that the value of the global entertainment and media industries will increase from $831 billion in 2000 to $1.3 trillion in 2005, an annual compound growth rate of 7.2 per cent (PriceWaterhouseCoopers, 2001). The global market for video games (not included in PriceWaterhouseCoopers forecasts) is estimated to be worth more than $17 billion and has more than doubled since 1995 (ELSPA, 2001). These are clearly high-growth industries.

In recognition of this, the UK government led the policy drive into the industries and made the first serious attempt to measure the economic importance of the creative industries in the UK (Department of Culture, Media and Sport, 1998). The first report has now been updated and shows substantial growth. In Scotland, SE identified the creative industries as being a potential emerging cluster and working closely with industry, developed and launched in 2000 a national strategy for the development of the sector, *Creative Scotland: Shaping the Future.* This strategy document lays out the priorities for growing the sector over the next 3–5 years and provides a framework for a £25 million investment plan.[1]

This chapter will attempt an overview of the creative industries in Scotland and an assessment of the global marketplace in which they are competing. Scotland can lay claim to some emerging strengths and a growing international reputation in some niche areas, but the future will bring considerable challenges. However, Scotland's creative industries can indeed survive and thrive in this environment by harnessing the opportunities offered by new technologies and markets. This chapter will also offer comment on policy implications and priorities for the development of the industries.

Definition of creative industries

Although the term 'creative industries' is widely used it is less well-understood. The Department of Culture, Media and Sport (DCMS) Creative Industries Task Force defines the creative industries as: 'those activities which have their origin in individual creativity, skill and talent and which have a potential for wealth and job creation through the generation and exploitation of intellectual property' (DCMS, 1998).

For the purposes of this analysis the following industries have been included within the umbrella term 'Creative Industries': Architecture, Advertising, Arts and Cultural Industries, Design (including Fashion Design and Crafts), Film, Computer Games and Multimedia, Music, New Media, Publishing, Radio, Television.

There are important differences between this and the DCMS sector listing. DCMS refers to interactive leisure software, interpreted here as computer games and multimedia. Software is also not included in the definition above. Software is an enabling technology and while it is a critical part of the supply chain it is not one of the creative industries *per se*. While creativity is used in other industries to add value to a product or service, in the creative industries creativity is the *raw material* for the product or service. It is this which principally links these wide-ranging sectors together. However, as this chapter will discuss, these sectors are being increasingly blurred by new technologies and converging markets.

Measuring the creative industries

The lack of robust and reliable economic data on the creative industries remains a *global* market failure. Existing statistical classification systems and survey data do not adequately reflect the structure of the industries and extrapolating figures from categories involves making numerous assumptions. As a result, different methodologies have been used in quantifying the industries.

The recently updated Department of Culture, Media and Sport, 2001 estimates that the UK creative industries generate revenues of around £112.5 billion and employ 1.3 million people. UK exports account for around £10.3 billion and between 1997 and 1998 output grew by 16 per cent as compared to 6 per cent for the economy as a whole (DCMS, 2001).

At the Scottish level data problems are compounded by the fact that information on turnover, exports, investment and sales are either not available or cannot be disaggregated from UK or broader industry classifications. For this reason, employment and business stock figures have proved more accessible, although as a means of tracking economic change they cannot be considered sufficient.

Research by EKOS Economic Consultants analysed data from the Annual Employment Survey. As a result of the aggregation within these categories, some cells contain employment not contained within the definition of the creative industries (for example, retail or manufacturing activity). Bearing these cautions in mind, Table 7.1 shows that up to 6.7 per cent of Scotland's employment is within, or related to, the creative industries, and this is higher than the rest of UK. Scotland in fact has a greater share of creative industries employment than any region in the UK outwith London and the South East of England (EKOS, 2001).

Another recent analysis carried out on behalf of SE by John Lord Associates demonstrated a 22.6 per cent increase in business stock between 1995 and 2000. This contrasts with 9.7 per cent growth in employment between 1995 and 1998 (John Lord Associates, 2001).

Table 7.1   Employment in the creative industries (1998)

CI Category	Scotland	South-East	London	GB	Rest of UK
Film	5 050	26 426	14 396	48 238	16 762
Television/Radio	27 238	107 709	57 873	254 341	119 394
News media	161	7 119	6 838	8 467	1 187
Other multi	3 212	11 226	6 145	33 801	19 363
Comp. games	10 590	139 145	49 935	241 070	91 335
Publishing	24 796	191 590	101 273	429 161	212 775
Music	271	5 627	4 349	9 075	3 177
Architecture	27 345	111 271	49 138	274 793	136 177
Cultural ind.	10 710	54 835	33 605	120 418	54 873
Advertising	2 662	58 309	35 694	87 852	26 881
Sport	23 967	72 584	22 740	213 757	117 206
Total	136 002	785 841	381 986	1 720 973	799 130
Percentage share of region's total employment	6.7	9.7	10.6	7.4	6.1

Source: EKOS, Creative Industries Baseline, 2001.

This implies that the average size of businesses is getting smaller, particularly in creative production and distribution. Growth across the industries has, however, kept pace with that of Great Britain as a whole.

Revenue and export figures are not readily available for the industries at Scottish level. A very rough estimate can be gained by 'calculating' revenue figures based on Scotland's share of UK employment and business stock figures. These estimates range from just under £7 billion to just less than £9 billion (1998 and 2000, respectively). These are both likely to be overestimates since the employment and business stock data on which they are based overestimate the industries and the two figures are not comparable. The largest estimated revenues are generated by the design, publishing and television and radio industries (EKOS, 2001).

Based on the share of employment (1998) the estimated level of exports is approximately £810 million. Based on the share of business stock it is approximately £625 million (2000). Therefore the range is between £625–810 million. Again, publishing and design emerge as having the greatest export earnings of the industries (EKOS, 2001).

Although this attempts a statistical baseline analysis for the creative industries in Scotland, the limitations of the data speak for themselves. Given the growing importance of the creative industries as a generator of wealth, the lack of robust statistical information constitutes a serious policy failure. This failure not only inhibits effective policy development and impact assessment, but also has a detrimental effect on the industries themselves, particularly when investors depend on being able to track reliable economic data.

While exact numbers are elusive, the overall picture is reasonably consistent. Scotland has the highest concentration of creative industries in the UK outwith London. That the industries make an important contribution to the Scottish economy is without doubt. The real question is how to grow this contribution.

Industry structure

Detailed analysis of the business stock in Scotland confirms that in all sectors Scotland has few businesses in the medium employment size-bands (50–499) and the largest percentage of companies in each sector have fewer than ten employees. This is an industry dominated by micro-businesses and there are few major companies (EKOS, 2001).

This pattern reflects both the nature of the industries and the fact that many sectors remain immature. Scotland does have a number of significant players, for example, BBC Scotland and Scottish Media Group in television, and Harper Collins and D.C. Thomson in publishing.

In newer sectors such as computer games, the industry is young, but has considerable market potential. In all sectors, Scotland's creative industries are very much focused on content production rather than distribution, an industry structure which brings both opportunities and challenges.

While there are a number of ambitious, fast growth companies in Scotland's creative industries, even the more substantial and established businesses do not have significant global presence and there is a need to develop more high-growth companies with international ambitions.

Global drivers

Whilst change is characteristic of these industries there is also huge growth potential. The creative industries are forecast to grow on average by 10 per cent per annum (Spectrum Strategy Consultants, 1998). Those in digital content production are forecast to grow at rates up to 20 per cent per annum (Digital Media Alliance, 1998). For Scotland this represents a substantial opportunity. Understanding the future opportunities for Scotland's creative industries means examining the global environment.

Technology drivers

Technological development is fundamentally reshaping the competitive landscape of the creative industries. The convergence of information and communications technologies through the Internet, along with digital broadcasting and the digitisation of music, publishing and film is a major step change. Digitisation reduces production costs and allows greater user interaction, thereby driving demand for new kinds of media content. There will also be further change with the emergence of third generation mobile networks, broadband internet access and increased consumer adoption of digital television.

It is however not only technological convergence, but the convergence of different *media* that is driving change in the creative industries. Barriers between previously separate domains of content are now being eroded. Digital broadcasting channels are evolving into interactive websites and sophisticated websites are effectively becoming broadcasting channels.

This convergence is not merely the unification of hardware systems as has often been suggested. It enables a particular user to move seamlessly from e-mail to Internet to games to broadcast material irrespective of whether they are using a personal computer or a television. It is therefore more about end-user choice than technology push and it is creating new markets for content developers and new business models for media companies.

As well as the convergence of media, the convergence of the digital entertainment markets will increasingly drive future change. This is introducing new players and new buyers of creative content. Device manufacturers (for example, Sony, Nokia, Philips), service providers (for example, Freeserve, Vodaphone, ntl, BskyB), e-commerce providers (for example, Tesco.com), portals such as Yahoo! and Lycos and tele-communications companies like BT and Telewest are all hungry for content.

The growth strategies of the major players look increasingly similar: all want to move their business towards platform-independent delivery of a wide range of broadband customer services. These strategies are based on a combination of new business models and revenue streams, strategic alliances and greater customer knowledge.

For Scotland, technological change brings both opportunities and threats. The rapid adoption of digital technology will be critical if we are to compete, but the introduction of new buyers into the market brings new revenue potential. The computer games industry in Scotland has a strong sense of community and a number of companies already successfully accessing international markets. The sector is also advanced in attracting company finance and investment in product development in order to retain intellectual property rights for future exploitation. Also, companies such as Digital Bridges are targeting the mobile games and entertainment market while others are taking up the opportunities offered by online gaming and interactive television platforms.

Scotland's academic sector is recognised for teaching and research excellence in a number of disciplines and the research base is strong in areas relating to creative industries. Virtually all of the major Scottish universities are active in research which can be applied in the creative sector. In Dundee, the University of Abertay is leading the way in computer games with degree courses and a R&D centre looking into the development of new technical platforms for multiplayer games. The Universities of Strathclyde, Glasgow and Edinburgh are all active in research into 3D computer modelling techniques and viewing systems. In terms of corporate R&D, some creative and technology companies are developing leading edge technologies for use in the production and distribution of digital content.

Scotland can therefore compete, but too few Scottish companies are fully embracing new technologies. In some sectors such as television production there is uncertainty about how real these opportunities will be, as a result investment in interactive digital media remains small scale. Other sectors are experiencing difficulties driven by investor nervousness about the Internet and telecommunications. Growth finance is urgently needed if the creative industries in Scotland are to keep pace with technology and compete on a global scale.

Market drivers

Figure 7.1 is a visual representation of the supply chain in the creative industries. This is an oversimplification, but the power in the creative industries supply chain rests with those who commercialise content, the publishers: games publishers, film distributors, television and radio channel managers, record labels and distributors as well as electronic and print publishers. It has been suggested that digital technologies threaten the dominance of this part of the supply chain by allowing content originators to reach customers without intermediaries. This may be true, but powerful companies entering the marketplace are fast dominating not just publishing, but large parts of the supply chain. Competition is converging.

This is in contrast to the recent past when markets were defined in product-related terms, for example, television, mobile phones and film. At a global level there are significant companies with the resources and ambitions to compete across traditional market boundaries creating competition at every level of the value chain from content to customers. The international media marketplace is becoming ever more complex and interlinked with technology companies, access providers and hardware manufacturers.

Companies do not easily fall into the categories above. The BBC has always been a content originator and a distributor, and Sony a publisher, distributor and device manufacturer, but now Nokia, ntl, Telewest and others are all active across this chain. The mergers of AOL/Time Warner

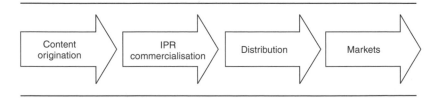

Figure 7.1   Creative industries supply chain.

Source: Creativity and Enterprise, 1999.

and Vivendi/Universal have created vast global media empires controlling the supply chain from content production to distribution. These
mergers drive efficiency and create economies of scale through enormous negotiating power and deep financial resources. Their ability to
distribute content across the world makes media companies well placed
to deliver effective platforms for advertisers. This will continue to be a
major market driver.

Scotland is somewhat disadvantaged, as none of the major publishers
and distributors have a Scottish presence – many do not even have
a base in the UK. Proximity to major content buyers and publishers
is advantageous not only in terms of access to their global networks
and markets, but also in terms of understanding their future strategies.
At least one major publisher surrounded by a growing supply sector
of small creative content developers is a model seen in Northern Europe
where there is a high degree of convergence within local media clusters.

Scotland's position is compounded by the fact that the creative
industries can be too focused on local markets. This results in intense
competition based increasingly on price not value.

The computer games market is dominated by a handful of large
publishers based in Europe, Japan and America. The film industry is
controlled by US distributors, while in television the power lies with
the broadcasters. The strategies of the UK broadcasters have important
implications for Scotland's creative industries.

The main terrestrial broadcasters (BBC, ITV and Channel 4) all
have, by law, to source a percentage of their programming from outwith
London. Scotland is under-performing in terms of securing its share of
these quotas. Forthcoming consultations on the future of the regulatory
framework may lead to changes in size of the quotas, but Scottish
companies will need to work more with the market grain in order to
ensure that they benefit.

Commercial broadcasters need to attract audiences attractive to advertisers to succeed. This can lead to formulaic scheduling and a reliance on
tried and tested formats. This strategy in turn has implications for
content producers and the kinds of programming which they require
to produce in order to stay profitable.

Digital and satellite channels are more focused on exploiting subscription and pay-per-view models. The tight cost models operated mean
that programmes must be made for less money hence thinner margins
for production companies. The new digital platforms also need interactive programming although there is no clear vision of what kind of
interactivity consumers will demand from television.

Television production in Scotland, whilst small, is looking towards new technologies. Leading companies such as Wark Clement[2] and Ideal World[3] are making investments in new and interactive media applications while expanding their programme experience into higher value genres such as television drama. Broadcasters such as BBC Scotland and Scottish Media Group are a key part of the supply chain and the decision of Channel 4 to locate in Glasgow its commissioning office for all programming outwith London is an encouraging development.

The powerful position of publishers, broadcasters and distributors raises the question of intellectual property rights. If opportunity lies in exploiting content across different platforms and channels, then owning the rights to the content is key to that strategy. Rights to content are almost always owned by those who bring the content to market – publishers, broadcasters and distributors.

Changing business models and new technologies are beginning to offer glimpses of how this might change. The development of technologies such as mp3 and Napster opened up the Internet as a means of distributing music and demand is growing for online books, music, newspapers and magazines. Protection of rights is a key issue and when the industries begin to understand how to convert Internet distribution of content from a free to a paying model while protecting copyright the patterns of media consumption will shift.

For content producers this offers opportunities. Companies who invest in content development are in a stronger position to negotiate on rights than the existing commissioning model where a company is given 100 per cent funding for a commission. Intellectual property rights are the assets on which companies can attract finance and generate profit through their continuing exploitation. The growing range of distribution channels for content and the convergence of different media expands significantly this market potential.

Business models

The early days of the Internet bred a belief that content should be free. The dot-com crash brought an end to business models built solely on advertising revenues and more and more companies now look towards subscription or pay-per-view revenue streams. So, in place of Napster there is PressPlay which offers similar file sharing services and access to a huge music catalogue for a subscription fee. What no-one knows is whether this strategy will bring sufficient returns. Amidst this uncertainty, advertising revenues still dominate and at the time of writing, spending on media advertising is experiencing a downturn. Advertising revenues are sensitive to macroeconomic conditions and Channel 4 recently announced, that as a result of falling advertising income, it will cut programme spending. This means less business for production companies. Advertising is fast becoming a necessary but not sufficient source of revenue.

Even multinationals have not yet reached consensus on the business models which will drive profits in the multi-platform market. Possibilities include subscription services, pay-per-view television, online transactions through interactive television, the Internet or mobile platforms, very small (micro) payments for content added to phone bills or advertising – or a combination. But which model will dominate and how will the revenue pie be divided between producers, publishers, distributors and access providers?

Changing business models, however, have important implications for smaller companies. Content originators are increasingly looking towards multi-platform content and are becoming more involved in financing development, allowing them to retain a larger portion of the rights. New finance models starting to emerge could be venture capital and equity funding or partnership and strategic alliances with publishers and distributors. Future success for smaller creative content companies will depend on their ability to negotiate new kinds of deals on their content and develop new revenue and finance models which allow them to retain control over their intellectual property.

Access and connectivity

Uncertainty also surrounds access to content and the availability of high bandwidth connectivity. There are two issues here.

- Companies involved in the production of digital content need affordable high-speed connections to send large files. This is a fundamental part of the infrastructure supporting creative enterprises.
- Consumer access to Internet content requires a sufficiently high-speed connection to allow a quality 'user' experience.

Cost is a critical factor and as more people get access to affordable broadband connections, more people will access the kind of content which depends on high-speed data transfer. This is a conundrum. As previously mentioned there is great uncertainty about the type of content that consumers will be willing to pay for. On the other hand, it can be argued that the availability of high-quality content will drive public demand for broadband services. But which comes first – connectivity or content?

In either case, the availability of affordable broadband connectivity is a major driver of competitiveness for the digital media industries. The US is leading Europe in broadband adoption by at least two years (*Strategy Analytics*, 2001) and countries such as Sweden and Finland have very high levels of connectivity.

Scotland has a communications infrastructure in the central belt at least, which is equal to anywhere in Europe excepting London. However, Scotland is still not cost competitive.

Regulatory drivers

The regulatory environment has potentially wide-ranging implications for the future of the creative industries. This varies considerably between countries although there is increasing pressure for global regulatory structures in areas such as digital rights protection.

In the UK, a new regulatory body, the Federal Office of Communications (OFCOM), is being created to bring together the nine previously separate bodies involved in the regulation of communications and broadcasting. Its position on media ownership restrictions will have potentially far-reaching implications. If the creation of larger companies continues, their greater resources will not only affect quality of programming, but larger broadcasters with greater audience reach will dominate advertising spend.

Plans by the BBC to launch free digital channels is also causing controversy amongst the private sector which is claiming that the licence fee causes unfair competition. The resolution of these questions will define the operating environment for the broadcasting and communications industries in the twenty-first century.

This will also affect spend on content which will impact on Scotland. The push into new media and interactive content will be driven by the large companies and the extent to which they commission this content or produce it themselves will dramatically affect the market for smaller companies.

Future opportunities and threats

To a great extent, the opportunities and threats for Scotland are defined by the market forces described already. Competition however is global and differentiation is a key challenge (Figure 7.2). Scotland's opportunities lie with companies in niche markets. Wireless gaming is poised for explosive growth over the next few years. It is estimated that there will be 107 million active wireless gamers by 2006 (*Strategy Analytics*, 2001).

Strengths	Weaknesses
• Good telecommunications	• Lack of major distributors
• Growing strength in niche sectors	• Lack of growth finance
• Strong academic sector	• Fragmented and immature sectors
	• Weak industry/research links
Opportunities	**Threats**
• Expanding markets	• Fierce global competition
• Leading edge companies	• Market consolidation
• Broadcaster presence in Scotland	• Talent drain

Figure 7.2   Scotland's creative industries: SWOT summary.

Embedded games have already proved to be effective differentiators for mobile handset manufacturers (for example, Snake for Nokia) but with the onset of next generation network technologies, wireless portals and network operators are hungry for new kinds of gaming content. Scotland already has companies active and gaining significant international profile in this market, providing a platform for their own future growth and the diversification of others into this market. One of these, Digital Bridges, is both a wireless content and platform technology developer and their wireless entertainment channel is carried on approximately 30 mobile networks worldwide. The company recently attracted $18 million in investment.

The opportunities in interactive digital television are also open to Scottish companies with the ambition to realise them. New channels and new buyers are entering the market and partnerships are there for those who can develop original and compelling cross-channel content. Furthermore, the international market for television formats is showing expansion. The success of programmes such as *Big Brother*, *The Weakest Link* and *Who Wants to be a Millionaire* have created demand for exportable format shows.

In order to realise these opportunities, greater focus on R&D is needed. Significant investment is needed in high growth creative companies so as to provide the resources to finance development work, and Scotland must be more active in promoting its academic research.

The biggest threat is that these market openings are not unique to Scotland, therefore it will be important in the future to define what it is that differentiates Scotland's creative industries. Scotland must project an international image of its creativity and champion high-profile successes. The linkages with related and supporting industries such as software and telecommunications are fundamentally important and information about the changing nature of the media marketplace is urgently required.

Another threat is the drain of talent from Scotland. This has always been a challenge for the creative industries, particularly in light of London's dominant position. This, however, can be seen as an opportunity. Scotland has a global centre for creative industries on its doorstep and the issue is not who leaves, but who can be attracted to work in Scotland.

Creating future success

Many of the priorities for developing a successful creative economy for Scotland by the year 2020 have already been mentioned but a number are worth emphasising.

The central underlying issue is business development in a broad sense. The creative industries in Scotland need more high-growth companies with the capacity to impact on global markets. New company formation must be stimulated and the business support infrastructure fine tuned to meet the needs of these sectors.

Greater access to finance is an urgent requirement and the industries themselves must professionalise and invest in management, creative and technical skills. Many are young companies in immature sectors and the opportunity is there right now for the public and private sectors to nurture and grow these companies and inject the required business and management expertise.

It will be essential to invest in developing and commercialising new ideas both in the company and academic contexts. Innovation and the development and rapid adoption of new technologies are hallmarks of successful digital media economies. Scotland cannot afford to fall behind in this respect. This requires not only investment, but also much greater co-ordination and co-operation between industry and the education sector.

The real priority in all of this is access to global markets. For many of the creative industries, building a strong domestic base prior to exporting simply does not work. For example, the start-up games developer or film production company is immediately in a global market. There is no domestic market and this requires new approaches to internationalisation, based more on partnerships, joint ventures and alliances.

The related question of access to markets and distribution channels is partly addressed by new international partnerships, but inward investment efforts should also proactively target companies who can fill key supply-chain gaps in the Scottish creative industries cluster. Publishers and distributors would probably be high on the list assuming that this will not create undue displacement in the indigenous company base. This will require clear propositions and targeted marketing of Scotland's capability, particularly in content production and R&D.

The creative industries will need support to meet these challenges and the response from the government at UK and Scottish level and from the public sector is encouraging. However, there are some areas in which public policy can make a difference.

Policy implications

The Creative Industries strategy published by Scottish Enterprise in August 2000 represents a positive step forward. It lays out four strategic priorities for the development of Scotland's creative industries:

- Develop a dynamic business environment;
- Develop and expand the talent and skills base;
- Increase innovation;
- Enhance the international reputation of Scotland's creative industries.

(Scottish Enterprise, 2000)

This is necessary but not sufficient progress. Areas of public and government policy can also have positive benefits for the creative industries.

First of all is broadband telecommunications infrastructure. The UK government has committed to making the UK the leading broadband nation in the G7 by 2005 (Lovegrove and Mombru, 2001). To do so policy must encourage competition and drive competitive pricing structures through the industry. Adoption of broadband connectivity will be a significant driver of future success in the creative and other industries. Thus far the focus has been on infrastructure, but new forms of content and services will also be key to driving uptake in the way that e-mail drove online adoption. Access providers have a central role in enabling new content and service innovations through partnerships and awareness of the need to differentiate customer segments in the broadband environment. One size will not fit all (Lovegrove and Mombru, 2001).

There are also important policy implications to emerge from the forthcoming Communications Bill and the development of OFCOM. Important areas here relate to UK broadcasters, the programming quotas discussed earlier and the question of cross-media ownership. In a market poised for widespread consolidation, the relaxing of the regulations governing media ownership could open the door to take-overs of Scottish companies. This could lead to a radical reshaping of the media landscape in Scotland.

Economic regulation will also fall within the remit of OFCOM and the challenge will be to create a truly competitive environment in which UK media can compete on a global stage. As potential for online content increases, the frameworks for the negotiation of rights between producers and broadcasters and access providers is an area where OFCOM could act in the interests of producers, encouraging growth in a competitive and innovative creative sector. Indeed, intellectual property in a wide range of fields must be protected so as to promote innovation while not creating barriers to the diffusion of new ideas and technologies. Public policy must engage more effectively with these issues.

Consultation on the Communications White Paper is still ongoing and predicting the outcome of that process is difficult. Certainly convergence creates a strong argument for the creation of a single regulatory body although this will bring considerable challenges. Effective competition policy will need to address the social and cultural issues in broadcasting and communications. In many ways this raises fundamental questions about the role of regulation and policy in a changing communication's world. The demands of both commerce and culture must be addressed and there is a need for clear thinking. Of course it is important to bear in mind that broadcasting and communication's policy are not devolved powers; therefore Scotland's creative industries must seek to engage in a way that ensures that the needs of the industry north of the border are represented.

Access to finance is a major challenge and future growth will depend on facilitating capital flows both from the UK and overseas. Rules on cross-media ownership and overseas investment currently act as barriers to the free flow of capital in the industries and policy will also need to address the issues surrounding public and private provision of new media services.

The possibility of extending into other digital media the kinds of tax breaks system currently applied to film investment could be examined. The current system operating for film allows investors to write off film finance against tax and pay this back only if a profit is realised. Should they prove feasible in other sectors, policy initiatives such as this could promote investment in creative companies and help provide the resource base which is so badly needed in the industries. Tax incentives for investment in the creative industries is certainly an area meriting further scrutiny.

While these are policy issues specific to the industries, wider economic policy matters remain relevant. The current focus on developing industry clusters is well-suited to the development of the creative sector. The underlying principles of creating inter-firm linkages and competition bound together by geographical proximity and formal and informal networks are consistent with the ways in which successful creative economies operate. Also important in this is the role of cities. Throughout the world successful creative clusters have emerged in urban areas, often sparked by public investment driven by regeneration goals (the development of Silicon Alley in SoHo in New York is a prime example). Creative companies tend to congregate in areas of low rent and as they grow, supporting businesses such as retail and restaurants emerge and a process of area regeneration is begun. A recent example of this is the Hoxton and Shoreditch area in London. Economic policy, therefore, must be broad-based and recognise the range of benefits that investment in creative industries can generate.

The areas of training and skills are devolved to the Scottish Parliament along with education and infrastructure and these are all areas in which policy can make a positive contribution to the development of the creative economy. The active promotion of creativity in school education is an area of great debate and policy support would benefit not just the creative industries, but the future well being of all Scottish industry. It is crucial that the creative industries are seen as a valid and valued career choice and that education at all levels is able to meet industry needs. In this respect a more productive dialogue between industry and education must be facilitated.

Small business support also has a key role to play and business starts is an area in which Scotland currently struggles. New creative businesses must be encouraged and they will need a supportive network of advice and assistance that understands the needs of the changing economic environment. This will require flexibility and speed of response.

Conclusions

This chapter has argued that the creative industries offer considerable future opportunities for Scotland. They have the potential to drive growth in a knowledge-based economy and can generate wealth and employment and contribute to the regeneration of our cities. There are also significant challenges which call for an integrated policy approach recognising the fast changing nature of the marketplace and the relative contribution to be made by a range of different areas of public policy. This will not be easy. Focus, commitment and sustained long-term investment are needed if Scotland is to compete in the next 20 years.

Notes

1 *Creative Scotland: Shaping the Future*, Scottish Enterprise (August 2000) is a national strategy for the development of Scotland's creative industries. The priorities laid out in the strategy were developed through extensive consultation with a wide range of industry, academic and other partners.
2 Wark Clements is one of Scotland's leading television production companies. The company has offices in Glasgow and London and has grown successfully through a combination of mergers and alliances with production and distribution companies, external investment into the company and development of new media capability.
3 Ideal World Productions is an independent television, firm and new media production company based in Glasgow and London.

References

Department of Culture, Media and Sport (1998), *Creative Industries Mapping Document 1998*, London: Department of Culture, Media and Sport.
Department of Culture, Media and Sport (2001), *Creative Industries Mapping Document 2001*, London: Department of Culture, Media and Sport.
Digital Media Alliance (1998), *Recommendations for Growth: UK Digital Media*, London: Digital Media Alliance.
EKOS Economic Consultants (2001), *Creative Industries Baseline*, Report for Scottish Enterprise, Glasgow (unpublished).
European Leisure Software Publishers Association (2001), *Screen Digest*, published online at http://www.elspa.com.
John Lord Associates (2001), *Creative Industries Skills Research*, Report for Scottish Enterprise, Glasgow (unpublished).
Lovegrove, N. and I. Mombru (2001), 'Broadband and the UK economy', *Culture and Communications*, London: Independent Television Comany, pp. 46–54.
PricewaterhouseCoopers (2001), *Global Media and Entertainment Outlook 2001–2005* (Second Annual Edition), New York: Calo Afron, LLC.

Scottish Enterprise (2000), *Creative Scotland: Shaping the Future*, Strategy Document, Glasgow: Scottish Enterprise.

Spectrum Strategy Consultants (1998), 'Interview with Janice Hughes, MD of Spectrum Strategy Consultants', *Independent on Sunday*, 15 February, London.

Strategy Analytics (2001), *Critical Challenges for the Wireless Gaming Market*, Viewpoint report by Strategy Analytics, published online at http://www.strategyanalytics.com.

8
The Future of ICT Industries in Scotland: Towards a Post-branch Plant Economy?

Ross Brown

Introduction

The electronics and ICT-related industries have undoubtedly been one of the central growth drivers in the Scottish economy during the second half of the twentieth century. Notwithstanding this, the electronics industry has generated a fierce debate regarding its contribution to Scotland's economic development (see Brown, 1996; Botham, 1997; McCann, 1997; Turok, 1993, 1997). During the 1970s, it was the nature of this and other such foreign-dominated industries which led John Firn to famously describe Scotland as a 'branch plant economy' (Firn, 1975). This term was used to depict a regional economy highly dependent upon truncated manufacturing operations of multinational enterprises (MNEs) with few decision-making powers, bringing little in terms of self-sustaining economic development to the host economy.

However, the industry is currently undergoing major structural changes which will fundamentally alter its shape over the next two decades; not least the rapid demise of low value-added manufacturing in Scotland and the closure of numerous branch plants. An assessment at the present time should help to identify possible steps which both firms and government might take to ensure Scotland makes a successful transition towards a 'post-branch plant economy'.

The evolution of 'Silicon Glen' in Scotland

With the demise of traditional industries in Scotland after the Second World War, the electronics sector assumed increasing importance in the

Scottish economy and has been the main source of new job creation in manufacturing. For example, in 1959 the electronics sector's share of total manufacturing employment in Scotland was 1.1 per cent; this had risen to 5.7 per cent in 1973 and to 16.4 per cent by 1994 (Brown, 1996; Botham, 1997). Broadly speaking, foreign investment in 'Silicon Glen' has taken place in four main phases (see Walker, 1987; Brown, 1996) (see Table 8.1 for major companies):

1 1945 and 1959: during this time overseas-owned firms – nearly all of whom were American – began locating across the industrial Central Belt of Scotland
2 1960 and 1975: this featured the emergence of a microelectronic components sector
3 1976 and 1985: a broadening range of electronics firms invested in Scotland
4 Late 1980s–present: particular growth has taken place in the data processing sector.

An overview of the current ICT sector in Scotland

The electronics industry is not a coherent single industrial activity, but a complex sector with widely differing supply chains, attributes and cultures (KPMG, 2001). It officially comprises data processing equipment, electronic components, electronic instrument engineering and other electronics (for further details see *Statistical Bulletin*, 1999). Main electronics products include: personal computers (PCs), laptops, servers, workstations, televisions, audio equipment, cellular telephones, photocopiers, microwave and instrumentation equipment, automated teller machines (ATMs) and active electronic components, such as analogue and digital semiconductors.

On a number of different measures, electronics and related industries is one of the most dynamic parts of Scotland's manufacturing sector. In 1998, the electronics industry employed over 40 500 in Scotland, with an estimated 30 000 jobs in supplier businesses (*Statistical Bulletin*, 1999). As we can see in Table 8.2, between 1993 and 1997 output in Scotland's electronics industry grew in real terms by an average of 20 per cent each year.[1] The sector also has an impressive export performance, accounting for 58 per cent of Scottish manufactured exports (£11 billion in 1999 – SCDI, 2001). The electronics industry is largely responsible for Scotland's average annual increase in exports of over 10 per cent per year since 1990 (Collinson, 2000).

Table 8.1 Leading companies in Silicon Glen

Company	Nation	Products	Location	Workforce	Opened
IBM	USA	Personal computers (PCs) and monitors, European Shared service centre	Greenock	5 000	1951
Motorola	USA	Semiconductors (Logic chips)	East Kilbride	2 000	1969
AT&T (formerly NCR)	USA	Automatic teller machines	Dundee	1 600	1946
DEC	USA	Workstations	Ayr	1 550	1976
Hewlett-Packard	USA	Communications systems	South Queensferry	1 500	1964
Solectron	USA	Electronics assembly	Dunfermline	1 000	1993
Polaroid	USA	Cameras, photographic film	Dumbarton	800	1950
Compaq	USA	PCs	Erskine	700	1987
Sanmina-SCI	USA	Electronics assembly	Irvine	650	1990
National Semiconductor	USA	Semiconductors	Greenock	550	1969
Oki	Japan	Printers, fuel injection systems	Cumbernauld	500	1979

Source: Author's analysis.

Table 8.2 Indices of output (1993–1997): by electronic groups and total manufacturing index values (1995 = 100)

Year	Data processing equipment	Electronic components	Electronic instrument engineering	Other electronics	Total electronics	Non-electronics	Total manufacturing
Weight	64.0	68.0	13.0	4.0	149.0	678.0	827.0
1993	69.5	59.1	96.9	69.3	67.2	95.5	90.4
1994	82.4	81.8	96.5	80.6	83.3	98.1	95.5
1995	100.0	100.0	100.0	100.0	100.0	100.0	100.0
1996	132.1	105.1	118.7	105.2	117.9	99.8	103.1
1997	151.0	130.6	110.3	123.5	137.3	101.6	108.1
Percentage change 1996–1997	14.3	24.3	−7.1	17.4	16.5	1.8	4.8
Percentage change per annum 1993–1997	21.4	22.0	3.3	15.6	19.6	1.6	4.6

Source: Statistical Bulletin, 1999.

The largest sub-sector in terms of total employment is data processing equipment with 14 400 employees in 1996, accounting for approximately 36 per cent of total electronics employment in Scotland (*Statistical Bulletin*, 1999). Another striking feature of Scotland's electronics industry is its high levels of foreign ownership: well over half of all employment is represented for by foreign-owned companies. Indigenous firms tend to feature more in specialist areas such as defence, opto-electronics and lower value segments of the supply chain.

Given that the most up-to-date official statistics highlighted above only cover the period up until the late 1990s, it is worth mentioning more recent developments. During 2001 there was a wave of major lay-offs and plant consolidations, especially by US firms located in Scotland. The closure of Motorola's two Scottish plants and NEC's plant in Livingston in particular will have major economic implications for Scotland both directly in terms of lost employment and exports and indirectly vis-à-vis the impact on supply chain across Scotland. The main reasons underlying these closures is the global downturn in demand for some electronic products, especially in telecommunications sector (for example, mobile phones). There has also been a wave of mergers and acquisitions throughout the industry, resulting in major consolidation across the supply chain in Scotland (Raines *et al.*, 2001).

In addition to this downturn which is fundamentally altering the nature of 'Silicon Glen', there has also been a relative slowdown in the level of new inward investment in this sector. On the positive side inward investors which have recently come have been of a higher quality but smaller than has traditionally been the case; for example, Motorola's new R&D centre at Livingston and projects linked to the Alba Centre, for example, Simutech.

Cluster analysis of the electronics sector

Scotland's electronics industry was one of the first Scottish sectors to be analysed using Porter's cluster model (*Monitor*, 1993). This initial analysis evaluated the key characteristics of the industry in Scotland as a whole using the 'diamond framework'. The *Monitor* study concluded: 'analysis of the cluster and its comparison with other globally competitive clusters, highlights a weak underlying competitive position, threatening both the cluster's near-term survival and its ability to adapt to changes in the competitive environment in the longer-term' (*Monitor*, 1993, p. 6). Many aspects of this report still seem valid today. As the cluster map in Figure 8.1 reveals, the industry as a whole is relatively

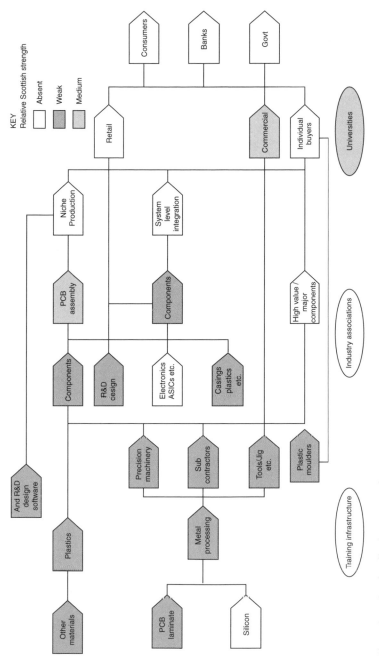

Figure 8.1 Scotland's electronics cluster map.

Source: Author's analysis.

Table 8.3 The cluster's main characteristics

Cluster characteristics	Electronics
Ownership structure	Mostly foreign-owned MNEs and first tier suppliers, few strong local firms
Local demand condition	Limited Scottish market, poor demand conditions
Nature of manufacturing	Mostly high volume and standardized
Type of supplier linkages	Mostly dependent, adversarial supplier relations, suppliers often highly dependent on one or two customers
Level of supply base internationalisation	Very low levels of internationalization
Technological capabilities	Some advanced R&D in a few plants, most Scottish suppliers have no meaningful technological capability
Impact on local economic development	Large amount of direct employment, high levels of exports, little indirect benefits such as supply-chain development or technology transfer
Cluster type and dynamics	Potential cluster: weakly embedded, low levels of innovation, at risk from external corporate decisions

Source: Author's analysis.

weak in Scotland and lacks several elements exhibited by strong more dynamic ICT clusters, such as 'Silicon Valley'.

At present, there are several main weaknesses in Scotland's electronics industry limiting the cluster's overall cohesiveness (see Table 8.3). First, the electronics industry is dominated by a handful of foreign-owned companies while Scottish firms tend to be smaller, less international suppliers. A dynamic cluster typically features well-rooted domestic and foreign-owned firms which are internationally competitive (Porter, 1990). Another key weakness is the focus on high volume, low cost manufacturing, making standardised electronic goods or components. In the main, the customers for products assembled in Scotland are nonlocal and have little direct interface with original equipment manufacturers (OEMs) in Scotland. Close interaction between producers and end-users (either public or private) is a key feature of strong high-technology clusters (Porter, 1990). Further, the standardised nature of production contrasts with other types of higher complexity electronics which require significant interaction with the customer (DTI, 1998). A further weakness is the lack of linkages between OEMs, local suppliers, government bodies and local universities. Strong networks and linkages are traditionally key advanced factors germane to dynamic sectoral clusters (Enright, 1998).

In sum, the electronics industry has had a very large direct impact on the Scottish economy in terms of employment, output and exports, but little impact in terms of indirect effects, such as supplier linkages and technology-transfer. This, together with the volume manufacturing nature of much of the industry in Scotland, means that the overall impact of the sector is reduced and places the industry at threat from divestment and eventual plant closure. Scotland has been slow to upgrade and develop the higher value end of the industry. In this respect Scottish policy-makers have ignored warnings dating back to the 1970s (Firn, 1975) and subsequent research during the 1980s and 1990s that a change in focus was required if Scotland was to have a successful future in this sector (*Monitor*, 1993; Turok, 1993; Brown, 1996). Notably, the lack of a coherent policy response seems to have become more acute during the 1990s, especially since the demise of the sectoral teams which existed within the Scottish Development Agency, the predecessor to SE (Halkier and Danson, 1997). Interestingly, SE has gradually dispensed with these teams in favour of more discrete cluster teams in areas such as communications technologies and opto-electronics.

SWOT analysis of Scotland's electronics industry

This section seeks to examine the industry in greater depth by evaluating the strengths, weaknesses, opportunities and threats within different components of the industry. Broadly speaking, there are six main categories of firms within the electronics industry (see Figure 8.2 for a summary):

Data processing equipment

The manufacture of data processing equipment, such as PCs and related peripheral products, is a central part of the electronics industry in Scotland. The main large-volume firms in this sector include, IBM, NCR, Compaq and Sun Microsystems. Indeed, these OEMs and local suppliers make up the single largest constituent of the electronics industry in Scotland. The nature of the main data processing equipment companies in Scotland varies quite considerably. At one end of the spectrum are extended value chain operations, such as IBM and NCR. For example, IBM operates a very large scale and diverse operation in Scotland, encompassing server and laptop manufacturing, software development and a shared service centre.

Similarly, NCR's plant in Dundee is the firm's main plant worldwide for ATMs, including having the firm's world product mandate for the

Strengths	Weaknesses
• Good supply of skilled graduates	• Dependency on data processing manufacturing industry
• Experience of high volume manufacturing environment	• Lack of plant level R&D
• Strong specialist electronics sub-sectors, such as opto-electronics, communications technologies	• Low skill intensity in certain sub-sectors (data processing and consumer electronics)
• High quality university research base	• Lack of local embeddedness

Opportunities	Threats
• Growing global market for electronics products	• Plant closures caused by global consolidation
• Higher skill intensity of new growth spin-off companies	• Migration of low cost manufacturing to Eastern Europe
• System on a chip design experience	• Component miniaturisation, especially SLI, could reduce employment in PCB assembly firms
• Very high quality academic research in various sub-sectors, such as communications technologies and opto-electronics	• UK outwith the euro may lead to divestments

Figure 8.2   SWOT analysis of the Scottish electronics cluster.

product and all associated R&D (Young *et al.*, 1994). Other data processing firms such as Sun and Compaq, operate more limited manufacturing operations in Scotland. Both firms have manufacturing-only operations which are often vulnerable to closure. Indeed, recent outsourcing at Compaq led to employment migrating to a Taiwanese supplier, Hon Hai, located in the Czech Republic in Eastern Europe. The long-term prognosis for these truncated branch plant operations looks bleak. Nonetheless, these are still central facilities in both firms global manufacturing operations. Indeed, Sun's server manufacturing plant in Linlithgow is its largest plant worldwide. If these plants are to survive over the next 20 years they may have to add additional service-related functions as IBM have done.

Electronic components

Semiconductors are the core technology at the heart of all electronic equipment.[2] This sector currently employs approximately 14 400 in

Scotland. The country accounts for 7 and 47 per cent of EU and UK semi-conductor capacity respectively. Chip-makers in Scotland manufacture a range of different products using various technologies. However, the recent closure of Seagate and the plans to close NEC and Motorola's plants, cast some serious doubts over the long-term future of semiconductor production in Scotland. In hindsight, the year 2001 may be seen as the beginning of the end of 'Silicon Glen', as the country's dedicated semiconductor plants halved in number from four to two. The two remaining plants in Scotland, Motorola and National Semiconductor, manufacture respectively, higher value-added chips (called Logic chips) for automotive systems, and analogue devices.

A number of particular issues face the semiconductor industry. For example, the reliance on inward investment has proved to be difficult in recent years. Scotland has very little private sector R&D activity in this area and most of the main foreign-owned chip plants manufacture high volume wafers. Semiconductor manufacturing is highly volatile due to the nature of demand. This part of the electronics industry more than any other faces huge demand swings and places policy-makers in a vulnerable position when committing huge sums of public money in capital intensive projects.

The industry is very weak in design and development activity, and the strength and quality of links within the cluster (especially between suppliers, manufacturers and universities) in Scotland are low. A significant area of potential in Scotland revolves around what is known as embedded software; this is the link between the silicon and the system. Indeed, SE has had some success at attracting specialist embedded software firms to Scotland through its Alba Centre (see Brown and Raines, 2000). If Scotland is to continue to prosper in this highly cyclical industry, initiatives such as the Alba Centre will have to be stepped up in the future.

Communications technology

The communications technology sector in Scotland is a collection of 150 or so companies which together employ approximately 15 000 employees. The industry in Scotland covers a wide range of activities and companies, ranging from the very high volume manufacture of mobile telephones to the bespoke production of one-off internet-signalling equipment.

In terms of manufacturing, inward investors dominate the sector in Scotland, notably Motorola and Agilent. Until summer 2001, Motorola operated a large-scale cellular phone plant in Scotland, but this closed down with the loss of 3000 jobs. Agilent also operate a large-scale plant employing 1400 employees manufacturing a range of telecommunications and microwave test equipment. Unlike Motorola, Agilent also undertake R&D within Scotland and employ a large number of engineers and graduates. The indigenous sector is concentrated on niche markets and companies and tends to be much smaller, such as Trak Microwave (microwave components) and Vision Microelectronics (videoconferencing/toys). In addition to employment within firms, Scotland also has very strong research strengths within the country's higher education institutions.

The communications technology sector in Scotland faces a number of challenges in the future. First, as with the rest of electronics production in Scotland, the country's position as a manufacturing location is under threat to lower cost countries in Eastern Europe. Second, Scotland in future will have to try harder to commercialise the first class R&D within universities. These research strengths coupled with its links with opto-electronics help to make the communications technology sub-cluster an area for strong growth potential. Maximising the country's academic intellectual property is as important for the sector's long-term future, as large-scale inward investment has been in the past.

Defence electronics/opto-electronics

Defence electronics has been a major part of the development and success of the electronics industry in Scotland. Indeed, it was UK-owned firms such as Ferranti and Barr & Stroud which formed the basis of electronics production in Scotland during the 1940s. Nowadays, the bulk of the indigenous electronics firms in Scotland are UK-based defence-related firms, most notably BAe Systems, Pilkington Optronics and RACAL-MESL. One of the positive features of the defence electronics sector is its concentration on high value, specialist production, which is often less cyclical than consumer electronics production. For example, the US-owned firm Raytheon, has managed to avoid some of the problems faced by traditional semiconductor manufacturers owing to its focus on defence electronics.

Another positive spin-off from the defence industry is the links this has with opto-electronics production. Opto-electronics is one of the most dynamic parts of the industry in Scotland, although still very small with 50 or so companies and approximately 4000 employees. However, a number of rapidly growing opto-electronics firms have spun-off from Scotland's university research base, such as Kymata, Kamelian, Microlase Optical Systems and Intense Photonics. Although very small at present these firms offer rapid growth potential and also provide very high quality employment, whilst undertaking high levels of R&D. For example, the University of Strathclyde spin-out, Kamelian, plan to base their R&D headquarters in Glasgow whilst undertaking manufacturing in the south-east of England, in direct contrast to UK's traditional spatial division of labour (Massey, 1984).

Consumer electronics

This is possibly the smallest aspect of the electronics industry in Scotland. In recent years, Scotland's consumer electronics industry has all but disappeared. The main reason for this has been divestment by MNEs in Scotland to reduce costs; the bulk of new foreign investment in this sector goes to Eastern Europe. A number of plant closures by Mitsubishi have reduced this sub-sector in Scotland to a single manufacturing plant in East Kilbride owned by JVC. The decline and withdrawal of OEMs producers has also had a knock-on effect on local suppliers and a number have recently closed (for example, Alps Electronics and Matsushita). There is some very small scale indigenous production left in Scotland, but this tends to be undertaken by highly specialist, low volume producers such as Linn Products, the makers of specialist audio equipment. It is doubtful if Scotland can compete in consumer electronics outside of such niche markets.

Suppliers and subcontractors

Although surveys show that the level of local sourcing in Scotland is relatively modest, there is still a considerable supply base (Turok, 1993), estimated to employ approximately 30 000 people.

There are three main tiers of suppliers in Scotland. First-tier suppliers undertake a range of manufacturing activities such as printed circuit board (PCB) assembly and full 'box-build'. Some have become high volume producers in their own right and frequently co-ordinate lower tier suppliers. During the 1990s, there was an increase in 'second-wave' inward investment by large foreign-owned PCB assemblers (for example, Jabil, Solectron and Flextronics). While these firms have clearly benefited from increased outsourcing from the OEMs in terms of employment growth, some of the bigger investors have also managed to develop strategic partnerships with their clients in Scotland, enabling them to move into higher value design-related activities. For example, the US-owned Solectron recently opened up a new design centre in Port Glasgow with the help of IBM.

Lower down the value chain are the second and third tier suppliers. Most of these firms manufacture basic components such as PCBs, sheet metal, cables, plastics, and so on. There has been some success in these areas by Scottish-owned suppliers (for example, Fullarton Computer Industries, Brands Electronics and Simclar), but these tend to be isolated examples (Brown *et al.*, 2000). These suppliers face growing price competition from East Asian and East European producers, which will no doubt increase further when EU enlargement offers tariff-free access to the EU market for the latter firms.

Key strategic trends and issues for the future

There are three main types of strategic challenges facing the electronics industry in Scotland over the next 20 years: changing factor conditions, technology and legislative issues.

Factor conditions

Many electronics products are becoming commodity items. Manufacturers therefore strive to get costs as low as possible. In the short-term this price orientation is leading OEMs to source further and further afield. Although this enables firms to remain competitive, this process can also act to effectively 'hollow out' the supply base in Scotland. In the longer term, the commodity nature of the industry is threatening the very existence of parts of the industry in Scotland. The future looks bleak for large firms who continue to view their operations as low cost manufacturing facilities (for example, Compaq and JVC). Manufacturing companies that will remain in Scotland will increasingly have to upgrade their knowledge-related activities (Peters, 2000).

Increasing globalization of the industry is also creating added pressure for electronics firms in Scotland. Unless Scotland's companies can reap the scale economies from further business internationalisation, they may face losing business with MNEs who increasingly demand global suppliers (Raines *et al.*, 2001). This is also an important issue for young technology-based firms who are effectively forced to 'go global' from the very outset of their existence to tap into key technology markets such as the USA (see Chapter 15).

Technological change

Technological change will also have a fundamental bearing on the future of the industry in Scotland. For example, a typical product cycle from concept to market launch is 18 months (KPMG, 2001). As product life cycles shorten further still, new product development becomes increasingly central to the success of any given company. Given the lack of R&D and weak co-operation between research, marketing, manufacturing and suppliers in Scotland, this would appear to be a serious threat in the future. This feature is especially true of Scotland's key manufacturing companies.

Another key technological trend in the industry is the move towards smaller, more portable products (for example, laptops and mobile devices), which require the miniaturisation of component parts, thereby impacting on the PCB assembly firms located in Scotland (because of the reduced requirement for electronic components on PCBs). At the same time, this trend increases opportunities for firms to advance systems level integration technology.

Legislative issues

The relaxation of trade barriers means that companies can go almost anywhere in the world to source products, people or technology. While this process is likely to proceed apace in the years to come, it will probably intensify with events such as EU enlargement and EMU. Furthermore, the UK's lax employment laws make it easier and cheaper to close plants in the UK than other parts of Europe (Raines and Brown, 2001). For example, the recent closure of Motorola's facility at Bathgate saw some of the work transferred to another of their plants in Germany. Electronics companies may, therefore, target closures on UK facilities.

The onset of European enlargement will clearly present opportunities as well as threats for the industry in Scotland. However, it will probably engender more intense competition for lower value-added parts of the industry in years to come. There is also a strong perception among inward investors that they could be at a disadvantage vis-à-vis firms inside the euro-zone owing to the problem of greater exchange rate fluctuations. This clearly would have major implications for electronics inward investment.

A final policy change which could impact the industry in Scotland relates to forthcoming EU environmental legislation. In particular, the industry faces greater pressure to recycle following the EU directive, Waste Electrical and Electronic Equipment (Weee). Due to come into effect in 2006, this Directive places greater responsibility on electronic producers to recycle electronic products. The Commission estimate that this could increase prices for electronic products by 1–3 per cent, but analysts reckon this could be as much as 20 per cent. While this clearly places additional cost burdens on the industry, it also opens up opportunities for firms to engage in recycling activities. Indeed, Scotland has already been successful in attracting one such firm, Citraya UK, to Ayrshire and a couple of home grown firms have also been established. There is clearly further scope for the growth of the recycling sector and other such 'green' electronics activities in Scotland.

Policy implications

Over the last ten years or so, public policy towards the electronics industry in Scotland has been reactive and incoherent. The reason for this situation has been a combination of the dominance of inward investment in the industry, the lack of a strong industry body, wavering levels of support for the industry by the Enterprise agencies and poor policy tools to develop and harness the industry's full potential (Brown, 1996). However, there are now some tentative signs that this situation is beginning to give way to a more coherent and co-ordinated approach for the industry.[3] In order to push forward the transition from a 'branch plant economy' to a 'knowledge-based economy', both firms and public policy will have to change direction.

There are a number of key institutional issues which will need to be examined.[4] First, SE should re-establish a dedicated national team to deal with the mounting problems facing the industry in Scotland. Second, Scotland should alter its traditional approach towards inward investment attraction. In future, the development of niche, R&D-intensive sub-sectors, such as opto-electronics, telecommunications and automotive-related electronics, should be the goal. Therefore, Scottish Development International (SDI) may have to widen the network of partners they traditionally work with (see Chapter 15). Plus overseas offices of SDI should be used as a conduit for attracting venture capital, people and technology to Scotland.

There should also be a comprehensive change to Scotland's policy instruments. At present, the most important form of assistance to the electronics industry is regional selective assistance (RSA) and by far the largest slice of RSA goes to electronics. For example, between 1995 and 2000 the electronics sector accounted for nearly half of all RSA awards (that is, £288 million out of a total of £626 million). One of the major criticisms of RSA has been its preferential treatment for inward investors, especially large scale capital expenditure by foreign-owned firms. Although it has proved itself to be a highly cost effective and resilient regional policy instrument (Armstrong, 2001), the Scottish Government is currently undertaking a review of RSA. This should aim to make the aid instrument more amenable to higher value, R&D-related projects which are often less capital-intensive. This should make smaller, indigenous firms more likely to qualify for awards.

In order to address the traditional weaknesses associated with the branch plant economy, it is absolutely vital that Scotland increases its indigenous stock of firms in this sector. In particular, more emphasis should be placed on the commercialisation of the existing science base (see Chapter 14). It is also important that the industry in Scotland forges stronger links to universities through secondments, and so on. Enterprise agencies will increasingly have to act as brokers between universities, entrepreneurs and venture capitalists. Another aim of the policy-makers should be to foster greater cross-cluster synergies between opto-electronics, semiconductors, defence electronics and communications technologies. This could be done by using R&D packages, such as the Proof of Concept Fund, to undertake an explicit interdisciplinary approach to funding.

Finally, other policy areas worthy of examination include supply chain and skills development. Policies to embed electronics companies in Scotland should be given a higher priority in future. Indeed, assessments of foreign direct investment (FDI) in Scotland have concluded that SE should consider developing a comprehensive supplier development programme (Firn Crichton Roberts, 2000). The procurement surveys previously undertaken by Scottish Enterprise to identify supply chain gaps should also be reintroduced. Skills shortages are one of the most chronic issues facing the industry as a whole, especially at the top-end of the market (KPMG, 2001). Attracting and retaining higher level skills in Scotland will be a key issue for the country over the next 20 years.[5] In addition, matching venture capital with the right people, technology, intellectual property and skills sets will be crucial.

Conclusions

During the last 20 years, electronics production in foreign-owned branch plants has been a cornerstone of the Scottish economy, especially in terms of output, exports and employment. Traditionally, Scotland's main competitive advantage has been its relative strength in basic factor conditions (low-cost flexible labour source, access to EU market, government incentives, and so on). However, in an era of increasingly mobile production and slippery space, these locational factors are no longer sufficient to make Scotland a 'sticky' place for electronics production (Markusen, 1996).

Structural changes currently unfolding across Scotland in this sector manifestly demonstrate that a new direction is required for the twenty-first century. Most importantly, if the industry is to have a long-term future in Scotland, we will have to shift away from the low-cost, high-volume production model and specialise and develop knowledge-based, higher value activities. Therefore, if Scotland is to successfully progress towards a *post-branch-plant economy*, the ultimate vision for electronics and ICT industries in 2020 should be to increase the proportion of people in electronics-related R&D employment, increase the stock of indigenous electronics businesses, increase overall skill levels and upgrade lower-value activities currently based in Scotland.

Notes

1   It is worth highlighting that the strong growth in electronics manufacturing has concealed an overall weak performance in the rest of the manufacturing sector in Scotland, however. Between 1993 and 1997, for example, output in non-electronics manufacturing merely averaged 1.6 per cent growth each year.

2   There are four main categories of semiconductor: application-specific integrated circuits (ASICs), memory, microprocessors and analogue devices.

3   In July 2001, a five-year action plan was agreed for the electronics industry in Scotland. The action plan was jointly drawn up by electronics Scotland, the main industry body in Scotland, the Scottish Executive and SE. The action plan has three main objectives: increasing R&D in the industry, improving the competitiveness of the supply chain, and improving skill levels within the industry. The action plan was formally launched by the Minister for Enterprise and Lifelong Learning, Wendy Alexander, on 30 October 2001.

4   I have concentrated on issues which are under the auspices of Scottish policy-makers, but clearly other factors will influence the future of the industry in Scotland. For example, a decision over whether Britain joins the Euro will clearly have a major bearing on the industry and Scotland's position outside the Euro may jeopardise the sector's future.

5   Another important issue for policy-makers to address over the next 20 years will be the development of new 'hybrid' skill sets, combining hard technical skills with softer generic and business-related skills (Hillage *et al.*, 2001). A move towards more bespoke production will also increase the demand for more intermediate 'technician-level' skills. Assistance with these issues will be greatest for smaller companies who traditionally neglect such human resource issues.

References

Armstrong, H. (2001), 'Regional selective assistance: Is the spend enough and is it targeting the right places?', *Regional Studies*, Vol. 35, pp. 247–257.

Botham, R. (1997), *Inward Investment and Regional Development: Scotland and the Electronics Industries*, Paper presented to the Regional Science Association (British and Irish Section) Annual Conference, Falmouth, 10–12 September.

Brown, R. (1996), 'Foreign direct investment and regional economic development: Backward electronics linkages in Scotland and Singapore', Ph.D. thesis, University of Strathclyde, Glasgow (unpublished).

Brown, R. and P. Raines (2000), 'The changing nature of foreign investment policy in Europe: From promotion to management', in J. Dunning (ed.), *Regions, Globalization, and the Knowledge-Based Economy*, Oxford: Oxford University Press.

Brown, R., P. Raines and I. Turok (2000), 'Supplier-investor linkages and the internationalization of the electronics and oil-gas sectors in Scotland', *Regional and Industrial Policy Research Paper*, No. 40, Glasgow: European Policies Research Centre, University of Strathclyde.

Collinson, S. (2000), 'Knowledge networks for innovation in small Scottish software firms', *Entrepreneurship and Regional Development*, Vol. 12, pp. 217–244.

DTI (1998), Electronics manufacturing, a report of a focus group of the foresight manufacturing, production and business processes panel, London: DTI.

Enright, M. (2000), 'The globalization of competition and the localization of competitive advantage: Policies toward regional clustering', in N. Hood and S. Young (eds), *The Globalization of Multinational Enterprise Activity and Economic Development*, Basingstoke, Hampshire: Macmillan, pp. 303–331.

Firn, J. (1975), 'External control and regional policy', in G. Brown (ed.), *The Red Paper on Scotland*, Edinburgh: Edinburgh University Press.

Firn Crichton Roberts (2000), *Inward Investment Benefits for the Scottish Economy*, Evaluation Report for Scottish Enterprise, Locate in Scotland and Scottish Executive by Firn Crichton Roberts Ltd., University of Strathclyde, and The Fraser of Allander Institute (unpublished).

Halkier, H. and M. Danson (1997), 'Regional Development Agencies in Western Europe: A Survey of Key Characteristics and Trends', *European Urban and Regional Studies*, Vol. 3, pp. 243–256.

Hillage, J., J. Cummings, D. Lain and N. Jagger (2001), *Skill Needs in Electronics*, Report for the National Training Organisation for Engineering Manufacture, Brighton : Institute for Employment Studies.

KPMG (2001), *Electronics in Focus: Lifting the Lid on the Industry*, Report for the Federation of the Electronics Industry.

Markusen, A. (1996), 'Sticky places in slippery space: A typology of industrial districts', *Economic Geography*, Vol. 72, pp. 293–313.

Massey, D. (1984), *Spatial Divisions of Labour: Social Structures and the Geography of Production*, Basingstoke, Hampshire: Macmillan.

Monitor (1993), 'A strategy for the Scottish software and electronics clusters', Report for Scottish Enterprise National, Glasgow.

McCann, P. (1997), 'How deeply embedded is Silicon Glen? A cautionary note', *Regional Studies*, Vol. 31, pp. 695–703.

Peters, E. (1999), 'Plant subsidiary upgrading: Some evidence from the electronics industry', in N. Hood and S. Young (eds), *The Globalization of Multinational Enterprise Activity and Economic Development*, Basingstoke, Hampshire: Macmillan, pp. 332–365.

Porter, M. (1990), *The Competitive Advantage of Nations*, New York: Free Press.

Raines, P. and R. Brown (2001), 'Does workforce flexibility affect foreign investment decisions? Germany and the UK compared', in M. Hughes and J. Taggart (eds), *International Business: European Dimensions*, Basingstoke, Hampshire: Palgrave.

Raines, P., Turok I. and R. Brown (2001), 'Growing global: Foreign direct investment and the internationalization of local suppliers in Scotland', *European Planning Studies*, Vol. 9, pp. 965–978.

SCDI (2001), *Survey of Scottish Sales and Exports 1999*, Glasgow: Scottish Council for Development and Industry.

Statistical Bulletin (1999), The Electronics Industry in Scotland, *Statistical Bulletin: NO IND/1999/C1.9*, Edinburgh: Scottish Office.

Turok I. (1993), 'Inward investment and local linkages: How deeply embedded is 'Silicon Glen'?', *Regional Studies*, Vol. 27, pp. 401–417.

Turok, I. (1997), 'Linkages in the Scottish electronics industry: Further evidence', *Regional Studies*, Vol. 31, pp. 705–711.

Walker, J. (1987), 'The Scottish electronics industry', *Scottish Government Yearbook*, Edinburgh: Edinburgh University Press, pp. 57–80.

Young, S., N. Hood and E. Peters (1994), 'Multinational enterprises and regional economic development', *Regional Studies*, Vol. 28, pp. 657–677.

9
Financial and Business Services

Jeremy Peat

Introduction

This chapter covers two distinct sectors, which are both very difficult to 'capture' in statistical terms – or indeed to define fully and formally. Financial services have a number of features in common with business services – not least relative significance in scale within the Scottish economy and importance in terms of pan-economy impacts, alongside limitations of data and analysis. Nevertheless the outlook for the two sectors must be examined separately, to some extent, if sound conclusions are to be drawn with respect to their key challenges in a 2020 context. However, the chapter has more to say about financial than business services. This is in part because the data and analysis of the former, while still limited, are better than for the latter. Also a number of components of business services, particularly professional services such as accountancy, law, management consultancy, property and computer services, are heavily dependent upon the major companies within financial services, which are likely to be their largest customers.

The starting position is that Scotland has significant potential to build upon an existing comparative advantage in these sectors, in particular in financial services. This sector has scope to continue to benefit substantially from strong branding – via well-respected names of public companies and major mutual organisations – and the reputation of the prudent, competent and highly educated Scot. It is reasonable to expect growing international trade in these service sectors. Unlike many parts of manufacturing, Scotland should not suffer any major transport disadvantage in exporting business and financial services to the rest of the UK or the rest of the world. These are sectors where being peripheral in Europe should not be a major cause for concern. Similarly the physical infrastructure requirements are relatively limited. These sectors are human rather than physical capital intensive.

The next section attempts to describe, statistically, the two sectors, on the basis of official data, such input–output material as is available and other sources. This is followed by consideration of the shape of the sectors and the key issues likely to influence their progress over the coming decades.

Statistical description

Financial services in Scotland incorporates banks, building societies, fund managers, life and general insurance companies and a range of other activities. Data have been brought together by Scottish Financial Enterprise (SFE) to show the scale of (for example) funds managed in Scotland and generally to demonstrate that the Scottish financial sector ranks sixth in Europe and fifteenth world-wide.[1]

Business services are more heterogeneous. The definition for statistical purposes often includes real estate and renting. Even excluding these activities, the business services sector is multidimensional, including accountants – large and small – lawyers, consultants, and so on, but also office cleaners!

Gross Domestic Product (GDP)

The latest data that permit comparisons between the share of financial and business services in GDP for Scotland and the share for other territories/regions of the UK are for 1998. These data show 'financial intermediation' as accounting for 5.1 per cent of Scottish GDP. This is more than for Wales and Northern Ireland; more than for the regions in the north of England and the Midlands; about the same as for the South West; but less than for London, the South East and the East of England. There has been considerable growth in financial services in Scotland since 1998. The share of 'financial intermediation' in Scottish GDP is now above 5.1 per cent.

For these regional data, business services are lumped together with real estate and renting. This aggregate sector accounted for 16.7 per cent of Scottish GDP in 1998. This was again more than for Wales or Northern Ireland, but less than for England. It was also a lower percentage of GDP than for most English regions.[2] Again this sector in Scotland has grown more rapidly than overall GDP since 1998.

There is no doubt that the combination of business and financial services has outperformed the economy as a whole, in terms of GDP growth, in recent years (see Table 9.1). From 1995 to Q2 2001, the output of 'business services and finance' has increased by 27 per cent, whereas growth in Scottish GDP as a whole, all at market prices, was 10.8 per cent[3] and 'all services' grew at 13.5 per cent. The relative scale of growth has been particularly impressive most recently. The quarterly GDP data from the Scottish Executive show an increase for business services and finance of 14.7 per cent from 1998 to Q2 2001, as compared to an overall Scottish GDP increase of 3.7 per cent in the same period.

These data are, as with the UK GDP data, disaggregated to distinguish 'financial services' from 'real estate and business services'. This latter classification is not ideal for present purposes – exclusion of real estate would be preferable for consideration of the business service sector – but the data are up-to-date. As again shown in Table 9.1, the increase since 1995 has been most marked in financial services (51.4 per cent), while growth in real estate and business services at 20.6 per cent has also substantially outstripped both GDP as a whole and total Scottish services. In the four quarters to Q2 2001, overall Scottish GDP increased at 0.3 per cent, while real estate and business services grew by 8.6 per cent and financial services at 9.6 per cent.

In summary, in terms of GDP, both business and financial services are major sectors contributing a significant and rapidly increasing proportion of Scottish output. It has been recognised by the Committee of Scottish Clearing Bankers (CSCB) that enhanced data on the activities of the major Scottish banks in Scotland would add to our understanding

Table 9.1 Scottish GDP: gross value added at basic prices by category of output

	Total	All services	Of which business services and finance	Business services and finance	
				Real estate and business services	Financial services
1995	100	100	100	100	100
1996	102.1	102.1	102.1	101.3	102.3
1997	104.9	104.6	106.8	106.5	108.0
1998	106.8	106.6	110.7	109.9	113.4
1999	108.8	108.1	111.7	107.3	128.3
2000	109.9	109.6	116.0	110.7	136.2
2001 Q1	109.9	111.9	122.5	116.9	143.7
2001 Q2	110.8	113.5	127.0	120.6	151.4

Source: Scottish Executive GDP Data for Q2 2001.

of developments within the Scottish economy.[4] Data on business and personal borrowing/deposits by the four banks in Scotland will provide an enhanced view of these activities, with implications for macroeconomic matters. Access to data in comparable form to the data available at the UK level will permit more meaningful comparisons with the UK, as well as examinations of trends at the Scottish level.

Employment

The latest official data put employment in 1999 in financial services as a whole at 65 900, down from 72 610 in 1997[5] (see Table 9.2). This is almost certainly a substantial under-estimate of the present level of employment in the sector, being out of line both with more recent quarterly data and estimates compiled by the FAI for SFE. Provisional estimates from the Scottish Executive, based upon these quarterly data, suggest that employee jobs in financial services amounted to between 87 000 and 89 000 in the first two quarters of 2001, a marked increase on the same period a year earlier. On the basis of these latest estimates, financial services in Scotland accounted for 4.2 per cent of the total number of Scottish employees, up from 3.9 per cent ten years earlier. Employees in employment in this sector in Scotland rose by 8.7 per cent over this ten year period, while the number of employees in all sectors declined by 0.2 per cent. At the Great Britain level, financial services in March 2001 accounted for a slightly higher share of employment at 4.3 per cent, down from 4.9 per cent a decade earlier.

Employment in business services, again defined to include real estate activities and renting, was estimated at 217 810 in 1999. By June 2001 this is estimated to have risen to over 246 000, an increase of over 13 per cent. Within this total 'other business activities', which may be a good proxy for what is normally taken as implied by business services, employed an estimated 157 970 in 1999, rising by 16 per cent to 183 151 in June 2001.

The largest sub-sector in financial services in 1999 was banks and building societies, accounting for 45.4 per cent of employees. Next came life insurance and pension funding (22.1 per cent) and then other financial intermediation (12.7 per cent). Life insurance/pension funding employment was 17.5 per cent higher in 1999 than in 1998, while employment in banking rose by 9.4 per cent.

Within the, broadly defined, business services sector 72.5 per cent of employment in 1999 was in the 'other business activities' category, with the next largest groupings being real estate (12.8 per cent), computer and related (8.1 per cent), and renting of machinery and equipment (4.8 per cent).

Table 9.2 Number of enterprises[1] with Scottish employment and their total Scottish employment for financial and business services (November 1997, 1998 and 1999)

Industry	Enterprises			Employment		
	1997	1998	1999	1997	1998	1999
Central Banks & Banks & Building Societies	60	60	65	35 590	27 330	29 910
Other Financial Intermediation	955	995	845	13 360	10 490	8 390
Life Insurance & Pension Funding	180	180	160	12 290	12 390	14 560
Non Life Insurance	50	55	40	2 340	1 530	2 240
Administration of Financial Markets	10	10	15	140	150	170
Security Broking & Fund Management	65	85	140	2 020	2 970	2 700
Other Activities Auxiliary to Financial Intermediation	95	125	165	1 160	2 020	1 390
Activities Auxiliary to Insurance & Pension Funding	445	445	470	5 710	8 230	6 550
Total Financial Intermediation	1 865	1 955	1 905	72 610	65 120	65 900
Real Estate Activities	2 970	3 160	3 305	19 200	24 150	27 920
Renting of Machinery & Equipment	900	1 020	1 065	11 210	11 310	10 540
Computer & Related Activities	3 135	5 050	5 560	10 680	14 200	17 730
Research & Development	175	185	170	5 560	3 330	3 660
Other Business Activities	15 265	17 620	17 695	143 730	149 620	157 970
Total Business Services[2]	22 440	27 035	27 800	190 390	202 610	217 810

Notes:
1 Excludes public sector.
2 Totals may not equal the sum of the constituent parts due to rounding.

Source: Scottish Executive National Statistics (IDBR data), 1997–1999.

It is evident from the data – again see Table 9.2 – that financial service enterprises in Scotland tend to be much larger than their business service counterparts. In 1999 – that is, before recent major mergers – there were 1905 registered enterprises in the financial sector, with an average level of employment of 35. There were 27 800 enterprises in business services, with on average fewer than eight employees each.

In financial services both enterprises and employment are concentrated in Edinburgh and Glasgow. Indeed together they account for over 68 per cent of enterprises and 63 per cent of employment. The remainder of the sector is broadly spread, but with significant representations in Stirling, Perth, Aberdeen City, North Lanarkshire, Fife and South Lanarkshire.

Inevitably, given the broad-based and small-scale nature of the sector, business services are more wide-spread. Edinburgh has the largest number of enterprises, followed by Glasgow, with the order reversed for employment. Aberdeen again comes third in both categories, but accounts for a far higher share than is the case for financial services.

Exports

The limited statistical information that is available on Scottish service sector exports comes from the annual survey by the Scottish Council, Development and Industry (SCDI). Their data from 1997 to 1999, for selected categories that appear to relate to business services, are shown in Table 9.3. Reported exports of most business service sector components are swamped by the figures for computer and software services

Table 9.3 Scotland business services sector exports (1997–1999)

	1997 (£m)	1998 (£m)	1999 (£m)
Accountants	15.0	15.1	16.2
Advertising	0.2	5.5	6.9
Architects	2.3	2.0	1.8
Chartered surveyors	1.8	2.1	2.5
Commercial R&D	46.4	53.2	56.3
Design services	0.6	1.4	2.6
Lawyers	4.9	9.6	4.7
Other business services	17.7	18.6	24.2
Total	88.9	107.5	115.2
Computer & software services	254.3	352.8	381.5
Oil & gas	638.9	814.6	958.8
Combined total	982.1	1 274.9	1 455.5

Source: SCDI, 2001.

Table 9.4 Scotland financial services sector exports (1997–1999)

	1997 (£m)	1998 (£m)	1999 (£m)
Banks	143.1	150.5	130.7
Auxiliary to banking	1.5	3.4	3.3
Insurance/assurance	196.4	235.9	245.8
Other financial institutions	35.4	38.2	45.1
Total	376.4	428.0	424.9

Source: SCDI, 2001.

and the service element of oil and gas. Indeed the total reported in this table for business services excluding these two latter categories, at £115.2 million, is only roughly one-half of the reported total for Scottish education and training exports and only 13.6 per cent of tourism exports in 1999.

The SCDI data for exports by the Scottish financial sector are set out in Table 9.4. These exclude profits made in international operations by Scottish financial institutions. SCDI estimate exports of Scottish financial services in 1999 at £424.9 million.

Clearly these export figures are small relative to exports of goods and services as shown in SCDI and Scottish Executive figures. One other source for export data is the Executive's work on input-output analysis. The tables from 1996 show Scottish exports of financial and business services as amounting to £2933 million, or 6.8 per cent of the total. These are clearly far higher than the SCDI estimates, but include exports to the rest of the UK as well as the rest of the world.

One interesting point to note from this source is that the gross value added (GVA) of these service sector exports is a higher percentage of the Scottish total than the percentage of total exports – at 8.3 per cent. This relative balance is very different from the picture for manufacture of office machinery and computers, where the share of exports was 13.6 per cent and that of GVA only 7.5 per cent. In other words the GVA in Scotland of exports of financial and business services in 1996 was markedly higher than that of office machinery and computers, reflecting relatively higher local content and value added.

Multiplier and head office impacts

In August 2000, an economic impact study on financial services in Scotland by FAI at the University of Strathclyde was published. This had been commissioned jointly by SFE and SE.[6]

The main conclusions of the study were as follows:

- The sector contributes just less than 7 per cent of Scottish GDP. This is a distinctly larger share than that implied by the weightings used by the Scottish Executive and makes the sector comparable with electronics in terms of GDP.
- Direct employment was estimated at 91 000 in full-time equivalent (FTE) terms, broadly consistent with the most recent Scottish Executive (quarterly) estimate given above.
- The quality of employment is high, with 34 per cent of employees classified as managerial/professional compared to 25 per cent for the overall Scottish workforce.
- Gross output of £7.18 billion generates a further £10 billion in indirect effects elsewhere within Scotland.
- The 91 000 FTE jobs support a further 89 000 FTE jobs across a broad spectrum of the Scottish economy.

These figures are extremely impressive. Note that the total, direct and indirect, gross output due to financial services is estimated at over £17 billion; and total employment, direct and indirect, due to this sector is 180 000 in full time equivalent terms. The multipliers for the sector are significantly higher than both those for the economy as a whole and those for most other key sectors.

However, even allowing for the multiplier effects can under-estimate the true value of the financial service sector to the Scottish economy. FAI estimated that ten of the largest 20 companies in Scotland are within this sector, accounting for 60 per cent of this group's sales and 63 per cent of profits. This was even though the survey was undertaken before the Royal Bank took over NatWest, with the head office retained in Scotland, and before Halifax merged with the Bank of Scotland, moving the new group's head office to Edinburgh. The Royal Bank of Scotland Group (RBSG) is now the second largest bank in Europe, in terms of capitalised value, and the sixth largest in the world. HBOS ranks eighth in Europe and fourteenth in the world. Both banks are significantly larger than such household names as Tesco, Diageo and Marks & Spencer (M&S) – indeed the capitalised value of M&S is only just over 20 per cent of that of RBSG.[7] In addition to these two very large plcs, Scotland is also the home for Standard Life and other significant mutual organisations.

Previous research by FAI and others has demonstrated the importance to our economy of large companies headquartered here. For example, such HQs attract high quality and well paid staff, with positive spin-offs to the economy and can provide clear career paths for indigenous and in-coming staff. Their presence should make it more likely that potential high flyers from Scottish universities develop their careers in Scotland, rather than heading down south or overseas, and also more likely that other high quality individuals can be attracted to develop careers in Scotland.

Large companies with Scottish HQs also demand high quality business services and other quality service sector inputs, services, yielding further potential benefits. These services will help to attract inward and footloose investment and be available to the benefit of smaller, Scottish based, companies. Further, it is inevitable that some people will move on from these large companies. Many will have the expertise and capital to set up new Scottish companies, adding to the extent of entrepreneurialism in Scotland. Finally, senior executives in such companies will provide a market for high quality personal services – retail, restaurants, theatre, sports facilities, and so on – in Scotland, the existence of which will then help to attract inward investment and top quality conference and tourism business.

No 'multiplier' or similar studies have been undertaken of business services. However, there is no doubt that the sector matters to the broader Scottish economy for many of the same reasons as outlined above. Enterprises in business services tend to be smaller and more heterogeneous. Their multiplier effects, broadly defined, may be less than for financial services, other than for the top stratum of the sector. Nevertheless it is evident that ready access to a broad range of high-quality business services is crucial to all large companies, indigenous and foreign based. Footloose investors will treat such availability, *in situ* rather than via video or the shuttle, as a necessary element of what they expect for any economy to be seriously considered for investment. That will be particularly the case for companies considering location options for HQ or high value-added activities.

The development of a number of significant companies headquartered in Scotland, including financial service companies, will have increased the extent to which such business services are available here and hence increased the probability of more major companies being attracted to or developing in Scotland. It is noteworthy that business service activity and employment has been increasing rapidly in recent years. Further investigation would be likely to show that this included a significant increase in high-quality business services, across the spectrum, to the wider benefit of the Scottish economy.

Business services – key issues and challenges for the sector in Scotland

Data on GDP and employment demonstrate that the business services sector is of increasing importance within the Scottish economy. The sector 'matters' for its own sake but it also matters because of its importance to other parts of our economy and its scope for dynamism in the years ahead. A high quality and vibrant business service sector is a necessary, albeit not sufficient, condition for development of businesses in Scotland, large and small, indigenous or incoming.

Three of the key challenges for this sector can be summarised as follows:

1 Which high-quality business services are the key priorities required locally by both dynamic Scottish businesses and actual/potential inward investors? Do they exist to the extent desirable and if not why not? How can we ensure that these key services will be available going forward?
2 Can we develop/are we already developing high-quality business services in sub-sectors that are actually/potentially tradable? How can our 'comparative advantage' in such sub-sectors be enhanced?
3 Are our business services playing an appropriate role in aiding and abetting the development of further new and growing Scottish businesses across the economy? How can this role be best stimulated?

Anecdotal evidence regarding the first challenge is encouraging. The Scottish Executive, Locate in Scotland, and so on have not suggested that any significant gaps in business service provision have acted to limit the attractiveness of Scotland as a business location. If major businesses, such as those in financial services, can operate quality business service-intensive Head Offices from Scotland, then there is no reason to believe that any paucity of such services should cause concerns for potential incomers.

For various reasons it is anticipated that international trade in business services will tend to increase substantially in the years ahead. Some of this trade will involve physical movements of personnel, to market their services overseas, while other elements will be sold abroad from a Scottish base – including here sales via the Internet. It is the combined impact of improved channels of communication and trade liberalisation, based upon the General Agreement on Trade in Services (GATS) that has opened up the opportunity for acceleration in service sector trade.

The only means of determining whether Scottish business service sector companies are gearing up for more exporting activity would be a specific interview-based survey of the key players within the sector. However, while the export potential in some fields may be limited – for example, for lawyers due to differences in legal regimes – the scope in other fields must be significant. In some instances this potential may be best realised by Scottish business services working in conjunction with Scottish financial services. The 'export' of Private Financial Initiative/ Public–Private Partnerships (PFI/PPP) to a number of countries in Europe, by consortia based in Scotland, is an example.

Turning to the third question identified above, there is no reason to believe that business service companies are doing anything other than working in their perceived commercial interests in determining how to inter-relate with business start-ups and growing Scottish companies. Nor is there any reason to believe that the Scottish business service sector is any less well placed or inclined to assist than its counterpart in the rest of the UK. There may, however, be issues related to overall organisation of contacts with potential start-ups that need to be addressed.

The Scottish business service sector has never been examined in any depth and data are limited. However, it would seem likely that the sector has in recent years moved up several notches, in terms of quality of local provision, in part as a reaction to the development of a number of large, Scottish-based companies. This enhancement should bring benefits for all Scottish companies, local or incoming, and should assist and act to facilitate both inward investment and business start-ups.

Going forward, exports may be a major source of dynamism. Data and relevant information are again significantly lacking. Given the importance of the sector, in itself and as an input to broader economic and corporate development, more study of its potential, domestically and internationally, appears merited. One focus of such study could be to examine whether there are any constraints on the sector *per se*, its potential growth or potential broader value-added, that could be addressed by public policy or via the Enterprise Agencies. While most of the momentum will have to continue to come from within, infrastructure, skills availability and the like do matter, and some implications for the public sector might be uncovered by further investigation.

The financial sector and the Scottish economy

Generally the outlook has to be remarkably positive. Scotland now has a range of very large companies in the sector (RBSG, HBOS, Standard Life,

Scottish Widows, Scottish Equitable and Scottish Mutual) either with large financial and skill-base resources of their own, or backed by well-healed parents. These companies are intent upon growing market share in the UK, Europe and further afield. Not all of the benefit will accrue to Scotland but, given the evidence of the multiplier studies and data on GVA of exports, a large proportion should.

Within this context, consolidation, which has often hampered Scotland in the past and in other sectors, has added to the strength in this sector. Thus the country lost the HQs of General Accident and Scottish Amicable, but held on to most of the rest. Scotland has gained hugely from retaining the HQs of the enlarged RBSG after the NatWest acquisition, HBOS after the Halifax/Bank of Scotland merger; and from the merger between Scottish Widows and Hill Samuel.

Domestically the largest Scottish banks are the key participants in both retail and corporate banking. The scope for expansion in the more traditional spheres of activity, beyond maintaining market share as the market expands, may be limited.

The contribution of the Scottish banking sector will be critical to economic development in Scotland in a number of broader areas, within which cost-effective progress will in turn be critical to the wellbeing of our economy in the decades ahead.[8]

Take first *new firm formation*. A variety of studies have been undertaken as to why the rate of new firm formation in Scotland is low relative to the UK as a whole – most recently by the FAI for SE. There is no hard evidence to demonstrate that shortage of the right type of private finance, on the right terms and at the right time is any more of a problem in Scotland than the rest of the UK. The strength of the Scottish financial sector, plus the proliferation of funds established by Scottish Development Agency/SE with European resources as well as blends of private and public funds, suggests that Scotland is better equipped on the financial front than is the UK norm. However, it must behove the Scottish financial sector to continue to work with the Executive, SE *et al.*, to determine the causes for such a shortfall and to assess how these causes could be addressed. At the least co-ordination is essential to ensure that potential Scottish entrepreneurs receive appropriate advice in a timely fashion.

The same applies to *commercialisation of research*. Scotland has a highly positive reputation for academic research. Yet a disappointing share of this research is being converted into commercial activity in Scotland – a huge disappointment for those seeking a more dynamic economy in the decades ahead. Why have commercial activities (for example, in oil and gas and IT/Telecomms) not inter-related with academic research and together generated a drive to more R&D intensive commercial activities in Scotland?

There is no *prima facie* reason why the Scottish financial sector should be any less innovative in this area and any less willing to work across the risk/reward balance than its counterparts elsewhere in the UK. If there are some Scotland-specific constraints, these look more likely to include some lack of mutual empathy between researchers and finance providers, and perhaps failure to attract sufficient head-office based IT/Telecomms activity, which would have more naturally led to R&D here. Nevertheless, to be a successful high value-added economy in the twenty-first century, Scotland must maximise the potential for building commercially upon the academic research base. Hence the financial sector faces another challenge, this time alongside academics and researchers.

Another frequently cited constraint for Scotland is on the *infrastructure* front. If Scotland is to flourish as a cost-effective location for high value-added activity, then infrastructure – broadly defined – has to be more than basic and adequate. Public sector resources are likely to be even scarcer in the UK in the decades ahead than in recent years; and such resources will tend to be particularly scarce in Scotland – whatever happens to the Barnett formula.

This implies that if Scottish infrastructure is to be markedly improved, then the PFI, or PPP in the latest parlance, will have a major role to play in the whole process from design and finance through to build and operate. The challenge will be to derive a Scottish model, which takes account of both domestic concerns regarding the concept and Scottish financial skills.

Then there is *education*. In an increasingly high value-added economy, enhanced education will also be critical. That implies yet more progression through to further education and higher education, but also substantially raising the standards at primary and preprimary, to reduce the share of those in the Scottish labour force with low qualifications and low skills. Public funds will be scarce. Going forward, education must be delivered cost-effectively, implying PFI/PPP in some instances, with a role for the financial sector. Increasingly individuals will require access to appropriate means of funding education and training. Again the challenge for the Scottish financial sector will be to develop innovative funding methods, in consultation with the Executive and others.

Some conclusions

Both business and financial services are substantive and growing areas of the Scottish economy. They are also relatively under reported, in terms of data, and under researched, in terms of more intensive study/analysis, than other less significant sectors. Depending upon precise definition, financial services must now be almost the largest single sector of the Scottish economy in terms of GDP and one of the biggest in terms of employment. It certainly has the best recent track record on growth and as strong a potential for growth as any Scottish sector of substance. It is truly remarkable how relatively little attention has been paid to the sector by the Scottish Executive and academic researchers. Indeed it was only in 2000 that the Executive appointed its first ever civil servant to specialise in financial services (Draper *et al.*, 1988).

Going forward the key questions are not simply related to how these sectors will develop, in terms of numbers directly employed in Scotland. Of equal importance will be issues such as, how can these sectors best contribute to enhanced dynamism and increasing value-added in Scotland?: and how can/should these sectors develop internationally, within the rest of the UK, in order to take full advantage of their comparative strengths and bring even greater benefits back home to Scotland?

While further data, research and analysis are desirable, there is every reason to be positive on both of these fronts. The multiplier impact of financial services has been shown to be large as compared to other sectors in Scotland. Business service provision is perceived to have improved markedly, in part due to demands from large corporate HQs in Scotland, and now provides the necessary services to aid inward investment and development in indigenous companies.

The financial and business service skills are there to be developed in other markets, with prospects of significant increases in exports in the years ahead. The skills extant in Scotland in fund management, pensions and banking, alongside improved communications and progress on GATS and the European single market, are such that the opportunities for external development of the Scottish financial sector must be substantial. Certainly SFE see the potential in Europe as enormous – not least in life insurance and pensions where they estimate that at present Scotland manages only 5 per cent of European pensions money.

The Scottish banks are also looking increasingly at European opportunities, for both corporate and retail banking. In this context innovation will continue to be critical. Internet delivery will be one part of the financial system, alongside a whole host of traditional and nontraditional delivery mechanisms. The Scottish banks have been at the forefront of the process of moving to a wider range of delivery mechanisms and innovative products. Standard Life Bank, If, Tesco Personal Finance, Sainsbury's Bank and Direct Line Financial Services all originated, and remain based, in Scotland.

These successful sectors make only limited demands upon the public sector. In June 2001 *Investing in our Future*, an 'Action Plan' for financial services was published by SE, Scottish Financial Enterprise and the Scottish Executive. Areas of examination included people and skills, property, e-business and infrastructure. The main issue for consideration was, correctly, not what the Executive and SE could do for financial services, in some 'support' manner. Rather, given the extent of actual and potential benefits for the Scottish economy from this sector, what can the Scottish Executive and SE do – along with others such as the Scottish Higher Education Funding council (SHEFC) and the Scottish Further Education Funding Council (SFEFC) – to get more out of the sector for Scotland?

In this context the two most crucial public sector roles must be: (a) how to ensure that required infrastructure provision, including and especially transport, is in place as and when required; and (b) assisting on education and training. The Action Plan includes a number of suggestions on skills and also notes that 'effective transportation will dictate major investment decisions, as the ability to move people to, from and around these centres (Edinburgh and Glasgow) will be critical to Financial Services companies' ability to do business.'

Prospects for private sector services in Scotland will be enhanced by more appropriate skill developments and enhanced transport. However, skilled management, dynamism and creativity from the key Scottish-based companies will be far more important.

Notes

1 Source: 2000 International Target Cities Report, Thomson Financial Investor Relations, 2000 as cited in 'Investing in our Future: the financial services action plan for Scotland', 2001: SE, Scottish Financial Enterprise and the Scottish Executive.
2 Source: Regional Gross Domestic Product, ONS media release of 27 February 2001.
3 Source: Scottish Executive Gross Domestic Product for Scotland for the 2nd Quarter of 2001; November 2001.
4 Work to improve such data has fallen into two main components. Efforts are being made to improve the quality and consistency of data on new business

formations and business closures in Scotland. In addition, the four major Scottish banks have agreed to develop data on personal and business sector borrowing and deposits in Scotland, along similar lines to those data for the UK prepared by the British Bankers Association and the Bank of England. Data on business lending, broken down geographically and possibly by category of activity, should be available in 2002. A template has been developed for personal sector lending and deposits, based upon a Bank of England model. This breaks down between lending secured on property (mortgage lending), bank unsecured lending and credit card lending. It is anticipated that large parts of this template should be populated in early 2002 for all four banks, with again the expectation of these data being placed in the public domain in due course.

5   Source: Inter Departmental Business Register (IDBR), Scottish extract for 1997, 1998 and 1999.

6   The FAI undertook two similar studies for RSBG in 1994 and 1999. The results of the studies for RBSG are thoroughly consistent with those from the SFE/SE study and hence not referred to in the main text.

7   Data as at close of business on 27 December 2001.

8   Some of these issues are discussed in more depth in other chapters. The reference here is to financial sector involvement and implications.

References

Draper, P., I. Smith, W. Stewart and N. Hood (1988), *Scottish Financial Sector*, Volume 5 in Scottish Industrial Policy Series, Edinburgh: Edinburgh University Press.

SCDI (1999), *Survey of Scottish Sales and Exports*, Edinburgh: Scottish Council Development and Industry.

10
The Scottish Food and Drink Industry

Susan A. Shaw and Jonathan Tait

Introduction

The Scottish food manufacturing industry makes a significant contribution to the Scottish economy, accounting for 17 per cent of Scottish manufactured output and 4 per cent (£2.8 billion) of UK food and drink output in 1998. It is a major outlet for Scottish agricultural production, worth £1.2 billion in 1998. Exports of Scottish manufactured food and drink products were £1.6 billion in 2000, 7 per cent of Scottish manufactured exports to destinations outside the UK. It is one of Scotland's oldest industries but like other Scottish industries faces many challenges if it is to survive in an increasingly competitive and global marketplace. This chapter describes the key features of the industry, identifies the external drivers of competitiveness and discusses its competitive position. The final section discusses current government strategies for the food industry, the progress being made and the critical factors that will determine future prospects.

The Scottish food and drink industry

The Scottish food and drink product chain, together with destinations, can be seen in Figure 10.1. This is a very heterogeneous industry with products ranging from lightly processed fish and meat to high value-added products such as whisky and meal solutions. Statistics are not available in a form which allows us to identify outputs by type of process or level of added value but the values of broad production sectors in 1998, the latest year for which data is available, can be seen in Table 10.1.

Forty-six per cent of output by value is production of whisky, gin and vodka, although the highly automated processes in this industry mean that it is less dominant as an employer. Bread and biscuits and other prepared

166

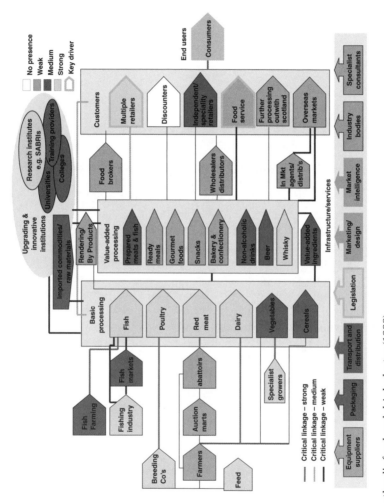

Figure 10.1 Scotland's food and drink cluster (1999).

Source: Scottish Enterprise, 1999.

Table 10.1 Manufacture of food products, drinks and tobacco (1998)

Sector	Value of output (£million)	Total employment (thousands)	No. of businesses
Meat processing	276.6	9.4	177
Fish processing	238.8	11.5	205
Fruit and vegetable processing	55.1	1.0	56
Oils and fats	14.2	0.3	8
Dairy products	112.4	2.9	87
Grain milling	52.1	0.5	19
Animal feed	149.1	1.2	60
Bread, biscuits confectionery and other miscellaneous foods	421.2	16.9	632
Whisky and other alcoholic drink	1320.4	11.5	222
Soft drinks & tobacco*	208.5	1.9	55
Total	2848.4	57.3	1521

* There is little production of tobacco in Scotland but further disaggregation of statistics is not possible.

Source: Scottish Production Database, 1999.

foods such as meal options account for a further 15 per cent of the total and processing of meat and fish and soft drinks production are also important.

There are some large businesses in the Scottish food and drink industry – for instance, one of the three major spirits companies, Allied Domeq, has a worldwide annual turnover of over £2 billion and an annual contribution to the Scottish economy of over £390 million. However, there is a striking contrast between the average size of food business in Scotland and in the UK as a whole. Average turnover of under £2 million per business in Scotland in 1998 contrasts with nearly £8 million for the UK. Only six of the largest 150 UK food manufacturers are based in Scotland. There is also a high proportion of family-owned businesses and a higher percentage (87 per cent) of UK-owned firms than any other Scottish manufacturing sector (Scottish Production Database). There are only 11 food and drink companies with headquarters in Scotland in the top 100 Scottish companies with Scottish headquarters and only one (Scottish and Newcastle) in the top ten (*Business Insider*, 2001). Even within the spirits sector, the size of Allied Domeq, Diageo and Seagram, none of whom have their headquarters in Scotland, contrasts with the average turnover of only £6 million in the sector because of the presence of smaller specialist companies.

Table 10.2 Sales by Scottish food and drink manufacturers 1998 – percentages to different destinations

Sector	Sales within Scotland		Sales outside Scotland	
	To Scottish Industries	For final consumption	Rest of the UK	Rest of world
Meat processing	26	12	38	24
Fish, fruit and vegetable processing	15	15	43	26
Oils and fats	45	3	42	10
Dairy products	40	16	35	9
Grain milling and starch	62	2	30	6
Animal feed	53	1	38	8
Bread, biscuits	19	14	52	15
Sugar	92	2	5	1
Confectionery	10	50	32	8
Miscellaneous foods	15	45	39	1
Alcoholic drink	2	5	4	89
Beer	15	53	24	8
Soft drinks	80	17	2	1

Source: Scottish Executive, 2000.

Capital expenditure was 9 per cent of net output, a smaller percentage than for manufacturing as a whole in Scotland (14 per cent). Again, however, there is considerable variation between food sectors from only 6 per cent in meat processing to 18 per cent in the dairy industry.

Forty per cent of output is exported outside the UK and a further 25 per cent is sold outside Scotland but again, averages disguise variations (Table 10.2). The whisky sector is consistently one of the UK's top five export earners, with a long-standing presence in over 200 export markets but export percentages, without whisky, are low. Table 10.2 also demonstrates the dependence of the Scottish industry on the rest of the UK for its consumer markets.

External challenges and the Scottish food and drink industry

Food tends to decline as a percentage of consumer expenditure as affluence increases so the main markets for Scottish products have grown only slowly in the last decade. In Western Europe demand grew by only 8 per cent between 1990 and 1998 (*Euromonitor*, 2000). This lack of growth and consequent high levels of competition are reflected in the relatively low profitability of, and low investor confidence in, the European food industry (*Euromonitor*, 2000). Growth opportunities are therefore defined by ability to take advantage of changes in patterns of preferences and by differentiation from competitors on product characteristics or price. The context is one in which affluent consumers have become more demanding in product variety and quality, handling methods and presentation. Changing lifestyles have led to growing demand for prepared products and switches from the retail sector to the food service sector as more food is consumed outside the home. A wider variety of products are also sought, so that markets for specialist high-quality products, often with regional/national identities, have grown.

Trends in demand have been accompanied by considerable structural change in downstream food channels. From limited concentration in grocery retailing prior to 1970, major UK retail customers are now based outside Scotland and are highly concentrated. The market share of independent retailers in the UK has fallen from 25 per cent in 1980 to 8 per cent in 2000 while the market share of the top five retail companies is now 50 per cent and of all multiple retailers over 90 per cent. (Shaw *et al.*, 1996). Sixty-five per cent of Scottish output goes to UK retail multiples (Scottish Enterprise). While more fragmented, there has also been increased concentration in the food service sector. The wholesale sector is less important because of direct supply to retailers and larger food service companies, but it has also become more concentrated. These changes have impacted on food manufacturers in Scotland in a number of ways (Table 10.3).

To these changes must be added the impact of rising sterling values over the past decade, particularly against other European currencies, which has made Scottish exports less competitive. On the supply side, cheaper agricultural inputs from other countries have adversely affected Scottish processors of Scottish raw materials (Urquhart, 1999). A further pressure is the globalisation of food markets, increasing competition.

The pace of development by sector 1992–1998

Trend analysis prior to 1992 is difficult because of changes in government statistical classifications. In the period 1992–1998 the net output of the industry in money terms rose by only 9 per cent (Table 10.4), rather slower than for the UK as a whole (Central Statistical Office, various) but again, attention must be drawn to the varied progress of different sectors.

In the meat sector, there has been growth in the production of poultry products and niche products such as processed venison, but offset by

Table 10.3 Scottish food manufacturers and changing downstream food supply chains

Changing demands	Implications for food manufacturers
Larger order sizes to smaller numbers of customers, although in recent years the scope for regional sourcing has increased	Scaling-up of production, problems for small suppliers with reorientation from local supply to Scottish or UK supply Need to invest heavily in ICT
Direct delivery, eliminating wholesale intermediaries	New skills in customer relationship management
Least cost global sourcing	Increased international competition Reduced competitiveness when using Scottish agricultural inputs
Stringent quality and handling requirements	Higher levels of investment in physical infrastructure
Continuous replenishment delivery	Higher levels of investment in manufacturing and delivery systems Low volumes of specialised product can be expensive to deliver on a daily basis
Innovative added value products	More investment in research and development

Table 10.4 Scottish food industry trends (1992–1998)

Sector	Changes in net output 1992 = 100	Changes in numbers of businesses
Meat processing	101	−25
Fish processing	221	+97
Fruit and vegetable processing	49	−7
Oils and fats	N/A	N/A
Dairy products	99	+19
Grain milling & starch	217	No change
Animal feed	159	−1
Bread, Biscuits, Sugar, Miscellaneous foods, Confectionery	96	+101
Alcoholic drink	107	+13
Soft drinks	127	+17

Source: Scottish Production Database, 2001.

declining red meat output, reflecting the Bovine Spongiform Encephalopathy (BSE) problems over the past decade. It is too early to predict the
long-term impact of the outbreak of foot and mouth disease in 2001.
Scotland was relatively unscathed, with only the area in south-western
Scotland affected. However, the closure of export markets to UK output
will undoubtedly have adversely affected confidence, especially in European export markets. It will take time to restore demand. The substantial
rise in the value of fish output reflects primarily high sea fish prices because
of buoyant demand in the face of static world output, rising production of
farmed salmon and trout and a higher proportion of added-value products.

The most notable decline was in fruit and vegetable processing which
reflects problems with the raw material base. As global competition has
increased, fruits and vegetables grown in Scotland for processing (soft
fruits, root vegetables, potatoes) have struggled to be competitive. Capacity to can and freeze fruit and vegetables in Scotland has declined as
a consequence, with companies either going out of business or multinationals closing Scottish branch plants. The static dairy output reflects
limited EU production quotas for milk and the emphasis on liquid milk
(low value-added) production at the expense of more highly processed
products, although outputs of speciality cheeses have been rising. The
increases in the value of processed grain and animal feed reflect buoyant
demand within the protected EU grain market.

Spirits output was static, reflecting sluggish world demand for whisky
in the face of strong competition from other spirits, not helped by the
high value of sterling. The sector has also been criticised for lack of
innovation, in the face of changing demand preferences. While the
malt whisky sector has increased ranges and improved marketing, less
change has been apparent in core bulk markets.

Survival and growth strategies 1992–1998

Research on a cross-section of Scottish companies in 1999, Shaw and
Young (2001) suggest a number of general ways in which, over the past
decade, Scottish companies have sought to define the markets they
want to service and the strategies to survive and grow.

Protecting the core business through range extensions

In line with food industries elsewhere, companies have tended to stick, or
retreat, to areas that are perceived to be the core business. There are few
examples of radical diversification, either out of the food industry or into
food areas that are not closely related. The most common changes

introduced by companies have been product line extensions. Typical examples are the moves of seafood processors to extend product lines horizontally and/or downstream extension of activities into the preparation of fish-based ready meals or other more highly processed fish products (for example, ScoFro, Strathaird and Pinney). The fall in the number of trade customers makes it difficult to grow sales by expanding the customer base. Instead range extension allows companies to increase sales with existing customers in areas where they can build on existing competence. Companies manufacturing intermediate products or ingredients have pursued similar strategies. For example, Oakwood Foods was set up in 1985 to manufacture sauce ingredients for ready meals and enjoyed rapid growth solely by expanding its range of sauces.

Range extension is also linked to the economics of plant operation. With growing use of more sophisticated batch production techniques or of continuous lines, there is a need to operate plants at high levels of throughput. Thus, companies originally established as whisky distillers and bottlers have now also become major bottlers of gin and vodka, with 75 per cent of UK production now in Scotland. These multinational companies have relocated facilities to optimise plant use (House of Commons, 2000–1). This case is unique in that, by law, Scottish whisky must be distilled and bottled in Scotland, so that rationalisation around a base in England or elsewhere was not possible.

Concentration on core markets

Most companies, particularly smaller ones, concentrate on the UK with a trend to increasing coverage of the UK market. This is a response to the national buying policies of large retailers. For exporters, patterns are also changing. Partly driven by improved management understanding and partly by pressure of competition, many exporters focus now on smaller numbers of key markets with less use of market spreading strategies. Exceptions are either those companies with very strong brands or companies targeting large numbers of narrow expatriate markets for distinctive Scottish products. This is linked to the need to provide high levels of service to large individual accounts, as the trend to retail market concentration has continued across Europe. It is also linked to the growth in demand for controlled temperature convenience products. The latter have a short shelf life which limits the geographical supply range largely to Western European markets.

Brands and Scottishness

Products with strong brand identities often have long histories and are ambient products such as biscuits, cakes, whisky, and canned soup.

At least originally, they had a strong local raw materials supply base. These brands usually make strong use of country of origin imagery in marketing but a much wider group of manufacturers also find this useful. This includes many of the food and drink manufacturers in Scotland with products that are sold under the brand name of others, particularly retailers. The Scottish image is a valuable mixture of tradition, naturalness and quality, because of the success of the whisky sector, Scotland's location as a tourist destination and Scottish cultural exports. For this reason, for example, at exhibitions in which the UK has a generic presence, the Scottish stands are separately and distinctively promoted.

Some food sectors have sought further differentiation through the promotion of distinctive industry-wide quality assurance schemes, (for example, Scottish Assured Beef and Lamb, Scottish Quality Cereals). The view of the authors is that the schemes have not yet built unique brand positions at premium prices. However, the schemes have been valuable in assuring trade customers of guaranteed standards and have kept Scotland at the vanguard of quality development. Quality Meat Scotland, the new Scottish meat marketing body, is using the strong underpinning which these schemes provide to start to create real brand values for Scottish red meat. Scottish beef in the quality assurance scheme is still trading at a premium.

Over the last decade the government through SE has also been involved in schemes to promote Scottish identity through generic branding. An early initiative to promote a quality mark for the food industry based on stringent quality assurance proved unsuccessful in the early 1990s, largely on the grounds of cost. This was followed by Scotland the Brand – a branding exercise for all Scottish products and services without quality assurance. The scope of this generic branding exercise extends to all Scottish products, but in 2001 most participants were food and drink companies. Scotland the Brand is now moving from a subsided scheme to a private scheme, so membership will cost more. The jury is still out on whether in the future the benefits of the scheme will be worth higher membership costs – the scheme has not had the scale of positive impact on markets that was anticipated. At this stage it appears most likely that the food and drink industry will emphasise a common food identity which is compatible with Scotland the Brand but is also distinctive and separate.

Abandoning the tartan

The brand values conveyed by Scottishness are not valued by all companies because different markets and market positions have different needs. One of the most striking examples is provided by one of the most successful Scottish exporters, Baxters which has recently chosen to play down Scottish themes in the promotion of its growing range of low fat products, seeing a confusion in brand values. The dilemma is most acute for companies like Grampian Country Food Group. Its recent acquisition of production bases outside Scotland, including the largest UK bacon plant Golden Foods International in Thailand, throws the emphasis on promotion of the company, not its origin. There are branding dilemmas for companies like A.G. Barr of *Irn-Bru* soft drink fame who are widening their appeal in young, non-Scottish markets where traditional Scottish imagery is a disadvantage. For some intermediate products such as the food casings business of Devro (which has its global headquarters in Scotland), where Scotland is one of a number of manufacturing locations for a nonbranded product, the issue is irrelevant.

The rise of niche products

A final feature of the past decade has been the development of many new speciality products, designed, at least initially, for small premium markets. This phenomenon is not unique to Scotland but reflects the willingness of affluent consumers to pay a premium for distinctiveness. Often the products are linked to tourism, but are also increasingly finding outlets within large retail groups because of the higher retail margins they offer. This is facilitated by the growing ability of retail multiples to source limited volumes for subsets of stores within their portfolio.

Evolving business structures

Structural change mirrors developments in the food industry elsewhere in Europe and the US. First, the growth in markets for high-value niche products has created opportunities for the entry of new businesses. During the 1992–1998 period the number of businesses in the Scottish food industry rose by 16 per cent, reflecting the ability of new firms to be competitive in small markets, provided that they have distinctive products. The fish processing (especially smoking), dairy (primarily new cheese and cheese-based products) and general food sectors all saw increases in number of new (small) businesses, although in some cases value-added is still low.

Secondly, existing firms have sought competitive advantage, through restructuring to improve market opportunities and/or to achieve greater production efficiency. Some private Scottish-based companies have been acquired by larger European food companies wishing to build a portfolio of related products (Pinney – smoked and prepared fish products – was acquired by Hillsdown, a multinational prepared foods company, now owned by a US venture capital group). Other Scottish-based companies have acquired smaller private Scottish companies in pursuit of similar strategies (MacPhie of Glenbervie – prepared foods and ingredients – acquired Oakwood Foods – sauces).

There are examples of Scottish companies who have sought to expand by acquiring other companies outside Scotland. Wiseman is developing as one of the UK's major liquid milk suppliers and Grampian Food Group, already mentioned, is now the largest privately owned company in Scotland with a turnover of £851 million. Others have expanded south by new build (Baxters have extended their product range from soups and ambient foods to chilled foods with a plant in England) in order to build competitive position in UK and European markets. It appears to be the case that when Scottish companies wish to grow and occupy major as opposed to minor market niches, organic growth or growth by acquisition involves acquisitions outside Scotland, to obtain more convenient access to larger markets or to absorb the plants of competitors. This mirrors the considerable restructuring elsewhere in the international food industry (*Euromonitor*, 2000). Companies have either sought to build portfolios of businesses which can compete globally, or, more modestly, to rationalise through mergers, acquisitions and the removal of surplus plant, particularly in commodity sectors such as milk, meat and bread.

Large spirit multinationals have sought greater production efficiency by moving bottling plant for vodka and gin to Scotland, as indicated earlier. Finally, some businesses have failed to make the transition to global markets, an example being Esk Frozen Foods, the largest frozen vegetable producer in Scotland which closed in August 2001.

A number of businesses have moved to private ownership from limited liability status via management buy-outs. Simmers and Paterson Arran are examples in this category. The larger plc parent sought to retreat to its core business, leaving the buy-outs to develop successfully as more specialist medium-sized operations.

Competitive position of Scottish food and drink

Despite the attempts to build stronger positions, there remain concerns about the competitiveness of the Scottish food and drink industry.

At the outset, the alcoholic drink sector should be examined separately. Its difficulties have already been noted and are primarily linked to problems with demand. The industry is seeking to address these problems through the development of specialist malt whisky products, adding value and encouraging consumption of whisky in new ways to new (younger) audiences and by seeking less punitive rates of sales tax. Although it can be criticised for lack of innovation, it is a successful industry with a skilled labour force, strong local supply linkages and sophisticated management.

Some high levels of performance can be found in other sectors, but overall an SE conclusion is that the sector could do significantly better (Scottish Enterprise, 1999). SE contrasts the performance of New Zealand and Denmark, both with smaller land area and similar agricultural exports, who have shown better overall export performance with high levels of market innovation and branding capability. The Scottish industry, facilitated and supported by SE identified the following weaknesses:

- Large numbers of fragmented, small businesses with a primary processing bias and low added value.
- Lack of industry leaders and lack of high-level marketing skills because of the absence of headquarters operations of large food companies.
- Lack of entrepreneurship culture and the low business birth rate in Scotland.
- A recalcitrant producer base with a 'subsidy driven dependency culture' and lack of customer orientation.
- Low levels of co-operation and collaboration to strengthen the value chain and offset the problems of small size in accessing national and international markets.
- Skills shortages.

To this can be added some concerns, hopefully short term about the raw material supply base. The problems of the red meat industry have already been mentioned. In addition, the salmon farming industry must address serious concerns about animal welfare and the environmental impact of current sea cage farming practices.

Nevertheless, there are inherent strengths that can be better exploited. There is mostly a strong raw material base in meat, fish, dairy, grain and game. Scottish products have positive international images. Experience in supplying the UK retail sector, one of the most demanding markets of the world in terms of innovation requirements and supply-chain efficiency, should be a benefit in other markets.

The research institutes, marketing and design networks in Scotland also offer a strong and potentially supportive base.

The food cluster strategy

The *Scottish Food and Drink Strategy* was launched by the industry (excluding spirits) in conjunction with SE in 1999 (Scottish Enterprise, 1999). The essence of the strategy revolves around the advantages of external economies enjoyed by industrial clusters in the same spatial location. No business works independently of others because success also depends on the quality of contacts which facilitate co-operation in marketing and the management of upstream and downstream supply networks. Networks create flexibility and high levels of innovation because of the speed with which members can respond collectively to new opportunities. Indeed the strengths of well-organised industry clusters (Porter, 1998) may be significant in determining the competitiveness of nations. The logic of the *Scottish Food and Drink Strategy* is that, in an industry primarily comprising small- and medium-sized firms, alignment of strategies and closer co-operation will strengthen the existing networks within the industry and hence international competitiveness.

An Industry Strategy Group was set up in January 2000. Its 20 members come from all sectors of the Scottish food industry. The largest group of members are chief executives from Scottish food companies of a variety of sizes, but support sectors such as research institutes are also represented. Two early objectives were identified. The first was to improve raw material quality with emphasis on sustainable farming and natural preservation techniques and on improved packaging and presentation. The second was to develop value-added meal components through better use of food technologies, and more efficient supply-chain servicing of retail and food service, with emphasis on the premium end of the market. Ambitious targets were set: an annual growth rate of sales of 6 per cent and annual growth rate of added value of 9 per cent, with a trebling of food exports. To achieve these targets there is a programme of action with six goals (Table 10.5).

These activities are supported by overall alignment of government support with these strategies – a package probably worth around £200 million.

The future

While initial signs are promising, it is too early to evaluate the success of the cluster strategy. The logic of the initiative is impeccable. Growth

Table 10.5 The action goals

Goal	Examples of Actions	Rationale
1. Develop industry leaders	Mentoring programme of small firms by their larger counterparts Continuing industry education by *Food Strategy Group*	Limited presence of major multinational food companies in Scotland has limited local supply of quality management capable of operating at international level
2. Attack premium markets	*Food Facts* advisory service launched and sophisticated consumer market intelligence on line centre at planning stage Development of *Scottish Food and Drink* brand – generic work to identify opportunities and translate to new products	The structure and location of the industry means that only premium markets will offer sufficient added value and are small enough to be targeted by the industry
3. Innovation	Current big push to develop healthy eating products Alignment of objectives of industry and centres of research	Added value and innovations go hand in hand
4. Efficient supply chains	Working on eating quality in red meats and seafood sector Work on consolidated transport systems to facili-tate movement of small volumes of specialist product	Continuous replenishment and other rising service demands by major downstream customers
5. Skills	*Food Learning Network* – ensuring wide access to specialist training, including use of com-munications technology to give distributed delivery	Need for improvement in production processes and other aspects of management, allied with current skills shortage
6. Communications	A range of internal ICT communications and development of information portals (see No. 3) via www.scottishfoodanddrink.com	Intra industry communication vital to embed the need for integrated thinking by all players

Source: Scottish Enterprise, 2000.

opportunities will be limited without better, more innovative products and better marketing, leading to higher added value. The cluster strategy is an ambitious attempt to overcome problems of lack of size, lack of skills and limited international experience. Whether it will be successful in meeting its targets will depend on a number of factors. First, there is the response of the sector itself and its willingness to work in new ways and to 'raise its game'. While possible, this is not easy. The predominantly small- and medium-sized Scottish enterprises face resource constraints and raising levels of innovations and marketing is a major challenge as a consequence. Secondly, transformation of the supply base is also vital. This issue is outside the scope of this chapter, but to capitalise on the strengths of the raw material base, a more businesslike and customer focused farming industry (Maxwell, 1999) is needed. This should deliver the quality inputs which will give distinctiveness to manufactured products. Similarly, the huge potential for Scottish seafood products requires more effective fisheries conservation policies than the European Community offers at present, together with more careful attention to welfare and environmentally friendly production processes in fish farming. Thirdly, there is the question of the pull of larger domestic and world markets. Aspirations for larger size may drive the decision-making and the largest businesses out of Scotland, taking with them the supply networks and relationships that together create a vibrant and innovative industry base. In this sense, the future prosperity of the overall Scottish economy, the quality of its physical skills and infrastructure and the quality of its communications with the rest of the world may well be deciding factors in determining the attractivenss of Scotland as a location for manufacturing and hence the future potential of the Scottish food and drink industry.

References

Business Insider (2001), 'Top 500', January.
Central Statistical Office (1999, 2000), production statistics.
Euromonitor (2000), Global Food Market Trends and Strategies, Global Market Information Database 3.1.1.
House of Commons (2001), 'The drinks industry in Scotland', Scottish Affairs Committee, Minutes of Evidence from the Gin and Vodka Association of Great Britain, Session 2000–1, London: Stationery Office.
Maxwell, F. (1999), 'Parliament calls business to help agriculture', *The Scotsman*, 5 October.
Porter, M.E. (1998), *On Competition*, Boston, Mass: Harvard Business School Press.
Scottish Enterprise (1999, 2001), various internal management documents.

Scottish Executive (1998, 2001), Scottish Production Database, Glasgow: Scottish Executive.

Shaw, S.A., I. McNicoll, and S. Dunlop (1996), *Wealth Creation and the Competitiveness of the British Food Industry*, study for the Biotechnology and Biological Sciences Research Council, May, p. 160.

Shaw, S.A. and S. Young (2002), 'Perspectives on firm growth and internationalisation: the case of the Scottish Food Industry', SIBU Working Paper No. 01/3, Glasgow: Strathclyde International Business Unit, University of Strathclyde.

Urquhart, F. (1999), 'Moonlighting farmers reveal crisis', *The Scotsman*, 26 May.

Appendix 10.1 Companies mentioned in Chapter 10.

Company	Interests	Turnover	Location of headquarters
A.G. Barr	Soft drinks	£112 mn (2001)	Glasgow, Scotland
Allied Domeq	Spirits and wines, food service	£2 620 mn (2000)	Bristol, England
Baxters	Soups, conserves	£46 mn (2000)	Speyside, Scotland
Devro	Casings	£46 mn (2000)	Moodiesburn, Scotland
Diageo	Wine and spirits, food service	£12 821 mn (2001)	London, England
Grampian Country Food Group	Meat processing	£851 mn (2001)	Aberdeen, Scotland
Hillsdown	Food manufacture	£271 mn (2001)	London, England
Paterson Arran	Biscuits and preserves	£11 mn (2000)	Livingston, Scotland
Sco-Fro	Seafood processing	£20 mn (2000)	Glasgow, Scotland
Seagrams	Whisky	£265 mn (2000) – Scottish Operations	Canada
Simmers	Biscuits	£6 mn	Edinburgh, Scotland
Strathaird	Farming and processing of salmon	£13 mn (1998)	Edinburgh, Scotland
MacPhie	Prepared foods	£26 mn (2000)	Stonehaven, Scotland
Walker's Shortbread	Biscuits & cakes	£51 mn (2000)	Aberlour, Scotland
Wiseman	Dairy operations	£300 mn	East Kilbride, Scotland

11
A Vision of Tourism in 2020

Brian Hay

Introduction

This chapter provides an analysis of the long-term trends in tourism in the 1990s; it also investigates possible future scenarios and policy implications for the development of the tourism industry in Scotland. Over the last decade there have been three National Strategic Plans for tourism in Scotland, the latest was published in 2000 (Scottish Executive, 2000), the first industry sector plan to be issued by the new devolved Scottish administration. The next plan will be published early in 2002. These plans are designed to help with the development of what is basically a privately delivered service to the public.

Overview of world tourism

It is important to remember that Scotland is a small country on a small island off the edge of Western Europe, and that tourism in Scotland in the 1990s was not immune from world events. The Gulf war in 1991, the steep rise in oil prices in 1992, the world economic recession of 1993/94, the demise of communism in Eastern Europe, explosion in the use of the Internet, the globalisation of companies, the opening of the Channel Tunnel in 1997, the financial crisis in the Far East in 1998 and finally in 2001 the attacks in the USA, all affected the growth of tourism in the last decade.

Despite these events, world tourism has grown relentlessly over the 1990s (World Tourism Organisation, 2000), with a 52 per cent increase in international trips and an 80 per cent increase in spending (Table 11.1). Europe and the Americas are by far the dominant world regions, but Europe's share of tourism in the 1990s declined from 54 per cent to

Table 11.1　International tourism in the 1990s

	1990	1991	1992	1993	1994	1995	1996	1997	1998	1999	2000
Trips (million)	458	464	502	518	553	568	600	620	635	650	698
Spend (US$ billion)	264	278	314	323	353	406	438	440	441	455	476

Source:　WTO, 2000, p. 6.

51 per cent, while that of East Asia and the Pacific began increasing as wealth started to spread to its emerging middle classes. It is not surprising that Europeans, with open land boundaries, ease of travel, wealth and highly paid holiday entitlement, account for over half of world tourism expenditure.

Tourism to the UK and Scotland

So how are the UK and Scotland performing in this period of worldwide growth in tourism? Overseas tourism to the UK, both in spending and trips (Table 11.2), has grown and shows every sign of continuing to grow (National Statistics, 2000). However, a more worrying trend is the travel account on the UK balance of payments, which increased from just over £2 billion in 1990 to over £11 billion in 2000. UK residents are spending more and more of their holiday expenditure on overseas tourism, rather than on domestic tourism, but this growth has not been matched by an increase in spending by overseas tourists to the UK. In terms of the 'big picture' the UK share of world tourism at 4 per cent is small, and Scotland's share of the UK market at 8 per cent is very small, and at best both are steady rather than growing.

Table 11.2　The UK share of world overseas tourist trips

	1990	1991	1992	1993	1994	1995	1996	1997	1998	1999	2000
Overseas tourists to UK ('000)	18 013	17 125	18 535	19 863	20 794	23 537	25 163	25 515	25 745	25 394	25 209
UK per cent share	3.9	3.7	3.7	3.8	3.8	4.1	4.2	4.1	4.1	3.9	3.7

Sources:　National Statistics, 2000, p. 18; WTO, 2000, p. 6.

Table 11.3   English residents holiday tourism in Scotland

	1990	1991	1992	1993	1994	1995	1996	1997	1998	1999
Trips (m)	2.7	2.8	2.7	2.6	2.6	2.7	3.1	3.3	3.1	3.0
Nights (m)	18.4	19.8	18.1	17.5	15.1	17.1	19.1	19.6	19.8	18.3
Spend (£m)	633	677	618	650	546	611	747	749	735	792

Source: UK National Tourist Boards, 2000, p. 6.

English residents tourism in Scotland

Over the last decade holiday tourism by residents of England in Scotland has grown (Table 11.3). The decline in spend in 1992 was associated with the increase in overseas trips by the English. The reason for this was that overseas trips, postponed because of the Gulf war in 1991, were taken in 1992. The decline in 1994 was linked to the economic recession that year. Overall, there has been a growth of 16 per cent in the holiday tourism market from England over the period 1990–1999.

Scottish residents tourism in Scotland

Scottish residents are an important market for Scotland. Between 1990 and 1999 there was an increase in their tourism activity in Scotland, and Scots did spend a very high proportion of their UK tourism spending in Scotland, over 40 per cent in most years (£410 million in 1999). The ratio of Scots' holiday spent at home compared to overseas trips is normally about 1:3 (Table 11.4). This is an important ratio as it suggests that any discretionary income available for holidays, is increasingly being spent overseas, and not in Scotland.

It is not surprising that the 1–3 night holiday trip was more important for the Scots than for the English in Scotland given travel distances.

Table 11.4   Scottish residents holiday tourism in Scotland and holiday spend overseas

	1990	1991	1992	1993	1994	1995	1996	1997	1998	1999
Trips (million)	2.2	2.6	2.8	2.9	2.8	2.8	3.1	3.5	2.6	2.9
Spend (£million)	280	360	340	416	339	362	313	449	265	308
Scots overseas holiday spend (£million)	756	890	1 003	1160	1434	1395	1157	1254	1346	1279
Ratio of Scots Spend in Scotland:Overseas	1:2.7	1:2.5	1:3.0	1:2.8	1:4.2	1:3.9	1:3.7	1:2.8	1:5.1	1:4.2

Source: UK National Tourist Boards, 2000, p. 7.

Expenditure on this type of trip has remained relatively constant, and as Scots already spend some 60 per cent of their 1–3 night holiday expenditure in Scotland, there is limited opportunity to increase this market. Although there is a clear long-term decline in their 8 plus night holidays, the 1–7 night trip accounted for over 90 per cent of all spending by the Scots on holidays in Scotland.

Over the 1990s we have seen a gradual decrease in the length of holiday trips in Scotland from 5.7 nights in 1990 to 5.1 nights in 1999, mostly due the decline in the Scots' holiday trips.

Overseas tourism in Scotland

Overseas tourism in Scotland has been a success, with trips and spending steadily increasing over the 1990s (Table 11.5). The USA with an expenditure of £186 million is by far the largest source market, followed by Canada (£95 million), Germany (£69 million), Italy (£53 million), Australia (£34 million), and Spain (£32 million).

Over the 1990s there has been a steady but gradual decrease in the length of stay of overseas visitors to Scotland from 9.7 nights per trip in 1991 to just 7.9 nights per trip in 2000. This trend is happening across the developed world as personal time is being squeezed by other demands. In the Scottish case, an increasing number of overseas visitors come from Europe and, because of proximity, take shorter trips. This has, for example, resulted in an increasing focus on overseas holiday tourism in Edinburgh and Glasgow.

Employment and structure of the tourism industry in Scotland

Despite all the changes in the tourism industry in Scotland the number of people employed in tourism has remained remarkably constant at about 160 000 (Table 11.6). Does this mean that as tourism has grown, the workforce has become more productive? Not really, as an increasing number of these jobs were converted from part-time to full-time.

Because tourism is difficult to define as a sector, it is difficult to provide a precise measure of the size of the industry. The best available data on two

Table 11.5   Overseas tourism in Scotland

	1990	1991	1992	1993	1994	1995	1996	1997	1998	1998	1999
Trips (million)	1.60	1.62	1.80	1.67	1.77	1.96	2.02	2.10	2.10	1.86	1.65
Spend (£million)	736	614	727	764	867	915	965	891	940	817	789

Source: National Statistics, 2000.

Table 11.6 Employment in tourism-related industries in Scotland ('000)

	1990	1991	1992	1993	1994	1995	1996	1997	1998	1999
Number employed	161	156	165	162	161	160	160	159	160	163

Note: Excludes the self-employed.

Source: Annual Employment Survey (1991–1998), Annual Business Inquiry Survey (1999).

of its most important sectors, namely accommodation and attractions, suggests there are over 13 000 accommodation units, and over 800 attractions in Scotland, but most of these are relatively small-scale enterprises. However, with stock utilisation rates (occupancy levels) of around 50 per cent, it must be difficult to be profitable (Table 11.7).

Table 11.7 Tourism businesses in Scotland

	No. of units	No. of bedrooms	Average No. of bedrooms	Average room occupancy*
Hotels	1 333	21 801	16	58
Guest houses	1 136	4 577	4	41
B&Bs	3 229	6 774	2	41
Self-catering	6 631			49
Camping & Caravan Parks	718			30
Hostels	173			50
Attractions: Less than 50k visitors	558			
Attractions: More than 50k visitors	142			

* Data refers to unit occupancy for self-catering, and pitch occupancy for camping and caravan parks.

Source: VisitScotland Research, Moffat Centre, Glasgow, 2000.

Tourism expenditure in Scotland has increased from just over £2 billion in 1990 to just under £2.5 billion in 1998, and by any measure this is a real increase (Table 11.8).

Review of past data trends

Past growth in tourism in Scotland cannot be taken for granted, and changes in marketing strategies are not necessarily the answer to

Table 11.8 Long-term data on tourism spending in Scotland (£million)

	1990	1991	1992	1993	1994	1995	1996	1997	1998	1999
Scots	368	429	437	620	488	465	413	573	353	412
English	938	956	895	928	795	878	1 033	1 068	1 110	1 176
UK total	1 380	1 458	1 435	1 645	1 348	1 421	1 586	1 744	1 536	1 667
Overseas	736	613	727	764	867	915	965	891	940	817
Overall Total	2 116	2 071	2 162	2 409	2 215	2 336	2 551	2 635	2 476	2 484

Sources: UK National Tourist Boards, 2000; National Statistics, 2000.

counteract these trends. Scotland is not immune from world events and although past trends can never be an accurate guide to the future, they do indicate some broad directions, which are unlikely to change in the near future. UK residents are spending more and more of their tourism expenditure on overseas trips. In the past this has traditionally been spent on their main holidays, but there are signs that the second, third and indeed fourth holidays of UK residents (previously spent in Scotland on short breaks) are now European short breaks. The focus of Scots' holiday tourism is the 1–3 night sector, but as noted Scotland has a high-market share of this (60 per cent of the 1–3 night UK spending), and there are therefore limits to its growth. In England the 4–7 night holiday looks to be the mainstay of their tourism spending.

Some of Scotland's competitor countries in Europe have clearly performed well over the 1990s compared to Scotland. They have somehow managed to grow at a much faster rate than Scotland; indeed the growth in overseas visitors to Ireland has often been quoted as a successful example, which Scotland should match. The explanations for this growth in tourism in Ireland can be attributed in part to the large capital investment in the product in the 1990s, mainly supported by EU development grants. Tourism also had strong political support, as articulated through their national economic development plans. Other more subtle but important factors also aided this growth, such as an established national airline which helped to spread national identity and an increasing number of direct ferry and air links to both Europe and North America (Table 11.9).

Overseas markets to Scotland are important for export earnings; however they are declining. Both the UK and Europe are losing market share and new markets and segments need to be developed. The decreasing length of trip of both UK and overseas tourists in Scotland is clear, caused by many more competing demands on our time.

Table 11.9   Growth in tourism in selected destinations (trips million)

	1990	1995	1998	1999	2000
1. France	52.5	60.0	70.0	73.0	75.5
2. USA	39.4	43.3	46.4	48.5	50.9
3. Spain	34.1	34.9	43.4	46.8	48.2
4. Italy	26.7	31.1	34.9	36.5	41.2
5. China	10.5	20.2	25.7	25.4	25.3
6. UK	18.0	23.5	25.7	25.4	25.3
7. Russia	–	10.3	15.8	18.5	21.2
8. Ireland	3.7	4.8	6.1	6.4	6.7
9. Scotland	1.6	1.9	2.1	1.9	1.7

Note: Ireland counts visitors from the England/Wales as international arrivals, but Scotland does not.

Sources: WTO, 2000; National Statistics, 2000.

Apart from these statistical trends it is important to be aware of the strengths and weaknesses of the tourism product in Scotland for they are unlikely to change at least in the short term (see Figure 11.1).

STRENGTHS	**WEAKNESSES**
Distinctive destination appeal	Short season resulting in low investment in the product
Quality products and natural produce	
	Poor service attitude compared to competitors
Culturally distinctive	
Hospitality of the people	Management skills
	High prices compared to competitors
OPPORTUNITIES	**THREATS**
Increase in short breaks	Impact of short breaks on remote areas
Growth in activity holidays and growing interest in culture	UK residents take main holidays overseas
	Competition for short breaks from overseas destinations
Trend towards green purchasing	
Growing domestic and international conference business	
Increase in the use of new technology	

Figure 11.1   Scottish tourism – SWOT analysis.

Review of key trends affecting the growth of tourism in Scotland

Consumers are changing, but the overall trend is of a growing market for tourism, underpinned by a number of global trends and developments.

Economic trends

The world economy has grown at an annual rate of over 3 per cent for the past 30 years, however, the *per capita* growth has been more modest at about 1.4 per cent per year. This lower rate means that on average people throughout the world are producing and consuming over 50 per cent more in real terms than in the mid-1960s (Scottish Tourist Board, 2000). The conventional wisdom about the future of the world economy is generally more sanguine. Most forecasters predict long-term growth of the world gross national product (GNP) in excess of 3 per cent per year, along with low inflation and relatively favourable business cycles. Assuming long-term stability in the USA economy, which is the main driver of the world economy, careful development of the former USSR countries and growth in spending in the Japanese economy, incomes should rise and this will allow people to spend more on leisure activities. As a result, tourism is expected to grow by about 4 per cent per year over the next 20 years (World Tourism Organisation, 2001). The emergence of the euro and the US dollar as the two leading world currencies will further reduce cost of travel and lead to fixing of travel costs across the world. The emphasis in the UK upon non-progressive taxation is expected to continue, and will be a contributing factor to the increasing disparity of wealth. It is expected that taxation on air fuel will be introduced, as a consequence holidays will become relatively more expensive, with holidays being increasingly only attractive to those with surplus income.

Information trends

Without a doubt the Internet is changing the way consumers access and book their holiday, with e-commerce fully developed in the USA and in many western economies. The question of how far it will penetrate the holiday market is dependent on its intrinsic appeal to different consumers with different holiday needs. The Internet is ideal for the independent traveller, with the majority of package holidays still being bought through conventional channels, such as travel agents. The Internet will be used for promoting a destination, although many independent travellers will use it for booking, as well as looking. What will drive its development will be the ease of access, booking and paying, and

Scotland must offer these services if tourism is to develop. Increasingly, home, work and leisure will be wired together resulting in little need to source information from one place, but the downside will be information overload. The introduction of digital and interactive television offers greater potential for targeting specific segments, but also presents the risk of increased 'noise' from competitors. By 2020 improved access by customers to information on tourism products will make it easier for them to compare products and prices.

Environment trends

Climate changes will evolve quite slowly across intense periods of extreme activity. Although the exact impact of climate change is open to debate, the initial impacts are expected to include: disruption to weather systems with warmer winters and wetter summers, increasing rainfall with more frequent intense rainfall, rising sea levels and increasing thaw rates of snow and ice.

Social trends

People are living longer than ever before, especially in the developed western economies, and are affluent and more active than previous generations. The present generations are therefore more aware of high standards of service and product quality. To entice them in a competitive market place, Scotland needs to work harder to attract such people, for these older travellers are more 'experience-focused' rather than 'destination-focused'. Such consumers are not time bound by school/work constraints, and are able to take their breaks throughout the year.

People are working harder, with less job security than ever before. Leisure time is being squeezed; we are taking fewer and shorter breaks than ever before, and are increasingly choosing destinations close to home. This creates a market with more disposable income but greater time constraints, and such people expect or want to achieve more and more from the little free time available. The consumer in 2020 will be prepared to spend money to avoid inconvenience and/or save their most precious commodity, time.

The average household size is falling with more and more people living in one or two person households. This creates a growing market of people with no dependents and high-disposable income. They may travel alone, but are more likely to travel with friends and family and/or take packages with like-minded people. They are also likely to choose a holiday with a specific interest. The advantage of this type of market is that people on such holidays are more likely to be repeat visitors as they are more likely to meet people like themselves.

With increasing pressures at work and little or no increase in free time, there is a growing search for an antidote to stress. The holiday or short break is recognised as a time to relax, indulge, pamper or self-reward. People are willing to pay for their indulgences, but do expect value for money. Although not at the forefront of their mind in the holiday decision-taking process, people are looking for destinations where they can get away from it all, even if it is just for a few days, in order to re-charge. The interest in breaks that promote fitness, health or alternative lifestyles is reflected in a growing demand for activity holidays and those involving spiritual retreats. The goal of a healthy and more balanced life will continue to be important for people, with more looking to grow emotionally and spiritually. Thus nature as an 'experience' and as a ready escape from everyday pressures, will be essential in 2020.

People are staying longer and longer in education, and well before 2020 it is likely that the government's stated objective of 50 per cent of 18 year olds in higher education will be achieved. Education is traditionally an indicator of the ability and willingness to travel. This group will generally have high disposable income and greater awareness of destinations. In the short term, there could be an increase in the backpacker market, and by 2020 there could be much greater interest in programmes such as the 'Elder hostel' market, which is already developed in the USA.

A 2020 scenario for tourism in Scotland

Given the above statistical picture and the overview of key trends, the author offers a personal interpretation of them and outlines a vision for the development of tourism in Scotland in 2020, based thereon.

With the decrease in household sizes, friends will be the new family. As social interaction changes and as more people live alone the importance of having networks of friends will be even further developed by 2020. Such friends will not be tied to one locality but, due to increased mobility and new technology, will likely be located all around Europe. The increasing costs of housing and the expansion of higher education will result in more young people living with their family. There maybe a re-emergence of family holidays, with three generation extended family holidays. The growing influence of females and gays and their expanding buying powers may result in the emergence of single sex hotels. The greater cultural diversity in Scotland will also result in the growth of a much larger ethnic population, and could result in Scotland becoming a popular destination for ethnic holidays, such as those focusing on Asian food.

The workplace is changing and given the rapid growth in information provision as suggested in the information trends section, and the merger of work and play, this will lead to a growth in portfolio working, which will offer personal liberation and greater earning potential for those with the skills to sell in the new marketplace. This could also lead to the creation of social economic and cultural exclusion; with many of these new jobs being service based, low paid and filled by the unskilled, school leavers and older people. The highly skilled portfolio workers could be looking for long holidays between jobs. It is also likely there will be a re-emergence of social tourism, whereby the government and unions recognise that holidays are a social right. Could the future include the emergence of hotels run by unions and government holiday camps? The downside of such employment trends is the decline in workplace loyalty, particularly among new workers entering the workforce for the first time. This may result in a decline in permanent employment as people become psychologically and emotionally separate from their employer.

There will be a blurring of the division between home and office, with less routine attendance at a central work place. Working from home at least part of the week is expected to be the norm in 2020. This will lead to a healthier balance between work and family life, and may lead to less pressure for families to holiday together. It is expected that licensing laws will be more relaxed, and with the development of the 7/24 society, leisure time will be taken throughout the day and night. There will also be a dovetailing of work and holidays, people will communicate with the work place when on holiday, for technology will chase us all over the world! The increasing use of social events will be an important way of gathering information – buying a social life – and tourism may well become a fashion statement, helping to define what we are as individuals.

There is little doubt that China will be the world's top destination by 2020. Tourism in Europe will grow, but perhaps by only 3 per cent per annum. Strong competition will come from previously closed countries such as Libya, Syria, Iran and other Middle East countries. It is expected that security in travel will be a major political issue, and terrorism or health alerts will continue to have a major effect on tourism destinations. The decentralisation of power in Scotland would be completed, but Scotland will still be part of the UK. The established Scottish Parliament will see tourism identified as a major economic development priority for Scotland, and afforded special status as a selected growth industry. The introduction of EU wide legislation will help to ensure a better quality of life, by restricting working hours and the adoption of family friendly policies and legislation. The interest in politics will shift from Westminster and Brussels to Edinburgh and other regional cities. The growth of regional co-operation will lead to a relaxation of border and exchange controls, and transport deregulation within Europe will boost regional co-operation. Tourists can and do move easily around neighbouring countries within one holiday trip, and this is a competitive advantage in attracting visitors to a region, rather than just a country.

The expansion in the use of Liquid Petroleum Gas (LPG) has helped Scotland be seen as an environmentally friendly destination. The continuing warming of the planet has changed the habitats of a number of Scotland's wildlife species, and the policy of establishing new habitats has again helped raise Scotland's environment profile. Unfortunately, Scotland has seen some coastal flooding, and tourism is seen as damaging some fragile environments. However, Scotland is seen as a safe environment particularly through the further development of the market for organic foods of all types.

Strategic implications for the devopment of tourism in Scotland

Within the context of the key trends and developments commented on above this will lead to new opportunities for Scottish tourism, which will complement rather than replace the current markets for Scotland.

New segments

1 *Active seniors*: The growing number of older people that have the time, and disposable income, to travel will create larger target markets for Scotland. These visitors will be better travelled than previous generations and will be more 'experienced' and destination focused, they will demand and expect quality products and services as standard. Their experiences will mean greater scope for specialist or niche markets, with soft accessible activities.
2 *Singles*: As the structure of households changes there will be more and more single households which will result in a growing market of people with higher disposable income, no dependents and who are relatively flexible and free in their holiday decisions. They will be looking for destinations focused on activities or special interest.
3 *Scottish descendants*: In the baby boomer market alone in the USA, there are 3.2 million people who claim to have Scottish ancestry. People want to know more and more of their 'roots' and this new market will be easier to reach with the new technology.

New products

1 *Health and wellbeing*: The development of the spa market has been well-established in mainland Europe, and is a popular activity with women. Scotland has in the past tried to capture this market through the development of our Victorian health spa heritage, and much upgrading has taken place with these developments. A new market aimed at the short break market will develop, particularly within two hours drive of the Victorian spa resorts. There could also be new spas developed in major cities, particularly those associated with high-quality accommodation. Given the resurgence in spiritual interest, holidays offering spiritual retreats could be developed, particularly those marketed with an escape theme or developed around a 'find oneself' theme. Scotland's international religious centres such as Iona, Whithorn and Callanish, are recognised places for retreats. Holidays which combine clean countryside and spiritual themes could provide a new basis for holidays in Scotland in 2020.

2 *Culture, history and heritage*: Inevitably, Scotland's cultural resources capture the growing interest in Scottish/Celtic culture thus ensuring a quality experience. Older travellers recognise the need for this experience. These holidays will be particularly attractive if they offer products with the ability to experience the 'real Scotland'. Activities such as tracing your 'roots' and understanding the 'real Scotland', are likely to offer some added value to a basic package. Holidays with specific themes, for instance archaeology, architecture, and our literary 'roots' (for example Burns, Scott, and other well-established writers, like Irvine Welsh) will grow.

3 *Green tourism*: General awareness of the importance of Scotland as a high-quality environment is well-established. The establishment of a National Park has further reinforced Scotland's image. Holidays built around an environmental education theme will be developed, such as dolphin and bird watching.

4 *City breaks*: Scotland's cities have always attracted and will continue to attract holidaymakers in their own right. The continuing pressure on consumers' time will result in these being attractive to tourists, particularly those with fast transport links, and which are able to offer simple condensed holidays, in which maximum experience can be offered in the minimum time.

5 *Activities*: A select number of activities will be well-developed by 2020, and those offering a mixture of education, different forms of activity and development of the mind, are more likely to grow.

'Soft' adventures especially for the older consumer, which offer the opportunity to experience thrills without danger, will expand, especially if associated with comfortable accommodation.

6 *Conservation*: A return to helping local communities will become more popular, and holidays associated with conservation (such as dry-stone dyking or repairing damage to peat lands) – particularly those linked with 'feel good' organisations, such as the Royal Society for the Protection of Birds (RSPB) and the National Trust for Scotland (NTS) – are likely to succeed, as will holidays where people learn new skills, while at the same time improve the environment. As work continues to be sedentary, holidays associated with manual labour, such as train driving and cleaning rivers, are also likely to be popular.

7 *Water focused holidays*: With so much concern associated with the development of land-based activities, it is possible that the waters of Scotland (both inland and coastal) could be developed as a new focus for holidays. Activities such as scuba diving are already very popular in the USA, and Scotland with so many shipwrecks has a unique selling point as a cold water destination. Sailing, particularly on the West Coast of Scotland, now that the Forth and Clyde Canal link has been restored, will be a popular activity, as well as barge holidays along the Canal. The waters of Scotland have always offered good salmon and trout challenges, but sea fishing could also be developed as offering new adventures to overseas visitors.

8 *Craft holidays*: As well as cultural and activity holidays, the growth of seeking 'yesterdays' experiences will offer new markets. There could be scope for craft holidays, for learning skills using one's hands. Activities such as painting, pottery or woodcarving could be developed, especially if these skills were being taught on residential courses by native Scots. Such courses may be particularly attractive in the more remote areas of Scotland.

9 *Gardens*: A niche market focusing around the theme of returning to nature, using gardens as a hook, could be developed in Scotland. Courses, which offer an educational theme, based around Scotland's horticultural assets will grow.

Policy implications for the development of tourism

There are many trends that could affect the development of tourism policy in Scotland by 2020. The world will be different in 2020, and not just an extension of the current trends, but the past and current national strategic plans for Scottish tourism assumes little change. They appear to focus on a relatively short time frame of the next five years, and focus more on delivering quick fixes such as new marketing initiatives in golf, genealogy or cultural tourism rather than on addressing the weaknesses in the tourism product in Scotland. These plans do not recognise the world is changing, and today's markets could easily disappear. The fundamental problem facing tourism in Scotland is that the consumer is changing, but the product is static.

There is an underlying assumption that the Government not only has a role to play in tourism, but it is essential it should take the lead role in what is basically a privately delivered service. The current national plans, perhaps because they are written by the public sector, focus heavily on public sector activities, such as national and local marketing, and that good old stand-by for justifying public intervention, namely 'co-ordination'. But why should this sector be afforded a special status with its own intervention body, the Scottish Tourist Board (STB)? Other mature tourism destinations such as the USA, or newer destinations such as Costa Rica, rely almost totally on the private sector to both develop and market their product (Scottish Tourist Board, 2001). So why this emphasis on public sector support for tourism? Perhaps it is because of a lack of faith or ability in the private sector to deliver, or the belief that public sector intervention equates to action? Or it could be that the private sector not only lacks an overall body to represent them in national discussions, but also they cannot act collectively – that is they work better as would be expected in competition with each other, rather than co-operating. From a consumer perspective it matters little who delivers a service, only that the service is delivered. The present body that purports to represent the tourism industry in Scotland, the Scottish Tourism Forum (STF), depends heavily on public sector funds to support its activities, and this limits its scope for action. If there is to be a distinctive new policy direction, there is a clear need for the private sector to fund, support and lead the development of the tourism industry. Indeed it could be argued that to achieve the goal of a vibrant private-sector tourism industry we should return to the days of the 1960s, when the STB was a private sector organisation, but in receipt of state funds to undertake and deliver on certain functions.

As more and more changes occur in the work environment, the movement away from self-seeking hedonistic pleasures of the early 2000s, to seeking self-fulfilment and a new view of life will develop as a counteract to the relentless pressures of both work and home life. Society by 2020 will be split into three groups: those who work, those who have retired, and those who are unemployed/in low wage jobs, with tourism markets developing to serve all three, and each will require a different set of actions by policy-makers.

1 For those in work, tourism will become focused on short breaks, offering intensive experiences such as city breaks, short educational visits, and challenging activity holidays. Here the government's policy actions will be that of an enabling and co-ordinating agency, for example, by ensuring that the historic infrastructure such as castles and historic houses are maintained to the highest possible standards, that activity adventures centres are licensed, and that their staff are qualified in the activities offered.

2 For those who have retired, holidays of a more spiritual or completive nature maybe the norm, as will those offering the chance to learn new practical skills. As people become more insular and inward looking, the chance to meet like-minded people, with similar sets of interests will become of more importance, and meeting people on educational courses will develop. Those between jobs will seek and expect long breaks which offer the chance to be pampered, and will be willing to pay for such pampering. Here the role of government is to act as an educational agency, by recognising that individuals will see tourism as a means of keeping the brain active. That is, tourism will be seen as public good like education, for it benefits the individual as well as the State.

3 The third market serving the unemployed/low waged will be looking for 'cheap and cheerful' holidays. A free market is unlikely to provide for this type of holiday, so it is just possible the government/union/ philanthropic bodies will see the importance of providing holidays for this group, as much for reasons of social control as wellbeing of the individuals. This could lead to the ghettoisation of holiday destinations, as seen today in the development of places such as self-contained destinations – like holiday centres.

The industry will have changed by 2020 through the introduction of a much more private sector approach, both in the development and marketing of tourism in Scotland. The government policy role will likely focus on policing actions and ensuring minimum standards. If Scotland is to develop a vibrant tourism industry, free of subsidies and independent of UK wide agencies, and grow in a very competitive world market place, there is a need to ensure quality across all aspects of the product. Over the next decade there will be a shakeout of poor quality operators, with those remaining adopting a more professional approach, with the customer as central to their marketing. With the development of new technology the industry needs to develop into a small number of marketing consortia, focusing on various product groupings, rather like airline alliances today, and will share customers and offer tailor made products that suit the needs of individual customers.

Government agencies will likely move out of tourism marketing and a new national marketing organisation led by the private sector with limited public sector funds, drawn from transport, accommodation and attraction providers, will exist. The mark of a successful tourism policy will be when a public subsidy will no longer be required. However, with the growing power of the consumer it is also likely they will have a direct say in the operation of this new body, through consumer representation.

As western society reaches a plateau in leave entitlement, and as work continues to dominate peoples lives, tourism in Scotland will contribute towards the wealth of the nation. The economic contribution of tourism to the balance of payments, rather than size of the industry in terms of numbers, should drive the industry. It will also be recognised by government policy that tourism has both a social and environmental responsibility. The need for tourism taxes to pay for both environmental improvements, as well as subsidising those who cannot afford to pay for their own holidays, needs to be debated. Social tourism could be viewed as an acceptable way of redistributing the recognised benefits of tourism, and as both an economic and social development policy tool working for the greater good of both visitors and residents.

References

National Statistics (2000), *Travel Trends: A report on the 2000 International Passenger Survey*, London: The Stationery Office.

UK National Tourist Boards (2000), *The UK Tourist: Statistics 1999*, Edinburgh: English Tourism Council, Scottish Tourist Board, Wales Tourist Board, Northern Ireland Tourist Board.

Scottish Executive (2000), *A New Strategy for Scottish Tourism*, Edinburgh: The Stationery Office.

Scottish Tourist Board (2000), *Future Prospects for the Scottish Tourism Industry*, Edinburgh: Scottish Tourist Board.

Scottish Tourist Board (2001), *Benchmarking of Scotland as a Tourism Destination*, Edinburgh: Scottish Tourist Board.

World Tourism Organisation (2000), *Tourism Highlights 2000 Preliminary Results*, Madrid: World Tourism Organisation.

World Tourism Organisation (2001), *Tourism Highlights 2001 Preliminary Results*, Madrid: World Tourism Organisation.

12
The Energy Industry
Stephen Boyle

Introduction

If the shape of Scotland's energy industries in 2020 is uncertain, the changes of the last 20 years are clear and stark. The period since the early 1980s has seen transformations in energy policy, enterprise ownership, economic regulation, technology, relative prices, union power, environmental concerns and geopolitics that have transformed the sector. Then, the principal object of policy was security of supply; something the market could not be trusted to deliver. Then, the public sector owned the electricity, gas and coal industries as well as Britoil and a significant proportion of British Petroleum. State ownership was the guarantor of secure supplies. It also reflected the prevailing belief that most energy industries were either natural monopolies or of such strategic importance that nationalisation was the only way to ensure effective control in the public interest. Then, economic regulation was limited to a recognition that in state-owned monopolies prices should be set as close as possible to marginal costs in order to minimise welfare losses. If the price happened to be lower than marginal cost, as in the coal industry, taxpayers provided subsidies in the name of security of supply or the nation's strategic interests. Then, dominant technologies included coal-fired thermal plants in the electricity industry and steel and concrete platforms for production in the offshore oil and gas industry. Then, the oil price had recently reached more than $80 per barrel in 2002 money. Then, the National Union of Mineworkers had extracted significant wage increases and investment for the industry from the Conservative government elected in 1979. Then, the environmental movement was a fringe interest, accorded little serious interest by people and politicians other than in its objections to the expansion of nuclear power generation.

Then, the prospect of a single market in energy in Europe remained distant. The Soviet Union was a superpower and there was no possibility of significat sums of private capital being sought for or seeking opportunities in the oil and gas-rich republics of Central Asia.

The last two decades teach two lessons about looking forward to 2020. First, change could be radical in ways that simply cannot be anticipated. Secondly, while the details of change necessarily elude analysts today, the likely sources of change seem predictable. The industry will evolve in response to developments in public policy, technology and markets. The ultimate aim of this chapter is to consider the most likely changes in these areas and to investigate how they may affect the Scottish energy sector. Before that, the chapter is structured as follows. The next section briefly defines the scope of the energy sector. It is followed by an analysis of the contribution of energy to Scotland's economy. Next, the distinguishing economic characteristics of the energy sector are identified, in part to permit the subsequent discussion of the strategic trends and issues that face the industry in the period to 2020. In addition to considering the outlook for energy in general, specific consideration is given to prospects for the oil and gas industry.

Defining the scope of the sector

This section defines the activities covered by the energy industry. It then identifies the main components of and companies in the sector in Scotland. The chapter is concerned with suppliers of energy services operating in Scotland. Thus, the focus is on companies that produce coal, gas, oil and electricity. Importantly, this excludes firms supplying the energy industries. This runs counter to some of the popular understanding of what constitutes the energy sector, particularly in the offshore oil and gas industry where suppliers of a range of services are commonly considered to be part of the industry.

The industry is dominated by a small number of large firms, making it easy to identify the leading companies in the sector. Although a number of small firms operate opencast coal mining sites, there is now only one deep mine, Kincardine, operated by Scottish Coal. In gas, as in the rest of the UK, the transmission system is owned and operated by Transco, once part of British Gas both pre- and post-privatisation. The 'supply' of gas – its procurement from physical producers, the purchase of the access to infrastructure that allows it to be delivered to customers' premises and the metering and billing of customers – takes place in a liberalised and competitive market. Customers are no longer restricted to buying their gas from a monopolist. Leading suppliers in Scotland are Scottish Gas – the brand name of Centrica in Scotland – and Scottish-Power. Centrica, like Transco, was once part of British Gas. The Scottish electricity businesses of ScottishPower and Scottish Hydro-Electric (SHE) are substantially those inherited on privatisation of the former South of Scotland Electricity Board (SSEB) and the North of Scotland Hydro-Electric Board. On privatisation, the nuclear generating assets of SSEB were not vested in ScottishPower but assigned to a third company, Scottish Nuclear Ltd. (SNL). Its equivalent in England and Wales, Nuclear Electric Ltd. (NEL) inherited the nuclear assets of the Central Electricity Generating Board. SNL and NEL subsequently merged to become British Energy and were privatised. The company is headquartered in Scotland. Finally, around 20 companies are directly engaged in oil and gas production as owners or operators of offshore acreage. BP Amoco and Shell account for more than half of production.

Energy and the Scottish economy

This section describes aspects of the sector's significance to the Scottish economy using the Scottish Input–Output Tables and employment data (Scottish Executive, 2001). In 1998, the year to which the most recent tables relate, the energy industries accounted for just over 4 per cent of gross value added (GVA), a measure of output similar to gross domestic product. To set the energy sector in context, it is smaller than public administration (8.1 per cent of GVA), retailing (6.8 per cent), education (5.1 per cent) and health (4.7 per cent), but larger than any individual manufacturing industry. In fact, both electricity production and distribution (1.9 per cent) and oil and gas extraction (1.8 per cent) contribute more to GVA than any individual manufacturing sector, including prominent industries like spirits (that is, whisky, 1.3 per cent) and all food processing combined (1.5 per cent) (Table 12.1).

A second measure of the role of the sector in the economy is the structure of demand for energy. Across the Scottish economy, 34 per cent of demand is 'intermediate' – that is, purchases of inputs by one industry from others – and 66 per cent of demand is 'final' – that is, purchases by Scottish consumers, export sales outside Scotland and investment demand. The pattern of energy demand is quite different, reflecting the fact that energy is a key input to the activities of other industries. Almost 96 per cent of coal demand comes from other industries and most of that is sales to the electricity generators. In electricity production and distribution and in gas distribution, too, a high proportion of demand arises from other industries

Table 12.1   Gross value added, Scotland (1998)

	£million	**Percentage of total**
Total	62 153	100.0
Coal extraction	79	0.1
Extraction of oil and gas	1 118	1.8
Electricity production and distribution	1 170	1.9
Gas distribution	225	0.4
Total energy	2 593	4.2

Source: Scottish Executive, 2001.

Table 12.2   Structure of demand, Scotland (1998)

	Intermediate (%)	**Consumption (%)**	**Exports (%)**	**Total final demand (%)**	**Total demand (%)**
Total	34.4	29.0	32.1	65.6	100
Coal extraction	95.9	1.0	6.2	4.1	100
Extraction of oil & gas	22.4	0.0	76.3	77.6	100
Electricity production & distribution	68.7	21.6	7.2	31.3	100
Gas distribution	60.0	37.0	2.6	40.0	100
Total energy	52.7	16.1	29.7	47.3	100

Source: Scottish Executive, 2001.

in Scotland, more than 60 per cent. The corollary is that the extent of exporting in coal, electricity and gas distribution is limited, no more than 8 per cent of demand compared with an average of 32 per cent across the economy. The exception to this pattern of demand is oil and gas extraction. Here, only 22 per cent of sales are to Scottish firms. More than three-quarters of sales are exports (Table 12.2).

The general importance of intermediate demand in the energy sector is reflected in another measure of the impact of energy on the economy, the value of sectoral multipliers. A multiplier measures the ratio of the total direct and indirect output, income or employment generated by an initial direct change in output, income or employment arising from a change in final demand. For example, as Table 12.1 shows, an increase in final demand for electricity of £1 million results in a total increase in output in the Scottish economy of £2.3 million. The multipliers for electricity production and distribution are notably high and those for coal extraction, and oil and gas extraction are in the top third of sectoral multipliers. High multiplier values reflect a high degree of integration between an industry and the rest of the economy. Thus, these multipliers indicate that although it may not be the largest sector, energy is central to the effective and competitive functioning of the Scottish economy.

The sector's direct contribution to Scottish employment is modest (Table 12.3). In 1998, there were around 34 000 jobs in the sector, less than 2 per cent of Scottish employment. Of the industry's components, oil and gas extraction accounted for most jobs, around 19 000.

A further important aspect of the industry's economic significance is that it provides Scotland with the headquarters of three FTSE 100 companies: ScottishPower, Scottish and Southern Energy (SSE) – of which SHE is part – and British Energy. The contribution of headquarters functions to the strength of regional economies is well-established. They tend to result in high proportions of inputs being sourced locally, especially high-value purchases such as legal, accounting and other business services. In the absence of headquarters functions demand for these services is lower, with adverse consequences for economic performance and prospects. That means not only lower income but also the absence of the dynamic and innovative influences that arise from the presence of key decision-makers. It is important to note, that the bolstering of Scotland's

Table 12.3 Employment in energy, Scotland (1998)

	Number	Percentage of total employment (%)
Mining of coal and lignite; extraction of peat	2 000	0.1
Extraction of crude petroleum and natural gas, service activities incidental to extraction; mining of uranium and thorium ores	19 000	0.9
Production and distribution of electricity	10 000	0.5
Gas; distribution of gaseous fuels through mains; steam and hot water supply	3 000	0.1
Total Energy	34 000	1.6
Total Scotland	2 160 469	

Source: Annual Employment Survey, NOMIS, 1998.

corporate base that the electricity sector provides was an unintended consequence of the electricity privatisation programme.

Economic characteristics of the energy sector

This section considers some of the economic characteristics of the energy sector. The brief summary of the leading companies above hints at its complexity. This complexity has a number of dimensions. First, the companies themselves are complex entities. Few of them supply only one type of energy. ScottishPower generates, transmits, distributes and supplies electricity and also supplies gas. Scottish Gas, through Centrica, owns and operates offshore gas fields, supplies gas to customers and also supplies electricity.

Secondly, few companies supply the Scottish market alone. The export figures understate the importance to the sector of markets outside Scotland. Internationalisation has occurred although not typically on the basis of previous trading activity. Thus, the electricity companies have 'supply' arrangements with customers throughout the UK. This activity involves procuring power from physical producers, arranging for access to the transmission and distribution systems of other companies and metering and billing customers. It does not entail the physical delivery of power from, for example, ScottishPower's generating stations to a customer in Wales. ScottishPower does have a physical interconnection with Northern Ireland and the Scottish transmission system enjoys a physical interconnection with England. The coal companies supply electricity generators in England. Most strikingly, ScottishPower owns an electricity company in the USA, PacifiCorp, and SHE has owned and operated a growing portfolio of generating capacity in the rest of Great Britain for almost a decade. In the oil and gas sector, none of the exploration and production companies operating off Scotland's shores is active in Scotland alone.

Thirdly, many companies supply services other than energy. Scottish-Power developed and continues partly to own Thus plc, the telecommunications company, and owns Southern Water plc. The principal oil and gas companies are integrated operations in which, within Scotland, the raw material is transformed into plastics, industrial gases and other products at the Grangemouth and Mossmorran refineries. As a brand of Centrica, Scottish Gas is part of a diversified household and personal services group that includes the Goldfish personal credit brand and the AA. A number of the opencast mining firms are engaged in general construction and engineering.

Fourthly, the sector combines elements of both aggressive, low margin competition – notably the supply of electricity and gas – and regulated monopoly, including electricity and gas transmission and distribution.

Finally, as the input–output tables show, there are very strong economic and functional linkages between parts of the energy sector.

These characteristics of the industry arise for a number of reasons, but two dominate. First, the industry demonstrates increasing returns to scale. Increasing returns typically obtain where the ratio of fixed costs to total costs is high. That, in turn, generally connotes a requirement for significant fixed capital investment before production can begin. Increasing returns are endemic to the energy industries. In oil and gas, increasing returns to exploration activity stem from the fact that drilling success rates are generally less than 10 per cent in the UK Continental Shelf. That is, fewer than one in ten of wells drilled yield commercially viable finds. In order to maintain a presence in such an industry, exploration and production companies need large portfolios of producing and potential fields to mitigate the risks of 'dry' holes. The industry also often requires fixed physical infrastructure such as pipelines to export its product from oil and gas fields. This needs substantial capital expenditure in advance of revenue as well as high volumes of production to make the investment viable. The electricity and gas industries were traditionally held to be models of 'natural' monopoly because of the investment required in network services like wires and pipelines that would only be supplied once. However, the recent past has demonstrated the presence of increasing returns in other areas. The supply of electricity and gas are competitive and contestable businesses that have seen new entrants in the market following liberalisation. Yet there are strong increasing returns because the capital costs of building and maintaining customer information systems for billing, metering and marketing are high. This explains the rapid rationalisation of the sector and the development of UK-wide supply businesses. It also partly explains the diversification of ScottishPower into the water industry – where incremental customers could be added to existing customer management systems – and SHE's merger with Southern Electric to form SSE.

Secondly, in the cases of electricity and gas, the form of economic regulation has provided firms with an incentive to diversify both spatially and in terms of product markets. Following privatisation, much of the electricity and gas industries were subject to regulation that constrained the scope for profit growth and, in some cases, reduced profitability. Under these circumstances the incentive facing businesses is to diversify into other markets, either the same activity in another place or another non-regulated activity or an activity subject to another form of regulation. ScottishPower's diversification into telecommunications and its overseas acquisition were partly prompted by the incentives presented by regulation.

Strategic trends and issues – looking to 2020

This section considers the factors that will influence the development of Scotland's energy industry over the next two decades from the perspective of 2002. It also speculates on what the outcomes might be. It considers two groups of factors that will cause change: public policy; and markets and technology. In terms of public policy, there are three key strategic issues:

(i)   the development of competition policy and economic regulation;
(ii) the evolution of environmental policy, both domestically and internationally; and
(iii) domestic policy with respect to nuclear energy.

Competition policy and economic regulation

The UK was in the vanguard of energy sector liberalisation from the 1980s. That involved a mix of privatisation and opening up to competition markets that had previously been the domain of monopolies. There is little more of the Scottish energy industry that could be subject to deregulation. Instead, the principal focus of deregulation will be at the EU level. Since the early 1990s, the EU has been committed to liberalisation across all sectors. In energy the main policy instruments have been requiring third party access to infrastructure and the removal of state aids to national energy companies. The introduction of third party access means that, for example, a new electricity generator can use the transmission and distribution systems of incumbent operators on the same terms that all similar companies use the infrastructure. This makes the market for energy services more contestable by granting access to infrastructure on identical terms and, almost, as a matter of right. The removal of state aids, notably in coal production – which indirectly subsidises electricity generation too – was also designed to reduce the barriers to entry facing prospective new entrants.

On both fronts progress has been slow in the energy sector as compared with a number of others such as civil aviation. However, much of this is attributable to the fact that the adjustment costs associated with introducing competition and removing subsidy are high in terms of job losses. Many of these costs have already been borne and the process of liberalisation will intensify.

The main implication for Scotland's energy industry is that new opportunities for mergers, acquisitions and joint ventures will emerge, particularly in the electricity sector. There will be opportunities for companies with experience of operating in liberalising and competitive environments as well as those with recent experience of procuring major infrastructure such as power stations and transmission system extensions. Thus, further deregulation at the EU level will present Scottish companies with opportunities for internationalisation, as well as an increased threat of external acquisition.

Environmental policy

Environmental policy will affect the sector at two levels. Internationally, the focus on reducing emissions of greenhouse gases is likely to intensify. Scotland will simply be a 'policy taker' in that context, as the UK government and the EU will negotiate agreements. Locally, the response of Scottish and local government and local communities to the environmental cost of renewables and the perceived risks of nuclear power will have a profound impact on the structure of the industry in 2020.

Producing and using energy has environmental consequences. The balance of scientific opinion is that very substantial reductions in CO_2 emissions are required to stabilise the world's climate. According to the UK government's Inter-Departmental Analysts Group on Long Term Greenhouse Gas Emission Reductions, on unchanged policies (including the expected progressive decommissioning of nuclear power stations), CO_2 emissions from UK energy consumption are likely to rise by between 0.1 and 0.3 per cent per annum by 2050. To achieve the reductions agreed at Kyoto will require a combination of greater energy efficiency, technological innovation, changes in the mix of energy produced and consumed, and changes in the economic incentives – prices and costs – facing producers and consumers.

In Scotland, environmental pressures will have a number of consequences. First, the share of energy – specifically electricity – produced from renewable sources will rise. Research conducted for the Scottish Executive has shown that Scotland has the technical potential to produce more than six times its electricity requirements from renewables in 2010 (Garrad Hassan and Partners Limited, 2001). However, delivering that potential comes at a cost. First, most of the technologies considered are of markedly higher cost than fossil-fuelled, nuclear or large hydro generation. Secondly, the local environmental costs of renewables projects can be high. These include damage to habitats, visual intrusion and noise.

The second related consequence is an absolute fall in the contribution of coal-fired generation and, possibly gas-fired plant, to energy production. As existing coal stations reach the end of their economic lives, they will be replaced by sources that emit lower levels of CO_2. To the extent that coal-fired electricity generation declines, the prospects for the coal industry will deteriorate.

Thirdly, policy-makers in Scotland may have to re-examine the scope for exploiting the country's longest-standing renewable resource, large-scale hydro-electric schemes. Although this is a wholly 'renewable' source, environmentalists and policy-makers have excluded large-scale hydro from the debate on renewables on the grounds that such projects have adverse local environmental impacts. The reason that the issue may be revisited is that individual large-scale hydro schemes provide hundreds of megawatts of capacity rather than the smaller contributions made by other renewable sources. Since the requirement will be to replace thousands of megawatts of fossil-fuelled generation, large-scale hydro cannot be ignored.

Finally, the need to reduce greenhouse emissions will be one reason why nuclear energy policy will be a key issue for Scotland in the next 20 years. It is the topic of the following section.

Nuclear energy policy

More than 50 per cent of Scotland's electricity supply is generated in nuclear power stations. The existing stations – Hunterston B, Torness and Chapelcross – are likely to come to the end of their economic lives during the next 20 years. That capacity will have to be replaced to meet electricity demand. The question is whether new nuclear power stations will be built or alternatives will be preferred. There are obvious countervailing pressures.

One of the strengths of nuclear power compared with generation based on burning fossil fuels is that it gives rise to no emissions of greenhouse or other gases. A decision to build new nuclear capacity would preserve that advantage for Scotland. The abandonment of nuclear power and its replacement by fossil fuel capacity would pose considerable problems for Scotland. The emissions that would be caused by substituting coal and/or gas plant for nuclear are unlikely to be acceptable or permissible under international agreements. Thus, for a given emission ceiling to be met, the alternatives are new nuclear generation and renewables. The case against nuclear generation is the – real or perceived – risk associated with the operation of nuclear plant and the subsequent decommissioning of stations and the disposal of waste. This will dominate public debate on the matter.

The decision about whether to commission new nuclear generation will be a political one. Energy policy is reserved to the Westminster parliament, not devolved to Holyrood. In 2001, the UK government's Performance and Innovation Unit, part of the Cabinet Office, began a review of long-term UK energy policy. One of the issues identified for consideration is how to replace the capacity provided by nuclear power when existing plant is decommissioned. Interestingly, while energy policy is reserved, planning consents for power stations are a devolved matter. Thus, while the UK government could decide to sanction further nuclear capacity, Scottish institutions retain an effective veto.

The outcome of this debate will have profound consequences for the Scottish economy.

Markets and technology

Two technological developments might affect the industry in Scotland. First, the further development and commercial application of hydrogen fuel cells. If this happens global demand for a range of conventional energy sources would fall. The impact on oil and gas is likely to be especially strong and such a development could lead to a reduction in the scale of the industry in Scotland. Secondly, relatively high production costs are the main obstacle to further expansion of renewables. Their wider use in response to government requirements that the proportion of electricity generated from renewables might lead to a fall in average costs as production volumes rise. However, significant progress is most likely to come via technical change. In both cases, technical change causes a shift in the supply curve and a corresponding response in demand.

Beyond technical change and the influence of public policy, it is difficult to envisage changes in markets that will affect the industry in Scotland. The size of the domestic market is fixed in the short-run and, in practice, in the longer-term. Population change will be modest and the bulk of the industrial restructuring that led to changes in consumption patterns – for example, the demise of steel production – have already occurred. Rising incomes will continue to boost energy demand, although the energy intensity of the economy will continue to fall as service activities continue to expand and the production industries' share of output falls.

The future of oil and gas

The imminent demise of the offshore oil and gas industry has been forecast since the 1970s, largely based on the assumption that a fixed and finite resource would be exhausted by production. The argument presented in this section is that the most likely outcome in 2020 is the continued presence of a smaller, more efficient but still significant offshore industry that plays a major role in the Scottish economy.

This conclusion is counter-intuitive in two respects. First, resources are finite and will be depleted further in the next two decades. Secondly, the UK continental shelf (UKCS) is a high-cost province. At a time when hitherto closed or unattractive but low cost regions are opening to investors – such as Central Asia and parts of the Middle East, Africa and South America – how can the UKCS continue to attract investment capital?

On the matter of resources, several points must be made. While the amount of oil and gas in the UK is fixed by definition, estimates of *recoverable* reserves reflect assumptions about the commercial viability of searching for and extracting the oil and gas. Commercial viability is not fixed. Rather, on the cost side, it is determined by a number of factors, principally technology and the tax regime.

Developments in technology have had a significant impact on the scale of recoverable resources. Thus, as Table 12.4 shows, the unit cost of producing oil and gas from new fields has fallen over time, in spite of the fact that average field size has also fallen, thereby reducing the scope for economies of scale. This has meant that the estimated volume of recoverable reserves has remained broadly constant during the last decade in spite of rising oil and gas production.

Table 12.4   Unit costs of fields at 2000 prices

	Oil fields[1] (£/barrel)	Gas fields (pence/therm)
Fields starting production before 1980	11	9
Fields starting production 1980–1985	16	23
Fields starting production 1986–1990	14	21
Fields starting production 1991–1995	9	14
Fields starting production 1995–2000	9	14
All fields in production	11	13.5

[1] Including condensate fields – and oil equivalent of associated gas. Excluding tax and royalties, and costs of abortive exploration.

Source: Department of Trade and Industry, 2001.

The range of technological developments has been considerable, but two related examples illustrate the effects of technology on commercial viability. The traditional method of production involved placing a fixed platform over a field and extracting the oil or gas using the equipment on the platform. Recent developments in: (i) pipes and tubes; and (ii) subsea equipment mean that a given platform can now extract oil or gas from fields a considerable distance away. These distant fields are not sufficiently large to justify dedicated platforms or transmission pipelines, but can become viable using these technologies. The effect has been to increase dramatically the volumes that can be recovered using existing infrastructure.

The industry in the UK is committed to continuing to drive down costs through the development and application of new technologies. While technological forecasting is perilous, the likelihood is that costs will continue to fall.

However, UKCS costs will remain towards the upper decile of the global production cost curve. With very low cost reserves in the Middle East and elsewhere, why should the UKCS be expected to compete successfully for investment, even if it manages to reduce costs from existing levels? Put differently, if there is so much potentially low-cost production in the world, why will prices not fall to $5 per barrel or less?

First, although the Middle East, Central Asia and elsewhere are low cost regions, developing fields there would require trillions of dollars of capital expenditure. Most of that would have to be funded from project finance debt rather than equity, whether new investment or retained earnings. The political and other risks associated with lending to projects in most of these countries mean that banks are unlikely to be willing to lend the sums required to develop the resources. Thus, in the continued presence of these risks, many of the resources in notionally low-cost locations will remain only a potential threat to the UKCS.

The second related point is that financial cost is not the only consideration facing investors making choices about where to allocate scarce capital. The UKCS offers two particular advantages that offset the higher financial costs of operating here. First, the political and regulatory regime is relatively stable and predictable. The probability of the UK government nationalising the assets of oil companies or imposing penal tax rates is markedly lower than in some other countries. That provides companies with greater certainty and security when planning investments that often run over decades. In the specific case of the tax regime, UK tax rates for the industry are among the lowest in the world and the UK government has demonstrated a commitment to making the tax burden consistent with the UKCS remaining a competitive location for new investment.

Secondly, the UK benefits from agglomeration effects. The concentration of oil industry activity in the north east of Scotland creates positive externalities. For example, there is a pool of labour with experience of the sector from which companies in the industry can draw. Similarly, an indigenous supply industry has grown that has led to the development of significant technical and professional expertise in areas critical to the industry. Conditions like these are found in only a few places in the world and are not easily transferred or created in other locations. Thus, although the total cost per barrel of operating in the UKCS may be high, it is offset by the benefits afforded by agglomeration effects.

A further reason for optimism about the oil and gas sector is that, until recently, it has largely been a North Sea industry. A handful of fields have been developed in Morecambe Bay and to the West of Shetland. However, the potential of the Atlantic Margin is considerable. Fields like Clair have long been known to hold potentially vast reserves. On some estimates Clair could be several times greater than the likes of Forties or Brent. Until recently, tackling geologically difficult reserves in locations remote from existing pipeline and processing infrastructure has been a barrier to development. New technologies mean that it is increasingly likely that the Atlantic Margin will be developed in the next few years and that it will be central to sustaining the industry in Scotland after the North Sea has substantially been exhausted.

There are two reasons to qualify this optimism. First, as discussed above, one possible technological change that would impact significantly on oil demand would be the development of fuel cells. If these become viable and if they substitute for oil, particularly in transportation, demand for oil may fall. Since the UKCS is a high-cost location, it is vulnerable to a decline in demand resulting from a shift in the demand curve. Secondly, the environmental lobby has for several years made clear its opposition to the development of the Atlantic Margin. If that lobby was able to muster sufficient political support it could succeed in blocking development to the west of the UK. In the absence of Atlantic margin developments and a much denuded North Sea, the industry would shrink considerably.

The 'North Sea' industry might play a final, different role in the energy sector in 2020. At present, a number of platforms are powered by electricity generated onshore and cabled to offshore installations. Some platforms could be remodelled to host windmills to generate electricity. The power could be cabled to the onshore transmission system. This approach has a number of attractions. For the oil and gas companies, it delays platform abandonment and the associated costs. It provides renewable energy, thereby contributing to emissions targets. Finally, since the installations are far from the public gaze, there are none of the environmental problems normally associated with wind farms.

References

Department of Trade and Industry (2001), *Development of Oil and Gas Resources 2001*, 'The Brown Book', London: The Stationery Office.

Garrad Hassan and Partners Limited (2001), *Scotland's Renewable Resource 2001*, Edinburgh: Scottish Executive.

Inter-Departmental Analyst Group (2001), Inter-Departmental Analysts Group on long term greenhouse gas emission reductions, *Preliminary report on work in progress*, London: Department of Trade and Industry, March.

Intergovernmental Panel on Climate Change (2000), Intergovernmental Panel on Climate Change, *Emission Scenarios*, Cambridge: Cambridge University Pess.

Scottish Executive (2001), *Input–Output Tables and Multipliers for Scotland 1998*, Edinburgh: Scottish Executive.

Part III

Corporate Scotland: Established and New Firm Strategies

13
Scotland's Established Corporate Base
Jonathan Slow and Diane Gordon

Introduction

This chapter explores how 'established' Scottish companies with over £500 million turnover, considered in the first section, may perform over the next 20 years. The second section outlines some of the strengths, weaknesses, opportunities and threats such companies face. The third section explores some general characteristics of success. The final section looks at policy issues that may impact on these companies.

Definition and impact

Definition

We have chosen to take £500 million turnover as a proxy for companies that have become established players. Table 13.1 reflects the time required and processes needed to become established and shows how these companies have fared over the last decade.[1]

There are six companies that appear in all the lists. Not surprisingly financial institutions feature quite heavily alongside ScottishPower, Scottish & Newcastle and John Menzies. There are a number of others who are still important but during the period from 1991 have seen control transferred elsewhere, for example, General Accident and Scottish Widows. Clearly, these companies are still important to the Scottish economy and the financial services industry in particular, but their ultimate destiny is now controlled elsewhere.

If we look further into the evolution of the list we see that although the number of companies at each snapshot point is around 15, the composition has changed. In 1991, seven of the top 10 companies were in financial services including insurance and life. In 2001 there were four under

Table 13.1 Top Scottish companies (turnover >£0.5 billion)

	Core business/industry	2001 (£million)
1 Standard Life	Life assurance	10 996.60
2 RBS	Banking & financial services	4 138.00
3 ScottishPower	Multi-utility services	4 115.00
4 Scottish & Newcastle	Brewing & leisure	3 571.90
5 Scottish & Southern Energy	Electricity generation	3 047.90
6 Bank of Scotland	Banking & financial services	2 371.00
7 British Energy	Electricity generation	2 058.00
8 Stagecoach Holdings	Public transport services	1 923.50
9 FirstGroup plc	Passenger transport services	1 817.80
10 Scottish Life Assurance	Life assurance	1 664.00
11 John Menzies	Wholesalers, aviation services	1 298.10
12 Grampian Country Food Group	Meat processing	796.48
13 Arnold Clark Automobiles	Vehicle hire/sale/servicing	783.02
14 Weir Group	Engineering	754.91
		39 336.21
Total 500		94 000.00
Percentage of total 500		41.85%

Source: *Insider* 500, 2001.

		1998 (£million)
1 Standard Life	Life assurance	8 614.10
2 General Accident	Insurance	6 066.00
3 Scottish Widows	Life assurance	3 881.68
4 Scottish & Newcastle	Brewing & leisure	3 349.20
5 RBS	Banking & financial services	2 952.00
6 ScottishPower	Multi-utility services	2 940.70
7 British Energy	Electricity generation	1 870.00
8 Bank of Scotland	Banking & financial services	1 765.70
9 John Menzies	Wholesalers, aviation services	1 417.40
10 Scottish Provident	Life assurance	1 153.04

11	Stagecoach Holdings	Public transport services	1 152.80
12	Scottish Life	Life assurance	998.70
13	Scottish Hydro-Electric	Electricity generation	951.10
14	Christian Salvesen	Distribution & Food processing	746.30

| | | | 37 858.72 |

| Total 500 | | | 83 000.00 |
| Percentage of total 500 | | | 45.61% |

15	Weir Group	Engineering	619.90
16	Watson & Philip plc	Food retailers	576.60
17	FirstBus	Passenger transport services	551.50

| | | | 39 606.72 |

| Total 500 | | | 83 000.00 |
| Percentage of total 500 | | | 47.72% |

Source: *Insider* 500, 1998.

			1996 (£million)
1	Standard Life	Life assurance	6 075.60
2	General Accident	Insurance	5 202.70
3	RBS	Banking & financial services	2 410.00
4	Bank of Scotland	Banking & financial services	2 283.40
5	Scottish Widows	Life insurance, pensions	2 185.19
6	Scottish & Newcastle	Brewing & leisure	2 021.50
7	ScottishPower	Multi-utility services	1 725.80
8	Scottish Amicable	Life insurance, pensions	1 619.12
9	John Menzies	Wholesalers, aviation services	1 258.00
10	Scottish Provident	Life assurance	860.00
11	Scottish Hydro-Electric	Electricity generation	833.10
12	Scottish Life	Life assurance	699.68
13	Christian Salvesen	Distribution & Food processing	646.00
14	Scottish Nuclear	Electricity generation	580.00

| | | | 28 400.09 |

| Total 500 | | | 61 253.44 |
| Percentage of total 500 | | | 46.36% |

Source: *Insider* 500, 1996.

Table 13.1   (Continued)

	Core business/ industry	1991 (£million)
1 General Accident		4 441.20
2 RBS	Banking & financial services	3 951.30
3 Standard Life	Life assurance	3 916.30
4 Bank of Scotland	Banking & financial services	2 201.90
5 Scottish Widows		1 478.52
6 Scottish Amicable		1 248.88
7 Scottish & Newcastle	Brewing & leisure	1 240.10
8 ScottishPower	Multi-utility services	1 132.10
9 John Menzies		902.20
10 Scottish Equitable		617.57
		21 130.07
Total 200		45 205.14
Percentage of total 200		46.74%

Source: *Insider* 200, 1991.

the definition adopted here. Interestingly, the biggest change has come about since 1998. This can be explained by significant consolidation in the global financial services industry as institutions want to build capacity, exploit economies of scale and build international presence and/or cement national presence as the industry slowly becomes more global (see Hood and Peters, 2000).

It is interesting to see those companies who have joined the list over the decade – again especially since 1998. Two new entries may provide examples of how the established firm base is broadening Grampian Country Food Group and Arnold Clark Group. The food industry has always been important to the Scottish economy, highlighted in the Scottish Enterprise Food Cluster Action Plan. Grampian may be just the first of a number of such companies over the next decade. Arnold Clark Group has also grown steadily over the last decade. There are a number of other motor groups in the *Insider* list and again we may see more growth here.

Similarly, the roles of utilities and transport companies are important. ScottishPower has always been a strong performer, but it is now joined by Scottish & Southern and British Energy (although in their former guises they were present, albeit on a smaller scale). Stagecoach and First

Group both joined the list in 1998. The importance of building on deregulation and having an aggressive acquisition strategy and building presence across a range of interlinked functions is important to all these companies. In utilities, we are now seeing that being transferred to an international stage. In transport, however, both Stagecoach and First Group have significant international presence already, and although this may have brought difficulties it is likely that first mover advantages will be important to longer term success. From the analysis of Hood and Peters both these areas still have a significant way to go in their ultimate globalisation. As we will see below this provides both opportunities and threats.

The final company is the Weir group, their continued presence shows their ongoing growth, especially in international markets, with strong growth between 1998 and 2001 (Weir Group, 2001).

Another interesting issue is the origins of these companies. The clearest fact that emerges is the importance of privatisation, deregulation and family businesses on the Scottish 2001 list. ScottishPower, Scottish & Southern Energy and British Energy have all been able to emerge in the way they have because of privatisation. Stagecoach and First Group have both grown through deregulation. Weir Group, Arnold Clark and John Menzies have all grown from family businesses. As will be shown below, this is a significantly different position to the US.

Impact

Almost by definition the impact these established Scottish companies have on the economy will be significant. In 2001 their combined turn-over was almost £40 billion. This has almost doubled since 1991 and has risen 40 per cent since 1996. The growth was particularly dramatic between 1996 and 1998, with a slowing to 2001. Remembering that the figures exclude the acquisition of NatWest by Royal Bank of Scotland plc (RBS), the slower growth may reflect a degree of consolidation by these companies, and planning for the next growth stage – in a number of cases on an international basis.

Although, turnover growth may have slowed, profits remain buoyant. In 2000 the average increase in profits across the 500 was over 23 per cent. This is again a feature of consolidation and improving per-formance through the embedding of acquisitions and mergers.

At a wider level we can see the on-going importance of these established companies. Their impact in the whole of the *Insider* 500 accounted for 42 per cent of total turnover in 2001. Interestingly, whilst this figure is high, it has dropped from 46 per cent in 1996.[2] This reflects the change in ownership of some of Scotland's largest companies (for example, General Accident).

It is also important to emphasise the other impacts these companies bring – not least of which are activities from having headquarters in Scotland. Clearly, there will be financial benefits to having such activities, but there are also impacts in terms of people, sponsorship deals and knock-on effects that may be spread wider when headquarters are elsewhere.

Moreover, there are other areas where they make a significant impact. Assessment of these was undertaken by Scottish Enterprise in 1999 as part of its Global Companies Enquiry (Scottish Enterprise, 1999), and although the companies studied as part of that research do not map exactly onto the established companies here, there are a number of similarities. The key areas identified were:

- Contribution to R&D and innovation levels in Scotland.
- Increased sophistication of alliances and technology transfer collaborations.
- Linkages to Scottish Higher Education Institutes.
- Raising the profile of Scotland internationally.
- Raising the quality of Scottish-based suppliers.
- Pulling through potential inward investment.
- Sponsorship of Scottish and community activities.

Even if it is assumed that most of the established companies here are involved with only one of these areas the impact will be substantial. For example, if, on average, 2.5 per cent of turnover goes towards this additional activity and a multiplier of 2 is realistic and pro-rating the overall turnover figure we find an additional impact of over £200 million per annum to the Scottish economy. If this is scaled up to include all 286 Scottish companies in the 2001 *Insider* 500 the total will be closer to £3 billion in turnover impact or around £1 billion in GDP. For this reason, strong performance in the established sector is vital to the long-term health of the Scottish economy.

How does this compare?

So far, the picture of Scotland's established companies shows on-going strong performance and a significant role in the economy in an absolute sense. However, it is important to consider this picture on

Table 13.2 Top 15 US companies (turnover >$0.5 billion)

	2001 ($million)
1 Exxon Mobil	210 392.00
2 Wal-Mart Stores	193 295.00
3 General Motors	184 632.00
4 Ford Motor	180 598.00
5 General Electric	129 853.00
6 Citigroup	111 826.00
7 Enron	100 789.00
8 IBM	88 396.00
9 AT&T	65 981.00
10 Verizon Communications	64 707.00
11 Philip Morris	63 276.00
12 JP Morgan Chase	60 065.00
13 Bank of America Corp	57 747.00
14 SBC Communications	51 476.00
15 Boeing	51 321.00
	1 614 354.00
Total 500	7 180 879.70
Percentage of total 500	22.48%

Source: *Fortune* 500, 2001.

	1998 ($million)
1 General Motors	178 174.00
2 Ford Motor	153 627.00
3 Exxon	122 379.00
4 Wal-Mart Stores	119 299.00
5 General Electric	90 840.00
6 IBM	78 508.00
7 Chrysler	61 147.00
8 Mobil	59 978.00
9 Philip Morris	56 114.00
10 AT&T	53 261.00
11 Boeing	45 800.00
12 Texaco	45 187.00
13 State Farm Insurance Cos	43 957.00
14 Hewlett-Packard	42 895.00
15 EI Du Pont De Nemours	41 304.00
	1 192 470.00
Total 500	5 518 510.40
Percentage of total 500	21.61%

Source: *Fortune* 500, 1998.

a relative basis too, not only to assess how large Scottish established players are compared to elsewhere, but also to see how dependent we are on them.

The US is perhaps the best comparator given the degree of data available. To provide some kind of snapshot comparison, the top 15 companies from the 2001 *Fortune* 500 list were analysed against the Scottish companies. The results are shown in Table 13.2.

Three points immediately jump out: firstly, the US corporations are significantly larger than their Scottish counterparts, secondly the US is far less dependent on these top 15 companies than Scotland and thirdly the sectors covered are different.

It is easy to dismiss comparisons with the US on the basis that the US economy is so much larger and because of this it will inevitably grow significantly larger corporations than Scotland. To some extent this is true, but there are also other arguments that should be considered.

Specifically, as the world economy is becoming more globalised, the regulations preventing market access to many countries are being reduced and the rate of mergers and acquisitions significantly increasing, companies of the size of these large US companies are now in play. Smaller companies, no matter how nimble, may become take-over targets.

The US top 15 account for around 22 per cent of the total *Fortune* 500, around half the Scottish rate. It is therefore less dependent on them in terms of overall impact on the economy. Interestingly, this figure increased between 1998 and 2001, but is still much lower than the Scottish figure.

Sectorally there are also differences. Clearly, financial services is an important sector in the US list too, reflecting the degree of concentration that has taken place there in the later part of the 1990s. However, we also see oil companies, motor and aircraft manufacturers, engineering companies, and technology companies. This is perhaps resonant of a large integrated economy but it also reflects companies with significant international interests and ones that have grown (over time) to this structure.

To assess how far this has gone, figures from the UN World Investment Report Index of Transnationality[3] (United Nations, 2001) are used. The sectoral breakdown of this grouping is shown in Table 13.3.

From this Index of Transnationality, it is clear that the areas where most of Scotland's established companies are in the 'less international at present' category, with utilities at 33 per cent (average of the proportion of overseas assets, sales and employment to the total). Financial services presumably in the 'other' category which at 66 per cent is moderately transnational, is not up with the highest, namely, media at over 85 per cent.

Table 13.3 Industry composition of the largest 100 TNCs for 1999

	Average TNI (%)
1 Media	86.9
2 Food/beverages/tobacco	78.9
3 Construction	73.2
4 Pharmaceuticals	62.4
5 Chemicals	58.4
6 Petroleum exploration/refining/distribution & mining	53.3
7 Electronics/electrical	50.7
8 Motor vehicle and parts	48.4
9 Metals	43.5
10 Diversified	38.7
11 Retailing	37.4
12 Utilities	32.5
13 Telecommunications	33.3
14 Trading	17.9
15 Machinery/engineering	0
16 Other	65.7
Total/average	52.6

Source: UN World Investment Report Index of Transnationality, United Nations, 2001.

This should not be taken to imply that Scotland's established companies are poor or weak – in fact quite the opposite is true. However, it does imply that there may be significant change in the markets these companies operate in. This is both an opportunity and threat in the medium to long term, but one that Scottish companies are already preparing for, and as we will see later, policy is also strongly positive towards international development.

Despite this, and irrespective of whether the Scottish companies are more or less than the figures in the UN report, it is a key issue that the sectors they serve are likely to increase in their international dimension – even if that is only at the European level.

The next section considers the strengths, weaknesses, opportunities and threats that the established Scottish companies may face over the next decade. It also shows some of the responses they have made and the success they are having.

SWOT analysis of established Scottish companies

The previous section has emphasised the importance of established companies to the Scottish economy. However, it is important that they retain that importance over the longer term – against some of the challenges posed by international business development, continuous innovation, critical mass and scale and scope economies.

This section explores the possible impact on established companies in terms of a simple and stylised Strengths, Weaknesses, Opportunities and Threats (SWOT) analysis. The overall implications are, we believe, positive despite the challenges posed.

Strengths

Adaptability, innovation, uses of technology, entrepreneurship and tenacity all feature heavily in the group of Scottish companies that have performed well. Interestingly, it is not necessary that all factors are present but they are very common in those companies.

Adaptability

The adaptability angle flows from the need to change rapidly in response to (or increasingly in advance of) macroeconomic events. Consider recessions of the 1980s and early 1990s, the withdrawal of sterling from the exchange rate mechanism (ERM), privatisation, EU legislation, opening of new markets (for example, from World Investment Report), and the need for an increasingly global mindset. There are a significant number of companies who have responded to these challenges and profited; the key issue now is to have more of them. One example of such a company is ScottishPower which has acquired PacifiCorp in the US. This story is a good example of how ScottishPower has developed itself as a utilities company rather than solely in electricity.

It is clear that this strategy of focusing on UK and US growth has been successful and delivered significant shareholder value. Moreover, they have also adopted a number of different forms to deliver their business, and have a good track record at acquiring and integrating businesses.

Innovation

Innovation in products and services is also commonplace. Success does not necessarily imply being the first mover, but being a fast, effective mover in order to secure gains. For success in terms of new financial services, the RBS and Bank of Scotland (now HBOS) are good examples. For example, the RBS has been successful in its joint venture with Tesco into Tesco Personal Finance: opening up a new market and using a different form of operation to do it.

According to a recent *Business a.m.* article, RBS is now worth more in the US than those stalwarts of the US economy Boeing, Ford, Du Pont, and 3M. In total the company is now worth over $60 billion (*Business a.m.*, 2001). The Royal Bank has also achieved significant growth through focused acquisitions in the UK and the US.

It has adopted a strategy built around growth from solid performance. Remaining small in an environment of banking mega-mergers has made the bank vulnerable, but it was not rushed into a potentially risky course of action. It waited and acted from a position of strength.

Following the NatWest success, the bank may look for more acquisitions in the future, but it is clear they will have a well-articulated strategy that operates from growth and performance.

Technology

For technology, again the financial services sector, and companies such as the John Wood Group are examples of established business using technology in new and innovative ways to grow new markets. Tenacity is a common factor in the strengths of the existing Scottish company base; a very good example of this is the Weir Group's transformation to a significant international player in its key markets. The title of the Weir Group annual report 2000 'Focussed Global Expansion, Increased Local Support' summarises this well.

Success in technology can often come through a focus on specialist niches, where success requires significant skills in addition to manufacturing excellence – for example, design and use of technology.

Weaknesses

No matter how successful the 'best' Scottish companies are, there is always the question raised: why do more not emerge? In answering this, common arguments around attitude to growth, the prevalence of 'life-style' businesses, failure to seize emerging opportunities, an unsympathetic financial community, too much bureaucracy, and government policy have all been offered as explanations. There are elements of truth in all these arguments. However, there is always a tendency to over-play the importance of them either singly or as a whole. There may be weaknesses, but whether they are significantly more prevalent or important in Scotland than in other countries is open for discussion, and is beyond the scope of this chapter.

There are some issues that have hindered Scottish corporate growth of which there is less debate. Low levels of corporate spending on R&D

(see Scottish Enterprise, 1999) and its general proxy for innovation, generally low levels of entrepreneurial activity within companies and corporate venturing as an outcome (for example, commercialising technology), where appropriate growing companies beyond export to become 'global' companies, risk-aversion, relatively poor marketing skills (McCall, 2001; Scottish Enterprise, 1999) and relatively low uptake of e-commerce are perhaps more pervasive weaknesses. There are also arguments that suggest a proportion of Scottish companies sometimes focus on being low cost manufacturers rather than value creators. This strategy may be flawed: there will always be some place in the world where it is cheaper to produce than it is in Scotland.

Another weakness that is evident from the *Insider* 500 data is the lack of technology companies in the list, although a number use technology as a source of competitive advantage. If you compare the Scottish list to that of the US, the differences become clearer. This could have potential downsides to the economy in that it may limit wider spending on R&D in the economy or the uptake of Scottish generated science and knowledge. There is conversion of technology into small companies, often operating in niche markets. A traditional weakness, however, is that these companies are often bought before they can become established in the sense discussed here.

Opportunities

There are many opportunities open to Scottish companies. Almost all of these are related to the way in which the global economy works in the twenty-first century. For example, e-commerce allows customers from anywhere in the globe to be serviced; globalisation and the reductions in trade barriers provides unprecedented opportunities for companies to grow globally, have overseas operations and become truly global players; creating new businesses and change markets through the clever use of technology and innovation; embracing new ways of doing business to create new and/or lower risk opportunities; accessing and using finance (from domestic or overseas sources) in new ways to build a solid platform for growth; and strategically using mergers and acquisitions to build scale rapidly and effectively and erect barriers to entry.

A good example of a company which has taken advantage of how other companies have embraced new ways of doing business is Aggreko. Since 1997, it has seen its turnover grow from £163.3 million to £325.8 million, whilst over the same time their profit has grown from £33.2 million to £67.1 million. Their business has grown on the back of the increased trend of outsourcing as companies focus on core competencies. In an outsourced market like power, however, reliability is paramount, and it is the combination of geographical coverage, an ability to meet rapidly growing demand and reliability that has contributed to Aggreko's success (see Aggreko Annual Report, 2001).

Their approach is based on providing solutions to problems in the most efficient way and developing long-term customer relationships.

To benefit from the opportunities seems to require a number of factors including: a clear strategy, focus on key niches, working in a growing market, having a clear approach to generating value, offering clear differentiation through service levels and problem solving mentality, and being flexible in operations for different markets.

Threats

Most of the main threats to established Scottish businesses come from not embracing or effectively undertaking the opportunities mentioned above. For example, not using e-commerce cuts off a large number of potential customers around the globe, or using e-commerce but not paying sufficient time to the logistics of fulfilling orders can lead to lost repeat sales (where the money is made in e-commerce). Likewise, not understanding the implications of globalisation may leave a company vulnerable to competition in Scotland from an overseas competitor who has reacted to the implications of lower trade barriers, improvements in logistics, and access to finance. Similar cases can be made for the other opportunities too. Finally, the whole area of education and skills, ensuring Scotland becomes an example of leading practice is vital – an inability to do this may make longer term success more elusive than is hoped.

Overall, there are many positive stories to be told surrounding the existing Scottish company base. The successful companies can build on their success provided they respond (and continue to respond) quickly, effectively and with sufficient scale to the opportunities outlined above. Other companies can join them if they do the same. Any potential problems for the future will come if businesses do not grasp the opportunities or deliver them in a half-hearted manner. Companies falling back into the 'tail' of economic performance will, other things being equal, reduce the performance of the Scottish economy overall.

A key threat could occur through the potential movement of headquarters away from Scotland. Although for the established companies here this may be less of an issue, it has happened before (for example, General Accident). Loss of headquarters functions is important. Although a significant proportion, if not all, employment remains high value added, functions like R&D can move to be close to the new headquarters, potentially compromising Scotland's innovative capability. The loss of key individuals can also be important in terms of future growth of companies – either established or emerging.

This discussion is driven by the degree of embeddedness of such headquarters in Scotland. It seems from the information available that the established Scottish base discussed here is reasonably well based in Scotland, although as noted it can never be certain (for example, General Accident). There are a number of key factors in this discussion: how attractive London is as a place for corporate headquarters, the bigger losses if a critical mass of headquarters is lost from Scotland, the ability to access finance, marketing and other resources at costs driven down by competition (again a function of critical mass), and the sheer scale of activity in certain areas.

If some companies move their headquarters then others may follow if there is a general perception that a critical mass is lost. Current trends do not seem to point to this happening (for example, the retention of the HBOS headquarters in Edinburgh), but it is always an issue to monitor.

Ameliorating some of the potential threats can be undertaken by continuing to respond to the economic challenges posed, to continue to look to grow internationally, to be adaptive and innovative, to embrace e-business, and to build shareholder value. In addition, the growth in broadband access, a growing pool of entrepreneurial talent, a highly open economy and a place to have a good quality of life are all factors that will be important in retaining and securing headquarters functions. They all lie at the heart of the Scottish Executive's 'Global Connections Strategy' explored in more detail in the Policy section below.

The other angle relevant to this chapter is how the existing Scottish company base will fare in the longer term. Many of the key issues mentioned above will continue to be important drivers of performance. However, there are some that override the others in their importance: the requirement to think globally and act globally as appropriate; the assimilation and use of leading technologies to maximise value; being a fast but effective mover (not necessarily a first mover); using R&D sourced internally or externally to drive innovation; and being flexible in using different delivery methods (for example, joint ventures) to spread risk but secure return.

The next section takes some of this analysis and outlines a series of activities that might constitute a wider list of characteristics of success for established companies, and also to others with desires to be established in the sense we have discussed here. They are certainly relevant to those companies that wish to be successful international players (see Scottish Enterprise, 1999; Slow, 2001).

Characteristics of success

Work undertaken by Scottish Enterprise (Scottish Enterprise, 1999; Slow, 2000) sets out what these characteristics may be:

- Adherence to clearly defined and articulated strategy for growth;
- Formulating strategy around defining and dominating market niche(s);
- Operating in markets with a small number of players or that can be highly segmented;
- Choosing core businesses carefully and operating them efficiently;
- Diversifying products and markets, but not on a sectoral basis;
- Disposal of non-core or non-performing businesses/business units;
- Differentiation from competitors by, for example, selling superior skills or technology;
- Operating to dominate market niches and generating significant barriers to entry for the competition both current and potential;
- When acquiring, acquiring strategically and aggressively;
- Valuing margins and not conducting business merely to maintain volume;
- In certain circumstances turning away low margin business to protect profit rates;
- Carefully managing risk, but with an eye on return to investment;
- Using flexible organisational structures to exploit available opportunities in the most beneficial manner – for example, joint ventures, alliances, and corporate venturing;
- Having a fully integrated financial and business strategy, with finance carefully managed, including the use of a range of financial sources.

These characteristics are related to the strategic direction followed by a company, and, as has already been seen, success can follow. However, a number of them are also influenced by policy. The final section considers how policy might impact on the established corporate base in the light of recent policy announcements and indications of wider policy direction in Scotland and elsewhere.

Policy effects

At a macroeconomic level, the general convergence of economic policies around the mantra of stability is likely to continue. It is also likely that over time, more countries will be adopting similar policies, either by choice or as a by-product of support from the IMF. The result of this is likely to be a greater convergence in policy measures and responses to external shocks – for example, a major slowdown in the US. To some extent this reduces risk for companies with international obligations. What it does not do is reduce variation: the same response to an external shock in one country may need a more aggressive reduction in interest rates than in another. It also does not remove the way in which shocks and changes in policy are transmitted, or the length of time the shocks will impact: gut feel is that the growth Internet usage in business and the volume of business transacted this way will lead to a faster transmission and more rapid impact, it will also lead to a more rapid recovery, probably with longer gaps between major shocks. The severity of the downturn will have implications for companies that are not sufficiently flexible to transform quickly.

The implications for and requirements of established Scottish businesses are:

- Flexibility in response to these shocks;
- A robust strategy with different options that can be implemented immediately in the face of changed conditions;
- Speed and effective operation to maximise opportunities;
- A continuous pipeline of innovation whether that be new products/ services or on-going improvements.

From the discussion earlier it seems there are a number of areas that should be reflected in such a policy range.[4]

- International expansion: exports, outward investment;
- R&D, innovation, and new product/service development;
- Technology adoption, especially Internet-related technologies (for e-commerce and business efficiency purposes);
- Encouragement for new forms of business operation (for example, spin-outs, commercialisation, joint ventures, corporate venturing and alliances;
- Mergers and acquisitions (M&A), especially cross-border;
- Skills development.

From a Scottish perspective, a number of these elements are now included in policy measures enacted by the Scottish parliament or the Westminster parliament.

Building on the *Framework for Economic Development in Scotland* (Scottish Executive, 2000), *A Smart, Successful Scotland* (Scottish Executive, 2001a) a broad framework for intervention by the Enterprise Networks is outlined and a number of areas of focus are highlighted. These areas reflect strongly the issues above. *Smart, Successful Scotland* (SSS) poses a challenge based around four key categories: productivity, entrepreneurship, skills and digital connections. This challenge will be crucial to rise to. In essence, they are all part of the wider issue of making the Scottish economy highly competitive in international markets and against international competition.

The response to the challenge is framed around three areas: growing businesses, global connections, and learning and skills. The key actions set out for the way forward are also strongly linked to the characteristics set out above. They set out clearly an agenda from which significant competitive advantage can emerge.

It is interesting to note that a number of issues identified in the first part of this chapter, have direct counterparts in SSS.

However, the international elements of this strategy are considered in the more in-depth *Global Connections Strategy* (GCS) (Scottish Executive, 2001b). The importance of this area of activity cannot be underestimated for the established Scottish company base, as many of them are already significant international players, expanding internationally or at the very least facing major international competition. Moreover, as set out in the GCS the areas covered span the key international priorities facing established Scottish companies:

- Digital connectivity – faces into the challenges of e-business and having the appropriate infrastructure to support it.
- Increased involvement in global markets – is concerned with promoting trade and international business development, particularly being able to respond proactively to the challenges posed by globalisation.
- Scotland to be a globally attractive location – is to ensure that as the nature and type of inward investment changes, so that Scotland is still able to enjoy the success it has enjoyed in the past.
- More people choosing to live and work in Scotland – focuses on the needs of responding to out-migration of skilled individuals, utilising the skills and connections of those overseas with a strong affinity to Scotland and enabling the benefits of global experience to be harnessed within the economy.

So collectively, policy at a Scottish level has many of the ingredients in place to respond to the challenges faced by established Scottish companies. However, this is not the end of the support available. At a Westminster level additional measures support R&D in terms of writing-off R&D investment, but also in terms of the R&D tax credits announced in the 1999 budget. The opportunity of cash-back against investment in R&D, thus levelling the playing field against many competitor nations (for the range of support available elsewhere see OECD, 1999), should increase UK investment in R&D. Scottish firms should be well placed to benefit.

The other area of reserved powers that may be relevant to the established Scottish companies are the rules on take-overs, and hence M&A. There are a number of positive aspects for Scottish companies, not least of which is the re-emergence of public interest as a key criterion in the decision to allow a take-over or not. In the past because the Scottish interest group has been well organised this has helped Scottish companies – for example, the Royal Bank possible take-over by Hong Kong Shanghai Bank (now HSBC), and the recent merger of Bank of Scotland with the Halifax Building Society. And the relative degree of lesser organisation in this regard elsewhere in the UK has also worked in Scotland's favour.

However, to expect this relative state to continue indefinitely is perhaps questionable: the growth of the Regional Development Agencies in the English regions, and the emergence of those regions as powerful economic entities in their own right (even without devolution) means that things may change. Moreover, with the EU increasingly taking a strong stand on mega mergers and looking to finally put in place a code on hostile take-overs, the process may become more difficult or at least more time consuming and costly. This may protect some Scottish companies, but it is possible that it will hurt more in terms of lesser expansion overseas than in the loss of Scottish ownership.

The overall openness of the UK economy and the generally high ratio of trade and outward investment to GDP (35–40 per cent and 27 per cent respectively, see United Nations, 2001; Scottish Enterprise, 1999), means that the UK is already well developed at an international level. However, the growth in international M&A (25 per cent per annum between 1989 and 1999 according to figures from the UN, see United Nations, 2000) and the overall encouragement of this activity in UK policy adds another level of support for Scottish companies wishing to grow further despite the caveats above.

From a policy angle, therefore, it seems that many of the issues could have a positive impact on established Scottish companies. Beyond providing a framework that allows organisations to flourish it also emphasises a number of directions organisations need to consider as part of their operations.

These areas of focus are important for the longer term growth of the currently existing corporate base in Scotland. Many companies already follow them, and if more can successfully adopt them, there is a significant opportunity to see major growth in the strength of the Scottish corporate base.

Conclusion

This chapter has examined the existing corporate base in Scotland. Some definitional work using the *Insider* 500 was required to clarify the type of company under consideration. There is strong representation in the banking/finance, utilities, transport, engineering and oil and gas sectors, and all sectors show success stories, some of which were examined in more detail in the case studies. It was also shown that these companies contribute a significant amount to the Scottish economy, both directly and indirectly. It can be argued that these companies are the backbone of the economy, and their continued success is vital to the health of the economy.

In considering the characteristics exhibited by the successful companies, some promising evidence for that future success is also found. The adaptability, innovation, use of technology, entrepreneurship and tenacity of the success stories, combined with their desire to expand globally, to 'be the best', adopt new ways of working, and create change in the markets they serve, bodes well for the future.

For the longer term, it is hard to say what will happen, but for the companies in this chapter, the net position will be positive, provided it is possible to build on existing successes. If we cannot, and the threats into competition increase, or by being reactive companies become takeover targets, the impacts could be reduced.

To finish on a positive note. An ever-increasing number of Scottish companies are 'taking on the world', the building blocks are in place for them to succeed/continue to succeed. Let us hope that when the question is reconsidered in 2020 the list of established Scottish companies is a very long one.

Notes

1 The figures used here are those of *Insider* magazine, and therefore do not contain the combined figures of the RBS and NatWest following their merger. Therefore, the actual figures for both turnover and profit are probably understated. For consistency of analysis across all companies in the 500 this figure has been used.
2 The figure of 47 per cent in 1991 was on the basis of the *Insider* 200 and therefore not directly comparable for the purposes of this analysis.

3   Based on an average of the proportion of overseas assets, sales and employ-
    ment to the total.
4   Reflected rather than included is the important word here because govern-
    ment intervention is focused on areas of market failure, and therefore some of
    the issues covered may only need a framework rather than direct support *per se*.

References

Aggreko plc (2001), 'Royal Bank now bigger than Ford and Boeing', Annual
    Report, *Business a.m.*, 18 May.
Fortune (2001), 'Fortune 500', *Fortune Magazine*, April.
Hood, N. and Peters, E. (2000), 'Globalization, Corporate Strategies and Business
    Services', in Hood, N. and Young, S. (eds), *The Globalization of Multinational
    Enterprise Activity and Economic Development*, London: Macmillan, p. 80.
Insider (2001), 'Insider 500', *Insider Magazine*, January.
McCall, W. (2001), 'Smart money and clean companies', Work (Research) for
    Scottish Enterprise, McCall Research (Unpublished).
OECD (1999), 'R&D, globalisation and governments', *OECD Observer*, December,
    Paris: OECD.
Scottish Enterprise (1999), *Global Companies Enquiry: research findings*, Glasgow:
    Scottish Enterprise.
Scottish Executive (2000), *Framework for Economic Development in Scotland*,
    Edinburgh: Scottish Executive.
Scottish Executive (2001a), *A Smart, Successful Scotland*, Edinburgh: Scottish
    Executive.
Scottish Executive (2001b), *A Global Connections Strategy*, Edinburgh: Scottish
    Executive.
Slow, J. (2001), *The routes to going global: a theoretical analysis*, Glasgow: Scottish
    Enterprise.
United Nations (2000), *World Investment Report 2000*, New York and Geneva:
    United Nations.
United Nations (2001), *World Investment Report 2001*, New York and Geneva:
    United Nations.
Weir Group (2001), 'Focussed global expansion, increased local support', Annual
    Report 2001.

14
The Growth and Development of New Firms

Neil Hood and Calum Paterson

Introduction and context

Viewed from the time of writing, if the Scottish economy faces one central economic development challenge, it lies in the area of accelerating the birth, growth and development rates of indigenous business. There are two basic reasons for this. For the past 30–40 years it has been highly dependent on the growth and development of inward investing companies. Factors such as heightened global competition for such investment, the role which different countries play in the manufacturing value chain and the relative competitiveness of the UK as a location for inward investment within Europe are among those factors which are already signalling a diminished role for inward investment in Scotland over the next decade or so. The desirable strategy of pursuing higher value inward investment with greater research design and development content further narrows the potential 'contestable' investment pool for Scotland. Thus taking a 2020 perspective, Scotland is likely to be much less dependent on inward investment by that time. This may be partially offset by an even more diverse ownership mix in the service industries by 2020, but whether this generates new firms in material numbers is another question.

The maxim that employment growth is not necessarily synonymous with business success applies to both foreign and indigenous business. It is an issue which points to the second reason for focusing more attention on the latter, namely the heightened search for 'high growth new businesses'. There is no simple or universally accepted definition as to what that means, since clearly turnover, employment or other accounting measures at specific points in time are limited, in that they fail to capture the characteristics of the firm which are likely to determine its medium to long-term success. Such characteristics include a high degree of innovation, the application of leading edge technology and practices, and the existence of actual or potential global competitiveness (DTZ Pieda, 1999). The search for growth companies is likely to accelerate dramatically in Scotland – from whatever source. This is reflected in the many approaches to the commercialisation of locally generated technology, in the expectations that universities will play an ever more central role in economic development by contributing spin-out companies on an increasing scale, the widespread efforts to foster entrepreneurial activity in all business contexts, and so on.

It should be recognised that Scotland is not alone in identifying these types of reasons for paying greater attention to indigenous business. This heightens the competitive challenge, but also requires us to think radically to achieve a 2020 vision of multiple sources of business creation and growth in the Scottish economy. The focus in this chapter is on what Scotland might need to do differently to achieve that. It is divided into four main parts. The first considers the business birth rate in Scotland; the second examines business growth; the third looks at technology, commercialisation and global companies; and the fourth section of the chapter reviews a number of cases of high-growth technology and other innovative companies which, as of 2002, exemplified one part of the innovation and growth agenda necessary for Scotland. The concluding section reviews some tentative policy alternatives leading up to 2020.

Business birth rate in Scotland

It has been recognised since the mid-1980s that Scotland has a problem of a low business birth rate. In 1992–1993, SE undertook an extensive enquiry to develop a deeper understanding of the problem. Among other things, this study quantified the under-performance relative to some other parts of the UK and highlighted the extent to which business births were critical to economic performance. For example, even with poor relative performance, the research showed that new starts accounted for some 125 000 jobs during the 1980s in Scotland, much more than alternative sources such as inward investment or the expansion of larger enterprises. This is consistent with other evidence showing that small businesses have accounted for a disproportionately high share of net new job creation in the UK from the 1970s – a product of the high rate of 'churn', whereby there is both a high rate of new venture formation and a high death rate. The 1992–1993 SE work also pointed to the existence of considerable interest in starting new businesses, but difficulties in converting this into action; to a perception of lack of finance; and to unduly negative cultural attitudes towards starting businesses. On the basis of these findings, Scottish Enterprise launched its *Business Birth Rate Strategy* (BBRS) in 1993 (Scottish Enterprise, 1993) with six priorities namely seeking to unlock the potential for setting up businesses (including more enterprise education); improving the environment for entrepreneurs; improving access to finance; widening the entrepreneurial base; increasing start-ups in key sectors (for example, manufacturing, high-technology and business services); and increasing the number of fast growing new starts. The strategy also contained an ambitious and, in the event, unrealistic target of raising the business birth rate in Scotland to that of the UK by the end of the 1990s. To achieve this the birth rate per head of population in Scotland would have had to increase by 3.5 times its historic growth rate.

Much credit goes to SE for initiating this enquiry, launching a policy initiative and raising the profile of this central economic development problem. The credit includes its extensive endeavours to secure broad support for addressing these issues as being central to both SE policy and that of Scotland as a whole. It failed in the latter regard and, in the following eight years (somewhat disappointingly), it was the grand target itself rather than the issue which was subject to most comment as it was progressively more evident that it was unattainable in the time scale (Scottish Enterprise, 1997, 2000; MacKay *et al.*, 2001).

Scottish Enterprise itself commissioned a thorough independent review of the BBRS (Fraser of Allander Institute, 2001) which serves as a useful point of departure for this chapter when looking ahead to 2020. To set this briefly in context, it is worth noting the general trends in Scottish relative birth rate performance in the 1990s:

- Measuring business density by the number of value added tax (VAT) registered businesses per 10 000 of the population, this improved in Scotland from 1981 to 1990, but has plateaued since then. The gap between Scotland and Great Britain (GB) as a whole has scarcely altered, but when London and the South East are excluded, it has considerably narrowed.

- Measuring birth rate by VAT registrations as a percentage of business stock, over the 1990s the Scottish rate was lower than the GB average, but that difference narrowed slightly in the 1990s. Within the GB regions only Merseyside and the North East had lower rates, with Yorkshire and Humberside broadly similar.
- Scotland has a low share of high growth or high performance businesses, largely as a consequence of its low business birth rate. In spite of the dramatic change in the 1990s in the numbers of high technology businesses emerging in Scotland, this deficit remains and it appears that areas such as South East England which produce the highest numbers of fast growing businesses also tend to have the highest rates of business start ups.

The Fraser of Allander (FAI) study is very useful in identifying the successes and failures of the BBRS and hence in establishing a base line for viewing 2020. Confirming the unrealistic target, it was noted that there had been a systematic but small underlying increase in the Scottish business birth rate, but that the BBRS strategy was only one of many factors influencing the number of new starts. The cyclical behaviour of the Scottish and UK economies was identified as having played a key role in influencing the Scottish/UK relative position on the VAT data. Moreover, many of the issues being addressed in this strategy were structural with much longer pay-off periods than anticipated. Among the favourable outcomes was the considerable improvement in the environment in Scotland for the promotion and sustenance of new firms in areas such as education, finance and the building of support networks. On the other hand it was evident that there was much still to be done in areas such as higher quality start-ups, business counselling, and the standardisation of multiple schemes of government related assistance. Perhaps above all, and with 2020 in mind, was the identified need to integrate public and private initiatives to make this a total strategy for Scotland. Looking forward, the Fraser study sets out issues to be addressed to put the new firm creation process at the heart of regional development (Best, 2000). These include placing emphasis on the creation of dynamic entrepreneurial firms, while leaving open to question whether there should be a continued emphasis on the promotion of high volume start-ups. The consequence of these observations and of the record on business start-ups will be further examined later in the chapter.

Business growth in Scotland

High growth businesses are key to developing a strong industrial base in Scotland. Before considering the specific topic of 'business growth', there are some other important issues to face. They surround the question as to whether 'growth' can be predicted. Clearly there is a presumption of growth potential from innovative activity in any business area, from a presence in a large and expanding market, or from the ownership of intellectual property which is in demand. It is tempting to correlate technology with growth from an economic development perspective, but this should be resisted. The more generic interest is in innovation, productivity and profitability enhancement in all types of business, whether this of itself creates rapid growth in revenues or employment. That said, the next section looks more narrowly at specific types of business development which are a vital part of the total mix of activity for both now and for 2020.

Scotland faces an additional challenge, namely that Scottish firms appear on some evidence to grow more slowly than in many comparable parts of the UK. In order to take a longer view of this, it is necessary to seek some explanations. Some recent data has emerged to shed further light on the underlying processes of job creation and distribution in Scottish firms[1] (Teasdale and Briggs, 2001). Using employment data, and remembering that this does not necessarily imply success, it shows that between 1995 and 1999 new firms accounted for some 40 per cent of all new jobs in Scotland. However, when analysed by firm size band, there was net job destruction during this period in every size band, except those with over 250 employees, this being consistent with their large share of the initial stock of employment, some 46 per cent in 1995. Overall between 1995 and 1999 over one-third of the panel of firms closed, and as at 1999, over 40 per cent of the employers in business had been formed in the preceding four years. The patterns of growth in Scottish firms, by other measures, was shown to be similar to that for all UK firms. There were two interesting exceptions. The large Scottish firms showed a net increase in employment while in the UK the figure was negative; and the net reduction of employment in the micro (1–9 employees) group was greater than in the UK overall. It was noted that the proportion of such firms achieving growth was the same, but Scottish ones grew by a smaller extent. This might be a function of market size, distance and market access for firms of this scale.

This latter point is powerfully emphasised in a parallel comparative study for Scotland and five counties in the South East of England (Trends Business Research, 2001). While the group of five South East counties is 70 per cent larger than Scotland in terms of employment, the growth of employment in the 1995–1999 period was 290 per cent larger. Whereas in the five counties there was a substantial contribution made by expanding firms, the largest single contribution to net change in Scotland was firm deaths. Moreover the Scottish economy was shown to be much more heavily dependent on sole traders and partnerships, rather than companies. 'Independent Scottish companies' plus Scottish controlled companies combined to account for over 50 per cent of employment in both years, thus highlighting the vital importance of local entrepreneurs. This is underlined by the fact that over this period, whereas the UK-owned companies showed a net decrease in employment in Scotland, this group accounted for a large proportion of expansions in the South East. This type of evidence continues to point to the substantial need to stimulate business growth within Scotland from all sources, but not least from the indigenous base.

The news in this area is not all bad however. The SE *Global Companies Enquiry* (1999) produced some useful evidence on high-growth companies.[2] The South East was chosen as a top performing region in this regard and the West Midlands as a proxy for the average. Scotland did well relative to the West Midlands in terms of number of companies per million of population and they grew faster, but both areas lagged the South East. Other data quoted in this report used different criteria and compared Scotland more widely across the UK.[3] It showed that Scotland was the third best area for growth companies in the UK over this period, after Greater London and the South East. Taking another measure related to business growth, according to British Venture Capital Association (BVCA) data, more Scottish firms received venture capital funding in the late 1990s than in any other UK region outwith the South East.

Technology, commercialisation and global companies

In the past decade in Scotland there has been a growing economic development policy focus on those three specific, and related, groups of new and developing businesses – a policy which has been assisted by broader UK government policy. Technology and commercialisation are related, though the latter are often linked to the realisation of gains from University and other R&D centres within existing companies.

Companies capable of emerging as global businesses, whether or not they have a specific technology bias, are a critical contributor to the extension of the stock of local headquarters, the provision of role models for Scottish entrepreneurship, extending the range and scope of indigenous Scottish businesses, and so on.

New technology-based firms (NTBFs), as they are often styled, can be regarded as a distinctive grouping within the overall subject of this chapter. In this case it can be argued that Scotland has made better progress than much of the rest of UK over the past decade, especially with regard to funding such enterprises. There is extensive UK literature on this topic. Among other things, it highlights how durable the funding problems are after decades of initiatives (Oakey and Mukhtar, 1999); the continued tendency to ignore 'early stage' investments in NTBFs (Bank of England, 2001); the financial barriers to exploiting innovations (House of Lords, 1997); and the alleged existence of bias against high technology in venture capital houses (Murray and Lott, 1995). However, the latter has changed dramatically. From 1996 to 2000, the number of technology companies receiving venture capital in the UK increased from 212 to 772 (20–65 per cent of total), £453 million to £1651 million (16–26 per cent according to BVCA data). By 2002 it was, however, evident that these figures reflected the peak of the cycle.

The stimulation of NTBFs has received considerable public and private sector attention in Scotland for the past decade. As regards the public sector, this has largely been justified in terms of different forms of market failure, including access to finance, the absence of sufficiently active clusters to stimulate such ventures in numbers, the specific and specialist needs of these emerging businesses and the potential for higher returns from public investment. Specifically on the early stage venture finance side there has been a large range of initiatives from both public and private sources. Among the former was the emergence of Scottish Development Finance (then part of SE) from the early 1990s as a manager of joint public and private funds for early stage technology ventures (Hood, 2000). This became a private company in 2000 as Scottish Equity Partners Ltd (SEP) and, established as such, raised a substantial new equity fund of £110 million, to continue this activity. 3i and several other institutions, together with a number of strong business angel groups, were also very active in this area in Scotland. The evidence from bodies such as BVCA has confirmed how well established is the Scottish financial infrastructure for NTBFs. Indeed 11 per cent of companies receiving venture capital in 2000 were in Scotland according to BVCA.

In the past decade SEP and 3i have been dominant supporters of early stage technology companies in Scotland, many still at the proof of technology and/or proof of market stages. They were joined by over 25 others in the period since 1998, many of these players doing single deals, but all reacting to the potential in the Scottish market. The focus has been on software, electronics, opto-electronics and life sciences, all in technically innovative companies. A further critical development of the 1990s in Scotland was the emergence of around 20 business angel groups (including Braveheart, Archangels, Virtual Realisation Networks and Hamilton Portfolio), not all of whom have, however, been active in this area. It is interesting to note that these and many of the high net worth individuals who both invest in these groups collectively and separately have supported NTBFs – although much of the money being reinvested has come from substantial fortunes made in applying innovative business models to traditional sectors such as retailing, transport, property and leisure. It is difficult to place a scale on this invest-ment, but in 2000 it was probably in the range £30–£50 million in Scotland (Don, 2001). Whether it will survive cyclical downturns such as those experienced from 2001 is another question, and there remains challenges at the lower end of the financing market where the economics and risk profile associated with seed capital provision continue to be challenging.

The final ingredient of support for NTBFs in Scotland lies in the wide range of nurturing and networking structures, many of which were stimulated by the business birth rate initiative by SE. These include early stage government funds in schemes such as SMART Awards, Support for Products under Research (SPUR), Innovation grants within the SE network and so on, the impact of which has been substantial. In addition, networking operations such as LINC Scotland, Connect, Entrepreneurial Exchange, Technology Ventures, and a variety of local enterprise company schemes have all played some part in adding to the milieux which fosters NTBFs in Scotland. There is some overlap in these activities and it is not clear whether all have had substantial impact, but overall they have probably had a positive role. Summarising the above, it is reasonable to conclude that Scotland is materially better served in 2002 than it was ten years previously and in better shape to build towards 2020 by promoting innovative, technology based businesses.

A critical dimension of the growth and development of new firms in Scotland and elsewhere lies in the more effective commercialisation of the country's science and technology base. That this was at the heart of developing a truly knowledge-based economy was recognised in the comprehensive study of this area by SE and the Royal Society of Edinburgh (RSE) (1996). This type of exercise was helpful in benchmarking the Scottish relative position, and in diagnosing a number of the problems of process, finance, corporate behaviour, and so on. While some progress can be identified, it has been relatively slow, not least because of the complexities inherent in moving it forward at a more rapid pace and the many factors involved in this ten-year programme. No single infrastructure of policy initiative could be expected to address all of the issues, but the challenge looking towards 2020 is whether Scotland is now set on a course which would sustain a marked scaling up of this activity. Progress has been made, not least stimulated by the reductions in public funding to universities and their need to exploit internal resources via further commercialisation. However, there is often a tension between the use of licensing technology to maximise revenues and minimise risk, and the need to incentivise spin-out companies, which may gave a greater economic development return. Among the early twenty-first century, innovations have been the introduction of 'proof of concept' funds to aid early stage development, the further support of commercialisation posts in universities, Royal Society of Edinburgh/SE fellowships, the examination of technology institutes operating on a commerce basis alongside universities, and so on.

Among other things, the SE *Global Company Enquiry* (1999) highlighted the economic importance of indigenous global companies[4] to the welfare of the Scottish economy and reviewed the many barriers and enablers to increasing the numbers of such businesses, including the prerequisite of high growth and high potential. While this type of initiative is welcome, its benefit perhaps lies most in attempting to set an agenda and assist in benchmarking aspirations for Scottish firms. As of 2002, companies in this category are a relatively rare breed. While government and its agencies can provide support, this is at the margin and for relatively few individual companies. Yet again the challenge lies more with management than it does with government.

Case studies

In order to provide some illustrations of the types of companies which Scotland requires in greater numbers and quality, this section is included. The five examples are NTBFs, but this is not to imply that innovation could not come from many other sources and in many other forms. Indeed there is a strong case for a diverse range of growth businesses. The evidence of the past two decades in Scotland shows that innovative and strongly differentiated companies with high growth have come from such diverse sectors as engineering (Wood Group), automotive repairs (Kwik-Fit), transport (Stagecoach and FirstBus), utilities (ScottishPower and Scottish & Southern Energy), financial services (Royal Bank of Scotland, Bank of Scotland, and Standard Life), and so on.

Throughout the 1990s, Scotland's reputation for producing innovative NTBFs, often exploiting scientific research undertaken within its universities, increased steadily. This was particularly evident in sectors such as software, communications, microelectronics, healthcare and biotechnology. Despite much promise, however, no Scottish technology start-up has so far gone on to achieve the level of growth on a global scale that is necessary to secure a winning market position. In that sense, it compares poorly with the likes of Finland (for example, Nokia) and Sweden (Erikson). The reasons for this are multifaceted and complex. It is, of course, difficult to grow from a technology start-up to a global business; the odds against doing so are massive, even when the technology involved is strongly differentiated. Success requires not just a strong competitive technology offering, but also a powerful commercial development strategy, executed by high calibre management. Nor is a public listing on the stock market a necessary route to stable development as events of 2000–2002 showed. Indeed many of the technology based Scottish companies have not performed well after a public listing over the past 10–15 years. Typically, the most successful Scottish NTBFs have been sold to larger corporate entities. This is almost certainly less to do with an inability to access growth finance or lack of ambition, two often cited reasons, than it has to do with the recognition that it is often the most logical course of action in industries that are dominated by multinationals with substantial marketing strength. This is not necessarily bad for the economy – entrepreneurship is closely related to wealth creation and often 'selling out' is the most realistic way to maximise value. Ultimately, however, an economic development policy objective is to have some NTBFs to grow into global companies which have strong roots in Scotland. In that sense, the task remains a volume one in that the more NTBFs that are formed, the more likely it is that some of them will evolve into larger enterprises led from a Scottish base.

The five examples provided here set out the profile of the businesses as of early 2002. They have several common factors, including their recent formations, innovative technological base, and the need to

Case study 14.1

Indigo Vision

Founded in 1994 by a young Scottish entrepreneur, Oliver Vellacott, Indigo Vision has developed leading technology to enable full motion real time video to be transmitted almost instantaneously worldwide, with digital quality and security, using the Internet, wireless links or local area networks. The technology allows manufacturers to develop their own visual communications products and performs all the functions between the device that acquires the input (for example, a network camera) and the network over which the video is transmitted. The market for video over intellectual property (IP) is significant and estimated to grow exponentially over the next five years in applications such as security, traffic services, environmental monitoring and entertainment. The company's product has been used for networked video cameras, traffic speed enforcement cameras and CCTV security systems. Like many NTBFs, the company designs, develops and markets, but does not actually manufacture products. It is seeking to gain market share by licensing its technology to manufacturers in various market segments, and designing and manufacturing its own products within specific sectors.

Having received substantial venture capital backing from Scottish-based investors, the company was floated on the London Stock Exchange in August 2000, raising approximately £35 million to fund future growth, most of which is being targeted at product development and marketing. Indigo Vision continues to be headed by Vellacott, but its management team has been augmented by high calibre individuals as the company has gone through its various phases of growth. The company's strategy is for its technology to become the industry standard for Video over IP between electronics products. Key to that will be its continued success in forming strategic relationships with leading global manufacturers.

---

extend that technology with a range of international customers at a very early and imminent stage in the company's life. All of these factors, together with the challenge of pulling together a suitably experienced

Case study 14.2

Kymata

Livingston-based Kymata was founded in 1998, accessing opto-electronics technology from the Universities of Glasgow and Southampton. Within two years of formation it had raised $160 million from private equity investors. The scale of this investment, unthinkable several years ago, is demonstrative of the substantial funding required to commercialise technology within the opto-electronics sector, as well as the remarkable enthusiasm for pioneering optical component companies, however early stage they may be. Kymata had been developing advanced silicon-based optical integrated circuitry for use in fibre-optic-based telecommunications systems within a market that is projected to grow exponentially. Within two years of its formation, employment had grown to 500, and the company had established offices in five other locations worldwide. Kymata secured more venture capital backing than any other technology company had previously done in Scotland at that time, and as the stakes increased, the company's backers were increasingly proactive in areas such as the strengthening of its core management team.

It was initially believed that Kymata would look to the public markets for additional access to capital and to achieve an exit for its early backers. However, by the second-half of 2000, there was growing concern that the previously predicted high-growth rates for optic components would be slower to take off than anticipated due to the delay in third generation (3G) licences and other technologies which have still to manifest themselves in the take up of large amounts of bandwidth capacity. This affected component companies such as Kymata. With a stock market flotation less likely, the company instead pursued a strategic partner and in July 2001 announced that it was merging with the US telecoms company Alcatel in a deal valued at less than the investment the company had raised.

management team, heighten the risks of these formative years. Evaluating such risks and the offsetting of opportunities is the essence of the contribution of venture capital in this part of the SME market. It is impossible to say where such companies will be in 2020, but the balance of probability will be as parts of larger international entities provided their technological and market assumptions are proven, and the way prepared for effective commercialisation. With good fortune, the headquarters of this division will be in Scotland, but the odds are against this.

Case study 14.3

TeraHertz Photonics

TeraHertz, based in Livingston, is another company within Scotland's growing opto-electronics sector. A spin-out from Heriot Watt University in 2000, it provides hybrid photonic integrated circuits combining active and passive components. Its key product areas are in optical polymer and sol gel glass; and SQAs which it is developing for use in switch arrays and tuneable filters. Having expertise and IPR across three different technology tracks is believed to be a major advantage in both a competitive and a risk sense.

The company's founders were academics at Heriot Watt, and recognised experts in their field. They were joined at the start-up stage by Ian Muirhead, a former senior executive of Motorola, who became Chief Executive and responsible for its commercial development. In early 2001 the company appointed Pearse Flynne, formerly president of the carrier networking group at Alcatel, the telecoms equipment corporation, as its non-executive chairman.

The company secured venture capital backing which it used to further develop its technology and to establish pilot production facilities. It does not intend to manufacture its own products, but rather to subcontract manufacturing and, where appropriate, to licence out its technology to manufacturers.

Case study 14.4

Quadstone

Founded in 1995 as a management buyout from Edinburgh Parallel Computing Centre (EPCC), a self-funded commercial department of the University of Edinburgh, Quadstone provides advanced customer behaviour modelling software solutions for its clients. The company is now recognised as a leading player in the customer relationship management (CRM) market. Still headquartered in Edinburgh, Quadstone has offices in both London and Boston, USA. From the outset, Quadstone's software was designed to take advantage of parallelism from earlier research at EPCC; it is therefore able to handle data on millions of customers and enables business users to access this through a highly visual interface. For example, its Decisionhouse can be used to interactively analyse a dataset with over 20 million customers and can be deployed against databases with over 100 million customers and billions of transactions.

By late 2000, the company had installations of Decisionhouse worldwide and an impressive base of customers in across-financial services, telecommunications and retail. The thrust of its commercial strategy has been to promote, develop and expand its technology leadership; expand sales and distribution capabilities through partnerships and aggressive marketing; and leverage and expand the strategic relationships it has formed. The company has attracted much attention among leading venture capital firms, and by late 2000 had raised more than £30 million to support its growth. A sharp downturn in software spending in the first half of 2001 was reported to have affected Quadstone as it announced a substantial cut back in its headcount, but the company's ambition continues to be to achieve global dominance in its sector.

Case study 14.5

Provis

In the early 1990s the Scottish entrepreneur, Ron Hamilton, established a contact lens company Award, having developed and patented an innovative process for lens production with co-founder Bill Seden. The process enabled lenses to be produced at a sufficiently low cost to enable them to be used on a daily wear basis. Having invested substantial personal resources and relocated the business from Southampton to Livingston, he raised substantial external finance in 1993. Product sales commenced a year later, and the company rapidly became the largest volume manufacturer of soft contact lenses in Europe. In 1995, Hamilton sold his business to US eye care company, Bausch & Lomb, for more than £20 million. Employment, which at that time had reached more than 200, subsequently increased to more than 1000 people, as production escalated to meet global demand for the product. The factory in Livingston remains an important manufacturing unit for Bausch & Lomb. Hamilton's involvement with the business ceased after a period of consultancy for the US parent.

Despite considerable commercial and financial success, Hamilton's entrepreneurial ambition was not completely fulfilled and, after a break of several years, he embarked on a second venture to exploit improved technology for soft contact lens production. Provis, based in Hamilton, has developed what is believed to be the highest specification daily wear lens on the market, and Hamilton's ambition appears to be to build the business into a major independent manufacturer for the global marketplace. He thus provides a good example of an entrepreneur continuing to develop another innovative business within the same sector.

Policy alternatives

To this point this chapter has explored many of the important issues surrounding the growth and development of new firms in Scotland. It has done so, on the firm assumption that while this is an area where government and its agencies can contribute in some important ways, the performance of Scotland is highly dependent upon the activities of individuals, entrepreneurs and managers, and on others in the private sector, including venture capital investors and company advisers. Moreover, there are some critical macro features of Scotland which are very material to this subject. Among these is Scotland's declining share of UK GDP and hence a lesser relative local market potential than 10 or 20 years ago; and the static nature of Scottish population and the loss of skills and talents through migration. In addition, Scotland's relative performance in both business birth and growth rates are affected by economic cycles, and not always responsive to micro-level programmes.

With all of this firmly in mind, and attempting to extend thinking over the period to 2020, Figure 14.1 attempts to view three-linked scenarios concerning the growth and development of new firms in Scotland. It accepts that 'policy' may be developed by government and agendas established, but the weight of implementation is with managers.[5] In the three stages each have illustrative scenarios, but they are all linked. They are not meant to be definitive and are designed to stimulate debate. They do, however, raise questions about the vision behind policy, the latent capabilities within the economy, and so on:

1 *Status Quo (SQ)*: This assumes that the progress in the 1990s has been on broadly the correct lines; that many of the central 1990s targets are still valid; but that this subject requires ever closer attention if this sector is going to make an enhanced contribution to the economy by 2010.
2 *Step Function (SF)*: This illustrates the challenges of 'scaling up' on a number of key indicators, in this case the growth in the numbers of science and technology based businesses. It assumes that the enhanced SQ makes this possible over a number of years and that Scotland has under-exploited assets in this area. By its very nature a step function requires radical and systemic change, as illustrated in Figure 14.1. There are substantial measurement problems on all fronts, not least in determining the base line for such an approach.
3 *Star Rating (SR)*: There could be elements of this already in existence on the supply side. For example, Scotland is probably already in a unique position within the UK and some parts of Europe, measured in terms of

a financial support structure for emerging high-technology businesses. The SR concept here implies that by 2010/2020 there will be several dimensions of 'excellence' evident in how new firms are grown and developed in Scotland, and that the net impact will be such as to be a model to be emulated. Again the seeds of these will be sown in the SQ and SF stages, and some may already have been sown. Expressed another way, the SR concept implies that Scotland will be at least as effective in the growth and development of new firms by 2010/2020 as it was in attracting inward investment in the 1980s and 1990s. To be effective this implies a substantial increase in the numbers of 'winners' (from whatever sector), where global success is evident and high class entrepreneurial managements are running these businesses. In some senses, all of these three scenarios are stretching. In reality, however, the SQ should not be regarded as a serious option because, without major effort, the gains of the recent past could readily be lost.

Conclusions

While much has changed over the past two decades and the policy focus on fostering entrepreneurship and the growth and development of new firms in Scotland is well established, there is much more to be done. This topic is not yet at the top of the mind of every part of the relevant Scottish infrastructure, and it has to be, to achieve the ambitions implied in the scenarios set out in Figure 14.1. Progress is being recorded with some of the systemic problems, such as developing a culture of entrepreneurship in schools and universities;[6] the commercialisation of academic research; and the training and retraining of business advisers; the growth in the mentoring process, and so on. But, critical to the 2020 vision is the greater alignment of individual aspirations towards establishing and growing businesses; the retention of cadres with appropriate skills within Scotland; and the widespread ambitions of existing businesses to more rapidly grow. Such combinations of events cannot be mandated, but they can be led, the infrastructure to support them enhanced, and the opportunities highlighted, not least by the existence of more successful role models.

A condition precedent for almost all of the required changes to achieve the goals discussed above is that of private sector engagement over the long term. To achieve this is challenging, but not impossible. As Scotland's larger companies become ever more international and the climate remains one of maximising shareholder value, their local focus could diminish even further. Yet it is evident that a successful and dynamic Scottish economy is vital to maintaining and enhancing the

	2002 Status Quo (SQ)	(Illustrative) 2010 Step Function (SF)	(Illustrative) 2010/20 Star Rating (SR)
Objective	To build on the directions of change in the 1990s, in terms of both business birth rate and growth; and in the stimulation of entrepreneurship	To seek changes in selected output measures by a factor of 5 or 10 in 2000, depending on the chosen platform[1]	To achieve a total national focus on the growth and development of new firms and see Scotland emerge as unique in Europe in selected dimensions[2]
Targets	(a) Offset decline in relative contribution from FDI in employment and productivity	(a) Multiple of 10 by numbers on commercialisation projects – ex Universities and other R&D sources	(a) Distinctive clusters of high-technology business, ranked in top quartile of EU locations
	(b) Eliminate BBR deficit versus UK by 2010	(b) Multiple of 5 on all other innovative company start-ups by number	(b) Distinctive support infrastructure in private sector to support SMEs
	(c) Scottish firms growth deficit versus UK removed by 2010	(c) Achieve up to 5 major Scottish technology based winners on European/world scale	(c) One of top UK locations for commercialisation, with lead institutions of world class
			(d) A higher number of 'winners' measured by global success and excellent management teams
Assumptions	Private sector leaderships: selected public sector funding: progress along this path and at 1990s pace is sufficient	Focus on private sector leadership: more selective government support but at factor of 5–10 levels of 2001: that demand and supply are in balance	Unique private/public sign on to this vision: recognise that other countries/regions will have similar aspirations to differentiate their locations, and for similar reasons

Activities	(a) Encourage Scottish business to penetrate the UK market as a whole	(a) Very substantial increase in SME management training, especially for technology companies	(a) Many as in the SQ and SF stages
	(b) Continue government funding of innovation, commercialisation and small firms advice, the latter largely by e-commerce	(b) Major programmes of recruitment of innovative entrepreneurs and retention of key skill base	(b) May require even more aggressive programme to attract and retain immigrant entrepreneurs
	(c) Accelerate entrepreneurship training at all levels	(c) Government and private sector 'innovation' funding up by factors of 10 – for product development, technology transfer	(c) Might require major elements of SE (or equivalent) budget directed towards entrepreneurship, growth and development of firms
	(d) Continued innovation on financing new, innovative businesses and so on	(d) Progress towards radical change in the output measures of universities to have a much stronger local economic development remit. This implies some redirection of government block grants.	(c) Might require major elements of SE (or equivalent) budget directed towards entrepreneurship, growth and development of firms
	(e) Experimentation with different forms of institutions to develop commercialisation	(e) Further major private sector drive for Scottish businesses to exploit their whole (UK) home market.	(d) Possibly would require greater focus of commercialisation around 'lead technology' universities, on US private University model.
	(f) Maximise integration of local SMEs into 'clusters' as they develop		
Commentary This implies a continuous building on the present foundations, with some radical thinking. Progress in this stage set the direction for a potential SF change en route to 2010		Scottish business as a whole have to 'own' this strategy. The selected SF above assumes that Scotland still has substantially under-exploited assets in this area. The targets are aggressive but require to be in order to have a material impact. the seeds of SR stage would have to be sown by this stage.	In the SR stakes, Scotland would be an exemplar as, for example, Israel, parts of US, and so on, are regarded in 2001/02.

No:es:
1 The platform would have to be determined by policy. For illustration it has been shown here as focused on growing science and technology based businesses. It must be recognised that there are serious problems about defining the metrics to measure the 2001 base line.
2 The areas of potential for 'uniqueness' would have to be set in the SQ phase, given the 10–15 year gestation period of similar types of initiative e sewhere.

Figure 14.1 Growth and development of new firms in Scotland: alternative policy scenarios leading to 2020.

character of the 'home base' for all such businesses, even though a relatively small proportion of their revenues and profits comes from within Scotland. Scotland's attractiveness for corporate headquarters is an important element of growing and developing businesses. But beyond that, it requires business in its many individual and institutional forms to align with this developing strategy. The vast preponderance of finance, advice and mentoring comes from (and will continue to come from) the private sector; with government continuing to play its part. In conclusion, we pose the question 'Is there another more central and more generic issue in economic development in Scotland?' and conclude that there is not, nor is there likely to be over the period to 2020.

Notes

1   This data refers to employment in Scottish firms (that is, those with a head office in Scotland), not to employment in Scotland. Many of the people employed by Scottish firms are elsewhere in the UK. The number employed by Scottish firms at the time of this survey was equal to about 60 per cent of employment in Scotland. (This study is based on TRENDS Business Research for the Department of Trade and Industry.)
2   Defined for this purpose as independent within Scotland with a turnover of at least £5 million and which increased its turnover by at least 210 per cent (approximately 10 per cent per annum) between 1985 and 1997.
3   This Deloitte and Touche data considered firms with a 30 per cent growth over a four-year period.
4   Defined as a company, strategically directed from Scotland and above a minimum size threshold for its sector, which conducts a substantial proportion of its business across international boundaries (through direct exports and licensing or franchising or locating operations or subsidiaries overseas) and which, possessing a relatively large and/or growing market share, has maintained a strong competitive position over a sustained period in responding quickly and efficiently to changing global market conditions (SE, 1999, pp. 10–11). A series of specific criteria were attached to this definition (see Figure 2.2, p. 11) to assess the extent to which they were global.
5   This is well illustrated in the fact that there are some 300 000 businesses in Scotland. In 2001, SE estimated that they were involved with some 15 000 existing businesses and around 7000 start-ups – namely some 7 per cent of the total.
6   In 2000/2001, it was estimated that over 30 000 school children in Scotland had some teaching about entrepreneurship, as had some 3000 university students.

References

Bank of England (2001), The financing of technology-based small firms, London: Bank of England, February.
Best, M. (2000), 'The capabilities and innovation perspectives', Research Monograph No. 8, Belfast: Northern Ireland Economic Council.

Don, G. (2001), Investment in Scottish Young Companies – Sources, Amounts, Methods 2000, Report for Scottish Enterprise, March.

DTZ Peida Consulting (1999), 'Evaluating high growth new ventures: main report', Report for Scottish Enterprise, July.

Fraser of Allander Institute for Research and the Scottish Economy (2001), 'Promoting business start-ups: A new strategic formula', Report for Scottish Enterprise.

Hood, N. (2000), 'The development of public venture capital in Scotland', *Venture Capital*, Vol. 2, No. 4, pp. 313–341.

House of Lords (1997), Select Committee on Science and Technology, The innovation exploitation barrier, House of Lords Paper 62.

MacKay, D. *et al.* (2001), 'Scotland's enterprise deficit', Edinburgh: Policy Institute.

Murray, G. and J. Lolt (1995), 'Have venture capital firms a bias against investment in high technology companies?', *Research Policy*, 24, 1, pp. 283–299.

Oakey, R.P. and S-M. Mukhtar (1999), 'United Kingdom high technology firms in theory and practice: a review of recent trends', *International Journal of Small Business*, Vol. 17, No. 2, pp. 48–64.

Scottish Enterprise (1993), *Improving Scotland's Business Birth Rate: A Strategy for Scotland*, Glasgow: Scottish Enterprise.

Scottish Enterprise and the Royal Society of Edinburgh (1996), Commercialisation Enquiry, Final Research Report, Glasgow: Scottish Enterprise.

Scottish Enterprise (1997), *Update: the Business Birth Rate Strategy: Five Years on*, Glasgow: Scottish Enterprise.

Scottish Enterprise (1999), *Global Companies Enquiry*, Research Findings, Glasgow: Scottish Enterprise.

Scottish Enterprise (2000), *Improving the Business Birth Rate: A Strategy for Scotland*, Discussion Paper, Glasgow: Scottish Enterprise.

Teasdale, P. and J. Briggs (2001), 'Job creation and job destruction in Scottish firms', *Scottish Economic Report*, June, pp. 96–103.

Trends Business Research (2001), *Components of Change in Scotland and the 5 Counties, 1995–99*, London: Trends Business Research.

Part IV

Policy Issues for the Scottish Economy

15

Globalisation and the Knowledge Economy

Stephen Young and Ross Brown

Introduction and context

This chapter examines the policy implications for Scotland emerging from new features of the world economic system, specifically globalisation and the knowledge economy. While globalisation is a multifaceted and ill-defined concept, it is used here to refer to:

> ... the growing interdependencies of countries worldwide through the increasing volume and variety of cross-border transactions of goods and services, and of international capital flows; and also through the rapid and widespread diffusion of ... technology.
>
> (IMF, 1997)

The related notion of the knowledge economy concerns the increasing significance of knowledge in company value and wealth creation, represented by the importance of intangible created assets (knowhow and information of all kinds) embodied in people, organisations or physical assets. Although the distinction between 'old' and 'new' economies is not useful, there is clear evidence of a progressive move away from physical and financial capital to intellectual capital in the value of corporations (Dunning, 2000). For the nation-state, this requires a fundamental shift from the 'national, monocultural' industrial age to the 'global, virtual, multicultural' digital age (Tapscott and Agnew, 1999).

The extensive literature on these subjects suggests five central paradigms which form the basis for the analysis in this chapter and their application to Scotland:

1 Liberalisation of internal and cross-border markets for goods and services, capital and knowhow.

2 Knowledge (principally in the form of human capital) as a key driver of wealth creation.
3 Alliances, networks and connections domestically and internationally as sources of knowledge and competitive advantage.
4 E-connectivity as a mechanism to facilitate integration of internal and cross-border markets and to overcome barriers to alliance and network formation.
5 Regional innovation and agglomeration drivers encouraging localisation, alongside the centralising forces of the global, knowledge economy.

Considering the first paradigm, while the liberalisation of markets in the last 50 years is indisputable, the future course of liberalisation is much less certain. Although the technological drivers of globalisation may be irreversible, the policy drivers may not be, witness the active anti-capitalism movement. The threat of protectionism will become stronger if recession deepens around the world, exacerbated by rising global insecurity. Regarding paradigm 2, the central importance of tacit knowledge is related in part to the international mobility of human capital, with relaxed visa controls in a number of developed countries being used to offset serious labour shortages, especially in IT intensive sector. Terms such as 'alliance capitalism' and 'relational capitalism' (Dunning, 1997; Cooke and Morgan, 1998) have been used to characterise the growth in the current era of domestic and international networks and alliances of value-adding activities (paradigm 3). Participants may include firms (as producers, suppliers, customers and competitors), governments, universities and other organisations and interest groups; and networks may operate domestically and internationally, physically and virtually.

A major facilitating factor in this process is e-connectivity (paradigm 4), which has potentially profound impacts on all aspects of the value-adding process. The latter include strategy and structure, technology development (global technology scanning, control of global R&D); procurement and supply chains (efficient and responsive supply chains and webs; in- and out-sourcing decisions; online exchanges; and, particularly relevant to Scotland, the potential marginalisation of small, national suppliers); manufacturing (production centralisation and relocation; global benchmarking); and marketing (new business models; interactive relationships with end-users through customer relationship management tools). Alongside these are the more obvious benefits associated with improved access to information and knowledge. The growth of e-business and e-connectivity is closely linked to other paradigms:

Thus knowledge is the key asset in the digital era; while transparency and openness in respect of trading, sharing and enhancing knowledge across networks are important in facilitating markets.

The final paradigm, which is also linked to e-connectivity, concerns the globalisation versus localisation debate and the notion of 'sticky places in slippery space' (Markusen, 1996). Globalisation is associated *inter alia* with production centralisation and relocation and reduced association with 'place'. Conversely, however, the regional clustering of innovative firms in related industries or technologies may encourage localisation and spatial immobility. More recently, however, there has been an upsurge of debate about the impact that the new ICT will have on regional development. Some commentators have predicted the 'end of geography' (Cairncross, 1997).

There are, however, real questions about whether new technologies will really fundamentally alter the centripetal and centrifugal forces of industrial and commercial life. There are numerous regional illustrations of forces of agglomeration working to develop and strengthen geographic clusters, but most are located in advanced industrial countries. Empirical studies of smaller peripheral industrial clusters highlight limited agglomeration tendencies and a continuing strong role for large, but weakly embedded MNEs (see, for example, Amin and Thrift, 1992; Brown, 2000).

Scotland's performance in the global knowledge economy

The paradigms set out above will have ubiquitous effects on Scotland (as on most other countries indeed) by 2020. To make the chapter manageable, however, the focus is primarily on the international business-related dimensions, specifically trade, FDI and knowledge. Figure 15.1 presents the core paradigms (liberalisation, alliances and networks, e-connectivity, and human capital) as facilitating forces which impact upon global patterns of business activity and the Scottish economy. Table 15.1 summarises these impacts upon Scotland in the form of a scorecard, showing clearly the challenges which face the country if it is to be a world player in this new era. Although the issue of localisation (implemented through, for example, cluster-based strategies) is critical to the overall performance of the Scottish economy, influencing corporate embeddedness, innovation and productivity gain, the topic is dealt with elsewhere in this volume.

An evaluation of Scotland's performance in the global knowledge economy is hampered by data deficiencies, especially in respect of intangibles – knowledge flows, alliances and networks, even services.

Figure 15.1 Scotland and the global knowledge economy.

Nevertheless, some important messages can be drawn from the partial information available.

Scotland's international trade

International trade has long been critical to Scotland's economic prosperity, and conventional wisdom (which perhaps needs to be queried in the light of protectionist tendencies in some traditional industries) is that Scotland is one of the most open trading countries in the world. Scotland continues to outperform the UK in manufacturing exports: the Scottish share in 1999 rose to 12.4 per cent – the highest share ever recorded and considerably higher than its share of manufacturing employment. More importantly, however, Scotland's manufactured exports were static over the three years to 1999 (Figure 15.2), and are likely to have continued to stagnate into the early 2000s.

Table 15.1 Scorecard for Scotland in the global knowledge economy

Interaction with global knowledge economy	Characteristics of global knowledge economy			
	Liberalisation	Alliance and networks	E-connectivity	Human capital
Trade: Exports	• Poor current performance outwith electronics (W) • Liberalisation of markets and trade growth (O) • Value-added services (O) • International brands exploiting Scottish image (O)	• Limited international networks and alliances (W)	• Unexploited potential (including new tradable products and services) (W/O)	• Outward-looking vision and mentality (W) • Language capabilities (W) • Pool of internationally experienced managers (W) • Utilisation of international graduates (W)
Imports	• Local producers no longer have protected home market (T) • Traditional manufacturing sectors still protected (W)		• Potential for foreign producers (T)	
Foreign Direct Investment: Inward	• Competition for FDI in mature/labour intensive sectors (goods and services); commoditisation (W/T) • Increased global flows (O)	• Poor internal networks in Scotland (W)	• Increased competitive pressure on local suppliers (W)	• In/out movements of people, building expertise and culture change (S)

Table 15.1 (Continued)

Interaction with global knowledge economy	Characteristics of global knowledge economy			
	Liberalisation	Alliance and networks	E-connectivity	Human capital
	• Exploiting true core competencies in FDI attraction (O)	• Few alliances (W) • Poor supplier linkages (W)	• Global benchmarking (O/T) • Intra-corporate project bidding (O/T)	
Outward/globalization	• Greater opportunities for Scottish companies (large and small) with world-class competencies, products/services (O) • Few Scottish multi-national/global companies (W) • Outsourcing and supply chain management potential (O)	• Poor internal and external networks (W) • Few alliances (W)	• Potential throughout value chain, but weak at present (W/O)	• Outward-looking vision and mentality (W) • Pool of internationally experienced managers (W)
Knowledge: In	• Technology transfer and diffusion (W)	• International academic/research partnerships (W/O)	• E-infrastructure and lack of broadband capabilities (W) • Technology transfer and diffusion (W) • R&D by foreign and domestic enterprises (W/O)	• In-migration (W) • Scots abroad (O)
Out	-	• International academic/research partnerships (W/O)	• Access to world-wide pool of knowledge (O)	• Out-migration (W)

Note: S = strength; W = weakness; O = opportunity; T = threat.

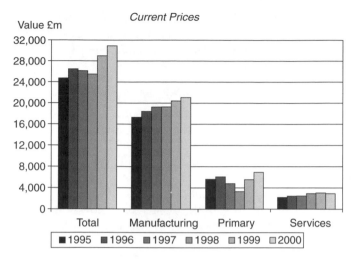

Figure 15.2 Scottish export performance, (1995–2000).
Source: Scottish Council for Development and Industry, 2001.

The sectoral composition of Scotland's exports is heavily skewed, with the electronics industry accounting for over 50 per cent of Scotland's manufactured exports (Peat and Boyle, 1999). This reflects the structure of the Scottish economy and the influence of export-oriented electronics inward investors. Indeed, non-UK owned companies now produce over 70 per cent of all Scottish manufactured exports (Scottish Executive, 2000). The export market is also dominated by large companies, with ten Scottish exporters accounting for some 50 per cent of total Scottish manufactured export sales; US-owned IBM itself represents approximately 10 per cent of all manufactured exports.

The other major export-intensive manufacturing sectors (oil and gas, chemicals, as well as whisky) are typically growing relatively slowly; while exports of traditional primary products such as agriculture, forestry and fishing are declining. Finally, Scotland's service sector exports are very low in comparison to manufactured exports, and accounted for a mere 4.7 per cent of total UK services' exports in 1999.

Dualism is thus evident in Scotland's trade performance: the export-oriented foreign-owned sector contrasts with the poorly performing traditional industries and many small firms. Scotland has thus responded poorly to the prospects offered by the global economy (as well as, in fact, to significant prospects much nearer at home – in the rest of the UK).

The scorecard in Table 15.1 suggests significant opportunities for the country, in respect, for example, of value-added services and new tradable products and services; but also major weaknesses in the ability to recognise and exploit these.

Inward Foreign Direct Investment (FDI)

Over the last 50 years, Scotland has very successfully capitalised on investment growth and liberalisation trends in the world economy (Peters *et al.*, 2000; Brewer and Young, 2000); and in particular managed to attract a significant share of greenfield electronics assembly and manufacturing investment flowing into Europe. The main reasons behind this success are well documented (Scottish Affairs Committee, 1999), including access to the EU, relatively low wages, inexpensive property, public subsidies and a flexible, English-speaking workforce. Scotland was also the first part of the UK to attract inward investment in a systematic and targeted manner (Brown and Raines, 2000).

In recent times, the nature of FDI coming to Scotland has significantly changed, however. Typically projects are smaller, involve lower capital expenditure, fewer jobs and smaller scale property requirements. More recent inward investment has also tended to be higher quality, such as electronics design employment, with an estimated one in eight planned new jobs representing R&D-related employment (Locate in Scotland, 2001). These changes are partly a reflection of loss of competitiveness, partly a function of a changing marketing strategy by the inward investment agency.

Another important development has been the emergence of service sector FDI, particularly in the shape of call centres, financial services and shared service centres. These firms tend to locate in urban economies which have access to good electronic communications and labour pools. However, some of the lower quality back office functions resemble the 'branch plant' jobs historically associated with the manufacturing sector. Many are low paid, with limited promotion prospects, and vulnerable to short-term cost fluctuations. As call centres evolve to multimedia contact centres, these jobs may migrate overseas, for example, to the Indian sub-continent. As in manufacturing, the key for the future is to capture knowledge-intensive service industries which are less short-term, and to upgrade the skills within current operations.

A number of factors will make inward investment attraction more difficult in the future. First, competition for new greenfield assembly projects is becoming increasingly intense, especially from Central and Eastern Europe and China. Second, although an increasing amount of inward investment is coming to Scotland through *in situ* expansions, intense intracorporate bidding is making these types of projects as difficult to attract as greenfield FDI. Third, Scotland no longer possesses the institutional first-mover advantages associated with FDI attraction (Brown and Raines, 2000).

In summary, during the last 30 years, there has been an excessive emphasis on attracting FDI to Scotland, irrespective of quality; and inward investment has not been sufficiently integrated within the overall economic development process. The vision for 2020 should be to make Scotland a global centre for technologically-advanced and knowledge-intensive FDI, supported by advanced factors and integrated within a knowledge economy. This is a much more challenging task than the former attraction strategy. It depends strongly on long-term investment in infrastructure and other public goods, aiding competence-building in indigenous enterprises and supporting networked and clustered regional development. To date the knowledge base in the country lacks the scale, depth and dynamism to achieve the desired large-scale shift to technology and knowledge-intensive FDI.

The potential to incorporate existing MNEs in Scotland within such a strategy also seems limited. Most foreign-owned subsidiaries have shown weak innovation tendencies, consequent on limited local R&D, and very restricted linkages (of all types) into the rest of the economy (Turok, 1993; Firn Crichton Roberts *et al.*, 2000). To date, therefore, the globalisation forces of centralisation and relocation are much stronger than the countervailing localisation influences in the Scottish case (Table 15.1).

Outward investment and global companies

Direct exports do not fully measure Scottish business performance in the global economy. The competitive penetration of international markets by indigenous Scottish enterprises may require other modes of market servicing, including licensing, strategic alliances, joint ventures, and wholly-owned greenfield operations or acquisitions. Although data are limited, it is evident that Scotland has not been very successful at internationalising its own corporate base. A recent survey of Scottish exporters revealed that a mere 119 (5 per cent) indicated they had some form of 'overseas presence' (SCDI, 2001). The most common form of overseas presence among these firms was an overseas representative office followed by overseas subsidiaries, manufacturing operations, joint ventures, licensing agreements and franchises. A further 88 firms (3.5 per cent) had less direct links overseas, such as commission agents, distributors and associates, linked to exporting. The geographic location of these overseas links is mainly in the USA and European markets, although a number of oil and gas firms have links with an overseas presence in Asia and former Soviet republics, such as Azerbaijan.

On the whole, therefore, there is relatively little direct outward investment or other non-export activity on behalf of the corporate base, especially outwith financial services and the oil and gas sectors. Additionally, there are few 'global companies' headquartered in Scotland. These are firms meeting the criteria of operational autonomy in overseas markets; a minimum 30 per cent of turnover from overseas; a presence in more than one market; global brands; and global vision (Scottish Enterprise, 1999). Increasing the level of outward investment and other equity and non-equity activity, and building more global companies is a key task for Scottish policy makers over the next 20 years. Weaknesses facing such companies include *inter alia* the limited pool of internationally experienced managers and the relative absence of an outward-looking vision and mentality. Moreover, the economy lacks the asset-augmenting and value-adding capabilities which internationalising companies can access and lock onto (Table 15.1).

E-connectivity

Cross-border flows of goods, services and investment represent traditional vehicles for the transfer of knowledge embedded in products, capital equipment and skilled personnel. Disembodied cross-border knowledge flows have, however, become increasingly significant, additional mechanisms for know-how transfer and diffusion, through patents, new organisations and organisational forms, partnerships and networks, and the explosive growth of cross-border information transmissions. Scottish data on these issues are restricted to the nature and extent of the country's digital connections. According to the Scottish Household Survey (SHS), 33 per cent of Scottish households own a PC, with just under half of these people connected to the Internet; and 14 per cent of households in Scotland have access to the Internet at home (SHS, 2001). There is, however, clear evidence of a 'digital divide' in Scotland, with Internet access of 27 per cent of all households in high income areas in Scotland comparing with just 7 per cent in disadvantaged urban council estates. On the basis of the SHS data the Scottish position compares reasonably with the rest of the UK but poorly with other small knowledge-based economies such as Denmark, Norway,

Sweden and Finland. Another survey by Oftel (2002) provides quite a different position of the Scottish relative position: Scotland had the lowest proportion of adults with Internet and PC access at home (30 per cent and 41 per cent, respectively) of any UK region; the UK averages were 45 and 52 per cent.

Of more importance is the extent of digital connectivity and ICT usage within the workplace. Since 1998, the DTI and SE, have undertaken an annual survey of companies in Scotland on ICT usage and uptake within Scotland.[1] The survey found that in 2001, 93 per cent of Scotland's labour force work in businesses connected to the Internet. While this figure compares reasonably well with other parts of the UK, Scotland lags behind major international competitors such as Germany (97 per cent) and Sweden (98 per cent).

At present, 20 per cent of Scottish businessses are trading online (defined as engaging in both ordering and paying online, with either customers or suppliers). Between 2000 and 2001, there was an increase in the absolute number of Scottish businesses trading online, from 33 036 to 38 651. This growth has been exclusively amongst micro businesses. Australia has the highest level of online trading (25 per cent) and Japan has the lowest (9 per cent). In terms of being able to purchase online, Scotland does not however compare very well with the rest of the UK: Only 25 per cent of Scottish businesses were able to receive orders online compared with a UK average of 29 per cent and 40 per cent in the East of England (see Figure 15.3) (DTI, 2001).

Other indicators of digital connectivity reveal that Scotland has a relatively poor record, the low investment in ICT infrastructure being

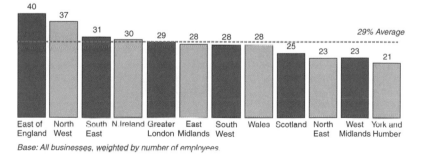

Figure 15.3 Businesses that allow customers to order goods and services online (%).

Source: DTI, 2001.

an especial cause of concern. High-speed Internet availability and access is low; and Scotland does not benchmark favourably against state-of-the-art in major metropolitan areas around the world where investment in cabling, trunking and highways provides significant locational advantages for firms.

Human capital

Factor markets (here represented by labour markets) are another form of market which has been affected by globalisation (Glover *et al.*, 2001). Skilled migration, in particular, is becoming a significant dimension of globalisation, with 'brain exchanges' being characteristic of all advanced economies (Lowell and Findlay, 2001).

The General Register Office for Scotland estimates that Scotland will suffer a net loss of 1000 people per annum between the present and 2020 (see Brown, 2001). Although this overall figure seems quite low, the composition is problematic. For example, the majority of young Scots leaving the country are young highly skilled people, especially young female graduates, while the majority of incomers tend to be elderly or retired people, indicating a net 'brain drain' among those of working age. This situation is particularly acute in certain key shortage sectors of the economy, such as microelectronics, opto-electronics and biotechnology. However, much more needs to be known about these

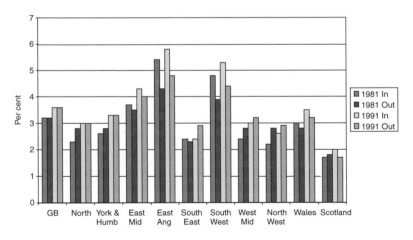

Figure 15.4 Migration rates in the UK.

Source: Glover *et al.*, 2001.

migration flows, including the composition of the outflows, and motivational factors underlying the trends; data at present are woefully inadequate.

Scotland is still a relatively closed society in terms of in- and out-migration compared with the rest of the UK (see Figure 15.4). Furthermore, the country is less cosmopolitan than the rest of the UK in terms of workers by country of birth. According to analysis of the Labour Force Survey, Scotland has less than 2 per cent of its population born outwith the country, whereas the Southeast of England has nearly 12 per cent of its population from overseas in terms of workers by country of birth. These two related phenomenon may engender a closed attitude in Scotland which could stifle creativity and close the country to new ideas, attitudes, and so on. Further, research elsewhere shows that high levels of in-migration is often associated with strong entrepreneurial behaviour (Glover *et al.*, 2001).

The 'international' policy of Scottish Enterprise and the Scottish Executive

Historically, policies to encourage inward and outward internationalisation have been operated quite separately within SE and the Scottish Executive and their predecessors, as shown in Table 15.2 (Scottish Affairs Committee, 1999). In the Global Connections Strategy (Scottish Executive, 2001), however, the changing global environment and the knowledge economy were recognised as blurring the boundaries between the different modes of inward and outward internationalisation.[2] The aim of the new organisation – Scottish Development International (SDI) – is to exploit inter-relationships and synergies in promoting international business in all its forms. This means a stronger role for policy makers in alliance formation, co-operative manufacturing, network building and brokering technology deals, and so on. In future, moreover, Scotland will have to attract human capital and entrepreneurial talent to Scotland as much as fixed capital expenditure, since knowledge has become the key resource.

There is no question that the thinking underlying SDI has many similarities to the approach in this chapter, and its establishment is strongly welcomed. The new strategy and structure do, nevertheless, face many challenges, as illustrated following:

- A critical question is whether the new organisation will be able to satisfy its very diverse customer base domestically and internationally.

Table 15.2   Policies and institutions for international development

	Year of establishment/ publication	Objectives/activities
Locate in Scotland (LIS)	1981	Maximise flow of inward investment and job creation
Scottish Trade International (STI)	1991	Trade promotion. Co-ordination of network of local support organisations
Global Companies Enquiry	1999	Strategy for increasing the number of global companies controlled from Scotland
Global Connections Strategy	2001	Support Scottish participation in the global economy[a]
Scottish Development International (SDI)	October 2001	New organisation to implement Global Connections Strategy[b]

[a] Meaning: Encourage investment into Scotland; increase investment in global markets; develop Scotland as a globally attractive location; and enhance digital connectivity.

[b] Operational divisions as follows: (1) Field Operations: all former LIS and STI overseas operations; (2) Inward Operations: most existing domestic inward investment functions; (3) Trade: most domestic export support operations of former STI; (4) Group services: strategy, planning, and so on; (5) International Business Development: internationalisation of Scottish companies beyond trade; (6) Scotland Europa: links with EU; and (7) Building International Networks: creating a network of Scottish business people to promote Scotland globally.

SDI will be dealing with client enterprises of diverse size, sector, value chain, technology and internationalisation characteristics, and with very divergent needs. An associated question is whether the large Scottish companies will support SDI, since the organisation has much to gain from their expertise.

- Regarding the corporate customers, particularly indigenous enter-prises, there is also a question mark over their own capabilities to participate in and benefit from the global knowledge economy and the services offered by SDI. Few Scottish companies are involved in international joint ventures, strategic alliances, licensing and franch-ising, and so on. This is partly related to low networking capabilities , partly to lack of expertise and awareness.
- The demands on the operational staff of SDI are going to be very considerable. Obtaining staff of the required wide-ranging capabil-ities becomes a major challenge.
- SDI must be integrated into the activities of SE in a way that the fiefdom that was Locate in Scotland (LIS) never was. This is particu-

larly relevant because of the importance to the competitiveness of the Scottish economy of created assets, represented by the transportation and communications infrastructure, education and other public goods; and because of the policy emphasis placed on cluster development. E-connectivity is a crucial facilitating tool for achieving SDI's goals and, therefore, integration with the e-commerce function is very important.

- Establishing objectives and targets for SDI represent further challenges. Since the organisation's role encompasses a wide range of global connections, then performance criteria need to go well beyond traditional measures, such as numbers of projects and jobs associated with inward investment, and levels of exports. Evaluation criteria need to be formulated to encompass knowledge flows in and out, networking arrangements and internationalisation capabilities, meaning new sources of information.
- Scotland needs to get closer to the policy-making institutions for international business at European and multilateral levels. Scotland Europa acts as a lobbying organisation in Brussels. There is no equivalent for the WTO, and yet questions of trade and investment liberalisation are of direct significance to internationalising firms. One possibility would be for Scotland Europa to take on a wider monitoring/briefing role in respect of the WTO?

Policy conclusions

Even with the formation of SDI, the underlying challenge of how to prepare Scotland for the global knowledge economy still remains. The country's fundamental weaknesses, as Table 15.1 has exposed, are principally in the broad area of soft skills and connections. They concern basic knowhow, but also the new skills concerning global mentality and vision, global networks and partnerships, and access to human capital resources wherever these reside. Converting the objectives into policy programmes in Scotland is complex, since the requirements are so wide ranging, and Table 15.3 focuses upon one particular issue, namely, education and training, as an exemplar. The programmes proposed should be regarded as complementary to SDI, providing the skills, awareness and attitudinal changes to capitalise on SDI's policy thrusts.

Applying these principles, first, to the objective of maximising trade, investment and knowledge flows, policy activity at a basic level needs to encourage greater global awareness and know-how among Scottish firms, especially for alliances and other non-export modes of operation.

Table 15.3   Policy guidelines for Scotland in the global knowledge economy

---

Policy objectives and aims

To maximise global trade, investment and knowledge flows, emphasising value-added products and services, through:

1 The stimulation of internal and cross-border wealth-creating alliances and networks.
2 The global exploitation of E-business concepts and applications across the value chain.
3 The development, retention and attraction of human capital with international awareness and capabilities.

Policy guidelines

- Promote awareness.
- Demonstrate benefits.
- Provide encouragement.

Policy focus:

1 Education
   - New aptitudes and skills training in schools/colleges/universities; specialised skills for computer and software industries, e-commerce, empowerment, and so on.
   - Training in language and culture.
   - In/out exchange programmes.
   - Academic partnerships.
2 Senior management programmes
   - Promote awareness/overcome resistance.
   - Recruitment from abroad.
3 Junior/middle management programmes
   - Promote awareness of global opportunities; new products/services; new business models; best practice globally.
   - Networking and ideas-sharing.
   - Recruitment of international students from Scottish universities.
   - Inward investors as mentors; placements in inward investing companies.

Greater efforts are required with the large group of 'non-international' Scottish companies.

With respect to the stimulation of wealth-creating alliances and networks, policy activity is underway in Scotland, in respect, for example, of tapping into Scottish networks abroad. But a much wider perspective needs to be taken. Internally, for instance, networks are insufficiently focused or inclusive: inward investors and young, dynamic Scottish companies may feel excluded or disconnected. The development of academic partnerships also requires much greater attention, both internally and externally. More radically, colleges and universities (even schools) may need to experiment with programmes designed to cultivate a network culture.

The foundations for the exploitation of the e-economy and e-business concepts and applications need to be laid in schools and further developed in tertiary education. This activity is ongoing and long-term. However, if Scotland is genuinely to engage with the global knowledge economy in the short term as well, it needs buy-in from senior industrialists in Scotland. For junior and middle managers, the policy requirements are different, namely, improving awareness and take-up for all value chain activities, promoting new business models, and assisting environmental monitoring and scanning capabilities directed at new opportunities and capabilities.

The required policies to develop, retain and attract human capital are broad-ranging. At one level, they focus upon raising skill levels (particularly in international business), including global awareness and cultural understanding, global strategy formulation, identification of global opportunities and of global best practice. There are major barriers of ethnocentricity to be overcome in bringing such expertise into Scottish companies. The challenges include the training of indigenous Scottish managers and workforces, which may include short-term placements with international companies (especially overseas). A stronger commitment to recruiting graduates with international business and language qualifications, and foreign students studying in Scotland is also important. Inward investors provide a (small) pool of indigenous Scottish managers who have undergone training abroad and worked with experienced multinational executives. Opportunities for using multinational affiliates in Scotland in a mentoring capacity with suppliers and customers or even local enterprises based in the same locality should be explored. All such human capital-related programmes have a positive contribution to make to the development of international networks and partnerships. They also pose the fundamental challenge for Scotland to accept and integrate people from anywhere in the world into the structure and fabric of society.

Conclusions

Using traditional measures of a global knowledge economy, such as export and inward investment levels, Scotland appears to be a moderately well-connected country. However, the evidence presented within this chapter reveals that performance in a number of areas is weak, linked both to lack of investment (as in e-connectivity), and particularly to problems surrounding human capital and knowledge in an era when face-to-face as well as virtual connections are so critical. Distance is far from dead, and Scotland faces fundamental challenges to improve connections and multiculturalism if it is not to sink from a position of European peripherality to global peripherality. The shift from a national, monocultural, industrial economy to a global, virtual, multicultural, digital economy is still a vision.

Notes

1 Two hundred interviews were conducted in each English region and in the devolved administrations of Northern Ireland and Wales. In Scotland, how-ever, the sample size was increased to 560 to provide a more concrete picture.
2 The *Global Connections Strategy* (Scottish Executive, 2001a) represents a follow on to earlier policy documents from the Scottish Executive, namely, *The Way Forward* (Scottish Executive, 2000) and *A Smart, Successful Scotland* (Scottish Executive, 2001b).

References

Amin, A. and N. Thrift (1992), 'Neo-Marshallian nodes in global networks', *International Journal of Urban and Regional Research*, Vol. 16, pp. 571–587.

Brewer, T. and S. Young (2000), *The Multilateral Investment System and Multinational Enterprises*, Oxford: Oxford University Press.

Brown, R. (2000), 'Clusters, Supply Chains and local embeddedness in Fyrstad', *European Urban and Regional Studies*, Vol. 7, pp. 291–305.

Brown, R. (2001), 'Demographic change, older workers and the 'new' labour market in Scotland', *Fraser of Allander Quarterly Economic Commentary*, Vol. 26, pp. 50–56.

Brown, R. and P. Raines (2000), 'The changing nature of foreign investment policy in Europe: From promotion to management', in J.H. Dunning (ed.), *Regions, Globalization, and the Knowledge-Based Economy*, Oxford: Oxford University Press.

Cairncross, F. (1997), *The Death of Distance*, Cambridge, MA: Harvard Business Press.

Cooke, P. and K. Morgan (1998), *The Associational Economy*, Oxford: Oxford University Press.

Department of Trade and Industry (2001), *Business in the Information Age: International Benchmarking Report 2001*, London: Department of Trade and Industry.

Dunning, J.H. (1997), *Alliance Capitalism and Global Business*, London and New York: Routledge.

Dunning, J.H. (ed.) (2000), *Regions, Globalization, and the Knowledge-Based Economy*, Oxford: Oxford University Press.

Firn Crichton Roberts, University of Strathclyde and Fraser of Allander Institute (2000), *Inward Investment Benefits for the Scottish Economy*, Glasgow: Scottish Enterprise (unpublished report).

Glover, S., Gott, C., Loizillon, A., Portes, J., Price, R., Spencer, S., Srinivasan, V. and C. Willis *et al.* (2001), *Migration: an economic and social analysis*, Research

Development and Statistics Directorate, Occasional Paper No. 67, London: Home Office.

International Monetary Fund (1997), *World Economic Outlook: Globalization-Opportunities and Challenges*, Washington DC: International Monetary Fund, May.

Locate in Scotland (2001), *Annual Report*, Glasgow: Scottish Enterprise.

Lowell, B. and A. Findlay (2001), *Migration of Highly Skilled Persons From Developing Countries: Impact and Policy Responses*, Geneva: International Labour Office.

Markusen, A. (1996), 'Sticky Places in slippery space: A typology of industrial districts', *Economic Geography*, Vol. 72, No. 3, pp. 293–313.

Oftel (2002), *Consumers' Use Of Internet*, London: Oftel, 29 January.

Peat, J. and S. Boyle (1999), *An Illustrated Guide to the Scottish Economy*, London: Duckworth.

Peters, E. and N. Hood (2000), 'Implementing the cluster approach: Some lessons from the Scottish experience', *International Studies of Management and Organization*, Vol. 30, No. 2, pp. 68–92.

Peters, E., Hood, N. and S. Young (2000), 'Policy partnership in the development of knowledge industries in Scotland', in J.H. Dunning (ed.), *Regions, Globalization, and the Knowledge-Based Economy*, Oxford: Oxford University Press, pp. 259–285.

Scottish Affairs Committee (1999), *Inward/Outward Investment in Scotland*, HC 84–I, Session 1998–99, London: The Stationery Office.

Scottish Council for Development and Industry (2001), *Survey of Scottish Sales and Exports 1999*, Glasgow: Scottish Council for Development and Industry.

Scottish Enterprise (1999), *Global Companies. A Strategy for Scotland*, Glasgow: Scottish Enterprise.

Scottish Executive (2000), *The Way Forward: Framework for Economic Development in Scotland*, Edinburgh: Scottish Executive.

Scottish Executive (2001a), *Scotland: A Global Connections Strategy*, Edinburgh: Scottish Executive.

Scottish Executive (2001b), *A Smart, Successful Scotland: Ambitions for the Enterprise Networks*, Edinburgh: Scottish Executive.

Scottish Household Survey (2001), *Scotland's People: Results from the 1999/2000 Scottish Household Survey*, Edinburgh: NFO System Three Social Research and MORI Scotland.

Tapscott, D. and D. Agnew (1999), 'Governance in the digital economy', *Finance and Development*, December, pp. 34–37.

Turok, I. (1993), 'Inward investment and local linkages: How deeply embedded is "Silicon Glen"?', *Regional Studies*, Vol. 27, pp. 401–417.

16
Strategic Partnership and the Future of Clusters in Scotland

Ewen Peters

Introduction and context

In the UK the cluster approach (Porter, 1990a) to regional economic development has been pioneered by SE, the government's main economic development body in Scotland. In many ways the cluster approach is a contemporary expression of the strategic partnership approach that historically has been the preferred working mode of both the private and public sectors in Scotland (Peters *et al.*, 2000). Accordingly, this chapter seeks to locate the adoption of the cluster approach within the history of that development; to summarise Scotland's experience to date of developing and implementing the cluster approach; to consider the future relevance of the cluster concept; and to draw conclusions regarding the future focus for strategic partnership in Scotland.

Developing and implementing the cluster approach

After a two-year consultation process, the government of the day established SE[1] in April 1991. In addition to its traditional role as an economic development service provider and institution builder, SE acts as a facilitator, broker, mediator, manager, advocate and leader of its external network of key stakeholders (the government), key partners (universities, local authorities, training providers, property providers, funding providers, and so on) and key customers (Scottish-based businesses and potential business investors). Accordingly, SE is accustomed to taking a systemic view of its interventions.

The cluster approach in particular was seen to provide an industry-specific context that enabled more 'fine grain' analysis of systemic market failures (that is, co-ordination failures, information deficiencies, and imperfect knowledge generation and exploitation, and so on) and provided a framework within which appropriate collaborative action could be taken to address these failures and thereby enhance local innovation. In short, clusters provided SE with a new opportunity to deploy and develop its strategic networking capability and to forge new and dynamic industry partnerships below the macro level.

Early developments

Early in its life SE began to consider how the cluster approach could be introduced in Scotland. With the help of *Monitor*, the consulting firm of Michael Porter, a modified version of the Porter method for identifying potential clusters with good long-term growth prospects (Porter, 1990b; Appendix A) was applied to the Scottish economy. No world-class clusters were found but over 30 emerging industry and service clusters were identified as potential targets for support (*Monitor*, 1993).

The *Monitor* analysis informed the cluster priorities set out in SE's Network Strategy published in 1994. These priorities represented a re-aggregation of the original *Monitor* target list into thirteen Scotland-wide constituencies that were larger and therefore more inclusive. From the outset progress was affected by competing resource issues, the need to create a widely shared understanding of the value of the cluster approach, and the need to develop a relevant and effective *modus operandi* for translating cluster strategy into action. More detailed work was, however, undertaken at this stage in electronics and oil and gas. This paved the way for a number of strategic initiatives such as the formation of the Scottish Electronics Forum in 1995 and the launch of the Alba Project in 1998.

Policy approval

Board approval for the wider adoption of the cluster approach was obtained 'in principle' in 1996. The relevant paper (Scottish Enterprise, 1996) also highlighted the organisational benefits[2] of adopting a cluster approach to economic development. The realisation of these was predicated not only upon wide acceptance of the concept but a deep embedding of the process across industry, area and organisational boundaries. In particular, 'deep embedding' was necessary to enable cluster linkages (both vertical and horizontal) to be strengthened, common infrastructure needs to be identified (for example, skills), and new synergies to be realised. A more fully integrated approach was also needed, if resources were to be mobilised on a scale commensurate with the demands of more broad-based cluster development. However, against the backdrop of the general tightening of public expenditure at the time, the paper also recognised the impracticality of pursuing the Porter ideal of providing in-depth support while trying to advance on all cluster fronts simultaneously. Accordingly, a further re-focusing of existing cluster targets was proposed to allow some progress to be made, at least in the short term.

Implementing the approach

Four clusters emerged as pilot initiatives namely: biotechnology, food and drink, oil and gas, and semiconductors. Together these clusters were estimated to support around 200 000 jobs in the Scottish economy and represented a mix of established and more promising industries and technologies. At the end of 1997, four dedicated cross-functional cluster teams were established as part of a new Cluster Development Directorate. These teams included representatives from across the Scottish Enterprise Network and were responsible for:

- producing action plans of 3–5 years duration for Board approval;
- promoting integration among national teams in SE; and
- extending the more holistic cluster approach to national team activities.

Once Board approval had been secured, budgets were allocated to the national team to deliver a National Cluster Strategy. The first phase of this process involved the R&D of individual cluster action plans. A communications strategy was also undertaken to formally introduce key partners and stakeholders to the principles of cluster development as conceived by Scottish Enterprise Operations, the main national operating division of SE at that time (see, for example, Scottish Enterprise, 1999).

In 1999, Network Directors were appointed to lead and facilitate action-plan implementation and budget for implementing action plans was also secured and ring fenced to encourage the SE Network to support cluster-enhancing projects. Responsibility for delivery (and therefore budget) could either be devolved to appropriate points within the SE Network or retained within the national cluster team according to the availability of resources and distribution of network expertise. The first full year of operation was 2000/2001 and in the context of preparing this book, this is very recent.

A second wave of cluster initiatives has also been selected and validated by SE. Five 'decision gates' were used, namely: growth potential, employment coverage, the existence of a 'window of opportunity' for

Scotland, industry readiness and the potential for the SEN to make a difference. Based largely on the *Monitor* list, the second wave includes: opto-electronics, forest products, creative industries and tourism. SE estimates that together these target clusters support around 250 000 jobs in the Scottish economy.

The first year in retrospect

It would be premature for SE to try to undertake formal impact assessment of the pilot clusters because of the long gestation periods inherent in cluster development. However, SE recently completed an internal review of the first full year of operation (Scottish Enterprise, 2001) for the most advanced pilot initiatives, namely: biotechnology, food and drink (excluding whisky) and semiconductors.

The objective was to examine operational progress, assess the benefits to participants and to draw lessons, especially in relation to SE's organisation and working practices. Data deficiencies and the nature of the data gathering methods employed mean that results are necessarily preliminary and indicative. Some of the main findings to emerge are set out below.

Achievements and business feedback

While there was clear evidence that each cluster had made progress (see Table 16.1), the rate of progress was found to be variable. The feedback from leading businesses indicated that: cluster-related institution building was helping to foster greater industry ownership; cluster-related events were stimulating more collaboration between businesses, inducing some additional commercial activity; policy co-ordination was improving; and that involvement in the cluster process had been a positive learning experience.

Various concerns were also highlighted: business collaboration was less successful around key areas of competitiveness; understanding and appreciation of the cluster concept was limited and the cluster approach had yet to win popular appeal – this was held to constrain participation by potential new entrants; lack of a critical mass of world-class companies to drive cluster growth was a common concern; and in the absence of more focused leadership, the cluster approach was in danger of losing credibility with business as a tool for more radical economic development.

Organisation and working practices

One of the main purposes of the national pilot initiative was to determine an appropriate *modus operandi* for working with clusters in

Table 16.1   Examples of main first year achievements against cluster action plans

---

Biotechnology:
- The number of biotechnology companies and jobs rose significantly (see Chapter 6)
- Increased industry ownership of the cluster process was reflected in the first-time establishment of an office in Scotland by the BioIndustry Association (BIA), the leading national trade body
- Commercialisation was further stimulated as a result of 14 biotechnology projects receiving Proof of Concept funding worth £2.5 million
- Cluster induced support for international trade development helped increase sales for Scottish biotechnology companies by £21 million, with further sales of £16 million projected
- The launch of the Biotechnology College Consortium and BioSolutions improved skills provision within the cluster

Food and drink:
- Despite the fragmented industry structure, a high degree of industry ownership of the cluster approach has been achieved – exemplified in the establishment of a new Industry Strategy Group
- Endorsement of the current cluster strategy was obtained from the Scottish Parliament and Scottish Executive
- Key projects have been implemented, including the Food Learning Network, CALMIC, Scottish Food and Drink International
- Progress was made in innovation and research

Semiconductors:
- Despite a difficult year, SE helped to secure a £20 million investment from Motorola for a new design centre at Project Alba
- The development of the Microelectronics Test Centre has helped strengthen the cluster
- Fifty-four students enrolled at the Institute for System Level Integration and a series of key vocational courses have been developed in conjunction with industry and Scottish Colleges of Further Education
- The establishment of the Microelectronics Website for Scotland has enhanced B2B communications

---

Source: Scottish Enterprise, 2002.

a Scottish context. Each of the three cluster teams has managed this process differently.[3] The Review highlighted a number of ways in which the SE Network was learning to better integrate the cluster model with established approaches and procedures. In particular there was evidence of freer sharing of information, greater collaboration and better co-ordination internally. Overall, however, progress was assessed to be slow and there were no early signs that cluster-related learning was helping to radically transform SE's working practices. A number of

contributing factors were identified. These included: the fact that ownership of the process was neither wide spread or deeply embedded; there was
no common appreciation of the value of the approach to the organisation;
a lack of clarity existed concerning how the chain of command for cluster
teams worked; and there was uncertainty over the amount of support that
existed for the approach at the top of the organisation.

Future policy

It could be two years before formal economic impact assessment of the
pilot cluster begins and more robust evidence of progress produced. In
the meantime, the view has developed inside the organisation that SE is
now less able to support the national development of many new broad
clusters, largely because of new emerging priorities associated with
knowledge economy, related resource issues and the perceived growing
risk of overlap.

A number of changes have already taken place. For example, the
development function of the Cluster Development Directorate has now
been disbanded and no action plans are to be prepared for the remaining
target clusters.[4] Operational changes can also be expected as the lessons
emerging from SE's internal review are incorporated into the implementation of the second wave of target clusters. Regarding more fundamental change, completion of the first wave of pilot clusters would
provide a natural breakpoint that could allow SE to undertake a more
fundamental assessment of the strategic benefits of its policy on clusters.

The future of the cluster approach

While many might agree that it would be desirable to have a greater
number of world-class clusters more widely distributed throughout the
global economy, their comparative rarity suggests they may well be
the exception rather than the rule. There is certainly no evidence from
the relevant literature to support any simple notion of a path dependence that automatically leads to convergence.

Accordingly, the use of well-developed clusters as a normative type for
public policy may be more limited than perhaps has generally been
recognised. This may change, however, as policy makers are forced to
address more of the challenges and opportunities associated with the
emergence of the knowledge economy. This is a fundamental change
that holds important implications for the future of clusters and
the strategic partnership approach in Scotland. Some of these will now
be considered.

Towards the knowledge economy

Over a decade ago Porter (1990b) acknowledged that many important industries, especially industries that were intensive in just one or two factors (for example, labour, capital, energy, and so on), or industries that choose to pursue non-differentiated, least-cost strategies, may not require to take advantage of the full range of proximity benefits associated with well-developed clusters. Since then innovation has come to the fore as a competitive theme that is increasingly important to many different kinds of firm in a great variety of industry settings. This would suggest, *a priori*, that a model of agglomeration explicitly founded on knowledge accumulation is likely to become increasingly relevant to a wider range of firms and industries and could emerge as the new dominant paradigm.

Though incomplete, there is a growing body of evidence to support this contention:

- A number of macro indicators[5] now point to the increased general importance of innovation and technological change (and therefore knowledge) in economic performance;
- Researchers[6] have also found that knowledge and innovation are becoming relatively more important for a number of single-factor industries and industries conventionally regarded as less knowledge intensive; and
- Empirical studies at the corporate level also show that stock market valuations are increasingly related to business expenditure on R&D and other intangible assets such as links to top scientists and the Internet.

Thus, while the future direction is becoming clearer, it is perhaps more difficult to assess the precise strength of these trends and to anticipate their differential impact on firms, industries and regions.

Knowledge accumulation and local milieu

The academic consensus related to the above is reasonably well-established and this is reflected in the models of economic development that have been developed more recently which place knowledge accumulation at the very heart of dynamic agglomeration. Moreover, the research (Aydalot, 1986; Maillat, 1995; Malmberg *et al.*, 1996) behind these models indicates that knowledge accumulation happens best in a 'local milieu' that facilitates the efficient generation and diffusion of valuable tacit knowledge by virtue of the amount, quality and uniqueness of the social capital embedded in the local system. Such social capital also acts as a barrier to wider diffusion while the existing pool of tacit knowledge attracts new entrants that add to it. Likewise, resident firms may add further to this pool by selectively tapping other external sources of knowledge.

These models give primacy to knowledge creation and diffusion (technological spill-over effects) over conventional economic linkages and associated local externalities (common pools of specialised skills, access to specialised services and common infrastructure, and so on) that reduce transaction costs and improve efficiency. An important conclusion here is that knowledge accumulation emerges as a potentially key advantage, especially for local firms and regions pursuing more differentiated competitive strategies based on innovation. This body of research also helps to make explicit what often remains implicit and therefore unrecognised in the Porter framework – as popularly presented.

Knowledge accumulation and Scotland's competitive advantage

Globalisation and the rapid intensification of place competition from fast-developing, least-cost locations have greatly reduced the surface friction and size of many economic spaces reliant on more static locational advantages such as efficiency gains and flexibility. In particular, the industrial districts, regional production systems and manufacturing belts of the peripheral and less favoured regions of the more advanced economies have been (and will continue to be) greatly affected by this competitive process. The recent sharp contraction in Scotland's electronics industry well illustrates this point (see Chapter 8).

Moreover, at that level of the economy, much of the new job creation has been in service-related investments such as call centres, customer contact centres, shared service centres, and so on. This trend is expected to remain positive, at least in the short to medium term (Quinn *et al.*, 2000; Keynote, 2002) and Scotland should continue to benefit from this. However, this type of investment seeks mainly to exploit advances in communications technology allied to various externalities (skills pools and infrastructure) that provide economies at the urban and regional level. By their nature, the transaction efficiency and flexibility benefits associated with these economies can provide little guarantee of a sustainable economic future for Scotland, especially if these services were to become more exposed to international competition (Hood and Peters, 2000).

These trends and issues suggest that if Scotland is to secure a significant stake in the global economy of the twenty-first century it must certainly look beyond the efficiency gains derived from traditional economies of agglomeration such as lower transport costs, flexibility, lower search costs, labour pool efficiencies, and so on. Moreover, the previous analysis suggests that knowledge accumulation will provide a more sustainable basis on which to build future regional and industrial specialisations. With respect to the latter, innovative local milieu could provide a more relevant sectoral focus for appropriate intervention than industrial clusters. However, the relevant literature (Bartlett and Ghoshal, 1990; Hedlund and Rolander, 1990; Doz *et al.*, 2001) highlights there could be a risk, longer term, that the future activity of multinational companies may undermine the key locational advantages on which such milieux are built[7] – and other policy options may need to be considered.

Towards a dynamic region

Early regional models that sought to capture the cumulative nature of agglomeration processes were largely based on assumptions about the persistence of scale economies and the sunk costs associated with large, capital intensive processes (Myrdal, 1957; Ullman, 1958; Estall and Buchan, 1961). However, a common feature of the regional models contained in the more recent literature is their focus on knowledge accumulation as a central feature and driver. These models include: the creative region (Andersson, 1985), the entrepreneurial region (Johannisson, 1987), the learning region (Saxenian, 1994), and the regional nexus (Cooke and Morgan, 1998). Their interest for policy makers lies not only in the central focus of these models (that is, innovation and knowledge accumulation) but their level of application (regional), the systems view they promote, and their focus on the key actors involved in the local innovation process. The emphasis on innovation and knowledge intensity, however, raises again the question of the general applicability of such models, especially to peripheral and less favoured regions that must contend with the 'regional innovation paradox' (Landabaso *et al.*, 1999). Some of the implications of this for Scotland will now be considered.

The regional innovation paradox

In the EU, advanced regions spend more public money, and do so in a more strategic way to promote innovation amongst firms, than less favoured regions. According to the EU's Seventh Survey on State Aid: Denmark, Finland and France spent over 200 Ecu per person employed in manufacturing on R&D; while Greece and Portugal spent 10 Ecu per person or less, and Spain did not reach 50 Ecu per person. There is a 'regional innovation paradox' associated with the innovation gap that these figures allude to. The paradox lies in the comparatively greater need to spend on innovation in less favoured regions, and their relatively lower capacity to absorb public funds earmarked for the promotion of innovation (for example, STRIDE). In other words, once an innovation gap has been defined, less favoured regions might be expected to have a bigger capacity to absorb the resources designed to meet this need, given the relatively low base they start from. In reality, less favoured regions face considerable difficulties in absorbing resources.

The main explanation for the regional innovation paradox is not primarily the availability of public money but rather the nature of the local innovation systems and the institutional settings found in less favoured regions that severely limit their absorption capacity (Landabaso *et al.*, 1999). The innovation system in less favoured regions tends to be characterised by a high degree of fragmentation; an absence of a critical mass of activity that constrains the development of both the supply-side and demand-side of the innovation system; key subsystems tend to lack coherence and are underdeveloped; the role of key innovation players is often not broadly understood or appreciated; there are different degrees of autonomy over the conduct of regional/industrial policy at regional level; and the absence of regional leadership makes the development of a the innovation system even more difficult. These points have been echoed in the conclusions of the most recent evaluation of Structural Funds (1994–1999) in less favoured regions (Higgings *et al.*, 1999). The major policy issues identified in this report included:

- Lack of co-ordination between the bodies in charge of public research and those in charge of private research;
- The disconnection between local Universities and local firms;
- Lack of co-ordination of the science and technology policy between departments of industry and departments of education;
- Overlap and inadequate co-ordination between national and regional measures; and
- Little involvement of the relevant regional actors, especially the private sector, in policy planning.

Devolution has provided Scotland with a new opportunity to address a number of these issues and to develop a more dynamic and effective regional innovation system that is better fit for the twenty-first century. The thrust of current government policy is beginning to push much harder in this direction (Scottish Executive, 2001) by encouraging local science, innovation and entrepreneurship. In particular, the emerging policy model assumes a larger role for Scotland's universities, colleges and research institutes in local economic development than is currently the case.

The challenge here should not be understated: a recent analysis of patent registrations in the US, for example, illustrates the size of the gap that currently exists between American universities and their British counterparts in terms of commercial involvement (Porter, 2002). More specifically, the relatively low level of expenditure on R&D by Scottish-based business that has been such a pronounced and persistent feature of Scottish economic performance remains a fundamental concern (see Chapter 17) that makes the challenge of gearing up the supply-side all the more difficult for policy makers.

In a Scottish context, however, regional models could provide a potentially more attractive, stable and effective framework to nurture and support local innovation. The absence of a specific industry focus, for example, would potentially allow more of the key actors involved in innovation to come together in new and perhaps more powerful strategic partnerships that are capable of commanding wide-spread commitment and support. This would clearly be a vital prerequisite to securing the level of resources needed to allow more effective implementation of long-run strategies and policies – a fundamental challenge that the present cluster approach has still to overcome in Scotland.

Conclusion

Implementing the cluster approach: some further lessons

Some of the lessons from the Scottish experience regarding cluster selection and assessment have already been documented (Peters and Hood, 2000). The present analysis illustrates a number of the operational challenges and benefits that implementation of the cluster approach can bring from the perspective of the local development agency. In particular, the analysis highlights that much of the steepness of the early learning curve has been to do with the difficulty faced in trying to establish broad-based understanding and ownership of the cluster concept and in integrating the cluster approach with pre-existing strategies, structures, programmes and initiatives during a period when discretionary expenditure was constrained. Given SE's pioneering role, the precise nature and extent of many of these challenges could not readily be anticipated.

The analysis also illustrates the fundamental problem posed by the long gestation periods inherent in cluster development. The local economic development body can easily end up on the horns of a dilemma where the level of resources needed to sustain cluster development cannot readily be justified by the short-term gains and benefits, while the policy itself becomes increasingly vulnerable to macro changes, especially the changing priorities of the government of the day. For these reasons alone it seems likely that SE's cluster approach in its present form will require some modification at some stage in the not too distant future.

Local milieu as a new focus for strategic partnership?

The above notwithstanding, the present analysis questions the continuing relevance of the cluster concept as a normative model for policy development, especially in less favoured and peripheral regions. Well-developed clusters that are genuinely world class are a relatively rare phenomenon and there is no evidence to support the notion of a general convergence towards higher order clusters. However, the emergence of the knowledge economy (see Chapter 17) highlights the growing importance of knowledge accumulation as a key agglomeration driver in the twenty-first century. Accordingly knowledge accumulation, rather than transaction cost efficiency and flexibility, will represent an increasingly important source of competitive advantage for Scotland in the future.

Contemporary models of network-based innovation focus on knowledge accumulation as a key driver and emphasise the particular importance of an innovative milieu where valuable tacit knowledge can be rapidly and efficiently generated and diffused locally. Because of its focus on knowledge accumulation as a key source of competitive advantage, the concept of a 'local milieu' could perhaps provide a more appropriate future focus for strategic partnership with industry – at least in the mid-term. Such a concept would represent a natural evolution that could build on what has gone before and incorporate many of the valuable lessons that SE has gained from its experience of developing and implementing the cluster approach. However, the implications of this would need to be considered further for a range of Scotland's key sectors and industries (see, for example, Chapters 6–12).

The analysis also suggests that the development of new and more powerful forms of corporate capital (allied to advances in information and communications technology) will enable multinational companies to overcome the barrier to wider diffusion that social capital embedded in local milieu can represent. While the development of appropriate forms of corporate capital would enable tacit knowledge to be codified and exploited more quickly on an international basis, the analysis suggests that this strategy also holds the risk of undermining the main locational advantages that such milieu offer.

Regional level strategic partnerships

In the light of the above, the analysis indicates that other long-term policy options may also need to be examined, and directs the attention of policy-makers to a number of the more recent regional models that have knowledge accumulation as their central focus. For policy makers in less favoured and peripheral regions that must contend with the 'regional innovation paradox', the interest of these models lies not only in their central focus and level of application (regional), but in the systems view they promote, and their focus on the key institutions and actors involved in the local innovation process.

Given the particular challenges of scale and integration that Scotland faces in this regard, the analysis suggests that these models probably offer greater scope than either industrial clusters or local milieu as a focus for the future development of new and more powerful strategic partnerships. In particular, their regional locus has the potential to enable *all* the key actors involved in the innovation process in Scotland to come together and define new collaborative approaches that are capable of commanding wide-spread commitment and support.

Much of this is consistent with the present thrust of government policy in Scotland that emphasises the importance of science, innovation and entrepreneurship. Related to this, an immediate priority for policy makers would be to find a new form of strategic partnership that will enable Scottish universities, colleges and research institutes to engage more positively and effectively with the strategic challenges that the emergence of the knowledge economy poses for Scotland. Regional models of knowledge accumulation could in future provide an appropriate intellectual framework that will assist this process.

The approach suggested here is consistent with much that emerges throughout the book and in the concluding Chapter 20. Scotland thus needs to continue to experiment with different approaches to economic development, yet avoid becoming a captive to any given methodology.

Notes

1   Subsuming the powers of the Scottish Development Agency (SDA) and Training Agency in Scotland, this new body was an attempt to fully integrate enterprise development and training for the first time in the UK. In Scotland, 13 new Local Enterprise Companies (LECs) were also established as part of the Scottish Enterprise network to provide an efficient and equitable delivery mechanism for more customised and better integrated economic development services, including business development support, training support, and physical and environmental improvement programmes. Scottish

Enterprise provides funding for the LECs through an annual process of competitive bidding and appraisal. Initially, Scottish Enterprise National provided leadership, support and accountability for the wider network and was responsible for key national and international programmes such as inward investment, exports, skills and business competitiveness.

2 The organisational benefits regarding the delivery of economic development services include reducing duplication of effort, improving co-ordination, fuller integration, creating new economies of scale and scope in the delivery of economic development support, and the realisation of greater synergies, and so on.

3 The biotechnology cluster team has established an integrated national team, based on seconded staff from across the network with each team member responsible for delivering a national priority project. By way of contrast, the semiconductor cluster team operates a centralised delivery structure with the majority of projects designed and managed by the core team located at SE's headquarters. Finally, the food and drink cluster team has taken a devolved approach to project delivery where all projects are designed, managed and delivered by the SE Network. These differences primarily relate to how the cluster team precursors (that is, SE's national sectoral teams) were organised and the distribution of relevant resources and expertise throughout the network.

4 The remaining target clusters include: chemicals (bulk and speciality), educational services, engineering (aerospace, automotive, marine, textiles and clothing and value added), power generation and whisky that together employ over 300 000 according to baseline estimates prepared by SE (1999).

5 For example: scientific endeavour continues to increase across the OECD and has a growing direct impact on innovation; growing proportion of R&D is business based; and the ratio of patents to gross domestic product (GDP) has increased significantly in most Organisation for Economic Co-operation and Development (OECD) countries – based on patents granted in the USA

6 For example, Chandler, Amatori and Hikino (1997) have highlighted the growing importance of intangible capital (including the knowledge, skills, experience and team work of organised human capabilities) that enable large capital intensive firms to fully realise economies of scale and scope; and the OECD (2000) has observed that financial and business services are accounting for a growing share of business-related R&D expenditure.

7 Essentially, the specialised corporate and organisational capital accumulated by multinational companies would over time be expected to nullify the 'barrier effects' of the unique social capital in local milieu. This in turn would enable the more rapid exploitation of valuable tacit knowledge on an international basis.

References

Andersson, A.E. (1985), 'Creativity and regional development', Papers of the Regional Science Association, 56, pp. 5–20.

Aydalot, P. (1986), *Milieux Innovateurs en Europe*, Paris: GREMI.

Bartlett, C.A. and S. Ghoshal (1990), 'Managing innovation in the transnational corporation', in C.A. Bartlett, Y. Doz and G. Hedlund (eds), *Managing the Global Firm*, London: Routledge.

Chandler, A.D., Amatori, F. and T. Hikino (1997), *Big Business and the Wealth of Nations*, Cambridge: Cambridge University Press.

Cooke, P. and K. Morgan (1998), *The Associational Economy: Firms, Regions and Innovation*, Oxford: Oxford University Press.

Doz, Y., Santos, J. and P. Williamson (2001), *From Global to Metanational: How Companies Win in the Knowledge Economy*, Cambridge, Mass: Harvard Business School Press.

Estall, R.C. and R.O. Buchanan (1961), *Industrial Activity and Economic Geography*, London: Hutchison and Co.

Hedlund, G. and D. Rolander (1990), 'Action in heterarchies: New approaches to managing the MNC', in C.A. Bartlett, Y. Doz and G. Hedlund (eds), *Managing the Global Firm*, London: Routledge.

Higgings, T. *et al.* (1999), *R&TDI Thematic Evaluation of Structural Funds 1994–1999*, Spain Country Reports, Brussels: Commission of the European Communities.

Hood, N. and E. Peters (2000), 'Globalization, corporate strategies and business services', in *The Globalization of Multinational Enterprise Activity and Economic Development*, London: Macmillan Press Limited.

Johannisson, B. (1987), 'Towards a theory of local entrepreneurship', in R.G. Wyckman, L.N. Merredith and G.R. Bush (eds), *The Spirit of Entrepreneurship*, Vancouver, BC: Simon Fraser University.

Keynote (2002), 'Call centre trends', London: Keynote.

Landabaso, M., Oughten, C. and K. Morgan (1999), 'Innovation networks and regional policy in Europe', Conference Paper, Karlsruhe: Fraunhofer Institute.

Malmberg, A., Solvell, O. and I. Zander (1996), 'Special clustering, local accumulation of knowledge and firm competitiveness', *Geografiska Annaler*. 78B (2), pp. 85–97

Monitor Company (1993), 'The competitive advantage of Scotland: Identifying potential for competitiveness', Internal Report for Scottish Enterprise.

Myrdal, G. (1957), *Economic Theory and the Underdeveloped Regions*, London: Ducksworth.

OECD (2000), 'A new economy: The changing role of innovation and information technology in growth', Paris: OECD.

Peters, E. and N. Hood (2000), 'Implementing the cluster approach: Some lessons from the Scottish experience', *International Studies of Management and Organization*, Summer, Vol. 30, No. 2, pp. 68–92.

Peters, E., Hood, N. and S. Young (2000), 'Policy partnership in the development of knowledge industries in Scotland', in J.H. Dunning (ed.), *Regions, Globalization and the Knowledge-based Economy*, Oxford: Oxford University Press, pp. 259–285.

Porter, M.E. (1990a), *The Competitive Advantage of Nations*, London: Macmillan.

Porter, M.E. (1990b), *The Competitive Advantage of Nations, Appendix A*, London: Macmillan.

Porter, M.E. (2002), 'Regional foundations of competitiveness', RDA Cluster Conference, Leeds, UK, 24 January.

Quinn, B., Cooke, R. and A. Kris (2000), *Shared Services: Mining for Corporate Gold*, London: Prentice Hall.

Saxenian, A. (1994), *Regional Advantage, Culture and Competition in Silicon Valley and Route 128*, Cambridge, MA and London: Harvard University Press.

Scottish Enterprise (1996), 'Cluster development: Taking the network strategy forward', Internal Board Paper, Glasgow: Scottish Enterprise.

Scottish Enterprise (1999), *The Clusters Approach: Powering Scotland's Economy into the 21st Century*, Glasgow: Scottish Enterprise.

Scottish Enterprise (2001), *Internal Report: Clusters Review*, (Unpublished).

Scottish Executive (2001), *A Science Strategy for Scotland*, Edinburgh: Scottish Executive.

Scottish Executive (2001), *A Smart, Successful Scotland*, Edinburgh: Scottish Executive.

Ullman, E.L. (1958), 'Regional development and the geography of concentration', Papers and Proceedings of the Regional Science Association (iv), pp. 179–198.

17
Commercialising Scottish Knowledge
Charlie Woods

Introduction

The exploitation of knowledge has always played a critical role in stimulating economic progress. With rapid technology development, growing globalisation and competition, and the increasing sophistication of consumers it is becoming increasingly important. The speedy application of knowledge is imperative for the economic success of firms, regions and countries alike.

Knowledge has been defined as the facts, feelings or experiences known by a person or group of people. It encompasses the technology behind a new product, through to how it is marketed and the quality of the service provided with it. This amply illustrates the breadth of what is involved in considering how the commercialisation of knowledge can be promoted in pursuit of economic development. Much of the most commercially valuable knowledge exists in the science and technology base of higher education and research institutes. This type of knowledge is at the heart of the commercialisation agenda and is where most activity has been focused to date. However, it is important to recognise that knowledge is broader and deeper than this and too narrow a definition runs the risk of underestimating the full potential of a place.

Knowledge can be tangible and codified, for example, within a patent. But more often it is tacit within an individual or group. Frequently the carrier of this tacit knowledge is unaware of its full potential. Often in itself it has little value and it is only valuable when combined with other pieces of knowledge. Chance can often play a key role here. Codified knowledge is much more open to trading than tacit knowledge. However, the intangible, less mobile, tacit knowledge, embedded in the individuals and organisations of an area, offers huge potential for regional differentiation and economic development.

This chapter looks at the factors that lie behind successful commercialisation in promoting development, in particular the role that place itself plays. It goes on to look at the issues and challenges facing Scotland and the initiatives that have been developed in Scotland in recent years to promote commercialisation. It is based on the premise that the design and delivery of effective policy in this area must build on an understanding of all aspects of the 'knowledge system' (creation, storing, sharing and exploitation) and the diverse institutions that make up the system.

Knowledge and place

On the face of it something as intangible as knowledge would appear to have little to do with place, but closer inspection suggests a different conclusion. For example, the 'institutional endowment' of a region can have a significant influence in shaping the environment in which knowledge is created, shared and used. This includes the rules, practices, routines, habits, traditions, customs and conventions associated with the way an economy operates in a particular area, as well as the wider culture and spirit that characterises a region. Not surprisingly this endowment is shaped by the history of a place and is embedded in the organisations, firms and institutions that exist in a region at any one time (see Maskell and Malmberg, 1999). The influence of the institutional endowment of a location has been used as an explanatory factor by a number of commentators in explaining differences in economic progress (Landes, 1998).

The concept of 'cumulative causation', developed by Myrdal to better understand the spatial balance of economic development is also relevant in this regard. This process involves vicious and virtuous circles. Development feeds off itself in some areas, attracting resources from those areas that are not as dynamic (backwash effects). There are some countervailing positive forces for poorer regions in terms of increased demand from the richer areas, and so on (spread effects), but these are usually more than outweighed by the backwash effects.

The most insidious of the backwash effects in the modern economy are the flows of skills and knowledge from weaker to stronger regions. The Local Futures Group (LFG) has recently illustrated a growing concentration of skills and knowledge in an analysis of the geography of the knowledge economy in the Britain. This study focuses on the proportion of the workforce with tertiary education qualifications in different industries and across different parts of the country. It shows:

- A strong concentration of graduate employment in the most prosperous parts of Britain – predominantly around London, but including Edinburgh and Aberdeen;
- An even stronger concentration of graduate employment in businesses in these regions – with the public sector relatively more important in less prosperous regions;
- A wider spread of knowledge-rich industries in the south and east of the UK;
- Big geographical differences in the proportion of graduates in smaller firms (under 250 employees): with over 25 per cent in London, 15–25 per cent in the area to the west of London, Bristol, Cambridge, Edinburgh, Glasgow and Aberdeen, and under 15 per cent in most of the rest of Britain.

The LFG analysis also looked at the movement of graduates within the UK after graduation. It shows significant net migration to London and the southeast (see Figure 17.1).

These trends are reflected in the overall proportion of working age population by highest and lowest qualifications in different parts of the UK (see Figure 17.2).

This concentration of talent appears to be in large part related to the corporate functions carried out in different parts of the country, for example, headquarters functions, marketing, design, research, and so

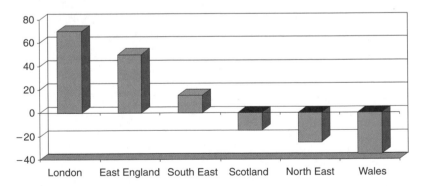

Figure 17.1 Net movement of graduates as a proportion of graduate output (1997–2000).

Source: The Local Futures Group, 2001.

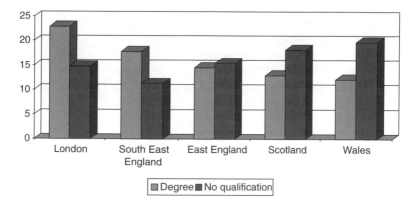

Figure 17.2 Proportion of working age population by highest and lowest qualification (2000).

Source: National Statistics, Regional Trends, 2000.

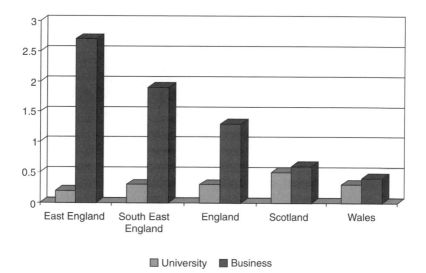

Figure 17.3 R&D spend as percentage of GDP (1998).

Source: National Statistics, Regional Trends, 2000.

on – all with high knowledge content. It is also probably a factor in explaining some of the significant regional differences in business R&D, particularly when compared to the level of University based R&D, across the UK (see Figure 17.3).

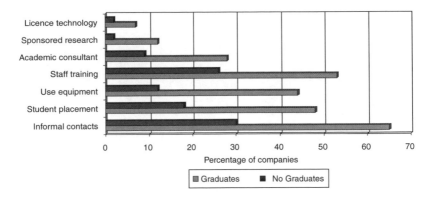

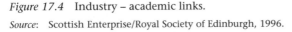

Figure 17.4 Industry – academic links.

Source: Scottish Enterprise/Royal Society of Edinburgh, 1996.

These differences in the business demand for knowledge, are likely to be a key factor in determining the 'industry pull' to commercialise the knowledge in university departments. The relationship between the skills in companies and academic – industry links was identified in the 'Technology Ventures' enquiry in 1995 into commercialising science and technology. It found significant differences in links with universities identified between those companies that employed graduates and those that did not (see Figure 17.4).

The number and movement of graduates and the associated flow of knowledge and talent also appears to be reflected in the entrepreneurial

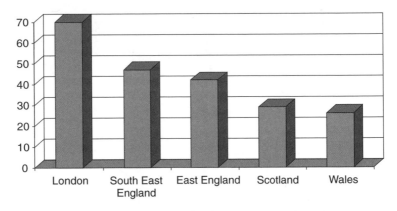

Figure 17.5 Business registrations (1998) (per 10 000 population).

Source: National Statistics, Regional Trends, 2000.

dynamism of a region – a key feature of the commercialisation process (Figure 17.5). Indeed there appears to be a very strong relationship between the number of graduates in the workforce of a region and the rate of business starts.

The cause and effect relationships involved are difficult to disentangle. Nevertheless, this analysis suggests that the development processes identified by Myrdal while studying the plight of poor Americans and underdeveloped countries in the middle of the twentieth century, could well be alive and well in the knowledge economy of the twenty-first century.

The connection between these factors highlights the systemic nature of the forces at play in commercialisation. They all help shape what has been referred to as the innovative milieu of a place. At its heart this is the complex web of relationships that tie economic actors together. This plays a key role in determining how potential investors and knowledge workers perceive a place. In many respects it is as important an element of the economic geography of a region as its physical attributes. It could be argued in the knowledge economy that it is even more important. An excellent example of this has recently been identified by the Silicon Valley Joint Venture – a public/private initiative aimed at keeping this part of California at the forefront of the knowledge economy. They have used the term 'habitat' of innovation and entrepreneurship to describe the environment of Silicon Valley, which provides a gathering place for researchers, entrepreneurs, venture capitalists and skilled workers to turn new ideas into innovative products and services.

These locational characteristics have been well described over a number of years. There is a strong relationship to the study of the contribution of 'social capital' to the economic development process and the way in which informal, personal networks complement more formal, impersonal market mechanisms (Dasgupta, 2000).

The way knowledge is applied within the process of innovation also has significant implications for regional development. Innovation is an interactive, iterative process, which is often stimulated and supported by face-to-face contact. Networks are of increasing importance. Fewer innovations are being introduced by firms working in isolation from one another. Coombs and Metcalf (2000) identify a number of reasons for this:

- A requirement for a wider range of technologies in many products and services, making technological self-sufficiency harder to achieve.
- Increasingly products and processes are themselves part of systems requiring consortia of firms to develop and deliver them.

- The increasing benefits from the combination of diverse technologies and business processes.

Relationships between individuals and the movement of individuals between different parts of a regional system are important transmission mechanisms. They are vital in building effective relationships between the research base and the firms in an area, and in developing a shared language and understanding. This ongoing inter-relationship is seen as a key feature of the 'Cambridge Phenomenon' (Lawson, 1999) and dynamic regions like Silicon Valley (Saxenian, 1994). It ranges from relatively formal contracts between university departments and firms, through the borrowing of equipment and sharing intelligence on key people, to the sharing of tables in a local restaurant. 'Simply recall the tales of the Wagonwheel restaurant during the semiconductor era, the Homebrew Computer Club during the freewheeling days of the birth of the personal computer and the sundeck on Sand Hill Road...where entrepreneurial deals are made over breakfast and lunch' (Silicon Valley Joint Venture, 2001). The complex web of relationships that exists in a region can, if properly nurtured and exploited, become one of the main assets of a region in commercialising its knowledge.

What drives the knowledge commercialisation?

The key drivers in commercialising knowledge can be considered in terms of supply and demand, sometimes referred to as 'technology push' and 'technology pull'. Although both of these concepts have to be treated with caution, because the interaction between the two is not always traded and it is not always technology that is involved.

Perhaps the most interesting dimension of knowledge commercialisation is how the supply and demand side interact with each other and how well the formal and informal transmission mechanisms between the two actually work. A strong relationship between the two requires that each understand the different cultures and motivation of the other. This does not mean that they have to become like each other – indeed this would probably be counterproductive (Coombs and Metcalf, 2000). They must, however, try to understand where each is coming from, no matter how frustrating that might be. The feedback loop from demand to supply is also an important part of the process. The demanding customer can often be a very creative stimulus in the generation of new ideas.

Supply – 'Technology Push'

Research and education institutions are at the heart of the supply side. Their primary responsibility is to create and disseminate knowledge. The very nature of this function, which is related to the creation of a public good, often creates difficulties in the commercialisation process – a process which is seeking to generate private benefits for those involved.

Corporate university policies coupled with individual and departmental attitudes and behaviours are important drivers of commercialisation. For example, the way in which a university deals with the intellectual property that its employees generate can have an important bearing on individual motivation. The culture and values of individual universities and the higher education system as a whole, alongside the discretion that individual departments and researchers have and their motivation will have a significant impact on any commercialisation process. For example, the relative *laissez-faire* corporate culture adopted by Cambridge University to date is cited as having a significant impact on the input of academics to the Cambridge phenomena.

Demand – 'Technology Pull'

The demand side is largely made up of the corporate base of an area (existing and potential). New firm formation can play a key role in providing the commercialisation vehicle, often involving researchers that created the knowledge, or someone that understands the idea involved and can see its commercial potential. However, spin-outs are not the only route and one of the key policy challenges is to stimulate the demand side from existing businesses. Key features of the demand side include its sectoral characteristics and the range and type of corporate functions. The level of strategic corporate decision-making in firms is likely to have a significant influence on the strength and dynamism of the commercialisation process of an area.

The role of key individuals

Key individuals play a critical part in the commercialisation process both within the demand and the supply side and in developing the 'social mechanisms' in which the demand and supply interact. For example, world-renown academics will not only have a big impact through their research, they will also act as a magnet for further research talent and funding or associated investment from those that want to be close at hand to try and exploit the work. The freedom and discretion given to key individuals within their corporate environment (be it university or company) to operate and interact with others can also be critical to the success of the process.

Personal relationships built up by individuals on the demand and supply side are at the heart of the transmission mechanisms in the commercialisation process. They can be particularly important in the early stages of a project where results may be uncertain or where a high level of trust is needed, say over how intellectual property might be handled. These key relationships are often built up within a local environment and are a key factor behind the importance of proximity to commercialisation. However, they can also be global, particularly with other specialists in a specific academic field.

A supportive business environment

Other actors in the economic environment of an area, such as financial and business advisory services, can play a key role in both stimulating and facilitating commercialisation. The more they have an understanding of the issues involved in taking ideas to the market, the greater the likelihood that this will happen successfully.

The role of the public sector

The rationale for public sector involvement in innovation and commercialisation relates primarily to the significant external economies involved, where the returns on investment accruing go to the economy at large rather than to private firms or individuals. A number of studies have estimated that social rate of the return from investment in R&D to be significantly higher than the private rate of return. For example, Griffith (2001) cites a conservative social rate of return to R&D in the UK of 30 per cent, against a private rate of between 7–14 per cent. This is because of the spillover from the firms making the investment into the wider economy, often as the result of the spread of tacit knowledge. If these rates of return are right they imply the UK should optimally be spending two to four times more on R&D as a share of GDP than currently occurs. This is a key determinant of the demand for research knowledge.

The public sector is often a primary funder – and hence shaper of the motivations and results – of research and education, recognising the important 'public goods' produced by both these processes. In Scotland this is via the Scottish Higher Education Funding Council (SHEFC) and the UK-wide Research Councils, with the former providing non-specific research funding to build up the research base in an institution, and the latter supporting specific projects that are built on this base.

There has been increasing interest from economic development agencies in recent years to fully exploit the commercial potential of an area's knowledge base. Their involvement can range from providing direct financial support to companies and academics, through to being broker or facilitator. This latter role involves putting in place mechanisms, which will help the differing objectives and motives of a commercial business and a research establishment find common ground for their own commercial benefit and the greater public good.

Policy should therefore be aimed at taking advantage of the positive externalities to nurture dynamic self-reinforcing systems, which can create, store and share knowledge and turn it into commercially successful products and services. A successful system will involve a strong teaching and research base, always looking to understand and disseminate more, that is well connected to, but distinctive from, a vibrant company base, which is driven by a desire to continually improve performance. They will stimulate each other to solve problems and identify opportunities in a way that is to their mutual benefit. This will involve researchers, teachers, students, entrepreneurs, and executives all interacting in an environment of learning, innovation and commercial success.

Key challenges for Scotland

Lissenberg and Harding (2000) have identified a number of factors that characterise the successful commercialisation of knowledge, based on an analysis of a number of countries and regions. These are set out below along with an assessment of where Scotland stands at the turn of the millennium with regard to each (in italics):

1 A strong industrial demand for innovation – *relatively weak, for example, low levels of business R&D investment compared to more dynamic and prosperous countries and regions little evidence of any significant recent improvement.*
2 A responsive and supportive university infrastructure with the right incentives for academics, along with an entrepreneurial vision in universities to understand the commercial potential of research – *this is an area where a lot of recent developments have taken place. A recent survey by the Scottish Executive highlighted some of the barriers to greater commercialisation within higher education which still exist. They included:*

 • *commercialisation not being part of the traditional career path;*
 • *research being focused on 'Research Assessment Exercise' success;*
 • *the workload demands of teaching and research;*

- *recruitment and promotion favouring teaching and research expertise over entrepreneurialism;*
- *a tradition of scholarly activity and academic publication, rather than user driven research;*
- *the desire to share knowledge resulting in inadvertent disclosure of intellectual capital before securing intellectual property protection.*

3 The appropriate intermediate institutions, which are championed and led by industry – *not well developed, although there is some activity here and further initiatives are planned.*
4 The synergy between university/business research and post experience education, which produces the individuals that can make the right connections – *not well established but developing.*
5 Strong regional clusters to spread innovation and make links – *emerging but still relatively weak.*

There have been some encouraging developments in Scotland over the last ten years. However, they have probably not been of sufficient scale or impact to turn a vicious circle into a virtuous cycle of self-reinforcing development.

Recent Scottish policy and initiatives

In response to the challenges outlined above a number of policies and initiatives have been developed in Scotland in recent years. This section outlines some of them. It is intended to be illustrative not exhaustive. Many of these initiatives were introduced on as standalone basis, however, they are increasingly being looked at and augmented as a more coherent whole, focused on developing the wider innovation system in Scotland.

Overarching policy and initiatives

The commercialisation of knowledge features prominently in a number of elements of the Scottish Executive's policy and reflects the much higher profile that has been given to the issue in Scotland over the last five years. This policy sets the framework within which the funding of universities and the promotion of economic development is set. Recent policy statements include:

- *The Framework for Economic Development* – the overarching 2000 statement of economic development policy covering all departments of devolved government in Scotland. Identifies the knowledge intensity of the economy in the future as a key challenge, gives priority to ensuring the dynamic competitiveness of Scottish enterprises with the promotion of science, innovation and commercialisation as vital.

- *A Smart, Successful Scotland* – the policy direction set in 2001 for the Enterprise Networks (the main economic development agencies in Scotland) identified 'Increased Commercialisation of Research and Innovation' as a priority.
- *A Science Strategy for Scotland* – published in 2001, this explicitly recognises the role of commercialisation in economic development with an objective to increase the effective exploitation of scientific research to grow strong Scottish businesses and provide cutting edge science to meet the needs of the people of Scotland.

'Technology Ventures' – SE and the RSE carried out a major enquiry in 1995/1996 across the business, academic and public sector. It focused on increasing the commercialising of Scotland's science and technology base in Scotland and involved an extensive research programme inside and outside Scotland. It played a major role in raising the profile of the issue of commercialisation and resulted in a strategy for Scotland whose objectives included: maximising the contribution of existing companies and the potential of spin-outs; improving the financing of commercialisation and the academic environment; and developing an effective infrastructure. A leadership group and executive team were set up to drive this strategy forward. Initial results came mainly in the academic environment, for example, in the stimulation of more spin-outs. Following a major review of the initiative in 1998 a stronger focus was put on securing more technology pull from the business sector.

SE/SHEFC Joint Task Group on Research and Knowledge Transfer – SHEFC and SE have begun to work ever more closely together to optimise the impact of their different, but related, policies and programmes which will influence commercialisation. One manifestation of this has been the establishment of SE/SHEFC Joint Task group on Research and Knowledge Transfer. One of the issues being addressed by this Group is 'third funding leg' for commercialisation in universities to go alongside funding for teaching and research.

Connecting universities and business

Industrial liaison/technology transfer offices – Nearly all of Scotland's universities have established offices to help commercialise their research with total operating budgets of over £5 million (an average of £500 000) and around 120 full time staff employed. Their activities include: the promotion of intellectual property protection, the assessment of the commercial potential of research, the management of patent applications, negotiation of licences, marketing of research capability and co-ordinating research grants.

Connect – formed in 1996 to nurture the creation, development and growth of technology enterprise throughout Scotland. It brings together researchers and technology entrepreneurs through workshops, seminars and conferences that give emerging companies the chance to meet and learn from specialists and from each other and stimulate opportunities for collaborative R&D between universities, research institutes and Scottish technology companies.

New intermediary research institutes – plans are being developed to establish new institutions to connect industry and research in industries and technologies offering significant economic potential, such as energy, communications technology and life sciences. It is envisaged that they will be focused on applied research – close to market, and be driven by industry. They will undertake some research themselves (possibly using key academics) and some under contract to universities. The intention is to make their funding additional to existing research funding, for example, from the European Investment Bank.

Industry clusters

Cluster development – one of the major economic development initiatives in Scotland in recent years, pursued by SE with a number of key industries. This approach is a systemic attempt to create, share and use knowledge to increase innovation and productivity (see Chapter 16 for a critique of this approach). It looks at an industry in its widest context and tries to get to the heart of what drives innovation in the industry. It focuses as much on the links and transmission mechanisms between parts of the industry, as in the individual parts themselves. Cluster plans have been developed for Biotechnology, Food and Drink, Semiconductors, Opto-electronics, Telecommunications, Creative Industries, Forest Industries, Energy, Tourism, Financial Services and Chemicals. SE is currently spending around £40 million a year (just under 10 per cent of its budget) on these plans. Many of the cluster action plans include a significant element focused on the commercialisation of world class research taking place in Scotland. The cluster plans have a strong local dimension, for example, Biotechnology in Dundee, Glasgow and Edinburgh, Creative Industries in Glasgow and Dundee.

AMCET Ltd is a specific cluster related project. It is a joint venture between the University of Dundee and Scottish Enterprise Tayside (SET) focused on the advanced materials technology developed by two academics at the University, with applications in the semiconductor industry. The university contributed the intellectual property and has a 76 per cent stake. SET invested nearly £2.5 million in the company and holds the remaining 24 per cent. They have also secured £1 million from the EU. They are about to spin out their first company.

Finance

Proof of Concept Fund – established by SE in 1999 to support researchers in universities, research institutes, and so on, to develop research to a stage where it is attractive to potential investors. It has focused on research to strengthen key clusters. A total of £30 million has been budgeted over a six-year period. By early 2002, 44 applications to the value of £7 million had been approved from 16 different universities/institutes. Biotechnology has accounted for the largest share of the successful applications (36 per cent by value).

Scottish Equity Partners Ltd – an independent, commercial venture capital company spun out of SE in 2000, marking an important milestone in the development of a vibrant venture capital industry in Scotland. Focused on technology based investments, often those that have had their genesis in Scottish research institutions. Its initial fund-raising round raised £110 million.

Stimulating academic enterprise

Enterprise fellowships – a SE/RSE programme to fund non-tenured academics to develop technology-based businesses. It provides personal development support to help participants increase their chances of entrepreneurial success. A total of £1.3 million has been invested in the programme – primarily in Biotechnology and Opto-electronics. The first phase involved 23 fellowships. A number of prominent Scottish technology start-ups have been assisted via the programme. Following a positive evaluation an extension to the programme is planned.

Scottish Institute for Enterprise (SIE) – established by the universities of Glasgow, Dundee, Edinburgh, Heriot-Watt and Strathclyde in 2000 (with plans to extend it to cover all of Scotland's universities). Supported by the UK Government's Office of Science and Technology (£4 million). SIE aims to stimulate and support the development of enterprising attitudes among those involved in science and technology at all levels.

Infrastructure

Science parks – one of the early initiatives in Scotland aimed at strengthening the links between academic research and industry. The first was at Heriot-Watt University and was followed by others in Glasgow and Aberdeen. The Technology Ventures enquiry concluded that successful science parks should: be part of a coherent and collaborative development strategy; be physically and institutionally integrated with a highly rated HEI; and offer support services to tenants, including privileged access to HEI staff.

The impact of commercialisation initiatives

It is difficult to draw definitive conclusions on the overall impact of the initiatives to commercialise knowledge in Scotland. And it is early days given the long-term nature of what is involved. The evidence to date appears mixed, but on balance it is encouraging. The key issue is whether the scale and pace of development is sufficient to secure Scotland's future in the knowledge economy – an issue considered in Chapter 14. In summary:

- There is evidence of an increasing number of spin-outs from Scottish universities. A recent Scottish Executive survey identified 107 spin-out companies from Scottish universities in the summer of 2000 – all but three of them were based in Scotland. Nearly all of these will have occurred since 1990 and the annual start-up rate appears to have grown significantly over the decade.
- The number of licensing agreements between Scottish Universities and companies more than doubled from 52 in 1996/1997 to 106 in 1998/1999. Of these 106 agreements just over 20 per cent were with Scottish-based organisations.
- The volume and value of company sponsored research rose from 3827 contracts worth £113 million in 1996/1997 to 4722 contracts worth £136 million in 1998/1999.
- R&D investment by business remains low at around 0.5–0.6 per cent of GDP (although the latest data on R&D does not go beyond 1999). This has hardly changed in recent years. It is well below the best performing parts of the UK and other comparable parts of the world. Other countries (Ireland and Finland) have also shown a significant increase over the past ten years.

Looking forward to 2020

Increasing the quantity and quality of the commercialisation of knowledge for the economic advantage of a country like Scotland is a complex issue, but one which will be critical to Scotland's future economic prospects. This chapter has tried to illustrate why policy and associated action in the years ahead must:

- take full account of the systemic nature of the process in which knowledge is created, shared and used and have regard to knowledge in its widest sense; and
- be based on an understanding of the different, but related, motivations and objectives (corporate and individual) of the various actors involved in the process and the way in which the connections between them work.

The balanced scorecard approach (Kaplan and Norton, 1996) to planning and managing business performance provides a useful framework to help a country or region think about progress in this area. It has four elements covering the end results sought, along with the relationships, processes and skills/culture needed to achieve these results. This approach explicitly recognises the systemic nature of what is involved and will help identify key connections. Using this framework it is possible to begin identifying the various elements (and the relationships between them) that must be in place in a country like Scotland if it is to be successful in commercialising its knowledge to maximum effect (Figure 17.6).

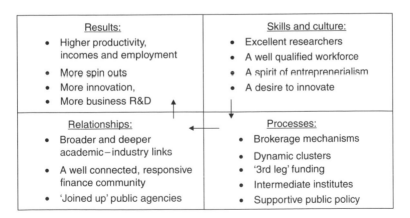

Figure 17.6 Balanced scorecard.

There is no one sufficient condition for success in commercialising knowledge but a series of necessary conditions. Therefore action to stimulate more commercialisation that has greater economic impact must go beyond a series of related but unconnected initiatives. Policy and associated programmes must be genuinely joined up and focused so that they reinforce each other to achieve a real step change. This is the only way to do more than simply tread water against the downward pressure of the vicious cycle that has characterised many less prosperous countries and regions in the past and build a virtuous upward spiral of development. Many of the building blocks are being put in place in Scotland and much has been achieved in recent years. But building an even stronger system is essential to allow the full economic potential of Scotland's knowledge to be realised.

References

Coombs, R. and S. Metcalf (2000), 'Universities, the science base and the innovation performance of the UK', CRIC Briefing Paper No. 5, Manchester: ESRC. Centre for Research on Innovation and Competition.

Dasgupta, P. and I. Svageldin (2000), *Social Capital – A Multifaceted Perspective*, Oxford: Oxford University Press.

Griffith, R. (2001), 'How important is business R&D for economic growth and should the Government Subsidise it?', Institute for Fiscal Studies, Briefing Note No. 12, London: Institute of Fiscal Studies.

Kaplan, R. and Norton, D. (1996), 'The balanced scorecard: translating strategy into action', Cambridge, Mass: Harvard Business School Press.

Landes, D. (1998), *The Wealth and Poverty of Nations*, London: Little, Brown.

Lawson, C. (1999), 'Towards a competence theory of a region', *Cambridge Journal of Economics*, Vol. 23, March, pp. 151–166.

Maskell, P. and A. Malmberg (1999), 'Localised learning and industrial competitiveness', *Cambridge Journal of Economics*, Vol. 23, March, pp. 167–185.

Saxenian, A. (1994), *Regional Advantage*, Cambridge, Mass: Harvard University Press.

Silicon Valley Joint Venture (2001), *Next Silicon Valley – Riding the waves of Innovation*, www.jointventure.org.

18
Economic Governance and the Scottish Economy: 1980–2020

John R. Firn

One of the interesting and enjoyable features of the past two decades, both in Scotland and its fellow developed economies, has been an exploding business and corporate lexicon as new management development concepts and policy concerns emerged from business schools and international consultants.[1] One of these concepts, namely *Corporate Governance*, may however have a longer shelf-life, especially if the narrower definition of governance is expanded to encompass the broader commercial and policy environment, ethos and framework within which stakeholders such as entrepreneurs, business managers, shareholders,[2] employees, and government departments and agencies combine in the process of economic development.

The purpose of this chapter is to use the newer concept of economic governance to review the evolution of the Scottish economy and business community since 1980; and to explore whether such an analytical framework might suggest policy lessons and implications for those in the Scottish Parliament and Scottish Executive charged with framing, funding and delivering such policy. This is a challenging and formidable task, especially as economic governance requires investigation of a range of complex inter-related economic development issues which are still imperfectly understood both in analytical isolation and within the bigger and more daunting policy environment.[3]

The starting point in this voyage through Scotland's recent business and economic development is an operational definition of economic governance which can then be used for a retrospective review of key governance issues that have (often unwittingly and unrecognised) been important influences in Scotland since 1980. It may then be possible to suggest economic development principles and priorities framing economic policy within Scotland during a period where both economic and corporate governance may become a global policy priority.

Corporate Governance and Economic Development

What is national economic governance, and why is it important to international, national and regional economic development in both policy and in operational terms? It is important to review these two separate but inter-related issues as a precursor to the governance in Scotland.

Corporate governance: an evolving concept

The notion of introducing managerial ethics into business affairs which lie at the heart of corporate governance can be seen as a slightly shame-faced reaction by the business community in the G7 group of nations to the emergence of the Masters of the Universe[4] in a post-communist world where only the market ruled. Corporate finance houses, banks, advisors, private investors and corporate executives (especially following Britain's Big Bang deregulation of its financial markets in 1987) actively and aggressively drove business and corporate change under the guise of improving shareholder value so that capital assets could be reinvested in higher yielding situations. Mergers and acquisitions (M&A) (increasing pursued by hostile Barbarians at the Gate, see Burrough and Helyar, 1990), venture capital promotion, the privatisation of state-owned enterprises, and the demutualisation of building societies, insurance and assurance institutions, all combined to radically reshape Scottish and world business. Companies and institutions in Scotland were regularly 'in play' despite occasional attempts to erect tartan ring fences to deter corporate raiders.

Such corporate reorganisation, often powered through the fee hunt of professional advisors, began to generate concern by national governments and international organisations that key groups of business stakeholders were being exploited, that corporate decisions were moving out with the influence of government, and that short-term capital gains had priority over long-term business performance returns. As a consequence both formal and informal (self-regulation) guidelines for ethical governance of the business community were accepted and adopted by the UK financial sectors.

Initially, governance improvements focused upon senior executives, Board members, financial advisors and banking partners of both quoted and private companies through such as the Cadbury Report (Irish

Association of Investment Managers, 1999).[5] During the 1990s, corporate governance has expanded to address environmental and sustainability issues; and will probably be further broadened to encompass global poverty and debt. Governance as a concept is thus continually evolving: governance in 2020 will have moved on from that of 1980.

In reviewing Scotland's post-1980 economic development, a broader definition of governance which includes:

- Structure and nature of the business community in terms of its ability to shape and influence its own corporate and institutional decision-making: *the degree to which it can govern, promote and regulate itself.*
- Culture, beliefs, probity and ethos of a business community as seen in its support for, understanding of, and participation in, market-driven business and economic activities: *the degree to which it encourages business.*
- Policy development and delivery framework in relation to a polity's effective capability to create, manage and maintain a continuing process of business, economic and community development in a genuinely sustainable manner: *the degree to which it supports business.*

Economic governance, in addressing these three aspects of economic and business development, lies at the core of national, regional and local economic development. It is this broader use of the governance concept that is used to explore Scotland's recent and prospective change and growth.

Economic governance and economic development

The rapid emergence post-1980 of economic development as a reasonably coherent and comprehensive academic discipline, has created a new profession and a policy area of international importance.[6] The explosion of research, experience and participation in all aspects of economic development has (as with economics in the 1950s and business management in the 1980s) spawned a portfolio of specialisms in a lead role. This is especially true in Scotland, where for over 30 years economic development has flourished and expanded into virtually every facet of the nation's existence – both a strength and a weakness as will be seen later.

The principal purpose of economic development must be to build and maintain national trade and investment competitiveness through the efficient and sustainable use of a nation's resources within the global economy. Experience suggests that this is probably best achieved through the decisions and investment of private sector businesses and their entrepreneurs. The economic governance within which business enterprises and organisations operate is thus fundamentally important. The three aspects of economic governance outlined above must thus always be taken into account by national policy makers and policy deliverers. The degree to which this has been achieved in Scotland over the past 20 years; and how might it be better promoted over the next generation is the core issue addressed below.[7]

Economic governance at local, regional, national and supranational levels is a complex area of research, policy and practice lying across the economics–politics interface. It has been perceived as simply too difficult to understand, especially within an international policy environment where technology has telescoped time and space and simultaneously generated a truly global economic, industrial and business consciousness. The emergence of the Single Global Market for many products and services, the advent of multinational currencies such as the euro and electronic transactions, the enlargement of multi-country economic clubs and zones, and the arrival of truly global business enterprises have led to an enhanced interest in economic governance, especially in Scotland which has traditionally seen itself as a 'taker' rather than 'maker' of governance. The issues addressed in this book should be seen in relation to economic governance: what do they mean for our national policy priorities?; what political and administrative framework can best pursue such policies?; and what will this mean in terms of building a genuinely sustainable economy?

Post-1975 economic governance in Scotland

Over the past quarter century, it is perhaps possible to distinguish seven inter-related economic governance trends important to Scotland's future. These are a limited and poorly defined vision for the national economy; a policy drift to supply-side issues; an increasingly confusing 'clutter' of economic development activities and agents; a penchant for continual re-engineering of organisations; a preference for consultation and evaluation rather than actions and decisions; a fascination with the new, the trivial and the image; and a declining capability in an age of informatics to measure, analyse and understand Scotland's national economy, its industrial and commercial sectors, and its businesses and organisations. These are all economic governance issues where radical improvements are essential over the period to 2010 if the national economy is to be better placed by 2020 to meet national expectations, especially in relation to economic sustainability.

The limited economic vision for Scotland

In retrospect, the post-1980 period has had few significant attempts to develop, promote and pursue a coherent long-term economic vision for Scotland, and certainly nothing as considered or as influential as the Toothill Report of 1961.[8] This is in contrast to the political vision where a common commitment to devolution emerged and was achieved, principally because of broad agreement in Scotland on the initial goal. There has instead been an explosion of strategies, action plans and initiatives throughout Scotland's economic sectors, local and regional communities and key organisations with little attempt to provide a set of national goals, a delivery framework, or co-ordinated resources for these. Whilst encouraging '. . . a thousand flowers to bloom' has much to commend it in encouraging innovation, there have perhaps been too many half-hardy annuals and insufficient perennials and fruit trees in the Scottish economic garden.

The significant changes in the global economy and its governance, especially over the past decade have not been fully understood or addressed within Scotland: this must be a national priority at the start of the new century. There is a need to examine and agree on a range of national governance issues: Scotland's international role and relationships; the minimum degree of centralisation of economic governance required; the policy contributions and role of the private and public sectors; and the longer term evolution and prioritisation for public sector expenditure and financing. A broad economic governance vision for the period to 2020 and beyond is thus the first priority. It will be a major challenge to secure agreement on policy priorities, but hard decisions are usually the important ones.[9]

The importance of the demand side

The ability of an economy to generate income, employment and wealth for its citizens in an increasingly linked global trading economy is always determined and driven by the creativity, determination, knowledge and investment of entrepreneurs, managers and owners of the nation's business community. Their success will build the demand for employment, capital and infrastructure, and make possible the public and community expenditure required by caring and responsible communities. An established feature of all developed nations is that government directly and indirectly supports its business communities (not always efficiently) to enhance their competitiveness and efficiency.

There is a long, and often little recognised, tradition of state and government intervention in Scotland's business and commercial enterprises and communities beginning in the seventeenth century.[10] The creation of the Highlands and Islands Development Board (HIDB) in 1965 and the Scottish Development Agency (SDA) a decade later have been the most direct twentieth century attempts to positively support the business community and thus build international competitiveness and demand through selective intervention. However, both these organisations have since been given much wider roles and remits which has resulted in their original focus being dissipated into a wide variety of supply-side areas such as training, knowledge management (what *is* this?), and supporting careers advice for school leavers.

The post-1990 parallel evolution of the Local Enterprise Companies (LECs) into devolved delivers and managers of national programmes (in hindsight) has generated so many activities and initiatives that no one, let alone businesses, can understand or engage with public support for demand-side initiatives in an efficient manner. There is an urgent need, within the national vision outlined above, to make a more effective use of public finances through targeting them on genuine and sustainable business, industrial and economic development priorities. The next decade must see a return to a greater demand-side rationale for our economic development agencies; the rest of their remits should return to Victoria Quay, the Councils or (in certain areas) to private sector providers.

The economic development community

An important (especially post-1990) feature of Scotland's economic governance has been the significant expansion of public, voluntary, community and partnership organisations with remits for planning, promoting, delivering and monitoring economic and community regeneration. It is difficult to keep count of the organisations, employment and expenditure involved, but in combination these activities represents perhaps the fastest growing sector in the national economy, especially following the arrival of significant European and Lottery funding throughout the latter part of the 1990s. What is of more concern is that the financial and budget costs of Scotland's present public and para-public economic governance framework are largely unknown (even excluding the capital cost of the new Parliament at Holyrood); and not normally compared to the value of the resulting benefits. This will become an increasingly important issue if Scotland's population contracts sharply over the next 50 years as is forecast, and is also relevant to future debate on the transfer of public finance from the UK and Europe, including the Barnett formula.

Whilst the early selective economic initiatives introduced a new and creative approach to regenerating industries, communities and organisations, the subsequent explosion of economic development funds, organisations and practitioners may have become self-defeating via the ubiquitous duplication of competitiveness concepts that target the same investors, markets, technologies and mechanisms. For some urban communities in Scotland, regeneration initiatives promising to bring sustainable economic and employment growth have become almost annual festivals celebrating the provision of clothes for the same naked emperor. Neither the initial Scottish Parliament's enquiry into the national economic development framework, nor the Minister's Bonfire of Quangos, has really addressed the major strategic governance issues associated with Scotland's biggest development clutter. This is a serious governance issue for the period to 2020.[11]

A further lesson is that once an economic development initiative has been established, it usually proves very difficult to end its existence, even when it has either outlived its usefulness or come to the end of its funding. Scotland is littered with Hamster Wheels containing lonely initiative managers running hard to secure further funding that will enable them to continue their existence to seek further funding. Future initiatives should always be time-limited, though perhaps of five-year rather than three-year duration. It is also worth remembering that the SDA in its early years had a policy perspective of doing itself out of existence as rapidly as possible, and of adopting this approach for its initiatives.

Policy and programme stability

An inherent problem of helping businesses, industries and organisations to anticipate, respond and drive competitive change in their products, markets, technologies and their employees is that a parallel absence of stability can be generated within the policy framework encouraging such change. This mirrors one important difference between UK and US companies over the past quarter century: underperformance in returns to shareholders in the UK (and especially Scotland) appears to be responded to through a sale or similar change of ownership of a company whereas US corporations tend to respond by replacing the chief executive and/or their senior executive colleagues. However, one Scottish difference is that not only do we not replace failed or poorly performing private and public executives, but we both tolerate them long past their sell-by date and sometimes rescue them from their failures.[12]

There are a number of examples of the economic governance costs associated with continual tinkering with the economic framework in Scotland over the past quarter century not being in the best interests of economic growth. Two prime examples of sequential short-term tinkering are worth noting:

1 Scotland has had three local government structures since 1975: an average existence of just over eight years. Every re-organisation has led to staff changes (and the loss of important intellectual capital); disruption to planning and business development frameworks; and a progressive centralisation of power.
2 The small business development framework has endured even more redesign efforts, predominantly by advisors and government clients with little or no direct experience of small business. Since 1985, owners and managers of small and medium enterprises (SMEs) in Scotland have successfully seen the SDA's Small Business Division succeeded by Local Enterprise Trusts, Business Shops and Business Gateways, together with a continual stream of local and national SME support programmes largely managed with a public sector ethos.

This comparative absence of policy and delivery stability (a feature of most economic development priorities) is one of the reasons why few consistent or coherent partnerships with the private sector have been maintained: 'It's not working yet, so let's change it'. This has implications for Scotland's future economic governance: patience and flexible persistence in policy and programmes must be given greater priority.

Consultation, evaluation and prevarication

The large-scale entrance of the public sector into economic development in Scotland (especially since 1985) and the emergence of the European Commission (EC) as the *de facto* policy-maker for business and industrial development, has encouraged the emergence and acceptance of a 'consultation for consensus' culture in many key areas of economic policy. Whilst consultation of those benefiting from, or affected by, emerging public investment decisions is right and proper (as an attempt at civic customer care), the 1990s saw such consultation processes at all levels of government consuming an increasing amount of public and private resources, thus diverting energy, enthusiasm and finance from more active uses.

Consultation processes, often involving dozens of organisations and individuals busily co-ordinating diaries already full with other consultations (often involving the same people) inevitably lengthen investment decision timescales; can generate lower common denominator compromise decisions; and sometimes lose the original sense of direction. Private sector eyes regularly glaze over at invitations to be consulted, even where this might benefit them. The Plant Director of a critically important multinational, long-established in Scotland, regularly sends junior managers to sectoral consultations with an admonition to them 'to keep us out of future consultations'!

An associated frustration is the parallel growth, often reflecting EC and Scottish Executive requirements, of evaluation studies designed to generate estimates of quantitative benefits to justify past policy and programme decisions, rather than to understand the impacts of the economic development process. Whilst some evaluations have made significant policy contributions, many end up knowing the price of everything and the value of nothing: of even more concern is that few longitudinal appraisals are considered, but simply cross-sectional snapshot evaluations. Consultation and evaluation often combine to result in a degree of prevarication that delays or prevents the making of hard decisions: the creativity and speed of decision required for investment decisions are regularly constrained as a result. This has implications for the framing and delivery of future economic governance. Scotland probably requires fewer and better economic development initiatives.

Out with the old, in with the new

An important innovation in Scotland's economic governance over the past quarter century has been the attempts to identify, secure and enhance new business models, industrial sectors, technologies, skills and management ethos into the national economy to counteract the long-term decline of traditional industries. Internationally, Eire and Scotland are oft-quoted as being comparatively successful small nations in pursuing this modernisation goal; but it is now becoming clear that much of the perceived success has been achieved by external investors and managers: this critical governance issue is returned to below. Whilst this pursuit of the new has much to commend it, the relative neglect and disdain for the 'traditional' industries and enterprises over the same period is increasingly recognised as misinformed and misguided.

Caution is also required with concepts such as *knowledge industries* (often simply tarted-up information technology activities), which often imply that there is no knowledge, intellectual property rights (IPR) or creativity in sectors such as engineering, shipbuilding, retailing or even agriculture. Some policy and programme initiatives have excluded long-established manufacturing and commercial enterprises from funding support in favour of concentrating on areas of technology where Scotland has little inherent defensible IPR. Look around at the products and services used daily by Scottish industry and consumers: the majority have been excluded or ignored in policy initiatives. As a Border farmer remarked recently: 'We'll be selling potato chips long after the silicon ones have gone'. There is an important governance issue in this bias, in that new organisations and budget lines to support sunrise sectors often crowd out development efforts for important established industries. It is always difficult to persuade government and financial institutions to support innovation in older sectors.[13]

The future policy environment must encourage a more inclusive approach to supporting Scottish-based entrepreneurs, businesses and industries than in the past. This will require reconsideration of the concept of sectoral clusters, which has become the new Millennium's policy priority, although Perroux and the 1963 White Paper for Scotland promoted this propulsive industry concept four decades ago. The principal electronics, chemicals, biotechnology and financial companies in Scotland all see themselves as being members of global rather than national or regional clusters: policy needs to recognise and reflect this over the next two decades. It is also perhaps not sensible to build a national economic strategy on dominant clusters driven by external investors; and a reconsideration of what Scotland is seeking to achieve through such an approach is an integral part both of the visioning priority referred to earlier and of the creation of more coherent economic governance.

Measuring, recording and understanding the economy

An important and worrying governance paradox over the past decade has been the comparative deterioration in the national capability to measure, record, analyse and report upon the nature, performance, comparative strengths and potential of the national economy, its sectors, enterprises and regions during a period when the hardware and software required to do this increased in speed and reduced in cost. Most economists have more computing power on their desks than was available to the whole of the Scottish Economic Planning Department (SEPD) in 1975; yet the quality and timeliness of national economic information in many key areas has not significantly improved. This is a seriously under-resourced area of the Scottish Executive: we can measure and analyse the molecular composition of the Crab Nebula more comprehensively and rapidly than the key economic variables for Scotland.

It is not just in the quality and quantity of economic statistics that our economic governance requires to be improved. Recent research into key policy areas such as FDI, new firm foundation and commercialisation of technology has encountered relatively sparse, incomplete, noncompatible and out-dated case files and information resources within Scottish Executive Departments and agencies with the relevant policy remits. This again reflects the present under-resourcing of a critical important component of our economic governance, with the consequence of limiting the value of the intellectual capital inherent in such information, reducing the efficiency and effectiveness of policy-making, and making it difficult to learn-by-doing. This is an important governance issue for early attention.

These are perhaps the principal generic economic governance features and lessons of the post-1975 period in Scotland that we need to take into account in planning Scotland's future economy. Many will be shared with other nations and regions, but in combination they represent an outline governance agenda for Scotland as it charts its course over the coming decades. There are other governance lessons in relation to the main components of business and industrial change experienced by Scotland in its recent past.

Key business and industrial governance issues

The past two decades have seen a significant improvement in our understanding of business, industrial and regional economic change in Scotland and internationally; and some of these emerging insights are important to future economic governance. There are four broad policy areas where past experience can shape future investment and policy: new firm creation; support for existing companies; mergers, takeovers and management buy-outs (MBOs); and the Scottish business establishment. A brief overview of the governance issues in each of these areas can help establish some governance priorities for the future.

Entrepreneurship and new business creation

It is worth remembering the advice of Baumol that the most important priority for a declining region is to increase the number of local entrepreneurs (Baumol, 1968), and this policy priority has been actively pursued in Scotland for the past two decades. There is, however, a continuing concern that despite significant investment in encouraging new business start-ups, Scotland's recent level of business creation compared unfavourably with other regions in the UK, Europe and North

America (Fraser of Allander Institute, 2001), that new firm survival rates are poorer; and that few new major international businesses have emerged since 1980. The growth performance of new technology based ventures in Silicon Glen has been especially disappointing, with no new indigenous global players to match those created over the same period in comparable areas such as Boston in the US or Cambridge in England. In the less glamorous sectors, a number of strong international companies have emerged in the oil and gas, retailing, financial services and transport sectors, yet such sectors are largely excluded from consideration by the venture capital community in Scotland post-1980.

The determinants of new start-ups in Scotland are still little understood. The long-term (that is, rolling 30 year) trend level of company formation is unknown; the nature versus nurture factors shaping new firm creation have never been properly explored; and there is uncertainty about the most appropriate route and mechanisms for encouraging entrepreneurs to create sustainable businesses. This is an especially important issue for Scotland's future economic governance, given that research consistently reveals that the most important source of advice investment and support to new firms comes overwhelmingly from family, friends and other businesses rather than from public sector organisations.

There is also the emerging evidence that the majority of Scotland's venture capital backed businesses, including those created to commercialise university R&D, have a short duration existence, and that most of the successful ventures lose their independence as investors recoup their rewards through trade sales to larger international companies.[14] New firm creation in Scotland must remain a policy priority over the decades ahead, but may require a different delivery framework.

Support for existing businesses

The post-1980 period has been marked by a patchy and constantly changing support framework for the nation's private sector businesses, although the core instruments of selective financial assistance provided by the Scottish Executive and its predecessor Scottish Office have played perhaps the single most important business investment role throughout the period. There have been major changes in the private sector's own development organisations: the Scottish Council Development and Industry (SCDI) is no longer the influential force that it was in the 1960s and 1970s; the Chambers of Commerce have not yet built a major development role or reputation; and the principal industrial, trade and sector organisations (including those representing the hi-tech enterprises) would find it difficult to continue without public sector partnerships and funding support. There is a further interesting govern-ance issue to be addressed in Scotland over the next decade, namely the potential restructuring of the private sector's representative organisa-tions within the context of a population of five million to create a strong, informed, influential and sustainable presence.

There are other important economic governance issues. Over 80 per cent of Scotland's private sector is made up of family businesses (often treated with scorn as 'lifestyle' existences by those living risk-free life-styles within public sector agencies). These have their own business priorities and challenges: self-support is beginning to emerge, but they remain generally unrepresented in the key national organisations and consultations. Rural businesses, like rural economic development, has been another neglected sector for much of the period: lowland Scotland's rural communities and sectors are beginning to fall behind England, where the Countryside Agency, working in partnership with the new English Regional Development Agencies, is actively supporting rural enterprise in all its forms. This is a further economic governance issue for the future, namely how best to secure rural representation in economic decision-making in a largely urbanised policy forum.

Mergers, takeovers and corporate restructuring

The past three decades has seen the independence of a large number of large- and medium-sized Scottish businesses disappear through mergers and takeovers; and as Ashcroft showed, such loss of independence had adverse linkage impacts on the Scottish economy (Ashcroft and Love, 1993). This is (with FDI) one of the two policy issues which has gener-ated most academic debate within Scotland, especially as globalisation of markets and share-ownerships makes the concepts of ownership and control difficult to understand or to shape. This is especially true in the context of the adoption of matrix management structures in many multinational corporations. Is it possible or even desirable to have a distinct Scottish policy addressing corporate change and corporate governance?

For a short period between 1979 and 1986, there was a consensus within Scotland's government and business community that major Scottish-based companies should (*ceteris paribus*) be helped to maintain their independence where no visible gains from mergers or takeovers could be demonstrated. Concerted efforts to make this case to the Monopolies and Mergers Commission were successful for Highland Distilleries, the Royal Bank of Scotland plc, and Scottish & Newcastle

Breweries plc: who would now argue that the prospects of these three companies would have been better as subsidiaries of Hiram Walker; Standard Chartered Bank or Fosters? The Conservative government 'Big Bang' effectively put an end to regional or sectoral considerations being taken seriously by the UK government; the regulation of mergers and takeovers has now passed to Brussels; and it is probable that a degree of global regulation may evolve through, such as the WTO. These economic governance changes should bear in mind that virtually all serious academic research suggests that there are no shareholder gains from mergers.

More recently Scotland's financial services sector has seen further losses of independence in banking, insurance and fund management; and a major decline in mutually-owned institutions, once a Scottish speciality, reflecting a strong co-operative ethos. It will be important for Scotland to retain and enhance its base of Scottish-owned companies, and thus the recent growth of MBOs in FDI plants and UK subsidiaries in Scotland is to be encouraged. However, maintaining corporate independence will always be difficult in the face of predatory corporate finance houses seeking M&A fees. Creative thought on this aspect of economic governance is necessary, especially as the acquisitive performance in other UK regions and in other countries has been so fundamental to the success of such Scottish champions as the Royal Bank of Scotland, Scottish & Newcastle Breweries and Stagecoach. What may be more important than a formal policy is the creation of a business ethos in Scotland which encourages the long-term growth of Scottish companies whilst maintaining their Scottish base, and provides appropriate finance to support this.[15]

The Scottish business establishment

An interesting feature of the post-1980 period has been the apparent weakening of Scotland's private businesses and their representative organisations to play a role in shaping economic policy and governance. The SCDI, the Chambers of Commerce, the Confederation of British Industry (CBI) and the Scottish industrial and trade associations had, by 2000, lost much of their real influence. The reasons for this are complex and beyond the scope of this review, but factors reducing the visible business voice include the increasing incorporation of business leaders within public sector agencies and quangos; the progressive takeover of Scottish-based companies; the relative dominance of the Labour Party in national and local governance; the cohesive impact on corporate decisions and behaviour of such public-sector led initiatives as the sectoral clusters,[16] and the centralisation of business regulation in London and then Brussels.

Able, aggressive and creative entrepreneurs have emerged in Scotland since 1980, some of them have become major UK and occasionally global business leaders. There is no reason to doubt that this inflow of new blood to Scotland's business establishment will continue through to 2020 and beyond; but also to recognise that as they mature and become decorated with equity-sale fortunes and civic honours they will maintain the continuity of Scotland's business establishment. The challenge is for economic governance to encourage more independent, confident and strategic inputs from this establishment into shaping the national economic vision. However, the plethora of self-congratulatory business awards and the advent of lists (such as Scotland's 100 most important business leaders) suggests that a degree of insecurity and inferiority must first be addressed.

Other economic governance priorities

Other important governance priorities to be addressed in Scotland over the period to 2020 include privatisation and outsourcing of public enterprises and agencies; the strategic long-term shifts in funding sources for economic development (especially in the context of the Barnett formula and EU enlargement); local economic development governance frameworks throughout Scotland; and the operational and strategic implications of moving toward a genuinely sustainable national economy.[17] All of these are important factors within the governance debate, and require to be addressed at length elsewhere.

Scottish economic governance to 2020

The argument advanced in this chapter is that the concept of economic governance enables a fresh look to be taken at the factors shaping both the policy framework and priorities of key economic stakeholders in Scotland, and at the strategic investment decisions of Scotland's business owners and executive managers. Many of these factors are shared with the corporate governance debate; others are specific to economic development at the national, regional and local level; and some represent responses to environmental and societal challenges of the post 9/11 global community. It will be important for the Scottish Parliament together with the Scottish business community to actively and continually seek more effective and efficient economic governance in Scotland that can encourage and support our inherent creativity and skills.

An initial step will be to secure agreement on what type of Scotland we are seeking by 2020; what are the strategic priorities to achieve this,[18] and what is then the post-supportive economic governance framework? The experience of the post-1980 period is that the framework will be significantly different both from that in 1980 and that which currently guides Scotland's economic evolution. Whilst Scotland's economic development over the period to 2020 thankfully cannot be forecast, thoughtful improvements to the nation's economic governance could enable it to realistically pursue the vision of being an influential and creative 'class act on a smaller stage' (Young, 2001).

Notes

1   Economic development policy, programmes and projects in Scotland have, especially since 1990, enthusiastically embraced and pursued business and economic change through such as business re-engineering, core competencies, benchmarking, economic value-added (EVA), sectoral clusters and whatever is the latest snake-oil remedy peddled by *Harvard Business Review, Fortune* or Arthur Anderson. An especial challenge over the period to 2020 will be to discover an economic sector that has not been the subject of a business park.

2   One of the emerging big issues for economic governance in Scotland will be the weakening power of ordinary shareholders in major corporations compared to the voices of analysts, corporate advisors and pension funds. Could such shareholders in Scotland have any influence on key corporate decisions: the experience of the past decade suggests not.

3   In particular, that of the EU which has emerged as a policy stakeholder of at least the same importance as the Scottish Executive since the mid-1990s. Unlike England, Scottish institutions have a positive partnership with Brussels.

4   A world best described in Tom Wolfe *The Bonfire of the Vanities* (1988). The 1986 Guinness plc bid for Distillers plc was known as the Bonfire of the Sanities in Scotland. The Guinness shenanigans had been piloted the previous year in its successful bid for Arthur Bell & Son, then Scotland's most aggressive private company.

5   This passed largely un-noticed in Scotland.

6   Much of economic development's conceptual emergence has been driven by development economics, itself a new discipline from the 1960s; and one where Scottish institutions have played an important role.

7   Many of Scotland's institutions, beliefs, attitudes and economic trends have their roots and influence far back in the past. Selecting analytical boundaries such as 'post-1980' is thus stamping hard on thin ice.

8   The time has come to transfer this and other key documents to the Web to make them more easily available, and to transfer on such valuable intellectual capital which remains important for future policy.

9   It is interesting that none of the economic strategy statements issued by the Scottish Parliament, the Scottish Executive and its executive agencies has set out a longer-term vision for Scotland: all are short to medium term

operational priorities. Scotland plc needs a corporate strategy as well as a rolling three year business plan.

10   The Scottish Parliament may be interested in the fact that James Law tried in 1704 to persuade an earlier generation of its Members to establish a national economic development agency.

11   The recent enquiries into Enterprise and Life-Long Learning by the Scottish Parliament (2000 and 2001) have not addressed this explosion in any detail, nor asked (let alone explored) economic governance issues.

12   This is a fascinating area in itself. Why, for example, do few of those in public agencies charged with promoting business start-ups lead by example? Further, might not it be an innovative policy initiative to limit employment contracts for such economic development activities to seven years?

13   In 1986, it proved impossible to secure equity investment from Scottish financial institutions in Europe's first oriented strand board (OSB) wood panels plant as they saw this as simply another chipboard plant, and thus an old non-competitive commodity technology. London and Scandinavian finance houses were better informed, and (together with SDA and HIDB) made significant profits from the subsequent sale of this start-up to Noranda of Canada (see also *Financial Times*, 2001; and A.B. Bernard and J. Bradford Jensen, 2001).

14   For a review of recent Scottish experience, see Firn Crichton Roberts Ltd 2001.

15   An especially important role has been played through the provision of Regional Selective Assistance (RSA) by the UK Government to support capital investment. RSA, currently under review by the Scottish Executive, may well be difficult to maintain at its current level through the period to 2020; and new long-term forms of investment support to private businesses are in prospect.

16   There is merit in having a final review of Scotland's local government framework within the next decade, and then leaving the resulting councils alone so that they can deliver their remits. Policy, budget and planning should be devolved wherever possible; Common Good and other funds returned to communities; and the spatial separation of major cities from their more affluent regions ended.

17   Scotland has the potential to be a leader in moving to a genuinely sustainable economy and society over the period to 2020; but this will require greater applied research and policy innovation than in the past (see Clement, K., 2000).

18   An initial checklist of eight necessary elements for successful change that require to be considered at the national level are the pressure for change; a clear shared vision; effective liaison and trust; the will and the power to act; capable people and sufficient resources; suitable rewards and accountabilities; actionable first steps; and a capacity to learn and adapt (see Eccles, T., 1994).

References

Ashcroft, B. and J.H. Love (1993), *Takeovers, Mergers and the Regional Economy*, Edinburgh: Edinburgh University Press.

Baumol, W.J. (1968), 'Entrepreneurship in Economic Theory', *American Economic Review*, Vol. LVIII, No. 2, May, pp. 64–71.

Bernard, A.B. and J. Bradford Jensen (2001), 'Who dies? International trade, market structure and industrial restructuring', National Bureau of Economic Research Working Paper 8327, Cambridge, Mass.: National Bureau of Economic Research.

Burrough, B. and J. Helyar (1990), *Barbarians at the Gate*, London: Jonathan Cape.

Clement, K. (2000), *Economic Development and Environmental Gain: European Environmental Integration and Regional Competitiveness*, London: Earthscan Publications.

Eccles, T. (1994), *Succeeding with Change: Implementing Action-Driven Strategies*, London: McGraw-Hill.

Financial Times (2001), 'Motorola and the cluster fluster', 25 April.

Firn Crichton Roberts Ltd (2001) 'The evaluation of the effectiveness of risk capital fund in the East of Scotland: A report to the Eastern Scotland European Partnership', Pittenweem, Fife: Firn Crichton Roberts Limited.

Fraser of Allander Institute (2001), 'Promoting business start-ups: A new strategic formula: Stage 1: progress review: final report', a Report to Scottish Enterprise Glasgow, Glasgow: Fraser of Allander Institute.

Irish Association of Investment Managers (1993), The Cadbury Report, Dublin: Irish Association of Investment Managers.

Wolfe, T. (1988), *The Bonfire of the Vanities*, London: Jonathan Cape.

Young, Alf (2001), 'The Tartan Ring Fence in a world where markets reign', *The Herald*, 23 April.

19
Networks and Relationships: The Scottish Diaspora

Alf Young

The simple fact that a substantial Scottish diaspora exists, scattered around the world, with major concentrations in North America and Australasia and strong traces in the furthest-flung corners of the former British Empire, tends to weigh heavily on any contemporary discussion of Scotland's economic future.

That the number of people living today of Scottish descent (variously estimated at upwards of 50 million) should so dramatically outnumber the 5.1 million resident population of modern Scotland raises profound questions about why they (or their ancestors) went, what their cumulative loss has meant for the continuing economic vitality of the small nation they left behind and what their going says about Scotland's dominant cultural and social values.

There is also a growing debate within institutional and political Scotland about what can be done to re-establish meaningful links with this diaspora and harness its residual sense of Scottishness and affection for its roots to the old country's benefit.

This chapter will look at why that diaspora happened, why the mere fact of it still matters and what we know about how modern Scotland is perceived by the rest of the world. It will also review the various initiatives that have been taken in recent years to harness the goodwill and influence of Scots abroad, people of Scottish descent and all others who hold Scotland, its achievements and its values in a positive light.

Population and growth

Let us start with a widely-shared assumption. Any economy that consistently, over time, leaks people has failed to provide its citizens with either an acceptable level of prosperity or all the economic opportunities and challenges they seek. Nations hit by sustained depopulation will almost certainly have grown less vigorously than their immediate neighbours, may even have suffered prolonged bouts of relative economic decline.

In the latter half of the nineteenth century Scotland's population grew steadily, thanks in large measure to medical advances and their impact on mortality rates. Between 1855 and 1900 it rose by 49 per cent or 1.46 million people. But the century that followed was one of relative stability. In particular since 1947, when Scotland first breached the psychologically significant 5 million people barrier, its population has never managed to top the 5.25 million mark. It peaked at 5 240 800 in 1974 and, apart from a brief rally between 1990 and 1995, has been in gentle decline ever since.

The latest projections from the Registrar General for Scotland see that downward trend continuing over the next two decades, to an estimated 4 926 000 by 2025. Longer-range forecasts by the government actuary point to a Scottish population as low as 4 590 000 by 2040. Some opposition Scottish National Party (SNP) politicians are even claiming Scotland's population could, on current trends, fall below 4 million by the second half of this century.

The latest official forecasts see a perceptible ageing in Scotland's population by 2025 although the trend is rather less pronounced than in many other economies at a similar stage of development. By 2025 the number of Scottish children under 16 is projected to fall to 78 per cent of the 2000 level, while the number of people of pensionable age is expected to grow by 15 per cent over the same period. Both trends pose significant challenges for the conduct of public policy over the next two decades.

The picture of continued population decline stands in stark contrast to predicted trends for the UK as a whole. The UK population is projected to increase from 59.8 million in 2000 to nearly 65 million by 2025. Some two-thirds of that long-term growth, around 135 000 more people a year, is expected to come from net inward migration from overseas. A continuing expectation of more births than deaths each year in the UK as a whole accounts for the rest of the projected UK population growth of 0.3 per cent a year.

The most significant factor influencing official forecasts of Scotland's future population decline is the changing balance of nature – a declining birth rate (down by one-fifth in the past two decades, for example) that no longer even compensates for the prevailing death rate among Scots. There is no convincing evidence that Scotland's declining birth rate is about to start growing again in the next 20 years. Nor, in contrast to the forecasts for the UK as a whole, is the Registrar General for Scotland expecting any net migration into or out of Scotland between now and 2025.

That implies that none of those additional 135 000 immigrants to the UK each year, who presumably include all the teaching and healthcare staff already being recruited from around the world to fill staff vacancies in schools and hospitals in England, will ever find their way to Scotland. It also suggests that recent talk of recruiting scarce technological skills from Eastern Europe, India and elsewhere to sustain the surviving elements of Scotland's silicon industries is unlikely to bear significant fruit.

The challenge of reversing Scotland's long-term population decline has, until very recently, featured only at the margins of debate about Scotland's economic priorities. Historically Scotland has been preoccupied not with boosting its population through promoting more in-migration but with the damage inflicted on its economy by failing to halt the persistent out-migration of many talented Scots. Indeed the history of mass emigration is seared deeply into the nation's collective psyche. The Highland Clearances – the mass eviction between 1790 and 1850 of countless tenants and their families from the crofting counties by lairds and clan chiefs in favour of the lucrative new sheep economy – sowed resentments and animosities that still fester today. Some of the dispossessed found their way to the slums of Glasgow. Many were scattered to the harsh new pioneering worlds of Canada and Australia. Some of their descendants have gone on to great achievements. But a sense of brooding injustice prevails and has ensured that subsequent mass emigrations by later generations of Scots have all been firmly rooted, in the popular consciousness, in a fundamentally economic rationale.

According to this prevailing consensus, Scots left their native land in large numbers not out of any sense of adventure or to seek their fortune, not because they found the society they left behind claustrophobically disapproving of their aspirations, but because the Scottish economy had consistently failed to produce enough jobs or pay decent enough wages to keep them all productively employed in the land of their birth.

From the middle ages Scots have willingly emigrated in search of enhanced education, to take up the life of a mercenary, to explore uncharted corners of the globe or to open up new trading channels. For centuries past the Scots have been decidedly internationalist in outlook. But ever since the spectacular failure in 1700 of the Darien scheme, with all that catastrophe was to mean for Scotland's material well-being and constitutional future, migration and economy have been inextricably linked. Darien was a hugely ambitious national venture, launched in 1695, to set up and populate a Scottish trading colony on the Isthmus of Panama in Central America. Its failure wiped out around a fifth of Scotland's entire national wealth. It also made the political union with England, which followed seven years later, all but inevitable.

Scotland has certainly lost millions of its most skilled people over the past two centuries, to England and to lands overseas. Like many other countries it has lost them when times were tough and deprivation widespread. But paradoxically it has also lost them when industrialisation within Scotland was thriving and Scottish companies formed a significant force in global export markets for ships, steam trains and other manufactured goods. A net 390 000 Scots left in the 1920s. Some 600 000 departed between 1951 and 1971. Many were highly skilled. No one had told them to go. Yet more of them have gone over the piece, as a proportion of national population, than anywhere else in Europe other than Ireland.

The pace has slowed in recent decades, as countries like Australia which were only too keen to attract scarce skills in the immediate post-war period, even to the extent of offering assisted passages for migrant families, developed and became more choosy about whom they would let in. Since 1980 net migration by Scots to the rest of the UK has continued, with the most recent peak of 16 600 reached in 1988. Net migration overseas had peaked earlier, in 1982, at 13 700 but continued at much lower levels for much of the rest of that decade.

The migration pattern with the rest of the UK went into reverse in the late 1980s and stayed that way for a period that coincided with the last significant UK recession, one that Scotland managed to avoid. By 1991 a net 12 400 people were moving north annually. That pattern has since reversed again although the net outflow is still running at below 7000 a year. In four of the seven years up until 2000, Scotland enjoyed a small net influx of migrants from overseas. Overall, combining flows to and from the rest of the UK with those from overseas, net migration has been running in Scotland's favour in 7 of the 11 years from 1990 to 2000.

It is difficult to prove statistically a definitive link between this rather complex pattern of migration and the prevailing economic climate of the time. Certainly between 1990 and 1992 when the rest of the UK and the United States were both in recession, Scotland (where growth had slowed sharply but stayed in positive territory) saw a short-lived but pronounced reversal of its usual migration losses to the rest of the UK. But in those same years it was still losing nearly as many people to overseas destinations as it was gaining from the rest of the UK.

On a longer timeframe, statistical correlations are no more conclusive. As we have already noted, some of the most significant migration from Scotland occurred in the 1960s, that so-called golden age when Scottish growth (as measured by gross domestic product (GDP) excluding oil and gas) pretty well mirrored growth in the UK as a whole. In 1964 Scotland's growth even soared as high as 8 per cent. That level of growth begins to rival the kind of double-digit rates which, in the 1990s, bestowed on Ireland its Celtic tiger status and saw it reverse decades of chronic depopulation, during which too many Irish men and women had had no alternative but to take the boat to Liverpool or Boston in search of work and prosperity. But, for Scotland in the 1960s, sky-high growth did not last. Within four years the annual rate was down to 1 per cent and painful industrial change was well under way. So an Irish-style reversal of population loss did not happen in Scotland in the 1960s.

Since 1974 annual Scottish GDP growth has never managed to top 4 per cent. Only in 1984 and again in the early 1990s recession elsewhere in the UK has Scotland's growth rate out-performed the UK as a whole. Over the past 30 years Scottish growth has averaged a modest 1.7 per cent a year, compared with 2.1 per cent for the UK as a whole. The latest GDP figures, for the second and third quarters of 2001, suggest Scottish growth is again falling sharply off the UK pace. Whether that divergence will persist and whether it will eventually be reflected in future migration patterns remains to be seen.

Despite the lack of a decisive statistical correlation between migration patterns and relative economic performance, issues of economic advantage undoubtedly play a highly significant role in where many people, particularly those of working age, choose to live and work. They are not the only considerations. Quality of life issues, family patterns, relative buying power (particularly in the housing market), ease and cost of transport links and, most recently, the ability of modern means of communication to shrink distance all come into the equation. That said, individual economic opportunity remains a fundamental driver in where many of us choose to put down roots.

While the direct challenge of reversing Scotland's historic population loss has never featured prominently in the policy debate, the parallel challenge of lifting the Scottish economy's growth rate above historic rates is now central to the 'enterprise agenda'. The problem, in the medium term, is that many of the initiatives being championed – such as persuading more Scottish companies to move higher up the value chain and releasing the commercial potential of more of the research being undertaken in Scotland universities – are unlikely to produce results quickly. If that emphasis on Scottish brains rather than Scottish brawn succeeds, we may see a step change in Scotland's growth performance by 2020. But the major pay-offs are likely to come towards the end of that period.

Images of Scotland

Very little serious research has been carried out into how modern Scots see themselves and how the rest of the world regards Scotland. We all recognise the anecdotal power of symbols like tartan, whisky, the Scottish football fan abroad, the Loch Ness Monster, links golf and, most recently, the film *Braveheart*.

Scotland's main economic development agency Scottish Enterprise (SE) and its predecessor the Scottish Development Agency have both carried out several studies into what, over the past 25 years has persuaded many multinational corporations to locate in Scotland. The ready availability of cost competitive skills, the quality of Scotland's educational system, the fact that our dominant language is English and our location within the EU (though not yet within the eurozone) have typically emerged as the strongest positives.

Indigenous Scottish businesses, notably in the financial services, whisky, textiles, food and tourism sectors have, for many years, used perceived aspects of Scottishness to market their goods and services. For many years the watchword of Scottish Financial Enterprise, the promotional body for Scotland's banks, life assurance offices and fund managers was 'Trust the Scots', a clear reference to our fabled reputation for thrift. Scotch whisky distillers regularly use heritage and the quality of Scotland's rural environment in promoting their brands. Craftsmanship lies at the heart of how Scotland's remaining textiles sector – cashmere and Harris Tweed – is marketed. And quality is the word most frequently attached to our meat products and seafood.

But research into the wider question of what kind of brand identity modern Scotland enjoys in the wider world is scarce. In the mid-1990s Scotland the Brand, a body set up by private initiative to develop a generic brand identity for Scottish goods and services, largely funded through SE, embarked on Project Galore. Research for Galore was carried out over a two year period by international brand development consultants CLK, who reported their findings in March 1999. The research, involving focus groups and in-depth interviews with individuals, spanned England, France, Germany, Spain, the United States and Japan as well as Scotland.

The research findings suggested Scots have a clear sense of their own identity, seeing themselves as civilised, educated, skills rich, astute and recognisably a nation. They admire their own value set but resent any sense of Scotland being dependent on its larger UK neighbour England. But when asked how the rest of the world sees Scotland, the Scottish respondents tended to default reluctantly to the haggis and bagpipes view of their country. Their aspiration was to be seen as inventive, modern and entrepreneurial. Their fear was that Scotland is still seen as irredeemably but wholesomely old-fashioned.

The non-Scots surveyed clearly identified Scotland as a country in its own right. Many could even draw a rough outline of its geography. Many saw it and its people in a very positive light. But they came to that conclusion because, from their perspective, Scotland represents a repository of traditional values in a fast-changing world. In spite of producing a significant proportion of Europe's personal computers and memory chips, Scotland is not associated with advanced technology or modern infrastructure. Some respondents thought Scotland had a second or third world economy, akin to South Africa or Poland. Germans were apparently surprised to discover modern Scotland has any dual carriageways. Americans, used to Heathrow as the sole gateway to the UK, did not know Scotland had any airports offering international connections.

None of this is entirely surprising. Those who have never been to Scotland are bound to form their impressions from unrepresentative evidence. Their principal encounters with Scottishness will have come from films like Mel Gibson's hugely successful *Braveheart* – a piece of hokum Scottish history. They may also have encountered the recreational preoccupations of the active elements in the great Scots diaspora – Burns clubs and Caledonian societies, with their inevitable emphasis on the past, on tradition.

Scots and non-Scots who took part in the Galore research could agree that Scots display a strong spirit of independence and show admirable integrity and tenacity. However, despite numerous studies claiming Scots have invented everything from the pneumatic tyre to television, only English respondents shared the perception that the Scots are an inventive people. For others Scotland remains a haven of tradition and tranquillity, somewhat out of step with the contemporary world and not at all the smart, successful economy today's Scottish politicians want it to be.

Tapping into the Scottish diaspora

Scots who can propose an arresting immortal memory at a Burns supper, have mastered Shetland fiddle music or can entertainingly build links to various other aspects of traditional Scottish culture have always known the world is their oyster. The more active elements of the Scottish diaspora provide ready audiences all round the globe for such performers. However Scotland as a whole has paid scant attention, until relatively recently, to Scotland's connectedness with the rest of the world and what people of Scots descent could do to assist economic progress of their homeland.

Decades spent pursuing mobile foreign direct investment helped create new global networks as generations of Scots-born managers worked their way up through the ranks of transnational corporations like IBM and Motorola. The focus on inward investment also uncovered earlier generations of expatriate Scots, keen to put something back into the land of their birth. But for a very long time the public response to these opportunities was lacklustre.

In the early 1990s, that partial vacuum was filled by private initiatives, notably the creation of the Scotland the Brand organisation in 1994 to develop a country of origin device and promote what were seen to be Scotland's distinctive brand values and the launch a year later of Scotland International, an annual gathering at Gleneagles designed to reconnect leaders of the Scottish business community with some of the most powerful players in the Scottish diaspora.

Scotland the Brand was rapidly absorbed into the formal machinery of economic development, receiving the lion's share of its modest funding from the government's principal development agency, SE. However it was much less clear what SE wanted from its new appendage. A new Scotland mark was launched in 1970 and, to date, some 350 Scottish companies and organisations in a wide variety of sectors have been accepted as licensees, able to use the device on their products and publicity material. The organisation has also been involved in a range of marketing and advertising initiatives, from food promotions in Paris to Tartan Weeks in Chicago. And it was responsible for the Project Galore research completed in 1999. The findings of that research were never properly exploited and now Scotland the Brand is to be privatised. When the process is complete it will be owned by the companies which have been licensed to use its mark. Its quasi-public role as the arbiter of Scotland's predominant brand values will be at an end.

Scotland International, the brainchild of Sir Charles Fraser and Sir Angus Grossart, has remained resolutely independent, although some of the initiatives it has spawned down the years, notably a £5 million plan to bring entrepreneurial education into the mainstream curriculum of every Scottish primary school was dependent on matching state funding. Other initiatives, like Scottish Knowledge and Scottish Medicine, have been launched as strictly commercial ventures but have again been dependent on an element of public patronage. Scotland International's links with the diaspora have dwindled since it first met. One weekend a year at the famous Perthshire resort hotel dissecting the state of Scotland and proposing initiatives to boost its performance has not proved sufficient to maintain momentum on that front. In recent years its relationship with SE has become more and more strained.

Scotland the Brand and Scotland International may have been the first to address issues around Scotland's global connections. However with the creation of the new Scottish Parliament in 1999 and the rapid reshaping of economic development strategy over the past three years, both the challenge of encouraging more people to live and work in Scotland and that of turning Scotland into a more globally attractive location have been placed at the heart of government policy. As the Scottish Executive's Global Connections Strategy puts it: 'Scotland needs to be a world class business location in order to retain and attract leading global companies and people as well as providing the environment for Scottish companies to grow and internationalise . . . We need to offer the jobs to encourage the young to stay and the more experienced to return. We need to tap into the network of Scots around the world to ensure that knowledge of Scotland and its opportunities is current and well understood. This will be one part of a broader programme of action to portray a more contemporary view of modern Scotland'.

The separate global outreach arms of SE charged with attracting fresh inward investment and promoting Scottish trade overseas have now been merged into Scottish Development International (SDI). However SDI comes into being at a time when mobile industrial investment has retrenched in the wake of the global economic slowdown and, where still active, is now looking for lower-cost locations than Scotland. Government is already reacting to these new realities by promising to put more of its financial support behind indigenous Scottish companies with high growth potential in quality business sectors.

The prospects of all these strategic shifts bearing some real fruit over the next 20 years is crucially dependent on delivery. And delivery, it seems to me, requires far greater focus and single-minded determination than institutional and political Scotland has displayed in the past. Take the renewed government interest in tapping into networks of expatriate Scots around the world. The Irish have exploited their diaspora brilliantly for decades past. By comparison, we Scots can seem like blundering amateurs.

Since the launch of the Global Connections strategy, SE has launched Global Scot, an attempt to build an international network of influential people of Scottish descent in business, industry and academia around the world. 'Scottish Enterprise believes that by encouraging key persons to share knowledge and expertise, everyone can benefit' says its website. Simultaneously Helen Liddell, the Scottish Secretary, used a banquet in London in November 2001 to launch her Friends of Scotland initiative. Liddell runs the Scotland Office, the constitutional link between the Edinburgh and Westminster parliaments. 'Tonight' she said 'I want to begin a process of reaching out to them (the Friends of Scotland) as we have never done before – with the aim of strengthening Scottish business, boosting tourism, but above all changing perceptions of Scotland and converting that changed perception into concrete benefits for our country.'

Liddell, who has been criticised for having a less than demanding ministerial portfolio, has already assembled a nine-strong advisory group, including the historian Professor Tom Devine and the former permanent secretary at the Foreign Office Sir John Kerr, to help her drive the Friends initiative forward. Quite how it relates to the Global Scot initiative being pursued by the Scottish Executive and SE is far from clear. It seems obvious that effective re-engagement with elements of Scotland's diaspora could yield tangible benefits over the next 20 years. But the history of under-resourced private initiatives, expensive research into perceptions of Scottishness that now gathers dust on a shelf, and competing ministerial initiatives to embrace Scotland's long-neglected expatriate communities suggests the strategy has yet to find a sharp enough delivery focus.

Part V

The Future of the Scottish Economy: International Perspectives

20
Conclusions

Neil Hood, Jeremy Peat, Ewen Peters and Stephen Young

Introduction

In drawing this book to a conclusion, we are conscious of the time in which we have been writing it. It is early days for our new Parliament, and there is evidence of a material shift in emphasis in economic development policies for Scotland over the past three years.[1] But time is not on our side, and the long term implications of the relatively poor performance of the Scottish economy, by both UK and other peer group measures, are already evident. Time series data shows that Scotland's gross domestic product (GDP) per head measured just below the UK average for most of the 1975–2001 period. For a short period in the mid-1990s the Scottish growth rate exceeded that of the UK. However, there are signs that the Scotland – UK gap has been widening since 1996.

The policy directions that are now established will, even if they are consistently and vigorously pursued, take a long time to deliver real economy-changing results. It is also critical to remember that many comparable countries are adopting similar strategies to address similar problems, and many of the industry-specific changes are in competition with others. The international orientation of the Scottish economy only adds to the challenge in that this results in its fortunes being much more dependent on what happens outside its borders than nations and regions of greater scale. So far we can only conclude that Scotland as a whole has not responded particularly well to global prospects, a situation that must change if its relative economic performance is to be enhanced. This raises the vitally important question as to what we should regard as a reasonable position for the Scottish economy to be in by 2020 – an issue that provides the starting point for the review of recurring themes that follows.

Recurring themes

We did not seek to impose a rigorous structure upon the contributors to this volume. Even if we had, they would not have complied. In any event that was not what we wanted; and we did not choose them for their record of compliance! Our interest was more in encouraging all parties to bear in mind the aims of the volume as set out in Chapter 1 as they addressed their assigned topic in the light of their experience and expertise. Thus the styles and formats are varied, but in every case they have had an eye to the future and to the direction that policy and behaviour should take over the next twenty years or so. Without forcing any of the analysis, it will be evident to the reader that there are a number of themes that regularly emerge.

What does Scotland want to be?

In various chapters, the matter of what Scotland is in economic terms is commented upon; in several others this is extended to the issue of what should be aspired to in terms of both corporate and country ambitions. As regards the former, Brian Ashcroft positions Scotland as 'by international and even UK standards, a mid ranking player'; Jonathan Star suggests that the aspirations should be for economic performance at the upper quartile level of the Organisation for Economic Co-operation and Development (OECD) nations; while Alf Young is quoted as viewing the realistic position as being regarded as 'a class act on a small stage'. There is an air of realism in these views. And none of us underestimate the seriousness of the situation and the major problems associated with stabilising or improving it. Moreover, benchmarking with others (Chapter 4) reminds us that all the relevant comparator nations and regions benefited from, among other things, concentrations of industries that have grown strongly in global terms, long term high levels of investment in productive capacity, education and other infrastructure, as well as effectively rooted foreign direct investment in most cases. One key aim has to be to raise the rate of investment and the share of investment in GDP, a double challenge when the high rates of investment associated with inward investment in Scotland in the past are taken into account. In short, the 'what future?' is one thing; the 'how to achieve it' is quite another. So even to attain to these appropriately scaled goals is not without its real challenges. One of the central parts of that challenge lies in both the continued existence, and further development, of major businesses in Scotland whose ambitions are truly global and whose commitment to developing a strong Scottish base is unwavering. This is a theme to which we will return later in this section, since it lies at the heart of much of the business potential within Scotland, and is picked up in several chapters. But suffice it to say that the overall quality of life in Scotland is critical if we are to foster the concept of an excellent home base for existing and emerging companies of all sizes.

Enterprise and business growth

The lack of entrepreneurship emerges as a central issue in many of the chapters. In Chapter 14 which specifically focuses on this matter, Hood and Paterson say that it is 'a topic that needs to be top of the mind of every part of the relevant Scottish infrastructure' and that 'private sector engagement in it is a condition precedent'. It is widely recognised that many parties need to continue to address the systemic problems associated with this deficit. The scenarios set out in Chapter 14 serve to show what it would take for Scotland to move ahead in this area, where even the 'step function' is very demanding of many of the relevant actors and institutions. Among the many aspects of this covered in the book are those with reference to benchmarking (Chapter 4); labour markets (Chapter 5); globalisation (Chapter 15); commercialisation (Chapter 17); networks and relationships (Chapter 19); and in all of the thematic chapters covering sectors and clusters (Chapters 6–12). It is rare to find such universal agreement among commentators. Chapter 14 shows that progress is being made, but there is much to do by 2020.

Flexibility and adaptability

Linked at times to enterprise and ambition, this is deemed essential in people, businesses and structures if Scotland is to have a better economic future. It is picked up in Chapter 2 as part of the critique of the economy's recent history; and it occurs in Chapter 4 as benchmarks are considered and where the need for Scotland to be flexible, adapt and be able to reconfigure itself is highlighted. In Chapter 5, David Bell spells out the specific labour market dimensions in his comment that 'without an adaptable, innovative and well trained labour force, the Scottish economy will be unable to support the changes needed to maintain competitiveness in an increasingly dynamic international market place'. The Scottish labour market has not performed well in the past decade, even where the existing policy framework has been consistent with the OECD Jobs Strategy. Questions remain, moreover, as to whether education strategy takes enough account of the needs of the economy and economic efficiency. Looking to 2020, the two key issues facing the labour market in Scotland are migration and ageing; while the country also needs effective strategies to get the substantial numbers in the non-participating groups into that market. New levels of flexibility and innovation are also essential in structures and institutions. This is evident with reference to higher education and commercialisation in Chapter 17; and as regards e-connectivity and internationalisation in business in Chapter 15. Being a more adaptive, cosmopolitan society is also behind some of the solutions offered for population decline and more capacity for building global businesses in other chapters. In the specific context of the latter, Stephen Young and Ross Brown say that 'increasing the level of outward investment and other equity and non-equity activity, and building global companies is the key task for Scottish policy makers over the next 20 years'.

Higher education and economic development

It is already evident that both politics and economics are likely to demand better linkages between these two activities in Scotland over the next two decades. This point emerges in several of the industry based chapters. Moreover, David Bell and others ask why the differentially larger proportions going into higher education in Scotland do not seem to result in relative economic benefit. Chapter 15 asks whether the knowledge base exists in Scotland to allow it to seek more knowledge-based foreign direct investment. Ewen Peters stresses knowledge accumulation as a central driver of dynamic regions in Chapter 16, also emphasising the role of higher education. As regards the vital issue of better commercialisation of R&D, Charlie Woods (Chapter 17) notes the low demand for innovation and therefore weak industry pull in Scotland. There is clearly much to do in effectively linking universities and the finance sector. At the same time he sets out a series of necessary conditions to change the commercialisation performance in areas of skills, culture, processes and relationships as the only way to avoid treading water 'against the downward pressure of the vicious cycle that has characterised many less prosperous countries and regions in the past and build a virtuous upward spiral of development'. The University system is seen to be responding, but much change has yet to occur; and expectations of an enhanced contribution are now much higher and seem likely to grow. This is brought out in Chapter 14 in the step function scenarios for innovation-based business birth rates. Failing to translate more of Scotland's research excellence into domestically based business between now and 2020 is not an option. But it is an open question as to whether the University sector can respond to these new demands; although it is imperative that it does.

Limits to government and the role of leading businesses

While most of the chapters consider and acknowledge the roles of the Scottish Executive and Scottish Enterprise (SE) in policy making and in many different programmes designed to change the Scottish economy, the limits to their contributions are also recognised. We are not short of such policies, indeed as John Firn observes 'economic development has flourished and expanded into virtually every facet of the nation's existence over the past 30 years'. That in itself is not enough to move forward. For example, looking to 2020 where services could be 70 per cent of GDP, Chapter 2 predicts that financial services and tourism are the most likely candidates to give both scale and growth, a view that many of our authors would share. Here, and in the services sector in general, more private sector champions are called for. Equally in Chapter 3, Gavin McCrone implicitly sees large business as part of realising many of the opportunities from European enlargement. Similarly, Jeremy Peat (Chapter 9) comments on the strength of the numbers of very large Scottish financial companies who are intent on growing market share in the (EU) and beyond. Equally, he stresses the vital role that business services have in the development of other businesses and as a sector with considerable 2020 potential. Tourism is seen to require many more large corporates (Chapter 8), as does creative industries (Chapter 7), biotechnology (Chapter 6), and food and drink (Chapter 10); while energy deregulation has allowed other major companies to prosper and show good growth potential (Chapter 12). Moreover, in several chapters, there is acknowledgement of the critical role of headquarters functions in the Scottish economy. Others go further and call for a new sense of co-operation between the public and private sectors in the ownership of Scotland's economic future. Indeed this is evident in many of the initiatives of SE in recent years as shown, for example, in Chapters 6, 8, 10 and 17. The chapter which specifically looks at Scotland's established corporate base (13) highlights some of the issues of strategy, ownership, innovation and global aspirations that will determine the way in which they help to shape the future. On the one hand there is some scope for encouragement over the past decade, but the Scottish public company sector is numerically in decline and in parts very vulnerable to takeover as at 2002.

Business development opportunities

The chapters in Parts II and III confirm that these exist. In sentiment, however, they vary considerably. Optimism at both the opportunity and managerial capacity available are evident in finance and energy. It is acknowledged that many of the larger opportunities are in the service sector – where innovative business models have already paid dividends for Scotland both in the growth of firms and in personal wealth. As regards creative industries, the potential is good in that Scotland has a high concentration of activity, but faces many challenges as to how to grow its contribution. Too few companies are fully embracing new technologies and growth finance is required – and often available if properly accessed. There are many micro businesses and few majors. For information and communications technology (ICT), whose importance continues and whose role in Scotland has been historically strategic, the question is what shape it will be in after its present transition. The evidence of Stephen Young and Ross Brown in Chapter 15 suggests that the globalising forces are now much stronger than the localising ones; so this outcome is particularly difficult to predict, but cannot be abandoned in policy terms: Scotland still needs inward investment. Everyone agrees that tourism has to succeed, but competition is fierce and our competitors continue to outstrip us. Chapter 11 calls for the private sector to shape a very different future for this key, diverse and fragmented sector. The tone in food and drink is cautious, and there are concerns about the competitiveness of much of it in Scotland. Potential there is, and inherent strengths, and ambitious attempts are underway to overcome some of the problems of lack of scale, skills and limited international experience. Finally to bio-technology in Chapter 6. Peters and Hood position this in these terms. 'With a premium on the more rapid formation and growth of specialised firms that are science-based, innovative and internationally oriented, biotechnology represents a relatively unique and growing opportunity.' Pursuing such options for Scotland in this and other similar sectors is crucial in order to test the capacity of the R&D base to sustain such development. Other countries have similar ideas, but taking such modest risks are essential and logical as part of charting a different economic future. It is accurately described as taking out an option of the future. At the time of writing it is encouraging to record that SE is now implementing a Business Partnership scheme with the top 100 Scottish owner companies to foster mutual engagement between their corporate interests and economic development. Hopefully this might assist in promoting further market-led approaches. And new forms of strategic partnership are at the heart of the review of the clusters approach in Chapter 16.

If the direction is right, stay on the policy track

This is an important point on which many of the authors comment. For example, Brian Ashcroft observes that current Scottish economic development policy is in line with modern thinking on supply side drivers. This does not of course in itself make it correct. But there is a good measure of agreement that the focus of attention reflected in documents such as *Smart, Successful Scotland* is about right, provided it can be adhered to and pursued over a longer period of time. The principal call thereafter is for just that. Gavin McCrone advocates the avoidance of reorganisation of economic development bodies for its own sake. Similar points are made by John Firn in Chapter 18 on economic governance, although here he appeals for greater simplification of organisations and procedures, as well as for more independent, confident and strategic inputs from the Scottish business establishment. Alf Young makes a powerful point in the same vein in Chapter 19 by his observation that the solutions to Scotland's problems will need better delivery, which 'requires far greater focus and single-minded determination than institutional and political Scotland has displayed in the past'. With that sentiment, we can all agree!

The shape of Scotland in 2020

In the introductory chapter we were honest enough to admit that the last time we conducted such an exercise we were only partially accurate when it came to looking forward and predicting some of the factors that would shape its economic destiny. There is no reason to think that it will be any easier this time, especially when we have a date in the book title. If anything, times are more uncertain in 2002 as we complete this book. So in this section we, as editors, have confined ourselves to speculating a little about the outworking of seven of the issues that have been identified as most material to Scotland's future prosperity.

European Union

There is little doubt that in various ways, the further integration and expansion of the EU will have a profound impact. The effects are likely to be both positive and negative. In many ways, it depends on what we make them. For example, as labour markets open further and as skills remain a critical determinant of economic development, an acceleration of migration towards the diversity of opportunity that constitutes Europe would be damaging to the delivery of much that is discussed in this book. On the other hand, more open capital markets together with better market access, could offer great development prospects for the financial sector and possibly for the growth of indigenous business. By 2020 it could even call into question what we mean by the use of that name to describe companies, if the EU is increasingly viewed as the home base for our Scottish businesses. The EU is important in other dimensions, not least in the likely decrease in the funding coming to Scotland as the enlargement agenda is worked out well within the study period. Enlargement will also lend to fiercer competition, and not only in electronics where problems have already arisen for Scotland.

Common European currency

It is highly likely that the UK will be part of the euro zone long before 2020. If Scotland remains reasonably competitive for inward investment in both services and higher value added manufacturing, this could be a substantial boost to the economy, but it is unlikely to be a major factor in our differentiation. However, as Gavin McCrone suggested, the single currency could also lead to US style intensification of competition, more concentration, large scale production and specialisation. This is turn would be both a threat and an opportunity for corporate Scotland, and it would be greatly aided by having a strong corporate base.

UK's relative position in the EU and world economy

It is unlikely that by 2020 Scotland will be any less an integrated part of the UK economy than it is at present. Indeed, it could be more integrated if further policy emphasis on locally based, high growth companies leads them more effectively to penetrate the UK market. Thus the relative position of the UK in terms of economic fundamentals like investment levels, growth, productivity, and so on, will all remain vital for Scotland. Vital, that is unless Scotland breaks the mould of the past in such indicators, and at best mirrors or out-performs the UK benchmarks. This would be a radical departure from the past. In the light of the analysis in this volume, it is hard to see from where such mould breaking would come. Within the UK, the position of London is particularly critical for Scotland: will the capital continue to suck young talent from this country, or will negative externalities (congestion, pollution, and so on) finally encourage greater decentralisation? However, there are competitive threats outside London too. Thus the Regional Development Agencies (RDAs) in the English regions will provide stiffer competition to Scotland than hitherto.

Ownership of Scotland's economic future

This book has been written in the context of a devolved Scotland. There are clearly several major political changes that could happen between now and 2020 and markedly different economic policies could accompany them. While acknowledging this, it is evident that much of the economic future of Scotland is determined elsewhere, whether at the micro level in multiples of board rooms or at the macro level by the UK government, EU, and by the outworking of global forces. Having said that, it is critical that all the relevant public and private sector interests have a sense of ownership of Scotland's economic future. In the early years of political change, this is not yet evident. Parliament as a whole needs to be much more engaged in economic affairs and provide the appropriate leadership. Yet it is necessary if this small, open economy is to be effectively differentiated in a way that generates greater economic wealth for its people and in so doing reduces net migration. In this very book, we reflect part of the problem. So much of our reference is to the activity of SE as the country's major economic development agency. While its leadership and policy setting role is vital, we should recall that it directly spends under 2 per cent of total public expenditure in Scotland yet seems to carry so much of the country's aspirations for economic change. On the face of it, this is both strange and unhealthy. En route to 2020, the existence of very much more effective public/private partnership in the development of the economy is a *sine qua non*. The public dimension has clearly to be as well designed and implemented as possible; but the vast majority of the strategic decisions that will make a difference are private. Without such partnership on a broad and enduring front, we might arrive at 2020 having argued around the parish pump more effectively than we have adjusted our business base to meet global challenges.

Higher education and economic development linkages

Economic development policy in Scotland has already (and we believe correctly) started to place higher expectations on its Universities and other Higher Education (HE) institutions. The extent to which these are realised will determine a number of important outcomes in the years ahead. Like many other countries Scotland is looking at this sector to further contribute to quality education and training, innovation, R&D, commercialisation, as well as diffusion and adoption of best practice. HE as a whole already has a major impact on the economy, but that in itself is ever more likely to be taken as read. While there is progress, substantial systemic changes will be necessary in the system if this sector is to deliver on such expectations and on the scale necessary to make a material impact by 2020. Such changes might include more differentiation within and between these institutions, different performance metrics, radical efficiency gains, different funding models and so on. In this vein, SE are assessing the possibilities of establishing Intermediate

Institutes in certain key technologies based on successful models in other countries. Whatever the outcome, the HE sector as with the business sector has to buy into the economic strategy for Scotland. But this is a sector where at best change tends to be gradual, and radical change is invariably resisted, sometimes for good reason. That said, perhaps this is the time for more radical thinking and an HE strategy which is more clearly aligned with the economic health of the country.

Clusters and infrastructure

Infrastructure issues have not been separately discussed in the book, but their importance cannot be over-emphasised. Beyond the question of HE, are those of internal and external transport systems of all kinds, telecommunications networks, and so on. On the softer side of these issues is a supportive planning regime that, among other things, encourages major indigenous businesses to grow and develop in Scotland when they choose so to do. It would be hard to argue that on any of these counts Scotland is particularly well placed as it looks to the next 20 years of economic development and towards the enhancement of its global connections. Thus an integrated transport policy is a pre-requisite for an enhanced 2020 performance for many reasons. For example, skill shortages can often be offset by commuting over greater distances in a country of Scotland's size, provided road and public transport systems fully enable this. Equally critical are direct air connections to major markets, an area where, as of 2002, provision had decreased over recent years.

Several authors have commented upon sectoral progress with cluster strategies, but Ewen Peters highlights the long gestation period required for effective cluster development. Thus eight years after the original clusters research study in Scotland, the three most advanced pilot initiatives had only completed their first full year of operation. Now new issues relating to the knowledge accumulation have begun to take priority; and Peters proposes that innovative local milieu could provide a more relevant focus for future policy action than industrial clusters. This means a need, for example, to look beyond the transport and communications infrastructure (essential though this is) to emphasise science, innovation and entrepreneurship.

Population, networks and relationships

Well explained in Alf Young's chapter, this is perhaps the most difficult issue of all to address. Difficult, because on the population side it is both a cause and an effect, and not readily reversible in the time scale without a major improvement in economic performance. Viewed from the perspective of this book, the best line of attack is enhanced opportunity and therefore greater skill and energy retention as well as the capacity to attract others to solve skill deficits. It is worth recalling that in the early 1990s Scotland had net in-migration at the time when its GDP growth out-performed the UK as a whole. Another way ahead is the effective tapping of other markets and really making international networks work for Scotland's good. Neither of these are trivial tasks; and both need that sustained level of community interest alluded to earlier.

Concluding remarks

Some important directions have been set for Scotland over the past three years. The outworking of these changes will take time, and have to be pursued with consistency of intent. This is a tall order, yet so vital. In reality, there are no longer major alternatives open to Scotland. For example, the long running dichotomy between supporting indigenous as distinct from foreign business has been addressed, and the policy framework is better balanced that it has been for two generations. Equally, the engagement of major Scottish business is essential, and cannot be ignored. Other countries face similar challenges, and the test will be less about their institutions than it will be about their will to succeed and their consistency. Meanwhile, Scotland as a whole, in its various constituencies, has to make good decisions in areas where it can control the outcomes, recognising that many other factors are beyond its control.

Is all of this doable? And can some of the corporate and individual optimism of the early twenty-first century be converted into a different economic future for Scotland? While we end in a positive vein about these issues, our conviction is that much will depend on a sense of common purpose and clarity of objectives. Business and political leaders will need to lead in their respective estates, share a measure of inter-linked ambition and support the fundamental changes necessary in attitudes, investment patterns and behaviour required to produce an improved Scottish economy by 2020.

Note

1 As reflected, for example, in Scottish Executive (2000), *The Way Forward – A Framework for Economic Development in Scotland*, Edinburgh: Scottish Executive; Scottish Executive (2001), *Smart, Successful Scotland: Ambitions for the Enterprise Networks*, Edinburgh: Scottish Executive; Scottish Executive (2002), *Measuring Scotland's Progress Towards a Smart, Successful Scotland*, Edinburgh: Scottish Executive.

Index

Access
  and connectivity 121–2
  to capital 103–5
Active Labour Market Policies
  (ALMPs) 79, 85–8
Ageing population 76–7
Agnew, D. 261
Amin, A. 263
Andersson, A.E. 288
Anglo-Saxon Model 69
Application-specific integrated circuits
  (ASICs) 135, 146
Armstrong, H. 144
Ashcroft, B 5, 13, 19, 22, 23, 26,
  325, 344, 348
Ashenfelter, O. 86
Audretsch, D. 30, 73
Automated teller machines
  (ATMs) 131, 137
Aydalot, P. 286

Bartlett, C.A. 288
Baumol, W.J. 323
Bernard, A.B. 329
Best, M. 23, 24, 25, 240
BioIndustry Association (BIA) 92, 284
Biotechnology
  Big Pharma and 101–2
  economic boundaries 92–3
Birkinshaw, J. 96
Blanchflower, D. 73
Boston Consulting Group (BCG)
  92, 99
Botham, R. 130, 131
Bovine Spongiform Encephalopathy
  (BSE) 171
Boyle, S. 7, 199, 267
Bradford Jensen, J. 329
Branch plant economy 130,
  144, 145
Brewer, T. 268
Bridgehead Technologies 97

Briggs, J. 241
British Venture Capital Association
  (BVCA) 242
Brown, R. 6, 8, 130, 131, 137, 139,
  142, 144, 261, 263, 268, 269,
  272, 346, 348
Burrough, B. 314
Business and industrial governance
  issues 323–7
  entrepreneurship and new business
    creation 323–4
  mergers, takeovers and corporate
    restructuring 325–6
  other economic governance
    priorities 327
  Scottish business
    establishment 326–7
  support for existing
    businesses 324–5
Business Birth Rate Strategy
  (BBRS) 239–40
Business
  birth rate in Scotland 238–40
  growth in Scotland 241–2
  models 120–1
  services and challenges for the
    sector 158–9
  structures, evolving 174–5

Cairncross, F. 263
Cambridge phenomenon 60, 302
Capability Triad 23
Carroll, M. 92
Clement, K. 329
Cluster approach
  developing and
    implementing 280–1
  early developments 281
  first year in retrospect 283–5
  future policy 285
  implementing the approach 282–3
  policy on 281–2

implementing 290–1
knowledge accumulation and local
milieu 286–7
knowledge accumulation and
Scotland's competitive
advantage 287–90
Cluster Development Fund (CDF) 62
Cluster
analysis of the electronics
sector 134–7
definition, measurement
and characterisation
93–7
pioneering the cluster
approach 93
Collinson, S. 131
Commercialising knowledge 302
role of key individuals 303
role of the public sector 304
supportive business
environment 304
'technology pull' 303
'technology push' 303
Commercialising Scottish
Knowledge 296–312
knowledge and place 297–302
Committee of Scottish Clearing
Bankers (CSCB) 151
Comparators, brief lessons from
63–4
Competition policy and economic
regulation 206–9
environmental policy 207–8
markets and technology 209
nuclear energy policy 208–9
Confederation of British Industry
(CBI) 326
Cooke, P. 262, 288
Corporate Governance and Economic
Development 314–16
an evolving concept 314–15
Country and regional
comparators 57
Cambridge UK 60–1
Denmark 59–60
Finland 58–9
Ireland 57–8
North Rhine Westphalia (NRW) 63
Singapore 61–2

Creative Industries 112–29
definition of 113
industry structure 115
measuring the 113–15
Cumulative causation 297
Customer relationship management
(CRM) 250

Daffin, C. 23
Danson, M. 137
Dasgupta, P. 301
Data trends, review of past 186–8
D'Cruz, J.R. 95
Demographic trends 74
Department of Culture, Media and
Sport (DCMS) 113–14
Don, G. 244
Doz, Y. 288
Draper, P. 162
Drivers
global 116
market 118–20
regulatory 122
technology 116–18
Dunning, J.H. 261, 262

Eccles, T. 329
Economic Development Board (EDB)
Singapore 61–2
Economic Development Board
Investments (EDBI) 62
Economist Technology Quarterly, The 99
Edinburgh BioComputing
Systems 101
Edinburgh Parallel Computing Centre
(EPCC) 250
Employment protection legislation
(EPL) 83
Employment
and unemployment trends 70–3
zones 86
Energy
and the Scottish economy 201–4
industry 199–213
sector, economic characteristics
of the 204–6
Enright, M. 96, 137

Estall, R.C. 288
European Agricultural Guarantee
     and Guidance Fund (EAGGF) 41
European and national policies 36
  European structural funds 41–4
  Scottish Enterprise, Highlands and
     Islands Enterprise 38–41
  UK regional development
     policy 36–8
European Commission (EC) 321
European Economic Area (EEA) 32
European Free Trade Association
     (EFTA) 32
European Monetary Union
     (EMU) 36, 143
European Regional Development
     Fund (ERDF) 41–2
European Social Fund (ESF) 41–2
European Union (EU) 2, 29, 347
Eurostat 33
Exchange rate mechanism (ERM) 226

FDA modernisation Act 98
Federal Office of Communications
     (OFCOM) 122, 126
Feldman, M. 30
Financial and Business Services
     149–64
  employment 152–4
  exports 154–5
  Gross Domestic Product (GDP) 16,
     150–2, 293, 335, 343
Financial Instrument for Fisheries
     Guidance (FIFG) 41–2
Financial Times 61, 329
Findlay, A. 272
Fingleton, E. 30
Firn Crichton Roberts 145,
     269, 329
Firn, J. 8, 130, 137, 145, 269, 313,
     329, 347, 349
Foreign Direct Investment (FDI)
     57, 145
Fortune 223, 224, 328
Framework for Economic
     Development in Scotland
     (FEDS) 21
Fraser of Allander Institute (FAI) 16

Future of Scotland
  ICT Industries 130–46
  oil and gas 210–13
  opportunities and threats 122–4
  policy, implications for 106–8
  success 124–5

General Agreement on Tariffs
     and Trade (GATT) 34
General Agreement on Trade in
     Services (GATS) 158
Ghoshal, S. 288
Global Connections Strategy
     (GCS) 233
Global knowledge economy,
     Scotland's performance in 263–4
  e-connectivity 270–2
  human capital 272–3
  international trade 264
  inward FDI 268–9
  outward investment and global
     companies 269–70
Glover, S. 272, 273
Griffith, R. 304
Gross National Product (GNP) 189
Gross Value Added (GVA) 20, 28,
     155, 201
Growth of tourism, trends
     affecting 189–91
  economic 189
  environment 190
  information 189
  social 190

Halkier, H. 137
Hampden-Turner, C. 65
Harding, R. 305
Hedlund, G. 288
Heidensohn, K. 34
Helyar, J. 314
Higgings, T. 289
High performance work systems
     (HPWS) 24
Higher Education (HE)
     institutions 351–2
Higher National Certificate (HNC) 84
Higher National Diploma (HND) 84

Highlands and Islands Development
  Board (HIDB) 318, 329
Highlands and Islands Enterprise
  (HIE) 36–8, 40, 44
Hillage, J. 146
Hood, N. 1, 2, 3, 4, 6, 7, 68, 91,
  96, 220, 221, 237, 243, 287,
  290, 343, 345, 348
House of Commons UK 37, 40, 172
Huggins, R. 17, 28

Industrial Development Act 1982 37
Information and communications
  technologies (ICT) 1, 6, 348
Initial public offering (IPO) 104
Intellectual property (IP) 105, 247
Intellectual property rights (IPR) 118,
  249, 321–2
Inter Departmental Business Register
  (IDBR) 164
International competition 105–6
International Institute for
  Management Development
  (IMD) 59
International Labour Organisation
  (ILO) 51
International Monetary Fund (IMF)
  69, 232, 262
International policy
  Scottish Enterprise and the Scottish
    Executive 273–5
International rates of return
  (IRR) 109

Johannisson, B. 288
Joint Performance Team 22

Kaplan, R. 311
Kay, J. 50
Keynote 287

Labour Market 68–88
  participation rates 77–9
Lanarkshire Development Agency 45
Landabaso, M. 289

Landes, D. 297
Lawson, C. 302
Leicester, G. 66
Levie, J. 56
Liquid Petroleum Gas (LPG) 193
Local Enterprise Companies
  (LECs) 36, 318
Local Futures Group (LFG) 297
Love, J.H. 21, 325
Lovegrove, N. 125, 126
Lowell, B. 23, 272

MacKay, D. 239
McCall, W. 228
McCann, P. 130
McCrone, G. 6, 32, 35, 347, 349,
  350
Malmberg, A. 286, 297
Management buy-outs (MBOs) 323
Market factors 97
Marks & Spencer (M&S) 156
Markusen, A. 145, 263
Maskell, P. 297
Massey, D. 141
Maxwell, F. 179
Mergers and acquisitions (M&A) 232,
  234, 314, 326
Migration 74–6
Mombru, I. 125, 126
Moore, B. 37
Morgan, K. 262, 288
Mukhtar, S.-M. 243
Multinational enterprises (MNEs)
  130, 136, 141–2, 263
Multiplier and head office
  impacts 155–7
Myrdal, G. 288, 297, 301

National and European
  Dimension 32–47
National Trust for Scotland (NTS) 195
Networks and Relationships: The
  Scottish Diaspora 331–40
New Deal for Young People
  (NDYP) 86
New firms, growth and development
  of 237–56

New technology-based firms
    (NTBFs)   243–5
Nomenclature for Territorial Statistics
    (NUTS)   47
North Rhine Westphalia (NRW)   63
Norton, D.   311
Nuclear Electric Ltd (NEL)   201

Oakey, R.P.   243
OECD jobs strategy   69–70
Office for National Statistics
    (ONS)   52
Oftel   271
Organisation for Economic
    Co-operation and Development
    (OECD)   50, 344
Oriented strand board (OSB)   329
Original equipment manufacturers
    (OEMs)   136
Oswald, A.   73
Oughton, C.   288

Path dependency   13
Peat, J.   6, 149, 267, 343, 347
Peters, E.   1, 6, 8, 91, 94, 142,
    220, 221, 268, 280, 287,
    290, 343, 346, 348, 352
Policy
    alternatives   252–3
    conclusions   275–7
    effects   231–5
    implications   125–8, 144–6
Population and growth   331–6
Porter, M.   93, 96, 102, 136, 177,
    280, 281, 286, 287, 290
Porter's cluster model   134
Post-1975 economic governance in
    Scotland   316–23
    consultation, evaluation and
        prevarication   320–1
    economic development
        community   318–19
    importance of the demand
        side   317–18
    limited economic vision for
        Scotland   317

measuring, recording and
    understanding the
    economy   322–3
out with the old, in with the
    new   321–2
policy and programme
    stability   319–20
Printed circuitboard (PCB)   135,
    138, 141
Private Financial Initiative/
    Public-Private Partnerships
    (PFI/PPP)   159, 161
Private sector employment   79–80

Quinn, B.   311

Raines, P.   134, 139, 142, 143, 268, 269
Recurring themes   334
    business development
        opportunities   347–8
    enterprise and business
        growth   345
    flexibility and adaptability   345–6
    higher education and economic
        development   346
    limits to government and the role of
        leading businesses   347
Regional innovation paradox   288–90
Reeves, R.   45
Regional Development Agencies
    (RDAs)   350
Regional Investment Company
    (RIC)   62
Regional Selective Assistance
    (RSA)   37, 144
Research and development (R&D)   4
Research Assessment Exercise (RAE)   85
Rice, G.   65
Robbins-Roth, C.   92
Rolander, D.   288
Royal Bank of Scotland Group
    (RBSG)   156
Royal Bank of Scotland plc (RBS)   221
Royal Society for the Protection
    of Birds (RSPB)   195
Royal Society of Edinburgh (RSE)   245
Rugman, A.   95

Saxenian, A. 288, 302
Scarpetta, S. 86, 87
Scientific and technological
    advance 99
Scotland Electricity Board (SSEB) 201
Scotland in context 51–7
    digital connectivity 54
    entrepreneurship 56–7
    exporting 54
    GDP growth 51
    labour productivity 52
    skills and knowledge 54
    spending on R&D 52
    unemployment rates 51
Scotland
    and the euro 35–6
    biotechnology cluster of 93–7
    challenges for 305–6
    clusters and infrastructure 352
    comparative performance 50–1
    European currency 350
    European Union 349–50
    global economy: the 2020 view 4–5
    higher education and economic
        development linkages 351–2
    ICT sector in 131–4
    images of 336–7
    ownership of Scotland's economic
        future 350–1
    population, networks and
        relationships 352–3
    shape of 349–53
    UK's relative position in the EU
        and world economy 350
Scotland's
    economy and benchmarks
        49–66
    established corporate base 217–35
    mediocre economic
        performance 17–28
Scott, A.J. 50
Scottish and Southern Energy
    (SSE) 203
Scottish Council Development and
    Industry (SCDI) 32, 131, 154, 324
Scottish Development Agency
    (SDA) 4, 160, 292, 318–20
Scottish Development International
    (SDI) 144, 273–4, 339

Scottish diaspora, tapping into
    the 337–40
Scottish economic governance 327–8
Scottish Economic Planning
    Department (SEPD) 322
Scottish economy 13–28
    and financial sector 159–61
    industry, policy and the 2–4
Scottish Enterprise (SE) 17, 36, 336
Scottish Enterprise Tayside (SET) 309
Scottish Equity Partners Ltd (SEP)
    243, 309
Scottish Executive and
    Parliament 44–7
Scottish Financial Enterprise (SFE)
    27, 150, 163, 336
Scottish Food and Drink
    Industry 165–79
    external challenges 168–9
    competitive position of 175–7
    food cluster strategy 177–9
Scottish Further Education Funding
    Council (SFEFC) 163
Scottish Higher Education Funding
    Council (SHEFC) 163, 304, 307
Scottish Hydro-Electric (SHE) 203, 204
Scottish Institute for Enterprise
    (SIE) 309
Scottish National Party (SNP) 332
Scottish policy and initiatives 306
    connecting universities and
        business 307–8
    finance 309
    industry clusters 308–9
    infrastructure 310
    overarching policy and
        initiatives 306–7
    stimulating academic
        enterprise 309
Scottish Tourism Forum (STF) 196
Scottish Tourist Board (STB) 196
Scottish Trade International
    (STI) 274
Segal Quince Wicksteed 60
Shaw, S.A. 7, 165, 169, 171
Silicon Glen, evolution of 130–1
Slow, J. 7, 217, 230, 231
Small- to medium-sized enterprises
    (SMEs) 59, 249, 254, 320

Smart, Successful Scotland (SSS)
    64, 233
Statistical
    bulletin   131, 133, 134
    description   150
Strategic issues and responses   91–108
    main economic features   91–2
Strategic trends and issues for the
    future   142, 206
    legislative issues   143–4
    partnership   280–92
    technological change   142–3
Strengths, Weaknesses, Opportunities
    and Threats (SWOT)   226
Support for Products under Research
    (SPUR)   244
Survival and growth strategies
    1992–1998   171–5
    abandoning the tartan   173
    brands and Scottishness   172
    concentration on core markets   172
    protecting the core business
        through range extensions   171–2
    rise of niche products   174
SWOT analysis of electronics
    industry   137–42
    communications
        technology   139–40
    consumer electronics   141
    data processing equipment   137
    defence electronics/
        opto-electronics   140–1
    electronic components   138–9
    suppliers and subcontractors   141
SWOT analysis of established
    companies   225–30
    adaptability   226
    innovation   226
    opportunities   228
    strengths   226
    technology   227
    threats   229
    weaknesses   227

Talbot, S.   45
Tapscott, D.   261
Taylor, C.   35
Teasdale, P.   241

Technology
    commercialisation and global
        companies   242–51
    enabling technology   92, 113
Thrift, N   263
Thurik, R.   73
Toolkit companies   99
Tourism in 2020, vision of   182–98
    development of   191–3
    policy implications   195–8
    strategic implications   193–5
Tourism to the UK and Scotland
    183–4
    employment and structure of the
        tourism industry   185
    English residents   184
    overseas   185
    Scottish residents   184
Trading environment   32–5
Training and education   83–5
Turok, I.   130, 137, 141, 269

UK continental shelf (UKCS)   210,
    211, 212
Ullman, E.L.   288
Urquhart, F.   169

Value added tax (VAT)
    239, 240
Van Reenan, J.   86

Walker, J.   131
Wolfe, T.   328
Working Families Tax Credit
    (WFTC)   85, 86
Working time, flexibility of
    80–3
World tourism, overview of
    182–3
World Trade Organisation (WTO)
    3, 34, 275, 326

Young, Alf   328, 331, 344, 352
Young, S.   1, 2, 3, 4, 8, 68, 92,
    96, 97, 101, 102, 105, 106,
    138, 171, 261, 268